Windows 95

Concepts & Examples

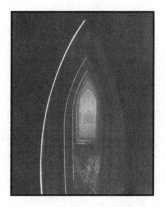

Carolyn Z. Gillay
Saddleback College

Franklin, Beedle & Associates, Incorporated
8536 SW St. Helens Drive, Suite D
Wilsonville, Oregon 97070
503/682-7668

President and Publisher	Jim Leisy (jimleisy@fbeedle.com)
Manuscript Editor	Eve Kushner
Production	Tom Sumner
	Karen Foley
	Susan Skarzynski
Cover Design	Steve Klinetobe
Marketing Group	Victor Kaiser
	Sue Page
	Eric Machado
	Laura Rowe
	Marci Calegari
	Cary Crossland
Order Processing	Chris Alarid
	Ann Leisy
Manufacturing	Publishers Press
	Salt Lake City, Utah

Contents

Chapter 1

Hardware, Software, and the Operating System

Chapter Overview

It is impossible to live in today's society without being affected by computers. Computers are found in public and private industry and are used in every sector of the business world. Computer software is what makes the computer useful for all types of applications. Computer usage will continues to grow.

While application software is what makes the computer useful to you, you must first understand how the operating system of a computer works. The operating system of a computer takes care of the mandatory functions for computer operations and allows the computer to run application software. Operating systems must keep pace with the technical advances of hardware and software, so new versions appear regularly. The focus of this textbook is Windows 95, Microsoft's newest entry into the operating system world.

Learning Objectives

After completing this chapter you will be able to:

1. Explain the difference between hardware and software.
2. Identify and explain the functions of basic hardware components.
3. Explain the purpose and function of the system unit.
4. Explain how a CPU functions.
5. Compare and contrast RAM and ROM memory.
6. Explain how the use of adapter boards increases computer capabilities.
7. List and explain the functions of the various peripheral input and output devices of the computer.
8. Explain the purpose and function of external storage devices.
9. Explain how the capacity of a disk is measured.
10. Compare and contrast the minifloppy disk, the microfloppy disk, and the CD-ROM.
11. Explain the purpose and function of the hard disk.
12. Compare and contrast the purpose and functions of hard and floppy disks.
13. Explain how and why a disk is divided.
14. Explain how disk drives derive their names.
15. Compare and contrast system software and application software.
16. Explain the functions of an operating system.

17. Explain how the user interface has changed in Windows 95.
18. Explain the docucentric approach developed for Windows 95.
19. List the hardware requirements for Windows 95.
20. Explain the advantages of using a network.

1.1   An Introduction to Computers

Computers appear in almost every aspect of life. These machines handle accounting chores (spreadsheets), write books (word processing), and organize and retrieve information (databases). In the visual arts computers have revolutionized the way films are made, games are played, and reality is perceived (virtual reality). Computers are even borrowing from other media to enhance the way work is done. It is hard to imagine purchasing a new computer without a CD-ROM player.

1.2   Computer Components

A computer is comprised of different pieces called components. Figure 1.1 shows the physical components of a computer, referred to as *hardware*. All computer systems have the same basic hardware. However, hardware by itself can do nothing. A computer system needs a program called *software.* Software is a set of detailed instructions that tell the hardware what operations to perform.

Data, in its simplest form, is related or unrelated numbers, words, or facts that provide information when arranged in a particular way. For example, if you wanted to add 2 + 3 using a computer, you would need the hardware to do the work. Next, you would need the software instructions to tell the computer how to add. Then, you would have to input the data, the numbers 2 and 3, so that the program would know what to process. Finally, you would have to enter the appropriate software instructions so that the addition could occur.

Figure 1.1   *Components of a Computer System*

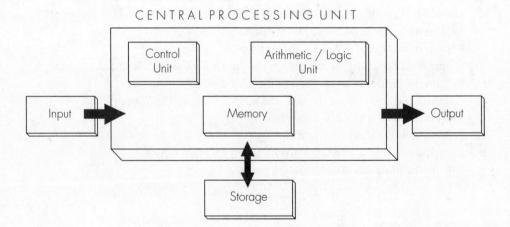

1.3   Microcomputer Hardware Components

This text is devoted to *microcomputers*. Microcomputers, which may be called micros, personal computers, home computers, laptops, notebooks, PCs, or desktop computers, are comprised of hardware components. Much like a stereo system, the basic components of a complete system (called the *system configuration*) include an input device (typically a keyboard) for entering data and programs; a system unit that houses the electronic circuitry for storing and processing data and programs (CPU, adapter cards, ROM, and RAM); a visual display unit (a monitor); storage units that store data and programs on disks (disk drives); and a printer for producing a printed version of the results. Today, when people purchase a computer, they usually want a multimedia computer. A multimedia computer includes a CD-ROM drive, a sound card, and speakers. Figure 1.2 represents a typical microcomputer system.

Figure 1.2   A Typical Microcomputer System

1.4   The System Unit

The system unit, as shown in Figure 1.3, is a case that houses the electronic and mechanical parts of the computer. If the outer case were removed and the unit were opened, it would look like the diagram in Figure 1.4.

Figure 1.3   The System Unit

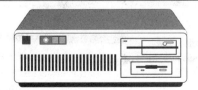

Figure 1.4   *Inside the System Unit*

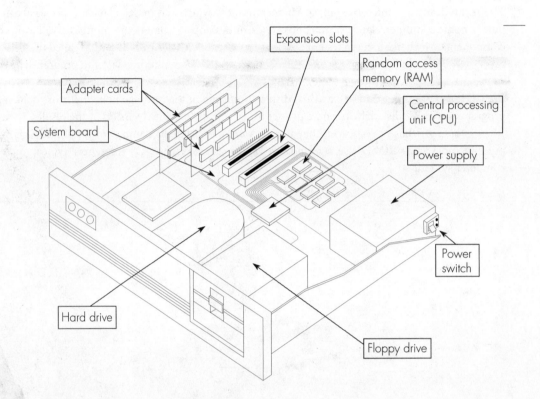

The system unit has some mechanical parts, such as the power supply (to provide the computer with power) and the disk drives. In addition, it contains many printed electronic circuit boards, also called cards, or *adapter cards*. One of these is a special printed circuit board called the *system board*, or the *motherboard*. Attached to the system board is the microprocessor chip that is the central processing unit (CPU), the random access memory (RAM), and the read-only memory(ROM).

1.5   Central Processing Unit

The central processing unit, most commonly referred to as the CPU, is the brain of the computer and consists of transistors on a silicon chip. It comprehends the instructions sent to it by a program and carries out those instructions for the computer.

The central processor has its own descriptive terminology. The first is numerical and relates specifically to the central processing chip. At present, the Intel 80486 processing chip is the most common one in use. It comes in an SX and DX version. It is easiest to remember SX as the standard model and DX as the deluxe model. Actually, an SX type of CPU is a scaled-down version of a DX. A DX type of CPU has more power. If a CPU is a DX2, it runs twice as fast externally as it does internally. It needs to slow down when it enters RAM. However, the most recent development is the 80586, or Pentium chip, which appeared in 1993 with tremendous performance potential. It is rapidly becoming the most popular chip.

The CPU speed is measured in *megahertz (MHz)*. Megahertz is the generally recognized unit of measurement used to compare clock speeds of computers. Simplistically, the CPU is like a clock. Every cycle of the clock allows the CPU to execute an instruction. If the clock is faster, more instructions are executed. This process makes the computer faster. The first personal computers had a rating of 4.77 MHz. Today, 100 MHz is common with 133, 160, and 200 MHz available.

All of these hardware devices must be connected in some way so that the CPU can deliver data. In computerese, output travels by *bus*. The terms *bus*, *internal bus*, and *local bus* refer to the electrical connections between the CPU and all of the output devices. Of course, the bus travels at a speed, one which depends on the processor. The classic bus was the standard ISA AT bus with a speed of 8 megahertz (MHz) and an electronic roadway 16 bits wide. The newest generation is the VESA local bus. Its speed also depends on the processor, and it has a roadway 32 bits wide. As with all aspects of computing, bus performance will continue to improve.

In addition, new standards are developing. There is the PCI standard, another type of 32-bit bus, which is competing with the local VESA. Because of its smaller size, the PCI may supplant VESA as the standard. There is also a bus called PCMCIA, which is the size of a credit card and is used in notebook computers. Presently, it is used to insert devices such as a modem or a networking card into a notebook. Some believe that PCMCIA will become the computing standard.

1.6   Random Access Memory

Often referred to as *memory*, or *main memory*, random access memory (*RAM*) is the workspace of the computer. The need for RAM in the last few years has been phenomenal. Where 1 megabyte (MB) of memory was satisfactory just a few years ago, software needs have made 8 MB of RAM commonplace, and 16 MB desirable. RAM is contained in many electrical circuits. However, a computer's memory is not like a person's memory. RAM is not a permanent record of anything. RAM is where the programs and data are stored while the computer is working. RAM is temporary (volatile) and useful only while the computer is on.

1.7   Cache Memory

Cache, or caching, is the latest in quick access memory features. Cache stores frequently used RAM data, making more rapid RAM access possible. Whenever the CPU needs data from RAM, it first visits the RAM cache to see if the data is available. If it is, rapid action occurs. If not, the CPU goes to RAM proper. Caching is especially useful for the MS Windows 95 interface because frequently used data is stored there, making data access much quicker. Caches may be found in video and printer memory systems.

1.8   Read-Only Memory

Another growth area in computer technology is read-only memory, or *ROM*. Originally, read-only memory was designed to hold permanently stored programs installed by the manufacturer of the specific computer. ROM has become the latest way to install software by using compact discs from audio media. More and more software is shipped on CDs and installed.

As with RAM, ROM is made from electronic circuits. "read-only" means exactly what it says. The CPU can read only the instructions from ROM; it cannot write, erase, or alter the contents of ROM in any way. ROM is nonvolatile, which means that when you turn off the computer, none of the information stored on ROM is lost. ROM actually has programs etched on it; it is a program on a chip. Here, however, is where the terms hardware and software blur somewhat. ROM is hardware because it is a chip. However, it is also software because it contains instructions. Hence, ROM is sometimes called *firmware*, something halfway between hardware and software. Nearly all computers use ROM to hold startup programs, including the instructions for loading the operating system into RAM. Most ROM is located on the system board, but some ROM can also be located on adapter boards.

1.9   Adapter Cards

Printed circuit boards, originally called adapter boards, are now called adapter cards or just boards. They are installed in the system unit when purchased or are added later. Adapter cards allow you to add more RAM, use a special video display, or use a modem or a mouse. These items are considered *peripheral devices* and are installed within the CPU in *expansion slots*. The number of adapter card options you can install depends on how many slots your system unit has. Inexpensive units usually have only one or two expansion slots, but a costly computer, especially one designed to be a network server, can have seven, eight, or more slots.

1.10   Input Devices—Peripherals

Software programs and data get into RAM via *input devices*. The most common input device is the typewriter-like keyboard attached by a cable to the system unit. By keying in instructions and data, you communicate with the computer, which places the information into RAM.

A mouse, or trackball, is used to manipulate data on the screen. A *mouse* is a hand-held pointing device with two or more lever-like buttons on top. On the bottom is a ball that rolls around on a flat surface to move an arrow-shaped cursor around the screen. Data manipulation is as easy as moving the cursor where you want it on the screen and pressing a mouse button. The *trackball* is another hand-held data entry device. In this case, however, the ball is on top and you rotate it with your hand or fingers. After you move the cursor where you want, you enter data by pressing one of the levers on the trackball. Another popular device is the *integrated pointing device*, which is a small, eraser-like object on the keyboard that you can manipulate to move the cursor. Glide pads are gaining in popularity as well. A *glide pad* is a small, smooth object on which you move your finger to control the pointer.

There are other input devices, such as a *light pen*, which has a light-sensitive cell. When the tip of the pen comes into contact with the monitor, it identifies a point on the screen. You may use the light pen to draw or enter data. You also may input data by scanning. *Scanners*, such as those in grocery stores, allow a clerk to wave an item across an electrosensitive plate, which reads the magnetic price code. This same technology has made scanners readily available to most computer users. Touch-sensitive display screens allow the user to touch the screen with a finger to input data.

1.11 Output Devices—Peripherals

In addition to putting information into RAM, you might also want to take it out of RAM. You may want to see what you have keyed in on the monitor or to print a "hard" copy of the data. These processes are known as output, or where information is written to. Thus, you "read" information in and you "write" information out, commonly known as I/O for input and output.

1.12 Output Devices: Monitors

A *monitor*, also called a terminal, display screen, screen, cathode-ray tube (CRT), or video display tube (VDT), looks like a television. The CPU writes information to the screen, where it is displayed for the user.

Monitors come in two basic types, monochrome and color. Monochrome monitors display in one color. The user can choose the color—green characters on a black screen, amber characters on a black screen, etc. Color monitors display in color. Most monitors display 80 characters across the screen and 25 lines down the screen. However, other monitors display an entire page. The clarity (resolution) of what is displayed is measured in picture elements (pixels). *Pixels* are little dots that light up to form images on the screen. The smaller and more numerous the pixels, the sharper the image or picture.

Information that the CPU writes to the screen needs a special kind of circuit board—a video display adapter card, commonly called a *video card*, which controls the monitor. In the early days of computing, the most popular adapters were the monochrome adapter and the color graphics adapter (CGA), which can display up to 16 colors. However, there was a trade-off. The monochrome adapter yielded good character resolution. If you wanted color, though, you lost the sharp resolution. The CGA was replaced by the enhanced graphics adapter (EGA), which can paint up to 64 colors. The EGA has since been replaced by the video graphics array (VGA), which can paint up to 256 colors. The Super VGA format can generate even sharper pixels for the 256 color spectrum, which is now the low end for colors. The Super VGA allows up to 64,000 and even 16.7-MB true color selection, depending on your video card. Super VGA is now the standard video card.

1.13 Output Devices—Printers

A *printer* is attached to the system unit with a cable that allows the user to have a *hard copy*, or paper printout, of information. The two major types of printers are *impact* and *nonimpact*. An impact printer works like a typewriter. The element strikes a ribbon, which in turn strikes the paper and leaves a mark. A *dot-matrix printer*, the most common type of impact printer, forms characters by selecting dots from a grid pattern on a movable print head. It may print in any style of letters or graphics (pictures). A dot-matrix printer operates from 80 characters per second (cps) to over 200 cps. The dot-matrix printer is being replaced by a new generation of ink jet and laser printers.

Nonimpact printers include *thermal printers*. Thermal printers burn images into paper using a dot-matrix grid. Some thermal printers heat the ribbon and melt ink onto the paper. *Ink jet printers* spray drops of ink to shape characters. The laser printer has become a popular nonimpact printer. With this type of printer, the computer instructs a laser beam to form characters by heating powdered toner and fusing it to the page by heat, as in a photocopying machine. This printer produces high-quality characters and graphic images. Laser printers operate noiselessly at speeds up to twenty-four pages per minute (ppm).

Color printers have become cost-efficient, even for the home user. Now, dot-matrix, ink jet, and thermal printers have color availability. Most color printers use a combination of four colors and are called *four color printers*. Each color is printed separately by either the spot color separation method (each color printed as a separate layer) or the process color separation method (each color is first separated into its primary color components, then printed). Both methods produce high-quality output. Color is available in laser printers, but color laser printers are very costly at this time.

1.14 Modems

A *modem* (modulator/demodulator) translates the digital signals of the computer into analog signals that travel over phone lines. The speed at which the signal travels is rated in baud, a unit of time. The rate of transmission has increased to 28,800 baud with even more rapid speeds available, but for this transmission to occur, the party on the other end must also have a modem that translates the analog signals back into digital signals. In addition, the computer needs special instructions, a software communication program, so that this activity can occur.

The growth of online services has made modems necessary. CompuServe, America Online, Prodigy, Internet, and Bulletin Board Services (BBS) make all kinds of information available. These services will be the libraries of the future.

1.15 Disks and Disk Drives

Since RAM is volatile and disappears when the computer is turned off, a computer needs *secondary storage media*, or *external storage media*, in order to save information permanently.

Disks and disk drives are magnetic media that store data and programs in the form of magnetic impulses. Such media include floppy disks, hard disks, compact discs (*CD-ROM*), and tape cartridges. In the microcomputer world, the most common secondary storage media are *floppy disks* and *hard disks*.

Floppy disks serve a dual purpose. First, disks provide a permanent means to hold data. When power is turned off, the disk retains what has been recorded on it. Second, floppy disks are transportable. Simply by inserting a disk, you can use programs or data developed on one computer on another computer. Without floppy disks, you could not use programs such as the operating system or other application packages. Each time you wanted to do some work, you would have to write your own instructions.

Storing information on a disk is analogous to keeping information in a file cabinet because both store information in files. When the computer needs this information, it goes to the disk, opens a file, "reads" the information from the disk file into RAM, and uses it. When the computer is finished using that file, it closes the file and returns (writes) it back to the disk.

1.16 Capacity Measurement—Bits and Bytes

A computer is made primarily of switches. All it can do is turn a switch on or off—0 represents an off state and 1 represents an on state. A *bit* (from **bi**nary digi**t**) is the smallest unit a computer can recognize. Bits are combined in meaningful groups, much as letters of the alphabet are combined to make words. The most common grouping is eight bits, called a *byte.* Thus, a byte may be thought of as one character.

Computer capacities such as RAM and ROM are measured in bytes. Originally, people referred to thousands of bytes, or kilobytes (KB or K), but now in millions of bytes, or *megabytes* (MB or M). A computer is binary, so it works in powers of 2. A *kilobyte* is 2 to the 10th power (2^{10}, or 1024). If your computer has 64 KB of memory, its actual memory size is 64, 1024, or 65,536 bytes. For simplification, a KB is rounded off to the nearest thousand, so 64 KB of memory means 64,000 bytes. Rapid technology growth has made megabytes the measuring factor. For example, just a few years ago, a satisfactory RAM system was 1 MB, or 1,024,000 bytes. Now, RAM expansion to 64 MB is not uncommon because so many software programs rely on RAM to perform effectively.

You should know the capacity of your computer's memory because it determines how large a program is and how much data the computer will hold. For instance, if you have 640 KB of RAM on your computer and you buy a program that requires 1 MB of RAM, your computer does not have the memory capacity to use that program. Furthermore, if your computer has a hard disk capacity of 20 MB and the application program you buy requires at least 25 MB of space on the hard disk, you cannot install the program.

Disk capacity is also measured in bytes. A double-sided 5 ¼-inch disk holds 360 KB (360,000 bytes); a 3 ½-inch double-density disk holds 720 KB. Because high-density and hard disks hold so much information, they can also be measured in megabytes. A 5 ¼-inch high-density disk holds 1.2 MB; a 3 ½-inch high-density disk holds 1.44 MB. Double-density disks are disappearing in favor of high-density disks. Hard disks range from 20 MB to over a *gigabyte* (GB), or a billion bytes. Today, most people consider a 500 MB hard disk typical; it has a capacity of approximately 500 million bytes. When referring to megabytes, most computer users use the term *meg.* A hard disk with 500 million bytes would be referred to as a 500 meg hard disk, whereas a hard disk with 1.2 billion bytes would be referred to as a *gig* drive.

1.17 Minifloppy Disks

Floppy disks come in two sizes: 3 ½-inch and 5 ¼-inch. The standard size used to be the 5 ¼-inch floppy, but it is now the 3 ½-inch floppy. The 5 ¼-inch floppy disk, technically known as a *minifloppy diskette,* is a circular piece of plastic, polyurethane, or Mylar covered with magnetic oxide (see Figure 1.5). It is always inside a relatively rigid, unremovable protective jacket with a lined inner surface. Like a phonograph record, the disk has a hole (called a hub) in the center so that it can fit onto the disk drive's spindle. The disk drive spins the disk to find information on it or to write information to it.

Once the disk is locked into the disk drive, it spins at about 300 revolutions per minute. The disk has an exposed opening called the *head slot* where data is written to and read from. Here the disk drive's magnetic heads actually touch the disk's surface. There is also a cutout on the disk's side known as a *write-protect notch*, which may be covered with a write-protect tab. If a disk is write-protected with the notch covered, the original programs and data on the disk cannot be written over and can never be lost. If the write-protect notch is not covered, data may be read from the disk as well as written to it. Some disks have no notch and therefore can never be written on. These disks are write-protected and can only be read.

Figure 1.5   A Minifloppy 5¼-Inch Disk

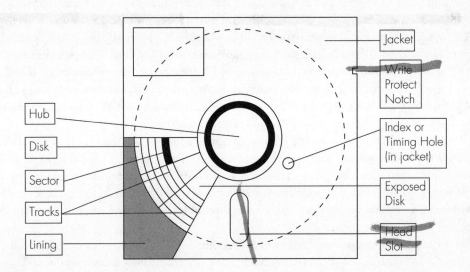

A 5 ¼-inch disk comes in two formats: double-density and high-density. The type of format you use depends on what kind of disk drive you have. Newer computers no longer use 5 ¼-inch disk drives. Furthermore, you will not see many double-sided, double-density disk drives or disks today. A 5 ¼-inch double-sided, double-density disk can store approximately 360 KB, whereas a 5 ¼-inch double-sided, high-density disk can store 1.2 MB of information. Usually, a high-capacity disk is called a *high-density disk*.

1.18 Microfloppy Disks

In principle, 3 ½-inch *microfloppy disks* work the same way as 5 ¼-inch disks, except that 3 ½-inch disks are smaller and are enclosed in a rigid plastic shell. In addition, each 3 ½-inch disk has a shutter that covers the read/write head. The computer's disk drive opens the shutter only when it needs access. When the disk is not in the drive, the shutter is closed. This disk does not use an *index* or *timing hole*; this function is performed by the *sector notch* next to the disk drive's spindle. The write-protect notch can be either a *built-in slider* or a *breakaway tab*, usually a slider. When the slider covers the hole, you may read or write to the disk. When you can see through the hole, it is a read-only disk. The 3 ½-inch disk also comes in two formats. A 3 ½-inch double-sided, double-density disk can store approximately 720 KB, whereas a 3 ½-inch double-sided, high-density disk can store 1.44 MB of information. There is also a newer size, the 3 ½-inch high-density disk, which can store 2.88 MB of information. Figure 1.6 shows the 3 ½-inch disk.

Figure 1.6   A Microfloppy 3 ½-Inch Disk

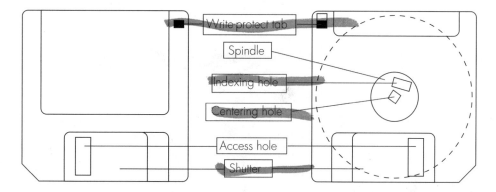

1.19 CD-ROM

The latest transport device for software is the ***compact disc.*** Borrowed from the music recording business, this disc can hold up to 600 MB of data. Like the recording compact disc, the disk accesses information with a laser. Although the compact disc is a read-only device at present, its write capabilities are well-known. CD-ROM drives are becoming commonplace in CPUs, and more software companies are shipping software on compact discs simply because it is cost-effective. Soon, read/write compact discs and read/write compact disc drives will be commonplace.

1.20 Hard Disks

A fixed disk drive, known as a hard disk, or a hard drive, is a disk that is usually permanently installed in the system unit (see Figure 1.7). A hard disk holds much more information than a floppy disk. If we compare a floppy disk to a file cabinet that holds data and programs, we can compare a hard disk to a room full of file cabinets. Both floppy disks and hard disks hold data and programs, but a hard disk simply holds more. Today, a common hard disk storage capacity is 300 megabytes, with 500 MB becoming the standard.

A hard disk is composed of two or more rigid platters, usually made of aluminum and coated with oxide, which allow data to be encoded magnetically. Both the platters and the read/write heads are permanently sealed inside a box; the user cannot touch or see the drive or disks. These platters are affixed to a spindle that rotates at about 3600 RPM. This speed can vary, depending on the type of hard disk. This speed makes data access much faster than a standard floppy disk drive. The rapidly spinning disks in the sealed box create air pressure that makes the recording heads float on a cushion of air above the platters' surfaces. Because the hard disk rotates faster than a floppy disk and because the head floats above the surface, the hard disk can not only store much more data, but it can also access it much more quickly.

Figure 1.7   A Hard Disk

1.21 Dividing the Disk

A disk's structure is essentially the same whether it is a hard disk or a floppy disk. Data is recorded on the surface of a disk in a series of concentric circles known as *tracks*, similar to grooves on a music disc. Each track on the disk is a separate circle divided into *sectors*. The amount of data that can be stored on a disk depends on the density—the number of tracks and the numbers of the sectors per track. Since a hard disk is comprised of several platters, it has an additional measurement—a *cylinder*. Two or more platters are stacked on top of one another with the tracks aligned. If you connect any one track through all the platters, you have a cylinder (see Figure 1.8).

A *cluster* is at least one sector. If it is composed of more than one sector, the sectors must be adjacent. The number of sectors in a cluster can vary from one to eight or more. The location and number of sectors per cluster are determined by the software in a process known as *formatting*. The reason a cluster is so important is that the cluster is the basic unit of disk storage. Whenever a computer reads or writes to a disk, it always reads or writes a full cluster, regardless of the space that the data needs.

A disk is a random access medium, which does not mean that the data or programs are randomly arranged on the disk. It means that the head of the disk drive, which reads the disk, does not have to read all the information on the disk to find a specific item. The CPU may instruct the head of the disk drive to go directly to the track and sector that hold the specific item of information.

Figure 1.8   Hard Disk Cylinders

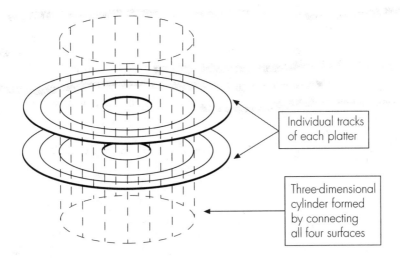

Individual tracks
of each platter

Three-dimensional
cylinder formed
by connecting
all four surfaces

1.22 Disk Drives

A *disk drive* writes information to and from a disk. All disk drives have heads that read and write information back and forth between RAM and the disk, much like the ones on tape or video recorders.

A floppy disk drive is the device that holds a floppy disk. The user inserts the floppy disk into the disk drive (see Figure 1.9). The hub of the disk fits onto the hub mechanism, which grabs the disk. When the disk drive door is shut or latched, the disk is secured to the hub mechanism. The jacket remains stationary while the floppy disk rotates. The disk drive head reads and writes information back and forth between RAM and the disk through the exposed head slot. Older disk drives are double-sided and can read and write to both sides of a disk, but cannot read or write to a high-density floppy disk. The new generation of high-density disk drives can read and write to both the old style double-density disks and the new style high-density disks.

Figure 1.9   A Floppy Disk Drive

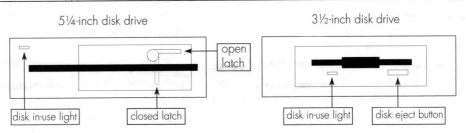

5¼-inch disk drive

3½-inch disk drive

open latch

disk in-use light   closed latch

disk in-use light   disk eject button

1.23 Device Names

A *device* is a place for the computer to send (write) or receive (read) information. In order for the system to know which device it should be communicating with at any given time, the system gives every device a unique name. Device names cannot be used for any other purpose. Disk drives are devices. A disk drive name is a letter followed by a colon. You must identify the disk drives you have on your microcomputer. Drive A is the first floppy disk drive. Drive C is the first hard disk drive. All other drives are lettered alphabetically from B to Z. You must be able to identify which disk drives you are using. Some common configurations are illustrated in Figure 1.10.

Figure 1.10   Disk Drive Configurations

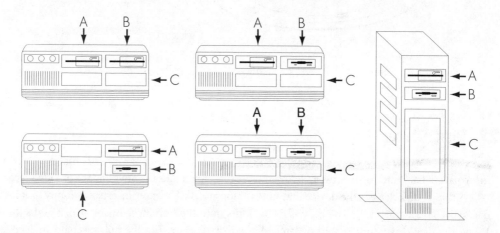

1.24 Software

To this point, primarily we have discussed hardware. However, software is what makes a computer useful. In fact, without software, hardware has no use. You can think of hardware as a box to run software. Software is the step-by-step instructions that tell the computer what to do. These instructions are called *programs*. Programs need to be installed, or *loaded*, into RAM, where the CPU executes, or runs them. Programs usually come stored on disks. The program is read into memory from the floppy disk or hard disk. Software may also be divided into categories. The most common division is system software and application software.

Application software solves problems, handles information, and is user-oriented. Application software may also be called packages, off-the-shelf software, canned software, software, or just apps. You may have heard of application software by brand names such as Word for Windows or Lotus 1-2-3. Thousands of application packages are commercially available. Most people purchase a computer to use application software.

System software coordinates the operations of the hardware components. The computer manufacturer usually supplies system software because it is needed to run application software. System software is always computer-oriented, rather than user-oriented. It takes care of what the computer needs so that the computer can run application software.

When you purchase a computer, you also purchase the operating system software. It is a manual with several disks or a CD-ROM disc. Running a computer is somewhat analogous to producing a concert. The hardware is like the musicians and their instruments, which do not change. Just as the musicians can play anything from Ludwig van Beethoven to Paul McCartney, the computer hardware can "play" any application software from accounting to a game. Like the conductor who tells the violins or trumpets when to play and how loudly, the *operating system* makes the computer work. The operating system supervises the processing of application programs and all the input/output of the computer. It is the first and most important program on the computer and *must* be loaded into memory (RAM) before any other program. Working with the operating system is known as being at the *system level.*

Typically, operating systems are comprised of several important programs stored as system files. These include a program that transfers data to and from the disk and into and out of memory and performs other disk-related tasks. Other important programs handle hardware-specific tasks. These programs check such things as whether a key has been pressed and, if it has, they encode it so that the computer can read it and then decode it so that it may be written to the screen. It encodes and decodes from bits and bytes into letters and words.

The term *operating system* is generic. Brand names for microcomputer operating systems include CP/M, Unix, Xenix, MS-DOS, Apple-DOS, TRS-DOS, and UCSD-P. The new operating system for microcomputers is Windows 95, which Microsoft Corporation developed and owns. Windows 95 is licensed to computer manufacturers who tailor it to their specific hardware, as well as to users who may purchase the product commercially.

Most people who use a computer are interested in application software. They want programs that are easy to use. If you are going to use a computer and run application packages, you are going to need to know how to use the operating system first. No application program can be used without an operating system. Since Windows 95 is the new microcomputer operating system in use today, this text is devoted to teaching the concepts of the operating system in general and Windows 95 operations in particular.

1.25 Operating System Fundamentals

Windows 95 is a program that is always working. No computer can work unless it has an operating system. When you boot the system, you are loading the system software or operating system programs into RAM. When you turn on the power to the computer, or "power up," the computer would not know what to do if there were no programs or sets of instructions. These most basic instructions are built into a chip installed in the computer called ROM-BIOS (read-only memory, Basic-Input Output System). Loading the operating system entails the ROM-BIOS checking to see if a disk drive is installed. The program then checks to see if there is a disk in drive A. If there is no disk in drive A and if there is a hard disk, the program will check drive C. It is looking for the operating system files, a file called the boot record. It reads the record from the disk into RAM and turns control over to this program. The boot record is also a program that executes; its job is to read into RAM the rest of the operating system. In essence, it pulls the system up by its *bootstraps*. Thus, you *boot* the computer instead of merely turning it on.

The purpose of the operating system files that are loaded into RAM is to manage the resources and primary functions of the computer. Once the operating system is loaded, it allows communication to and from the CPU and RAM by the use of the peripheral devices. When you key in a character on the keyboard, that character moves *to* the CPU and RAM; this is input. When a character is displayed (written) to the monitor or the printer, it moves *from* the CPU and RAM; this is output. Input and output take place within the CPU, memory, and the different peripherals. Then, the application program can concentrate on doing its job, such as word processing, without having to worry about how the document gets from the keyboard to RAM and from RAM to the screen. The operating system takes care of those critical functions. This whole process can be considered analogous to driving an automobile. Most of us use our cars to get from point A to point B. We would not like it if every time we wanted to drive, we first had to open the hood and attach the proper cables to the battery and to all the other parts that are necessary to start the engine. The operating system is the engine of the computer that allows the user to run the application in the same manner that a person drives a car.

1.26 Why Windows 95?

The most popular operating system was MS-DOS. Windows 3.1 was developed as the graphical user interface to be used with MS-DOS. Why, then, did Microsoft develop a new operating system? One of the problems with DOS is that it is a command-line interface and is perceived as unfriendly to users. Windows 3.1 was developed to provide, among other things, a friendly user interface, or graphical user interface (GUI, pronounced *gooey*). Windows 3.1 was not an operating system as such, but an operating environment. You still had to run DOS when using Windows. The Windows 3.1 interface changed how you communicated with your computer by using icons (pictorial representations) and menus. In addition, Windows allowed you to install hardware, such as a printer, rather than on an application-by-application basis. Windows 3.1 and applications written for Windows 3.1 had a standard look and feel. Windows 3.1 introduced multitasking, which is the ability to accomplish more than one task at a time. However, since Windows 3.1 was based on DOS, an old technology, there were problems.

In August 1995, Microsoft began selling Windows 95 to the public. Windows 95 replaces DOS and Windows. It is called a true 32-bit operating system, which means that Windows 95 can take advantage of the power and speed of the new microprocessors. Built with new architecture (design), Windows 95 is faster, handles computer resources better, improves the system capacity to run more applications, and is more robust. Robust means, among other things, that if an application program does not work, your system will not crash (cease to function). Instead, Windows 95 will close the aberrant program and will allow you to continue your work.

Windows 95 supports Plug and Play. Prior to the introduction of the Windows 95 Plug and Play standard, adding devices to a PC was a very painful process. A lack of coordination between the hardware and software caused devices to conflict with one another. Furthermore, the application software had no idea what devices were on the system. The different bus standards for different devices complicated the issue further. Plug and Play lets the devices talk to Windows 95, which then handles how the programs can and will use the devices. This feature allows users to buy new devices and plug them into the computer allowing Windows 95 to handle the "dirty" work.

Although the design of Windows 95 is important in terms of new hardware, what has dramatically changed is the user interface. The new Windows 95 user interface is intended to be easier and more intuitive and easier to use. Thus, features like Wizards lead you through things you do not know how to do. Windows 95 allows you to use both the right and left mouse buttons and provides context-sensitive menus at a mere click of the mouse.

Object linking and embedding (OLE) was introduced in Windows 3.1 and was much improved in Windows 95. OLE is a standard that application programs use to make sharing data among different applications easier. One of the improvements in OLE is in-place editing. When a user creates a document, he can use many application programs to create different types of data to appear in that document. For instance, he can use a word processor to create text and a drawing program to create a picture. Both the text and the drawing will appear in the same document. With in-place editing, the user can edit either the picture (an object) or his text (an object). The appropriate application program that created the object will appear without the user ever leaving his document. This process makes sharing data among programs much easier and more transparent for the user. The docucentric approach is further enhanced and refined in Windows 95. Now, almost everything in Windows 95 is considered an object that the user can manipulate.

1.27 Hardware Requirements for Windows 95

Windows 95 is a very powerful operating system. Although you can run your old programs under Windows 95, you will find yourself buying the new, improved versions of your favorite application programs. Because these programs are powerful, they are also very large. To run Windows 95, you need at least a 386 or higher processor, at least 4 MB of memory, a high-density disk drive, and a hard disk drive with at least 35 MB available. Furthermore, you need a VGA monitor and VGA display adapter. With this hardware, you can run Windows 95 and applications written for Windows 95. This is the bare minimum.

If you really want to take advantage of Windows 95, you will want at least a 486DX2, 66 MHz processor, 8 MB of memory, a high-resolution Super VGA monitor, and a Super VGA display adapter with special memory (2 MB) on the video board for processing graphics. You will want the largest hard disk you can afford—at least 500 MB. You will also want a CD-ROM drive and probably a modem with a speed of at least 14,400 baud. In the computer world and especially in the Windows 95 world, more is better—more memory, more disk space, a faster processor, and so forth.

1.28 Networks

Today, it is likely that you will be using a network in a work or lab environment. A *network* is two or more computers connected together, and requires special hardware and software. In addition, networks usually have various peripheral devices such as printers connected to them. A network helps users share expensive devices, such as laser printers or modems. A network provides many advantages such as allowing to share data. Several users can access information on the hard disk, located on the main network computer, which is called the *server*. Networks also enable users to send electronic mail, e-mail, to other users on the system.

There are two kinds of networks. A local area network (LAN) encompasses a small area, such as one office. The hardware components, such as the server, terminals, and printers, are directly connected by cables (see Figure 1.11). A wide area network, or WAN, connects computers over a much larger area, such as from building to building, state to state, or country to country. Hardware components of the WAN communicate via telephone lines, fiber-optic cables, or even satellites. The Internet is an example of a wide area network.

Figure 1.11   A Typical Network Configuration

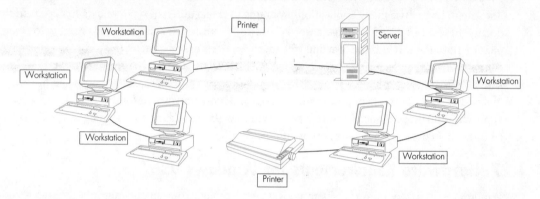

Chapter Summary

This chapter discussed the fundamental operations of a computer. The various hardware components were also examined. In addition, the concept and purpose of software was introduced. The differences between application software and system software (operating systems) were presented. Application software solves problems, whereas system software handles the integration of the hardware and the interface between the hardware and the software. A computer cannot run without first having an operating system loaded into RAM. Windows 95, the newest operating system in use today, is a graphical operating system that is user friendly, making the use of operating system commands easier for the user. What has changed for the user is the user interface. Windows 95 has a new, docucentric approach, and it requires powerful hardware to operate successfully.

Key Terms

Adapter cards	Breakaway tab	Cluster
Application software	Built-in slider	Compact disc
Bit	Bus	CPU
Boot	Byte	Cylinder
Boot record	Cache	Data
Bootstraps	CD-ROM	Device

Disk drive	Kilobyte (KB)	Pixels
Dot-matrix printer	Laser printer	Printer
Expansion slots	Light pen	Programs
External storage media	Loaded	RAM
Firmware	Local bus	ROM
Floppy disks	Main memory	Scanners
Formatting	Meg	Secondary storage media
Four-color printers	Megabyte (MB)	Sectors
Gigabyte	Megahertz (MHz)	Sector notch
Glide pad	Memory	Server
Hard copy	Microcomputer	Software
Hard disk	Microfloppy disk	System board
Hardware	Minifloppy disk	System configuration
Head slot	Modem	System level
High-density disk	Monitor	System software
Impact printers	Motherboard	Thermal printers
Index hole	Mouse	Timing hole
Ink jet printer	Network	Trackball
Input devices	Nonimpact printer	Tracks
Integrated pointing device	Operating system	Video card
Internal bus	Peripheral device	Write-product notch

Discussion Questions

1. Define hardware.
2. Define software.
3. What is data?
4. What is the difference between hardware and software?
5. What is meant by the system configuration?
6. Describe a typical microcomputer configuration.
7. Compare and contrast the SX and DX models of the microprocessor.
8. What is the purpose and function of the bus?
9. Compare and contrast RAM and ROM.
10. What is an adapter board?
11. List two input and two output devices and briefly explain how these devices work.
12. What are pixels?
13. Compare and contrast impact and nonimpact printers.
14. What purpose do disks serve?
15. What is the difference between disk storage and memory capacity?
16. What is the difference between high-capacity and double-density floppy disks?
17. What is a CD-ROM? What is its purpose?
18. How many types of disks are there? Describe them.
19. What is the difference between a hard disk and a floppy disk?

20. What are tracks and sectors? Where are they found?
21. What is a cluster? What is it comprised of?
22. What is a device?
23. Compare and contrast application software and system software.
24. Can application packages run without an operating system? Why or why not?
25. What is the function of an operating system?
26. Compare and contrast internal and external commands.
27. What is the purpose and function of a network?
28. List the two types of networks and explain differences.

True/False Questions

For each question, circle the letter T if the question is true and the letter F if the question is false.

T   F   1. Booting the system simply means turning on the power.
T   F   2. The bus is the electrical connection between the CPU and all of the output devices.
T   F   3. The compact disc may only be used in Windows 95.
T   F   4. Windows 95 replaces both DOS and Windows 3.1.
T   F   5. By themselves, the hardware components of the computer can do nothing.

Completion Questions

Write the correct answer in each blank space.

1. A common name for the single-user computer is the _____.
2. Components of a complete computer system are also called _____.
3. One of the most common input devices is the _____.
4. People purchase a computer because of the availability of _____.
5. Clusters are comprised of _____.

Multiple Choice Questions

Circle the letter for the correct answer to each question.

1. The physical components of a computer system are called
   a. software.
   b. firmware.
   c. hardware.
   d. none of the above

2. Memory that disappears when the computer's power is turned off is considered
   a. volatile.
   b. nonvolatile.
   c. vital.
   d. nonfatal.

3. The ability to plug in a device and let the operating system handle the configuration of the device is called
   a. configuring the system.
   b. Plug and Play.
   c. playing a device.
   d. none of the above

4. The central processing unit
   a. is the workspace of the computer.
   b. comprehends and carries out instructions that by a program sends it.
   c. is volatile.
   d. all of the above

5. The purpose of having printed circuit boards is
   a. so that the user can add peripheral devices.
   b. to cut down on the amount of electricity a computer uses.
   c. to have a means of permanently storing data and programs.
   d. none of the above

Chapter 2

Exploring Windows 95

Chapter Overview

In this chapter, you will be introduced to the primary features of Windows 95. You will learn how to use the desktop and the taskbar, and you will familiarize yourself with menus and their uses. You will learn about windows, the different techniques to manipulate them, and the proper terminology and concepts behind the basic features of Windows 95, such as objects and properties. You will also learn to prepare a disk and how to start and exit Windows 95.

Learning Objectives

1. Explain the purpose and function of the desktop.
2. Explain the purpose and function of the objects found on the desktop.
3. Explain the purpose and function of pointing devices.
4. List and differentiate among the four types of pointing devices.
5. Identify the items found on the Start menu.
6. Explain the purpose and function of cascading menus.
7. Compare and contrast dialog boxes and message boxes.
8. Explain the purpose and function of sizing and moving windows.
9. Explain the difference between minimizing and sizing a window.
10. Explain the purpose and function of a property sheet.
11. Explain the purpose and function of an object.
12. Describe the difference between a parent and a child window.
13. Define the term *docucentric* as a Windows 95 paradigm.
14. Explain the purpose and function of multitasking and multithreading.
15. Compare and contrast foreground and background windows.
16. Compare and contrast cascading and tiling windows.
17. Explain the purpose and function of formatting a disk.

Student Outcomes

1. Start and exit windows.
2. Open the Start menu and use the cascading menus.
3. Identify by name and function the basic components of the desktop.
4. Move and resize a window.
5. Change the location and size of the taskbar.
6. Access and use the taskbar property sheet.
7. Open and close child and parent windows.
8. Move between foreground and background windows.
9. Use the taskbar to tile and cascade windows.
10. Format a disk.

2.1   Starting and Exiting Windows 95

Software is always being improved. Almost all the software you buy will, at some later time, be updated. In order to stay current with the latest changes in the software, you purchase upgrades. An *upgrade* is the newest version of software which replaces old software.

An operating system is also software. Thus, if you were using DOS or Windows 3.1 and you purchased Windows 95 as an upgrade, it came on either many floppy disks or on one CD-ROM disc. You should know that the CD-ROM and floppy disk versions of Windows 95 are different. The floppy disk version does not include all the programs and files that the CD-ROM version does. In either case, you must upgrade Windows 95 to the hard disk first.

You may install or upgrade an operating system or programs. To *install* is to copy new files to the hard disk. Usually an operating system upgrade is a special process that you only do once. Essentially, an upgrade means copying, sometimes referred to as installing, the new operating system files from the disks to the hard drive. An upgrade replaces old files with new files. Once you install the new operating system to the hard drive, you have completed the upgrade process.

However, if you purchased a new computer or are in a school or work environment, most often, installing Windows 95 has already been done. Just having Windows 95 installed is not enough to do work. Remember, you must also place the operating system files in memory, or boot the system. *Booting the system* means the operating system files are copied from the hard disk to memory. Fortunately, it simply means turning on the computer. In Windows 95, when you are done working, you do not turn off your computer. You must follow the proper shut-down procedure which you will learn at the end of this chapter.

2.2   The Desktop

When you want to work, you usually work at a desk that contains *objects*, the tools you use when you work. If you want to work on your taxes, you place the income tax form on your desk as well as the instructions on how to fill out the form. You may also have a tool such as a calculator to help you with your task. In Windows 95 you also have a desk, but you must boot the system in order to see it. Your desk is called the *desktop*, which in Windows 95, is your primary work area (see Figure 2.1). Like your desk, it is a convenient location to place objects such as your tools, your program files, your document files, and your physical devices. It can also provide access to a network, if you are on a network.

Figure 2.1   The Desktop

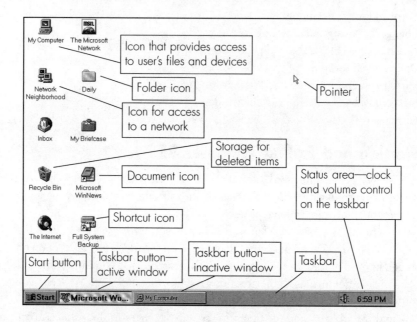

Although the desktop varies depending on what objects have been placed on it, certain items are always present.

Taskbar   The major focal point of Windows 95 is the taskbar. Typically located at the bottom of the screen, the taskbar contains the *Start button*. This button, when clicked, displays a menu that allows you to launch programs, open documents, alter the look of the desktop, and find files. It also allows you access to help if you are unsure of what to do. Lastly, it is the location of the command for shutting down the computer.

Taskbar buttons   Whenever you open a program, a document, or any window, a labeled button is placed on the taskbar. You can use this button to move quickly between the windows you have to open. By clicking the desired button on the taskbar, you easily switch to a different task. The button can be an application program, a folder that holds programs and files, or a device such as a disk drive. Any window that is open appears on the taskbar. The active window is identified by its button being in a three-dimensional highlighted view.

Status area   The status area is on the opposite end on the taskbar. Any program can place information or notification of events in the status area. For instance, if you were connected to the Internet via modem, an icon of a modem would appear in the status area whenever the connection is active. Windows 95 also places information in the status area. In Figure 2.1, the Clock and Volume control icons appear in the status area. The digital clock indicates what time it is. The sound icon controls the volume of the computer's sound system.

Icons   An icon represents a pictorial representation of an object. An icon may be a program, a document, or a folder that holds programs or documents. A shortcut icon provides convenient access to other objects that are stored elsewhere. Icons appear on the desktop and in a window, and they also open into windows. A window is the primary way you work with and interact with data.

Pointer   The pointer is the visual representation of your location on the screen.

2.3   Pointing Devices

A graphical user interface allows you to select and manipulate objects on the screen. The arrow, ⌖ called the *mouse pointer*, or *cursor*, tells you where you are on the screen. You manipulate the pointer by moving the pointing device. The most common pointing device is the *mouse*. As you move the mouse on a flat surface, it responds by moving the arrow on the screen. When you position the arrow over an object, you are pointing to it.

When you position the arrow over an object and click the left mouse button, you are selecting or activating that object. *Clicking* is the process of pressing and then immediately releasing the left mouse button one time. When you double-click an object, you are usually about to take some kind of action. *Double-clicking* means quickly pressing and releasing the left mouse button twice. Sometimes the left mouse button is called the *primary mouse button*. Whenever you press the right mouse button it is called *right-clicking*. Thus, when you are instructed to click, it means press and release the left mouse button. Remember, click refers to the left mouse button; right-click refers to the right mouse button.

When you select an object and then press and hold the left mouse button, you are preparing to drag an object across the screen. *Dragging* is the process of moving an object. When you release the mouse button, you will place the object in another location. This process is called *drag and drop*. Dragging means holding the left mouse button while you drag. *Right-dragging* means holding the right mouse button while you drag.

This text will refer to a mouse, but the same instructions may be used for a *trackball* or *integrated pointer*. In addition, when the text refers to placing the mouse pointer on an object, it will use the term mouse, though technically it is the cursor.

The shape of a pointer changes. When it is an arrow, you can move it on the screen. When it changes to an hour glass shape, it is telling you to wait while Windows 95 completes a task. If you work with text, the shape of the pointer becomes an I beam. If the pointer changes its shape to a circle with a slash through it, the standard international symbol for NO, it is telling you that Windows 95 cannot do what you asked.

2.4   *Activity—Starting Windows 95 and Using the Start Menu*

Note: Some networks require a disk in drive A. Check with your network administrator for the procedures in your lab environment.

1   Locate the on/off switch for the monitor and turn it on.

2   There should be no disks in any drive. Power on the computer by locating the power switch. The type of switch and location will vary from computer to computer. Sometimes the switch is a lever that you lift; other times it is a button that you press. The location of the power switch may be on the front, side, or back of the computer.

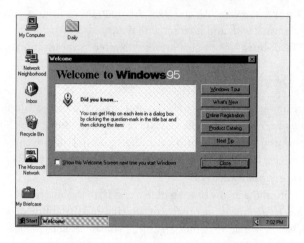

What's happening? How long the system takes to boot depends on the speed of your processor, how much memory you have, and other such factors. When the booting process is complete, you will see a Windows 95 logo on the screen. However, Windows 95 is still not finished loading. The number of programs that are loaded automatically when you start Windows 95 will affect the time it takes to get to the desktop. The Welcome Screen, which contains helpful hints, may appear on the screen. If you do not want to see the Welcome Screen every time you boot the system, click the box next to Show this Welcome Screen next time you start Windows so that a check mark does not appear in the box. Then your screen will look as follows:

3   Click the **Start** button on the taskbar.

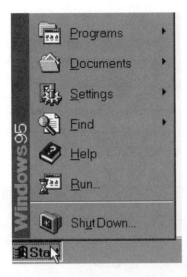

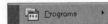

You have opened a *menu* which presents a list of items from which you may choose. The Start menu lists the major functions on your system:

Programs   Takes you to another menu that lists the application programs on your system.

Documents   Takes you to another menu that lists the last documents on which you were working.

Settings   Takes you to a menu that allows you to alter your Windows 95 environment.

Find   Takes you to a menu so that you can locate files, folders, computers, or a network.

Help   Takes you to the help program so that you can learn how to accomplish tasks.

Run   Allows you to execute a program when you know the program's name.

Shut Down   The proper way to exit Windows 95.

Windows 95 uses cascading menus. A *cascading menu* is a menu that opens another menu. In the cascading menu structure, the first in the series is a parent to the menu that follows. Each subsequent child menu becomes a parent to next menu. Thus, a cascading menu is also referred to as a *hierarchical menu* with *parent* and *child menus*, so that each time you make a choice, another menu opens. Since not all menus are cascading menus, a right-pointing triangular arrow ( ) appears to the right of any menu that can be cascaded. You can identify a cascading menu by the triangular arrow on its right shown below:

As you move the mouse pointer, you can tell which item is selected on the menu because it is highlighted. The purpose of highlighting is to identify a selected item. *Highlighting* alters the appearance of the selection usually by displaying the selected item in a different color.

4   Move the mouse pointer to **Programs** on the **Start** menu.

To *point* is to place the mouse pointer on a specified item. Since Programs has a triangular arrow, another menu opened.

One of the nice features of Windows 95 is that you do not have to press the mouse button when selecting cascading menus. You simply point the mouse to the next menu. What is on your Programs menu will vary depending on what software you have installed on your computer.

5   Point to **Accessories**.

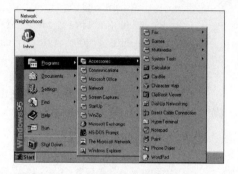

> ■hat's
> happening? Again, the highlighting told you that you selected Accessories. When you pointed the mouse on Accessories, it opened the next menu.

6   Point to **Games**.

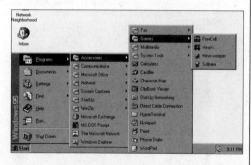

> ■hat's
> happening? Although in this example the menus continued cascading to the right, the placement of the cascading menus may vary depending on your screen resolution.

Sometimes the cascading menus appear on top of the other menus, especially when there is not enough room on the right to display them. The Games menu displays a list of games that come with Windows 95. Since not one of the choices on the Games menu has a triangular arrow, there are no more menus. Now you want to choose something to do. In this case, you want to play a game.

7   Click **FreeCell**.

> ■hat's
> happening? FreeCell is an application program. When you clicked on it, you loaded the program file into memory. When a program is in memory, it may be used. You can now play a card game called FreeCell. Playing this game will allow you to become familiar with your mouse as well as introduce you to some of the common elements of an application program.

Every application program has a *title bar* with the name of the application program on it. In addition, an application program will usually have a menu bar. The FreeCell menu bar has two menu choices: Game and Help. Game has the letter G underlined, and Help has the letter H underlined. Whenever you see an underlined letter, you may open, or *drop down*, the menu by pressing the [Alt] key and the underlined letter, or you may select the menu of interest the usual way by clicking it. Most people prefer clicking the mouse.

8   Click **Game**.

What's happening? → You have several choices on the menu. If an item is dimmed, it is unavailable. For instance, Undo is dimmed. You have not yet done anything, so there is nothing to undo. Many choices have a keystroke, or combination of keystrokes, next to the menu choice. Rather than mouse clicking, you may use the keyboard commands. You are going to select a specific game to play. You could press the [F3] key on the keyboard, but you are going to use the mouse.

9   Click **Select Game**.

What's happening? → A *dialog box* appears. A dialog box either presents information to you or requests information from you. Most dialog boxes have a default choice. This dialog box default choice is the number of a specific game. If you do not key in other information, the game number in the box will be selected. If you do not want to use the default selection, you may override it by keying in the number of the game you wish to play.

10   Key in the following: **5500** [Enter]

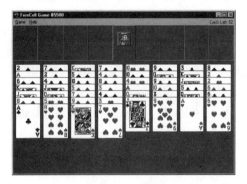

What's happening? → Now you may play the game of your choice. The object of the game is to place all the cards beginning with the ace in order within the currently empty right-hand squares. You may temporarily place cards in the left-hand empty squares as you move the cards around. On the playing field, you must place the red and black cards in alternate order.

11 Click the ace of clubs.

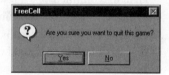

> **What's happening?** You can tell that you have selected the ace of clubs because it is highlighted.

12 Click the empty square farthest to the right.

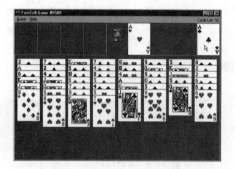

> **What's happening?** You moved the ace of clubs to the top. At the same time, the ace of hearts also moved.

13 Click the queen of spades, and then the king of hearts.

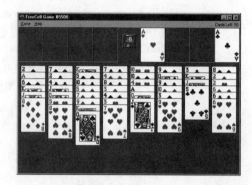

> **What's happening?** You moved the queen of spades on top of the king of hearts. If you wanted more information on how to play the game, you would select Help on the menu bar. At this point, you are going to close the program and return to the desktop.

14 Click **Game** and then **Exit**.

> **What's happening?** You are presented with a message box. A *message box* is a type of dialog box that informs you of a condition. It interrupts your current task to alert you to a problem with your system, to inform you of an error you have made, to request a confirmation on a command that could have serious consequences, or to explain why the command you have chosen will not work. These message boxes usually display a graphical symbol to alert you to the problem.

A Question:

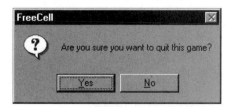

Information:

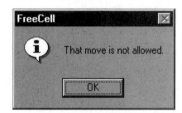

A critical error:

Message boxes most often ask you to confirm, cancel, or retry an action after you have corrected the problem. Dialog boxes provide command buttons to accomplish these tasks.

A *command button* is an example of a control because it controls what happens. In this case, you have two choices—Yes, which acknowledges that you do wish to carry out your command of Exit FreeCell, or No, you do not want to quit this game. Command buttons also have default values. If you look carefully at the Yes command button, you will see two signs that it is the default button—its border is darker than the border of the No button, and a dotted rectangle surrounds Yes. With a mouse, you choose a button by clicking it. If you are using the keyboard, you may use the **Tab** key to move between the buttons. An easier way to carry out the selected action (the default) is to press **Enter**.

15 Click **Yes**.

What's
happening? → You have closed FreeCell and returned to the desktop.

2.5   Activity—Exploring The Desktop

1   Hold the pointer over the **Start** button until you see the following ToolTip.

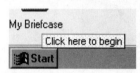

What's happening? ➔ Whenever the mouse pointer pauses over a button on a toolbar or on the taskbar, a ToolTip appears. A *ToolTip* is a brief description of either the function of the button or simply its name.

2   Right-click the **Start** button.

What's happening? ➔ You have opened a pop-up menu. A *pop-up menu* provides an efficient way for you to perform an operation on an object. The object in this case is the Start button. Pop-up menus, sometimes called *shortcut menus*, are displayed at the location of the pointer. They eliminate the need to move the pointer to the menu bar and then select from the menu. Usually, pop-up menus open with a right-click on the object.

3   Click the desktop to close the short-cut menu.

4   Hold the pointer over the time.

What's happening? ➔ In this instance, the ToolTip is the display of the current day and date. ToolTips reveal information about the selected object. To use ToolTips, hold the mouse pointer over the object for a few seconds.

5   Right-click the time on the taskbar.

What's happening? ➔ You have opened another pop-up menu. The object in this case is the Time. You have choices such as the ability to adjust the data and time from the pop-up menu.

6   Click the **Volume** icon. (*Note:* If you do not have a sound card, this option will not be available. If you have a sound card but do not have this icon, click **Start**. Point to Settings and click **Control Panel**. Double-click the **Multimedia** icon. You will see the location to display this icon.)

What's happening? ➔ Here is another example of a control. *Controls* are graphic objects that represent the operations or properties of other objects. This one is a slider control. A *slider* lets you adjust or set values when there is a range of values. You set or adjust the control by moving the slider with the mouse. In this case, the action is changing the volume level from high to low.

Another control in this dialog box is the check box. A **check box** is a **toggle switch**. A toggle switch is either on or off, much like a light switch. You click in the check box to turn the feature off or on. When there is a ☑ in the box, it is set (enabled) or "on." When it is empty, as this one is, it is not set, (disabled) or it is "off." Your choice here is to have no sound (the Mute check box with a ☑ in it) or have sound (the Mute check box with no ☑ in it).

7   Click the check box.

What's
happening? → You have turned off the sound.

8   Click outside the **Volume** box to close it.

What's
happening? → On the taskbar, the international symbol for No (the circle with a bar through it) shows that the sound is off.

9   Click the **Volume** icon, and then click the **Mute** check box to set the sound.

10   Right-click the **Sound** icon.

What's
happening? → You have opened another pop-up menu. The object in this case is the Volume. You have two choices. You may open the Volume Controls dialog box or the Audio property sheet.

11 Double-click the **My Computer** icon.

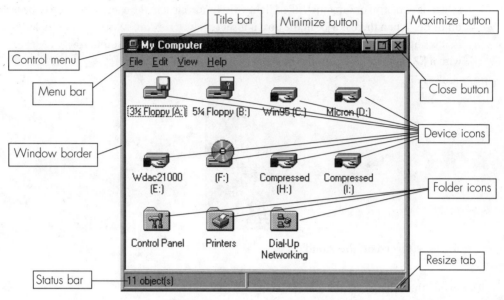

> You have opened a window with objects in it. If you look at the Taskbar, you will see that My Computer appears as a button. The button is highlighted, indicating that it is active. The title bar of the My Computer window is also highlighted, indicating that is the active window. The My Computer window allows you access to your storage devices, such as disk drives and folders that contain objects that control your system. The My Computer window has the following items:

Control menu   When clicked, it will allow you to drop down a menu to control the window by using the keyboard or mouse. In some instances, if you right-click a control-menu, it will open another menu to locate files and create shortcuts.

Title bar   The name of the window.

Minimize button   When clicked, it will keep the window open but minimize it. It will still appear on the taskbar as a button.

Maximize button   When clicked, it makes the window fill the entire screen.

Close button   When clicked, it will close the window. Since it is closed, it will no longer have a button on the taskbar.

Device icons   Represent the devices on your system. Each icon shows what type of device it is, whether a floppy disk drive, a hard drive, or a CD-ROM drive.

Resize tab   By dragging on this corner, you can make the window larger or smaller. This is called sizing a window.

Folder icons   Represent folders which contain objects that let you control your system.

Status bar   Provide information about the window, in this case, how many objects are in it.

Window border   Identifies the boundaries of the window.

Menu bar   Contains available menus for this window. Clicking on a menu choice will open a menu with more choices.

12 Click the Minimize button on the **My Computer** window.

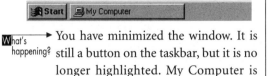

What's happening? → You have minimized the window. It is still a button on the taskbar, but it is no longer highlighted. My Computer is open but not active.

13 Click the **My Computer** button on the taskbar.

What's happening? → You have restored the window to its previous size. It is now open and active.

14 Click the Maximize button on the **My Computer** title bar.

What's happening? → The window now fills the entire screen. Look at the buttons on the right side. You have a new button, the *Restore button* instead of the Maximize button.

15 Click the Restore button.

What's happening? → You have restored the window to its previous size.

16 Click the Control-menu icon on the **My Computer** title bar.

What's happening? → You have dropped down the Control menu. You can, minimize, maximize, move, or size the window by either clicking a selection or pressing the **Alt** key and the underlined letter. Restore is dimmed out because the window is already in its restored position.

17 Click outside the menu to close it.

18 Click the **Close** button on the **My Computer** title bar.

What's happening? → You have closed My Computer and have returned to the desktop. You could have also closed the window by selecting the Control menu and choosing Close or by pressing **Alt** + **F4**.

2.6   Moving and Sizing Windows

In addition to minimizing, maximizing, and closing a window, you can move a window to other locations on the screen. You may also change the size of the window. Moving windows allows you to arrange your desktop just as you would move items such as a phone or address book on your desk. Sizing a window differs from minimizing or maximizing a window. Minimizing a window shrinks it to appear only as a button on the taskbar, but it is still open. Maximizing a window fills the screen. Sizing a window means changing its size and shape. If you wanted to have two or more windows visible on the screen, you could adjust, or size, both windows.

2.7   Activity: Sizing And Moving Windows

1 Double-click **My Computer**.

2 Place the mouse on the title bar of the window. Hold down the left mouse button and drag the mouse downward.

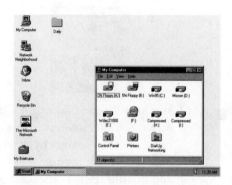

What's happening? → As you see, you moved the window. To move any window, you use the title bar as a handle and grab it with the mouse. If you place the mouse anywhere else within the window, the window cannot be moved.

3 Move the window back to its original location.

4 Place the mouse on the left window border. The pointer should change to a double-headed arrow.

5 Press and hold the left mouse button down on the border and move the pointer to the left. The window should expand to the left. When you have expanded it about an inch, release the left mouse button.

What's happening? → The window is now larger. Once you have adjusted the size of the window, this new size becomes the default which is the restore size.

6 Place the mouse on the left window border. The pointer should change to a double-headed arrow.

7   Press and hold the left mouse button on the border and move the pointer to the right. The window should contract to the right. When you have contracted about an inch, release the left mouse button.

What's happening? →   You have returned the My Computer window to its original size which is now its default and restore size. Another way to size a window is to use the Resize tab which allows you to move two sides at the same time.

8   Place the mouse pointer on the Resize tab in the lower-right corner of the window. Hold the left mouse button and push inward and upward.

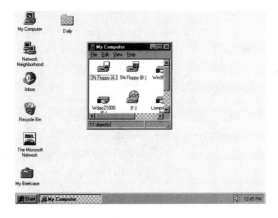

What's happening? →   You have made the window smaller by adjusting two sides at the same time.

9   Place the mouse pointer on the Resize tab. Hold the left mouse button and drag out and down.

What's
happening?   ➤ You have returned the window to its previous size.

10   Close the **My Computer** window.

2.8   Manipulating the Taskbar with a Property Sheet

A *floating* taskbar or floating button bar can have its size or location altered. Not all taskbars or button bars float, but the Windows 95 taskbar does. You may also manipulate the taskbar in other ways. You may hide it, always have it on top, choose to display the clock, or change the size of the icons. In order to manipulate the settings of the taskbar, you use a property sheet.

A *property sheet* is a type of dialog box. Almost every object in Windows 95 (folders, files, desktop, taskbar, devices, etc.) has properties associated with it that can be viewed or altered. The settings in an object's property sheet affect how the object looks and, sometimes, how it works. A property sheet allows you to look at or change information about an object. Property sheets can be accessed easily by right-clicking the object and then clicking Properties on the short-cut menu. When you open a property sheet, there may be multiple sheets. Each sheet has its name on a tab, much like the tabs on file folders. To access the sheet of interest, click the tab.

2.9   Activity—Working With The Taskbar

1   Place the mouse on the taskbar in an empty location. Click and hold the left mouse button and begin to drag the taskbar to the right.

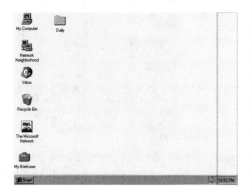

 You see the line moving as you drag the taskbar. This is the outline of the taskbar.

2   When the line is at the right side of the screen, release the left mouse button.

What's happening? The taskbar changed locations. You may drag, or "float," the taskbar to the top, left, or bottom of the screen. You may also change the taskbar width.

3   Place the pointer on the edge of the taskbar. When it becomes a double-headed arrow, drag to the left. When the taskbar is about two inches wide, release the left mouse button.

What's happening? The taskbar is much wider. You can make it narrower by moving it in the opposite direction.

4   Place the pointer on an empty location on the taskbar and hold the left mouse button. Drag the taskbar to the bottom of the screen.

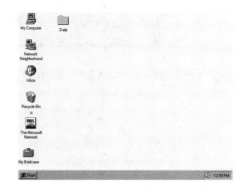

What's happening? The taskbar returned to its default position and size.

5 Click **Start**. Point at **Settings**.

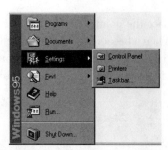

What's happening? → You have opened the Settings menu which then presents another menu.

6 Click **Taskbar**.

What's happening? → You are looking at the Taskbar Properties sheet which contains settings that control the taskbar. An object could have more than one series of settings to view or change. If it did, it would have multiple property sheets. Each sheet would have a labeled tab. You click the tab of the sheet you wish to use. The Taskbar Properties sheet has two choices: Taskbar Options and Start Menu Programs.

7 Click the tab for **Start Menu Programs**.

What's happening? → By clicking the tab, you brought the Start Menu Programs property sheet to the front.

8 Click the **Taskbar Options** tab.

What's happening? → In this example, certain check boxes contain checks, indicating they are the set, or enabled, choices. Always on top and Show Clock are enabled. Neither Auto hide nor Show small icons in Start menu have checks and are thus disabled. The taskbar is hidden and the icons are large. (*Note:* Your settings could be different.) If you would like a description of a property sheet feature, it is readily available.

9 Click the **Question Mark** icon on the **Taskbar Properties** title bar. A question mark attaches itself to the cursor . Drag the cursor to **Always on top** and click.

> Ensures that the taskbar is always visible, even when you run a program in a full screen.

What's happening? → A pop-up description appears, telling you the function of the Always on top feature. Whenever you see a question mark icon on the title bar of any window, you may click it and drag it to the item in question. The question mark on the title bar is known as the What's This? command.

10 Click outside of the description to close it.

11 Set the **Show small icons** in the **Start** menu check box by clicking inside the box.

What's happening? → The example shows smaller icons in the Start menu.

12 Click **OK**.

13 Click the **Start** button.

What's happening? → The icons are smaller in the Start menu. You may also access property sheets by right-clicking the taskbar.

14 Click outside the **Start** menu to close it.

15 Place the pointer on the taskbar in an empty location and right-click.

What's happening? → You have quickly opened the pop-up menu that relates to the taskbar. The only item available is Properties.

16 Click **Properties**. Click **Show small icons** in **Start** menu to disable it.

<u>What's</u>━━▶ You have again opened the Taskbar Properties property sheet and altered the characteristics of an
happening? item.

17 Click **OK**.

<u>What's</u>━━▶ You have returned to the desktop.
happening?

2.10 Objects

In Windows 95, nearly every item is considered an *object*. In general, objects can be opened and have
properties. An object can be a program item icon which represents an executable program file. An
executable program is a tool that allows you to accomplish some task. FreeCell is an example. When
you double-clicked it, it opened and became a game you could play. An object can be a document icon
that represents a data file created with an application program. When you launch it, you are launching
the program that created the data file as well as opening the document. An object may be a device such
as a disk drive or a printer, or it may be a folder that can hold program-item icons, document icons,
files, or even other folders that hold further objects or folders.

In Windows 95, objects have properties, settings, and parameters. Each object usually has a property sheet which is a collection of information about the object's properties. Usually, properties can be
changed or adjusted. Properties of an object affect what the object does or what you can do to the
object. For instance, the desktop is an object. It has properties such as its background color. You can
alter the colors of the desktop—the object.

Objects can be manipulated in various ways, depending on what the object is. Object behavior is
supposed to be consistent. Once you know how to deal with a specific kind of object, all other similar
objects will behave the same way. A folder is an object that can be opened. In it can be other objects
such as other folders, files, or devices. The folder itself has properties such as its location. You can
manipulate the folder by moving it, copying it, or deleting it. All folder objects can be manipulated in
the same way. Remember though, what you can do with the object depends on what the object is.

2.11 Activity—My Computer as an Object

1 Double-click **My Computer**.

What's happening? → The object called My Computer opens into a window, called a *parent window*, because it is the owner of the objects within it. A parent window may have one or more child windows, but a child window can have only one parent. This relationship is called a hierarchy because there is a dependency relationship among the objects. The objects in your My Computer window will be different from the example presented here. In the above example, the My Computer parent window has 11 objects or children. As indicated on the *status bar*, eight of the objects are devices—the drives on the system. There are two floppy drives (drives A and B), one CD-ROM drive (drive F), two hard drives, (drives C and D) and two compressed drive (drives H and I).

In addition, all systems will have two child folders, one called Control Panel and the other called Printers. These fold-

ers also hold objects. Control Panel allows you to control your system, whereas Printers manages the printers on your system. This example has another folder called Dial-Up Networking which allows the system to make connections to outside computers or online services. If you performed a complete installation of all Windows 95 features, you will also have this folder. (*Note:* If you want your settings to match the screens in this text, click View on the Control Panel title bar. Click Options. Click the Folder tab. Set Browse folders using a separate window for each folder. Click OK.)

2 Click **Printers**.

What's happening? → When you click an object, the status bar confirms that you have selected it. To activate, or choose it, you must double-click the object.

3 Double-click **Printers**.

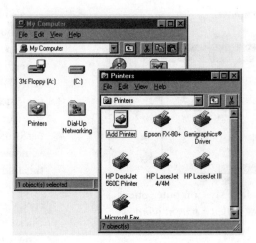

You have opened the Printers window. The Printers window is a child window to the My Computer window. The Printers window is subservient to the My Computer window, and therefore beneath it in the hierarchical structure. This child window contains objects but no children. It has only one parent, My Computer. The Printers folder shows the printers installed on your system. Here is where you add a new printer. Both the Printers window and My Computer window are open. The Printers window should be the active window.

4 Press the **Backspace** key.

→ When you press the **Backspace** key, you make the parent window of the child active without closing the child window. In this case, the active window became My Computer, the parent of Printers. The Printers window may be hidden behind the My Computer window. If you do not see the Printers window, you may drag the My Computer window to a different location.

5   Click the **Printers** window to make it active. If you cannot see it, click the Printers button on the taskbar. Click the Close button on the **Printers** window title bar.

6   Double-click the **Control Panel** folder.

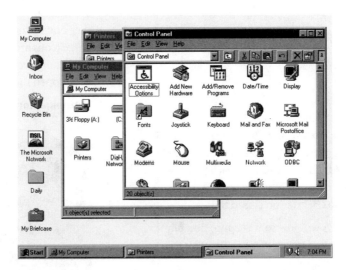

→ You have displayed an object that controls your system. Control Panel is a child window to My Computer, the parent. Control Panel contains objects. In the Control Panel you have icons that allow you to add hardware, add and remove programs, change the way your display works, customize your mouse, and other such system related tasks. Both My Computer, the parent, and Control Panel, the child, are open windows. You can close each window individually, but there is a shortcut for closing the current window and all its children.

7   Hold down the **Shift** key and click the **Close** button on the **Control Panel** window.

My Computer

→ You closed both the child window, Control Panel, and the parent window, My Computer, in one action.

8   Place the disk that came with the text in drive A. (*Note:* In this text, drive A will be referred to. If you are using drive B, substitute drive B every time the text says drive A.)

9 Double-click **My Computer**. Double-click the drive A icon.

 You are looking at what is on the disk in drive A. Windows 95 will always remember the last size and the last way you arranged the display for each window you opened. Thus, the look of each window will vary, depending on the last action you took before you closed the window.

10 Size the drive A window so it is approximately the size of the text example. Click **View** on the menu bar.

 You have dropped down the menu and can see all the different ways to manipulate a window. In this case, Status Bar has a check in front of it, indicating that the status bar is enabled. When a check mark is used, it means that all, some, or none of the items may be set. There is also a dot by Large Icons indicating its enabled status. The dot means that this feature is on. When you see a dot, it is an option button. An *option button* means that only one item can be selected. Options are mutually exclusive choices; it is either one or the other. If Status Bar and Large Icons are not enabled, set them on by clicking each. Each click requires that you reopen the menu.

11 Point to **Arrange Icons**.

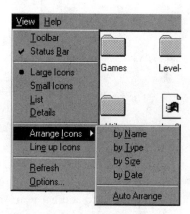

 Arrange Icons has a triangular arrow so it has a cascading menu. You can arrange your icons by Name, Type, Size, or Date. The default choice is by Name. In this example, Auto Arrange has no check mark and therefore is not enabled. Auto Arrange means that, when you open a window, the icons will automatically be fitted into the window in the most efficient way.

12 Click **by Name**.

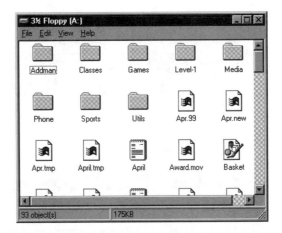

W̲h̲a̲t̲'̲s̲
happening?
→ The title of this child window is 3½ Floppy (A:) [⊟]. The taskbar tells you which windows are open. Look at the taskbar.

W̲h̲a̲t̲'̲s̲
happening?
→ The Taskbar shows that the open windows are My Computer [⊞] and 3½ Floppy (A:) [⊟]. The 3½ Floppy (A:) button is highlighted and indented indicating that it is the *active window*, the one in which you are currently working. There may be many open windows, but only one window may be active at a time. In the drive A window are folders and document icons. The folders are children to the drive A parent.

13 Double-click the **Level-1** folder.

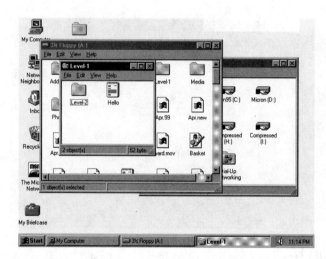

▶ Look at the taskbar. You will see that My Computer, the drive A window, and Level-1 are all open, but Level-1 is the active window. Level-1 contains a child, the folder called Level-2. It also contains a document called Hello.

14 Double-click the **Level-2** folder.

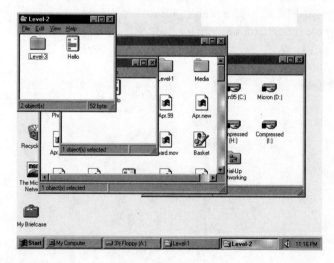

▶ Look at the taskbar. You will see that My Computer, the drive A window, Level-1, and Level-2 are all open, but Level-2 is the active window. Level-2 contains a child, the folder called Level-3. It also contains a document called Hello.

15 Double-click the **Level-3** folder.

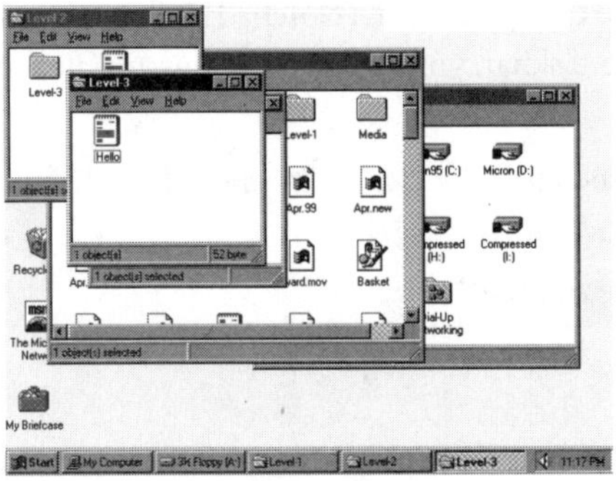

What's happening? Look at the taskbar. You will see that My Computer, the drive A window, Level-1, Level-2, and Level-3 are all open, but Level-3 is the active window. Level-3 contains no folders but does contain a child, a document called Hello.

16 Click the **Close** button on the **Level-3** window.

17 On the taskbar, click the **3½ Floppy (A:)** button making it the active window.

18 Hold the **Shift** key down and click the Close button on the 3½ Floppy (A:).

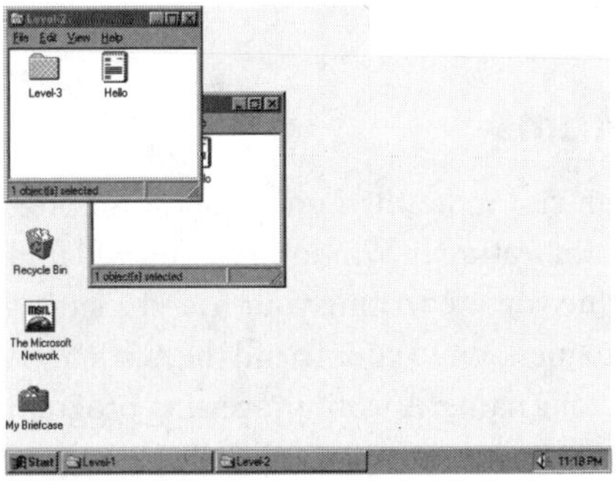

What's happening? The hierarchy of parent windows to children windows was My Computer, then 3½ Floppy (A:) window, then the Level-1 window, and then the Level-2 window. Since you made the 3½ Floppy (A:) the active window and then held the **Shift** key, when you clicked the close button, you closed the 3½ Floppy (A:) window and its parent My Computer. Since you started in the middle of the hierarchy, you did not close the Level-2 or Level-1 window.

19 Click the **Level-2** window to make it active.

20 Double-click **Hello**.

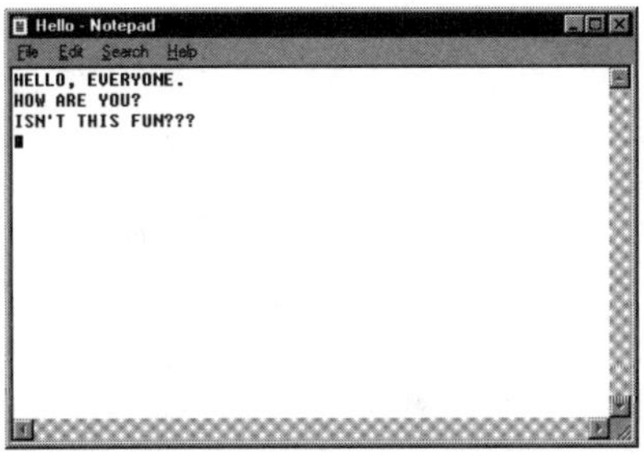

What's happening? You have opened a program called Notepad so that you may look at the document called HELLO. The document's name is actually Hello.txt, but the .txt is not displayed in this setting. Notepad is an ***application window***, which is a program that does some task. In this case, as the name Notepad indicates, it is a "pad of paper" to create or view short documents. The document in question is a data file called Hello.

Windows 95 employs a docucentric approach. ***Docucentric*** means that what is most important to a user is the data that he creates, not the program that generated the data. However, there is a catch to this approach. You cannot open a document without also opening the program that created the document. Thus, on the title bar is first the Control menu icon, which is represented along with the icon of the Notepad program, followed by the name of document (Hello), followed by the name of the application program that created the document (Notepad). Applications that were not written for Windows 95 and are not docucentric will have first the name of the application (Notepad) followed by the name of the document (Hello). If you look at the taskbar, you will see buttons for all these open windows.

21   In the **Level-2** window, hold down the [Shift] key and click the **Close** button on the title bar.

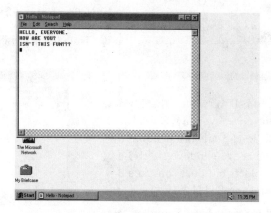

What's happening? → You closed all the child and parent windows. However, you did not close the application program Notepad with its open document Hello. You must close application programs separately. When you open a folder window, you are seeing what files and folders you have on disk. When you open an application program, you are planning to do work.

22   Click the **Close** button for Notepad.

What's happening? → You have returned to the desktop.

2.12 Working With Application Programs

Windows 95 allows *multitasking* which means it can run more than one application program at a time. Multitasking is an extremely useful and important feature in Windows 95. You will find yourself using it often. To see how multitasking works, imagine you are writing your friend a letter using the application program, Word for Windows. You want to mention to your friend the Academy Award for Best Actor of 1988, but you do not remember the actor's name. A word processing program, such as Word, will not have answers to questions, but another program you own, called Bookshelf, will. Bookshelf is a reference tool that includes a dictionary, almanac, thesaurus, atlas, and other common reference books. While Word is open, you access the almanac and find your answer—Dustin Hoffman won for *Rain Man*. When using two programs at the same time, it appears you are multitasking

In reality, you move from one task to the another. Windows 95 is also concentrating on different tasks. It let's lets you key information into Word and open the almanac. It also performs some operating system tasks, such as accessing the disk or drawing the screen. Windows 95 is switching from one task to another very rapidly, giving you the impression that you are doing many things simultaneously. Remember, your computer has only one processor (CPU) and can do only one task at a time. Windows 95, as the operating system, manages the time allocation so that the CPU can process each task.

Windows 95 also allows *multithreading*, which means that within an application program, tasks are divided into smaller tasks called threads. For instance, one thread in a program could be devoted to printing so you can continue to work while your document is printing. Another thread could automatically correct typing errors. A third thread could perform calculations. The purpose of multithreaded applications is to help you work faster. Applications must be written specifically to support multithreading. As applications are written or updated for Windows 95, they will more than likely be multithreaded.

In the multitasking Windows 95 environment, you may have many applications open and running, but there is only one active application. Considered the *foreground application* or *active window*, the active application has its title bar highlighted and is above all of the other applications. If all of your applications are minimized, the active application is the button that is in contrasting colors with a three-dimensional appearance on the taskbar. You may only work in an active, open window. When it is open, it is the active or *foreground window*. Objects such as My Computer also appear in windows.

2.13 Activity—Moving Between Foreground and Background Windows

1 Click **Start**. Point at **Programs**. Point at **Accessories**. Point at **Games**. Click **FreeCell**.

2 Click **Start**. Point at **Programs**. Point at **Accessories**. Point at **Games**. Click **Solitaire**.

3 Click **Start**. Point at **Programs**. Point at **Accessories**. Click **Calculator**.

4 Click **Start**. Point at **Programs**. Point at **Accessories**. Click **Notepad**.

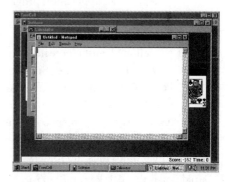

What's happening? You have opened four programs. Notepad, the last one you opened, is on top. It is the foreground and active window. Look at the taskbar. All the open windows are listed on the taskbar but only Notepad has its button highlighted. You can move among the open windows making each one active in turn.

5 Click the **Solitaire** window.

> **What's happening?** By clicking on a window, you make it active.

6 Click the **Calculator** button on the taskbar.

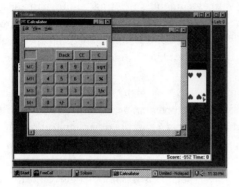

> **What's happening?** Calculator is now the active window. The taskbar can become very crowded. In fact, sometimes you will not be able to read the entire name. Remember, if you hold the pointer over the button, the full name of the window will appear. Since Notepad is an application program, the document name (Untitled) and the program name (Notepad) become visible. Not all applications create data documents. For instance, Solitaire and FreeCell are games. They have no document windows. Calculator is a tool and it also has no documents. A button can also be a window such as My Computer which holds files and folders.

7 Hold down the **Alt** key and tap the **Esc** key until you have cycled through all the application windows. End with Notepad, the active application.

> **What's happening?** Look at the taskbar. As you cycled through the open applications, the buttons depressed indicating the active application. If a window is minimized, only the button on the taskbar will be highlighted. This technique for switching among open applications is the slowest method because it requires drawing the entire screen. A faster technique is to use the **Alt** and **Tab** key combination.

8 Hold the **Alt** key and tap the **Tab** key so you cycle through all the open applications.

> **What's happening?** When you use the **Alt** + **Tab** key combination, you also cycle through the open windows. However, rather than drawing the window of the application, the **Alt** + **Tab** key combination displays the icon and the name of the application. It also shows you all the open application icons with a box around the current selection.

9 Right-click **Solitaire** on the taskbar.

> **What's happening?** You opened the Control menu from which you may manipulate the window by moving, sizing, minimizing, maximizing, or closing it. Restore is dimmed because Solitaire is already an open window.

10   Click **Close** on the menu.

11   Close all the open application windows.

What's happening? → You have returned to the desktop.

2.14 Manipulating the Display

When you have many applications open, you may display them in several ways. You saw how to make each active in turn, but what if you wanted to see all of them at once? In Windows 95, you may display all of the open windows in a cascaded or tiled fashion. *Cascaded* means that the open windows will be stacked on top of one another with each of the title bars visible. *Tiled* means that the screen will be divided between the windows. If a window is minimized, it will not be included in the tiled or cascaded display.

2.15   Activity—Using The Taskbar To Manipulate Windows

1   Click **Start**. Point at **Programs**. Point at **Accessories**. Point at **Games**. Click **FreeCell**.

2   Click **Start**. Point at **Programs**. Point at **Accessories**. Click **Notepad**.

3   Right-click the taskbar in an empty spot.

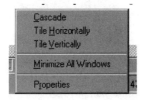

What's happening? → You have opened the pop-up menu for the open objects on your screen.

4   Click **Tile Horizontally**.

What's happening? → When you tile horizontally, you divide the screen between the two open windows. The active window has the title bar highlighted. If no title bar is highlighted, no window is active.

5   Click **FreeCell**. Click **Notepad**. Click **FreeCell**.

What's happening? → As you click each window, it becomes active.

6   Right-click the taskbar in an empty spot. Click **Undo Tile**.

What's happening? → You have undone the tiling. You may not be able to see the Notepad window, but if you look at the taskbar, you will see that Notepad has a button.

7   Right-click the taskbar in an empty spot. Click **Tile Vertically**.

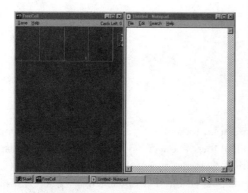

What's happening? → You have tiled the windows side-by-side.

8   Click **Notepad**. Click **FreeCell**. Click **Notepad**.

What's happening? → As you click each window, it becomes active.

9   Right-click the taskbar in an empty spot. Click **Undo Tile**.

What's happening? → You have undone your tiling.

10   Right-click the taskbar in an empty spot. Click **Cascade**.

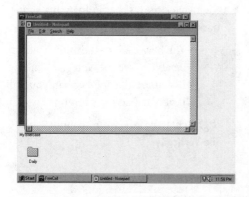

What's happening? → You have cascaded the open windows, making them stack upon one another with all the title bars visible.

11   Click **FreeCell**. Click **Notepad**.

What's happening? → As you click each window, it becomes active. If you cannot see the window, you can click the button on the taskbar.

12   Right-click the taskbar in an empty spot. Click **Undo Cascade**.

13   Right-click the taskbar in an empty spot. Click **Minimize All Windows**.

What's happening? → Now all the windows are minimized. If you look at the taskbar, you can see buttons for all the open windows. If you are not sure which windows are open, minimizing all of them will give you this information.

14   Right-click the taskbar in an empty spot.

What's happening? → Minimize All Windows is unavailable. However, you now have a new choice, Undo Minimize All.

15   Click **Undo Minimize All**.

What's happening? → Your windows are restored again.

16   Right-click the taskbar in an empty spot. Click **Minimize All Windows**.

17   Double-click **My Computer**. Double-click **Control Panel**.

18   Right-click the taskbar in an empty spot. Click **Undo Minimize All**.

19 Right-click the taskbar in an empty spot. Click **Tile Horizontally**.

21 Click the **Close** button on the **Control Panel** window.

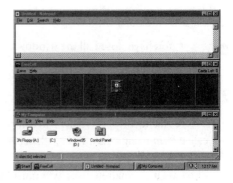

What's happening? → Now you have two application windows open (Notepad and FreeCell) and two object windows (My Computer and Control Panel). Your windows are equally divided on the desktop. Notice that an application window and an object window behave in the same way.

20 Right-click the taskbar in an empty spot. Click **Tile Vertically**.

What's happening? → The screen display did not change. When you tile, you divide the desktop between the open windows. You only see the difference between vertical and horizontal tiling when there are fewer windows open. You can make any window active by clicking it.

What's happening? → You closed the Control Panel window. Now your screen has three windows open.

22 Right-click on the taskbar on an empty spot. Click **Tile Horizontally**.

What's happening? → Now the three windows are divide the screen horizontally.

23 Right-click the taskbar in an empty spot. Click **Tile Vertically**.

What's
happening? ➤ Now the windows are arranged side-by-side.

24 Right-click the taskbar in an empty spot. Click **Undo Tile**.

25 Right-click the taskbar in an empty spot. Click **Cascade**.

26 Close all the open windows.

What's
happening? ➤ You have closed all the windows and returned to the desktop. There are no menu choices such as Close all windows or Close all applications. Each must be closed independently.

2.16 Formatting a Disk

Before placing files and folders on a floppy disk, you must first prepare the disk for use. This process is called *formatting* a disk. Today, when people purchase floppy disks, they tend to purchase preformatted disks which are ready to use. Nonetheless, if you wish to erase all information from a disk or if you purchase unformatted disks, you must format them.

2.17 Activity—Formatting a Disk

1 Get a blank disk or a disk with information you no longer need. Place a label on the disk and write "Data disk" on it, your name, and today's date. It is wise to place a date on a disk so you that know when you created it.

2 Place the disk in drive A.

3 Double-click **My Computer**.

4 Right-click the drive A icon.

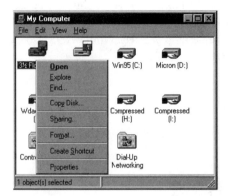

→ You have opened the menu for the disk
happening? in drive A. One of the choices is Format.

5 Click **Format**.

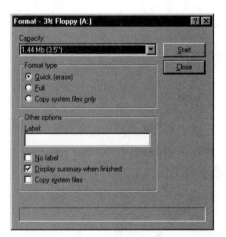

What's → You have opened the Format dialog box.
happening? In this example, drive A is a 3½-inch
floppy. You can see the capacity of the
disk. You also have some choices. In Format type, the default option is Quick
(erase). This choice can be used only on
a previously formatted disk.

6 Click the **Full** button. Click the **Start** button.

What's → If you look at the bottom of the dialog
happening? box, you see a progress indicator. A
progress indicator reports to you the
progress of a task. When the disk is formatted, you see the following report:

What's → This disk is now formatted. It is ready to
happening? receive files and folders.

7 Click **Close**. Click **Close** again.

8 Close the **My Computer** window.

9 Remove the DATA disk from drive A.

2.18 Exiting Windows

To leave Windows 95, do not simply turn off the power. You must complete a shutdown process. The process allows Windows 95 to close files and write the information it needs to disk so that, when you use your computer again, you will be returned to the desktop you left. Windows 95 also has other housekeeping tasks it must perform before shutting down completely.

2.19 Activity—Exiting Windows 95

1   Click **Start**.

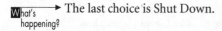 The last choice is Shut Down.

2   Click **Shut Down**.

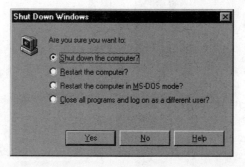

What's
happening? The Shut Down Windows dialog box contains several choices, but you may have fewer choices depending on how your system was set up. The default choice is Shut down the computer? The other choices are Restart the computer? and Restart the computer in MS-DOS mode? If you are on a network or your computer was set up with multiple users, you will have another choice: Close all programs and log on as a different user? This dialog box presents you with option buttons, so choices are mutually exclusive; you can select only one option.

3   Be sure **Shut down the computer?** is selected. Click **Yes**.

What's → You see a screen telling you that Windows 95 is preparing to shut down. Do not turn off the
happening? computer until you see the message:

It is now safe to turn off your computer.

4   When the safe message appears, turn off your computer and monitor.

Chapter Summary

This chapter introduced the basic features of Windows 95. You learned about the work area, called the desktop. You acquainted yourself with the taskbar, the primary way to see what windows are open. You learned how to manipulate the floating taskbar and move among windows using the taskbar buttons. You were presented with the features of pointing devices. Knowing the meaning and use of mouse terms such as click, double-click, drag, right-click, and right-drag is important to work effectively in Windows 95.

Menus are an important feature of Windows 95. One of the most important is the Start menu that, as its name implies, gets you started. You identified and used cascading menus. You familiarized yourself with the keyboard and mouse by making selections from a menu. By pressing the **Alt** key and the underlined letter, you selected a menu item. When you used the mouse, you clicked your menu choices. Since everything in Windows appears in a window, you focused on the techniques to manipulate windows. These techniques include the ability to move, size, minimize, maximize, and restore a window. Sizing a window is adjusting the borders of a window, whereas, minimize, maximize, and restore refer to making a window a button on the taskbar, filling the entire screen, or restoring the window to its default size.

You were introduced to the concept of objects which can be opened and have properties. Properties of an object are accessed through its property sheets, collections of information about the object. Property sheets allow you to view or alter properties of the object and are most often accessed by right-clicking the object and choosing Properties from the Shortcut menu.

You learned about parent and children windows and the hierarchical nature of windows. You were introduced to application windows, and you learned how to open and close windows and shortcuts.

You used the Format command to prepare a disk for use because all disks must be formatted before you place information on them, and you learned the proper process to exit Windows 95.

Key Terms

Active window	Clicking	Device icons
Application window	Close button	Dialog box
Booting the system	Command button	Docucentric
Cascaded	Control menu	Double-clicking
Cascading menus	Controls	Drag and drop
Check box	Cursor	Dragging
Child menu	Desktop	Drop down

Floating
Folder icons
Foreground application
Foreground window
Formatting
Hierarchical menu
Highlighting
Icons
Install
Integrated pointer
Maximize button
Menu
Menu bar
Message box
Minimize button
Mouse

Mouse pointer
Multitasking
Multithreading
Objects
Option button
Prent menu
Parent window
Point
Pointer
Pop-up menu
Primary mouse button
Progress indicator
Property sheet
Resize tab
Restore button
Right-clicking

Right-dragging
Shortcut menus
Slider
Start button
Status area
Status bar
Taskbar
Taskbar buttons
Tiled
Title bar
Toggle switch
ToolTip
Trackball
Upgrade
Window border

Discussion Questions

1. What does it mean to boot the system?
2. Explain the purpose and function of the desktop.
3. Explain the purpose and function of the taskbar, start button, icons, window buttons, and status area.
4. What is the purpose and function of pointing devices?
5. List and explain the major items found on the Start menu.
6. What is a cascading menu? How can you determine if a menu is a cascading menu?
7. What is the purpose and function of a dialog box?
8. What is the function of a command button?
9. What is a ToolTip?
10. What is a Control? Give two examples of a control.
11. Explain the purpose and function of moving a window.
12. Explain the purpose and function of sizing a window.
13. What is the difference between minimizing and sizing a window?
14. Explain the purpose and function of property sheets.
15. Name one way a property sheet may be accessed.
16. How can you display the taskbar property sheet on the screen?
17. Compare and contrast a parent window and a child window.
18. Compare and contrast multitasking and multithreading.
19. Compare and contrast foreground and background windows.
20. Open applications can be displayed either tiled or cascaded. Explain.
21. Compare and contrast tiled and cascaded windows.
22. When multiple windows are open, how can you identify the active window?
23. How can you quickly close parent and children windows?

24. Why is it necessary to format a disk?
25. Why is it important to go through a shutdown process rather then just turning off the computer?

True/False Questions

For each question, circle the letter T if the statement is true or the letter F if the statement is false.

T   F   1. Tiled windows divide the space on the desktop equally.

T   F   2. Folders may contain only programs.

T   F   3. To select a cascading menu, you must click the mouse button.

T   F   4. To change two sides of a window simultaneously, you may use the resize tab.

T   F   5. The Printers window is a child window to the My Computer window.

Completion Questions

Write the correct answer in each blank space.

1. A pictorial representation of an object is known as a/an _____.
2. To select an object, you must click the _____ mouse button.
3. To allow you to look at or change information about an object, Windows 95 uses a type of dialog box called a _____.
4. To determine what windows are open, buttons are placed on the _____.
5. The approach of Windows 95 to treat the user's data as more important than applications is called a _____ approach.

Multiple Choice Questions

Circle the letter for the correct answer to each question.

1. Booting the system is the process of
   a. copying system files from CD-ROM to your hard drive.
   b. copying system files from your hard drive into memory.
   c. placing a data disk in drive A.
   d. attaching the CPU to the other components.
2. The day and date can be displayed by
   a. choosing Show Day/Date from the Start menu.
   b. double-clicking on the time icon.
   c. holding the mouse over the time icon.
   d. right-clicking on an empty area of the taskbar.
3. You may access the taskbar's property sheet by
   a. choosing Settings and then Taskbar from the Start menu.
   b. right-clicking on an empty area of the taskbar.
   c. both a and b
   d. neither a nor b
4. Menu items which are unavailable
   a. have no alternative keystrokes.
   b. are dimmed.
   c. are not shown on the menu.
   d. have no underlined letter.

5. The My Computer icon represents:
    a. a diagnostic program that describes your system.
    b. a document that lists the current settings for your system.
    c. a utility program for controlling the desktop.
    d. a folder containing device icons and folders.

Application Assignments

Problem Set I—At The Computer

Problem A

Click the **Start** button.

1. You have opened a
    a. menu.   b. dialog box.

Open FreeCell.

2. In order to open FreeCell, you used
    a. cascading menus.   b. only a dialog box.

Choose game number **555**.

3. The only ace on the fully exposed cards is the
    a. ace of clubs.
    b. ace of diamonds.
    c. ace of hearts.
    d. ace of spades.

Play FreeCell if you wish. When you are finished, you must exit or close the program.

4. Which button must you click to close FreeCell?

    a. [_]   b. [🗗]   c. [✕]

5. When you close FreeCell, you are
    a. immediately returned to the desktop.   b. first presented with a message box.

Problem B

Double-click **My Computer**. Maximize it.

6. The title bar contains the word(s)
    a. My Computer.   b. File.

7. The menu bar contains the word(s)
    a. My Computer.   b. File.

Click the Control menu in the left corner of the **My Computer** title bar window.

8. Which of the following commands are unavailable for use?
    a. Restore.   b. Minimize.   c. Maximize.

9. You knew the command was unavailable to use in the menu you opened above because it
    a. was dimmed.   b. was highlighted in red.   c. does not appear on the menu.

Minimize My Computer.

10. My Computer
    a. is closed.   b. is open.

Right-click the **My Computer** button on the taskbar. You will open a pop-up menu—the Control menu. Different choices are on the Control menu.

11. You may close My Computer on the menu you opened by clicking Close or pressing the
    a. **Ctrl** + **F4** keys.   b. **Shift** + **F4** keys.   c. **Alt** + **F4** keys.

Click **Restore** on the Control menu, then click the **Close** button on the **My Computer** title bar, and then close My Computer.

Problem C

Double-click **My Computer**. Move the **My Computer** window to the lower right corner of the desktop.

12. You moved the My Computer window by placing the mouse on the
    a. My Computer title bar and double-clicking it.
    b. My Computer title bar and dragging it.

Expand the **My Computer** window by about an inch.

13. By expanding the My Computer window, you are
    a. maximizing it.   b. minimizing it.   c. moving it.   d. sizing it.

14. When you expanded the My Computer window, the pointer changed shape. It became a
    a. double-headed arrow.   b. single-headed arrow.

Return the **My Computer** window to its original size. Move it back to its original position. Close the **My Computer** window.

Problem D

Open the property sheet from the taskbar. Click **Taskbar Options**. Click the **Question Mark** icon and drag it to the **Start** button in the property sheet. Click it.

15. The following description appears:

> Shows how the settings on this tab affect the way Windows displays the taskbar. This image changes as you select different settings.

    a. True.   b. False.

16. A property sheet is a type of
    a. menu.   b. cascading menu.   c. dialog box.

Close the property sheet.

Problem E

Place the Activities disk that came with the text into drive A. Double-click the **My Computer** icon. Double-click the drive A icon.

17. Arrange the icons by date in the drive A window. Which folder is first?
    a. Addman   b. Classes   c. Games   d. Utils

18. Arrange the icons by size in the drive A window. Which file is first?
    a. Addman   b. Y.fil   c. Games   d. File2.czg

Arrange the icons by name. Open the **Media** folder by double-clicking it.

19. Does the Media folder have any child folders?
    a. Yes.   b. No.

20. The parent of the Media folder is
    a. My Computer.   b. 3½ Floppy (A:).

Close all the windows.

21. Which window is on top?
    a. Media.   b. My Computer.   c. 3 ½ Floppy (A:)

Undo the cascade. Close all the windows.

Problem F

Exit Windows 95 properly.

22. The fastest way to exit Windows 95 correctly is to
    a. turn off the computer.   b. click Start then click Shut Down.

Problem Set II—Brief Essay

1. Describe the purpose and function of a pointing device. Then agree or disagree with the following statement and explain why you chose your position: *To use Windows 95 effectively, it is important to be able to use a pointing device.*

2. You may open, close, minimize, maximize, or move windows that are on the desktop. Describe briefly the purpose of each of the functions.

Problem Set III—Scenario

1. You have been directed to design a standard placement of items on the desktop for all newly purchased computers that came with Windows 95. Wisely, you have decided to interview the users of these newly acquired machines to establish a standard organizational scheme so that if one person needs to use another's computer, the transition will be easy and no time will be wasted with desktop reorganization. You must decide, among other questions, what windows should be open and how the windows should be arranged. Prepare a plan for this investigation and include questions relating specifically to the desktop.

Chapter 3

Using Help

Chapter Overview

Windows 95 provides extensive online Help capability, which means that rather than looking up how to accomplish tasks in a printed manual, you can access the information directly from the computer. Help in Windows 95 is a hypertext utility, which means you can jump between logically connected items.

One feature of Windows 95 is that once you learn a task in one application, it will be the same in other applications. Applications written for Windows 95 will also have an online Help facility that looks and works the same way.

Learning Objectives

1. Explain the purpose and function of online Help capabilities.
2. Explain the purpose and function of a hypertext utility.
3. Describe how to add missing Windows 95 components.
4. Compare and contrast accessing Help using Contents, Index, or Find tabs.
5. Describe the purpose and functions of the controls found in a dialog box, such as command buttons, option buttons, list boxes, drop-down list boxes, check boxes, and spin boxes.
6. Explain the purpose and function of scroll bars and scroll boxes.
7. Explain the purpose and function of the Question Mark icon when found in a dialog box.
8. Explain the purpose and function of animated demonstrations.
9. Explain the purpose and function of the annotation feature of Help.
10. Discuss the use of Help in other Windows 95 applications.

Student Outcomes

1. Access Help.
2. Use the Contents, Index, and Find tabs in Help.
3. Use online Help for a specific topic.
4. Use animated Help, if available.
5. Use online Help for a specific topic.
6. Use Help to learn about dialog boxes.
7. Use Help to solve problems.
8. Create annotations.
9. Print a section of online Help.

3.1   Adding Windows 95 Components

Windows 95 has an interesting feature. The type of Help available depends on what features were selected when you installed Windows 95. Many users choose Typical when they install Windows 95. Typical means minimal. Minimal means that many features and programs included with Windows 95 are not installed. You may add the missing components later, but you must use the original CD or disks. There is another facet to the installation of Windows 95. If you purchased the floppy disk version, you will have several missing components, such as animated Help and Quick View, which are standard on the CD version. If you want the complete Windows 95, you may order the missing components from Microsoft. If you are working in a lab environment, the complete installation has been done for you. The following activity will demonstrate how to identify and add the missing components. If you are in a lab environment, read but *do not do* this activity.

3.2   Activity—Adding Windows 95 Components

1   Click **Start**. Click **Help**. Click the **Contents** tab.

2   Double-click **Introducing Windows**.

What's happening? The Help Topics window opens. In it, you see three tabs: Contents, Index, and Find. The Contents window is arranged by category. Each category is represented by a closed book icon. This is an example of the Help Topics Contents window when not all Help components are installed. To see what topics are in a category, you must open the book icon.

What's happening? By double-clicking you expanded the entry so that the book icon is now an open book. Double-clicking displays the topics that are in a category. In this example, the topics in this category are represented by two other closed book icons. Each closed book icon can be expanded to show other related topics.

3   Double-click **Introducing Windows** again.

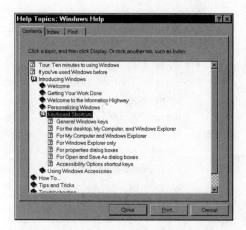 By double-clicking the icon, you col-
lapsed it to its highest level. Its icon is
again a closed book.

4   Double-click **Introducing Windows** again.

Note: If your screen looks like Figure 3.1, all
Help components have been installed and it is
not necessary to complete the activity. However,
you should read the activity to learn how to add
and remove components.

Figure 3.1   Fully Installed Help

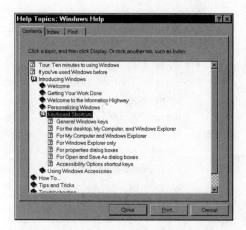

5   To continue installing the missing components,
double-click **Using Window Accessories**.
Double-click **For General Use**.

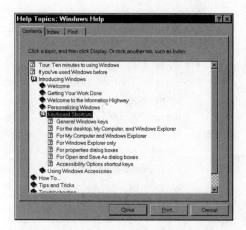 This entry is fully expanded. There are
no further topics. You may now go to the
item of interest.

6   Double-click **Windows games**.

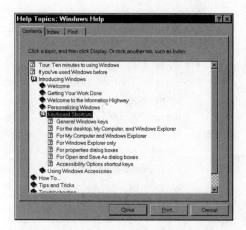 You see the instructions for playing a
game. If you tried to follow the instruc-
tions and found no games to play on
your system, the Note tells you why. It
tells you the games were not installed.

7   Click the **Related Topics** button.

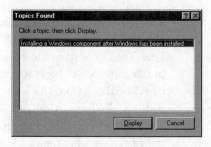

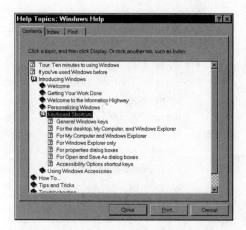 One topic was found and highlighted.

8   Click **Display**.

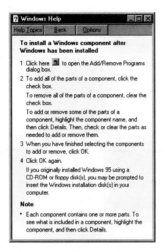

> This is an example of using hypertext. Remember, *hypertext* allows you to jump from one logically related topic to another. Thus, each time you clicked a command button, you were taken to the topic of interest. You did not have to return to the categories as you would in a sequential search for information.

What's happening?

Windows Help often provides a ***shortcut button*** ⌐. When clicked, the icon, a purple arrow pointing to the upper-left corner, takes you directly to the location to accomplish the task.

9   Click the shortcut button.

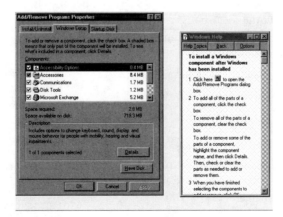

What's happening?
The shortcut button took you to the correct dialog box, Add/Remove Programs Properties. (You may also access this property sheet by double-clicking My Computer. Double-clicking the Control Panel folder and then double-clicking the Add/Remove Programs icon.) The instructions remain on the screen so that you may refer to them. Your entries may differ in the Add/Remove Properties dialog box, depending on what was installed on your system. If you look at the property sheet, you see that the highlighted entry Accessibility Options has a check in the check box. The check means that Accessibility Options are installed on your system. If you do not see a check mark in the check box, Accessibility Options were not installed. If installed, Accessibility Options will occupy .4 MB of disk space. If you look in the Description box at the bottom of the dialog box, you see a description of the option indicating that one out of one components was selected. If you look at the next entry, Accessories, you see a check in the check box, but the check box is grayed. A grayed check indicates that some of the options are selected but not all.

Note 1:   **Working on your own computer**—The following steps will demonstrate how to add missing Windows 95 components. If all the items are checked in the Components window, you do not need to take these steps. If you want to take steps to add a component, you must have the CD-ROM or floppy disks available.

Note 2:   **Working in a lab**—If you are in a lab environment, you *must not* take these steps. Simply read the steps so that you understand how the procedure is done.

10   Click **Accessories**.

What's happening?
In this example, Description tells you that only 13 of 16 components were installed. Your Description might be different.

11   Click **Details**.

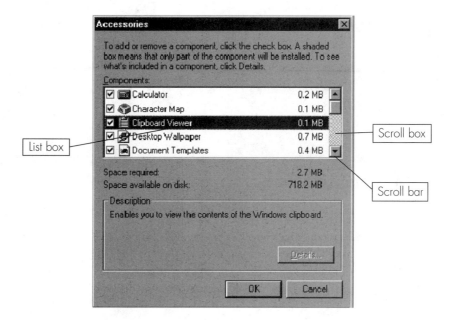

What's
happening? ► In this example, Calculator has a check in its check box, but Clipboard Viewer does not, indicating that Calculator was installed but Clipboard Viewer was not. If you clear a check mark in a box, you will remove an item. If you click an empty box and add a check mark, you will add the item.

12 Click **Clipboard Viewer**.

What's
happening? ► The items to choose from are in a list box. A *list box* is exactly that, a list of items from which you select what interests you. Sometimes, the list is far larger than the list box and will not fit into one window. If the entries will not fit into one window, a scroll bar appears. A *scroll bar* allows you to move up or down through the list so you can see all the items. If you click the up arrow, you move up one entry, and if you click the down arrow, you move down one entry. In addition, you see a scroll box. A *scroll box* allows you to use your mouse and drag the box to move rapidly through the list, rather than to move an item at a time.

13 Scroll through the list until you see the entry **Online User's Guide**.

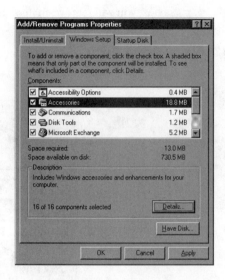

16 Click **OK**.

What's happening? In this example, the check box does not have a check mark in it. If Online User's Guide is not installed, you do not get the full benefits of Help.

14 Click the **Online User's Guide** to place a check mark in it if it does not already have a check mark.

15 Scroll until you see **Windows 95 Tour**. If it does not have a check mark, click it to place a check mark in the box.

What's happening? Now you have selected sixteen of sixteen components or all the available options in the Accessories component.

17 Click **OK**.

What's happening? You are asked to insert the correct disk.

18 Insert the correct disk. Click **OK**.

What's happening? You see a progress box indicating that the missing files are being copied to the hard disk.

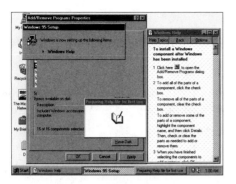

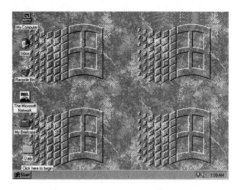

19 If the above screen appears, click the **Close** button.

What's
happening? ➤ Windows 95 prepares Help for you.

What's
happening? ➤ You may also find that your wallpaper (background) has changed. If it has, take the following steps:

20 Right-click the desktop. Click **Properties**.

What's
happening? ➤ You may get the above screen.

What's
happening? ➤ You see the Background tab for the Display property sheet.

21 In the Wallpaper list box, scroll up until you see the option **None**. Click **None**. Click **OK**.

What's
happening? ➤ You are returned to the desktop. You have installed the components that you selected.

3.3   Help

Now that you have the fully installed version of Windows 95, you may continue to explore your options. Help dialog boxes will often have a question mark on the right side of the title bar. The question mark will provide a definition of an item. When you see the question mark, you click it and point it at your query. The question mark will then provide you with a What's This? pop-up description of the process in question. You may also right-click an item in a dialog box and the What's This? will pop up so that you can click to get a brief description of the item.

Help also includes shortcut buttons. As you have seen, these buttons allow you to jump quickly to the area you need. For instance, if you wanted to change the time, Help would tell you how to do it as well as provide a shortcut button that takes you to the Date/Time property sheet where you change the time.

Help is organized by sheets with tabs labeled Contents, Index, and Find. The Contents sheet is organized by category. You double-click the book icon to see what topics are in a category. Often these topics will have tips and tricks. The Index sheet is an index with a pre-determined list of words and phrases. You key in the word or phrase and double-click to display Help about it. If you do not know the word or phase you need, you may use the Find sheet to build an index for all the words and phases within the Help topics.

3.4   Activity—Using Help

Note: The remainder of the text is based on the assumption that Windows 95 was completely installed. If your screen display is not the same, you need to install the missing components.

1   Click **Start**. Click **Help**. Double-click **Introducing Windows**.

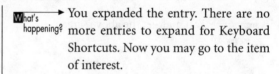 You have expanded the entry. You see many book icons.

2   Double-click **Keyboard Shortcuts**.

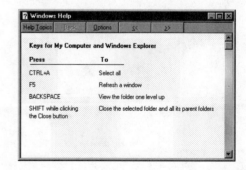 You expanded the entry. There are no more entries to expand for Keyboard Shortcuts. Now you may go to the item of interest.

3   Double-click **For My Computer and Windows Explorer**.

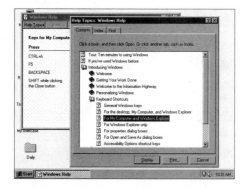 You see information about the different keystrokes you may use, such as pressing the **Shift** key and clicking the Close button which you learned in Chapter 2. You will see that Windows Help also appears as a button on the taskbar. Help is an application program because it "does" something, namely providing help. You may close the Help window by clicking the Close button, or you may return to the Contents window.

4 Click the **Help Topics** command button.

5 Double-click **General Windows keys**.

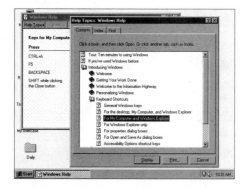

 You now see only the General Windows Keys window. When you opened this window, you closed the For My Computer and Windows Explorer window. Pressing the **F1** key is an alternate way to get Help.

6 Click the **Options** command button.

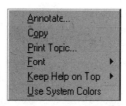

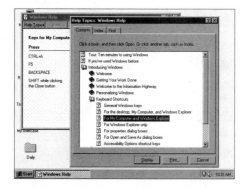 You opened the Options menu which has several choices. Each item with a right-pointing arrow indicates that you have further choices. Print Topics does not have an arrow, but does have three dots. These three dots are called an *ellipsis*. When you choose an item that has an ellipsis, it means that a dialog box will open. Be sure that the printer is turned on.

7 Click **Print Topic**.

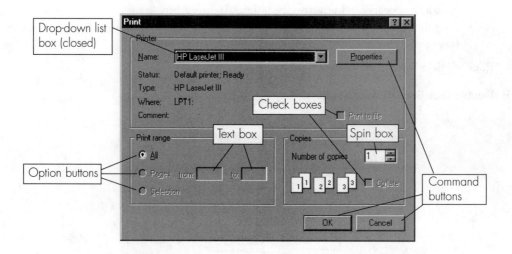

What's happening? ▶ This dialog box presents information about the printer. In addition, the dialog box has many elements common to most dialog boxes. Your dialog box choices may differ depending on what printer you have installed. The choices that are available are generically called controls. A *control* is a way that a user can interact (provide input) with the available choices. Usually a control is a way to initiate an action, display information, or set the values that you are interested in. The controls in this dialog box are:

Command buttons
A *command button* carries out a task. The OK command button will cause printing to occur. The Cancel button will take no action and will close the window. The Properties button has an ellipsis, indicating that, when you click it, you will open another dialog box.

Drop-down list box
A *drop-down list box* contains a preferred (default) choice. In this case, the default printer is a Hewlett-Packard LaserJet III. If you wanted to choose another printer, you would click on the down arrow. This opens the drop-down list box and presents you with a list of other of printers.

Option buttons
Option buttons present mutually exclusive choices; you may choose only one option at a time. The selected option contains a black dot. In this example, the Print Range option buttons have only one option available, All. The other options are dimmed, and therefore unavailable because there is no range of pages to print. If this were a multiple page document, you could choose to print all the pages, a selection within a page, or a range of pages.

Text box
A *text box* allows you to key in information. If this were a multiple page document, you could determine which pages you wanted to print by clicking the Pages option button and then keying in a range of pages in the From and To text boxes.

Check box   A *check box* provides a choice that may be enabled or disabled. You may
                 have many check boxes from which to choose. They are not mutually
                 exclusive. In this example, the Collate check box is dimmed and cannot
                 be enabled because a one-page document does not need to be collated.

Spin box   A *spin box* is available for the number of copies in this dialog box. A
                 spin box allows you either to key in a number or to click on the up or
                 down arrow to increase or decrease the number of copies you wish to
                 print. When you have a numeric quantity to choose, you will usually see
                 a spin box. The Number of Copies spin box may not be available to you,
                 again, depending on the printer you have installed.

8 If your printer allows you to alter the number of copies printed, you will see a spin box. If the spin
     box is available to you, click the up arrow in the **Number of copies** until it reaches **5**. If it is not
     available, read only, do not execute, Step 8 and Step 9.

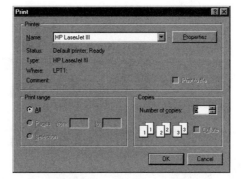

What's → By clicking the up arrow, you increased the number of copies that will be printed. The number
happening? 5 is highlighted. Windows 95 has a feature called *typing replaces selection*. This means that
             when an item is highlighted (as the number 5 is), you may key in another number, thus replac-
             ing the old number with a new one without having to delete the old one.

9 Key in the following: **1**.

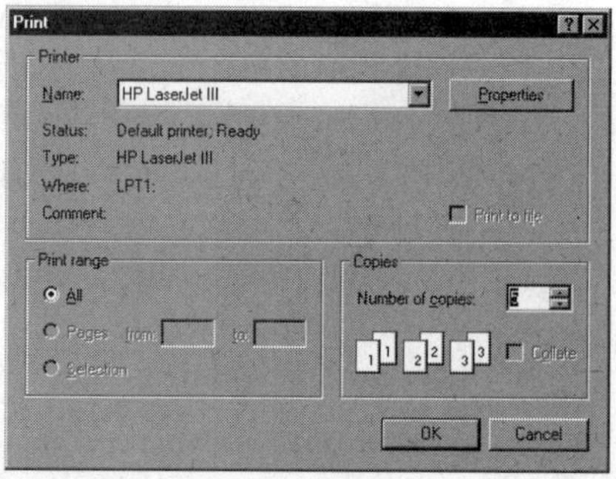

What's happening? When you keyed in the number 1, you replaced the number 5. You did not have to delete the 5 first. The item to be replaced must be highlighted.

10 Click the **Properties** command button.

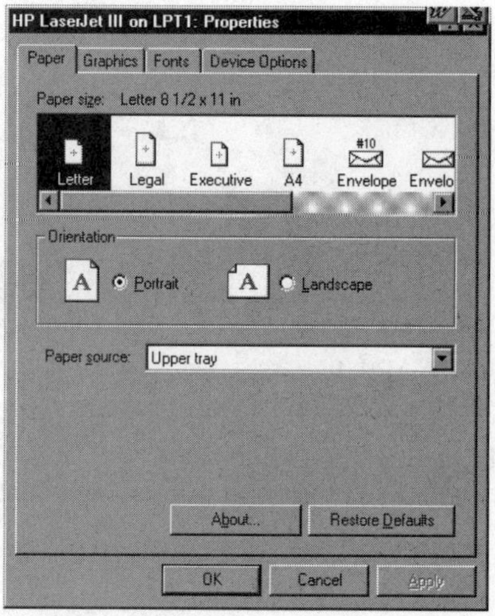

What's happening? You are looking at the property sheet for the specific printer attached to your system. Your properties may vary, depending on the installed printer on your system. In this example, the Paper property sheet is selected. This property sheet has option buttons. You either print in portrait or landscape; you cannot print in both. ***Portrait printing*** is the typical way a document prints in an 8½- by 11-inch mode. When you print in ***landscape mode***, you are printing in an 11- by 8½-inch mode, or "sideways." This property sheet includes a drop-down list box that allows you to choose the Paper source. You also have a scroll bar. As you saw earlier, a scroll bar allows you to move through a document. A scroll bar automatically appears, vertically, horizontally, or both whenever a document is too large to fit into the window. See Figure 3.2.

Figure 3.2   Scroll Bar

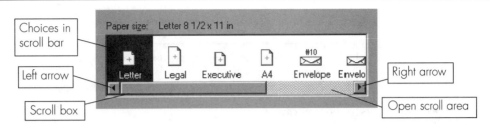

Left arrow	When you click the left arrow, you move in small increments to the left.
Right arrow	When you click the right arrow, you move in small increments to the right.
Scroll box	When you drag the scroll box, you can move quickly through the document. The scroll box indicates your relative position in the document.
Open Scroll area	Clicking the open scroll area to the right or left of the scroll box will move you in larger increments through the document.
Choices in scroll bar	The selected choice is highlighted. When you click an icon, you make your choice.

11 If you have a scroll bar, click the right arrow.

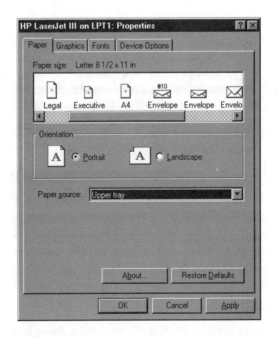

What's → You moved to the right to view the paper size choices.
happening?

12 Click **Cancel**.

13 Click the question mark on the Print title bar. Click **Print range**.

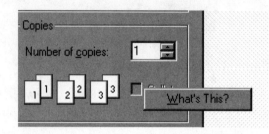

Specifies whether to print the entire document, specific pages, or the selection you highlighted.

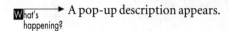 A pop-up description appears.

14 Click outside the pop-up window to close it. Right-click the **Collate** check box.

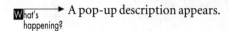 You see the What's This? pop-up window.

15 Click **What's This?**.

If you have selected more than one copy, specifies whether you want the copies to be collated.

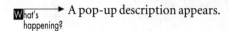 This is another way to see a definition or description of an item that you are interested in.

16 Click outside the definition to close it. Click **OK**.

Print Topic ☒

Printing "General Windows keys"

Cancel

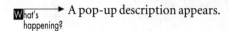 An information status box quickly appears, informing you that the document is being printed. If you look quickly at the taskbar, you will see an icon of the printer, indicating that the printer is working. Now you have a hard copy of the shortcut keys.

17 Close the **Windows Help** window.

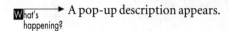 You have returned to the desktop. If you open other dialog boxes, you will see the same types of controls available. Figure 3.3 is another example of a dialog box with controls.

Figure 3.3   Controls in a dialog box

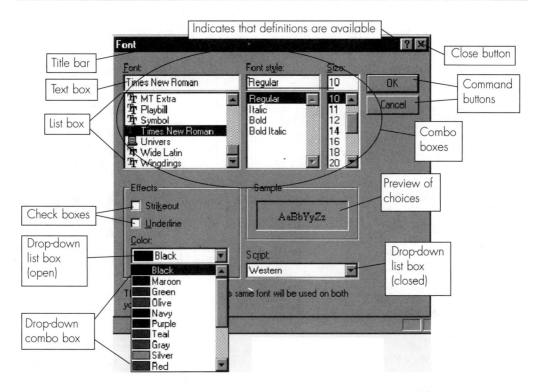

As you can see, most of the elements are the same even though this is a different dialog box. There are two new features.

Combo box   A *combo box* is a standard Windows 95 control that combines a text box and an interdependent list box.

Sample box   If the choices you make will alter the appearance of an object, then a *sample box* is displayed to show the results of your changes.

Drop-down combo box Again, a drop-down combo box is a standard Windows 95 control that combines the characteristics of a text box with a drop-down list box.

3.5   Animated Help

In addition to the Help you just used, in certain cases, Help also includes animated demonstrations. These demonstrations are animated so that a Windows 95 feature may be shown to you. You will also find the animated Help feature in different application packages. If you did not do or do not have a full installation of Windows 95 (the Online User's Guide and the Windows 95 Tour in the Accessories), animated Help will not be available to you.

3.6   Activity—Using Animated Help To Learn Dialog Boxes

1 Click **Start**. Click **Help**. On the Contents page, double-click **Introducing Windows**. Double-click **Getting Your Work Done**.

2 Double-click **The basics**.

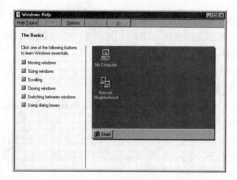

What's happening? → If you cannot see the entire window, size it so you can. This window introduces you to some tasks you have already accomplished, such as moving and sizing windows.

3 Click **Moving windows**.

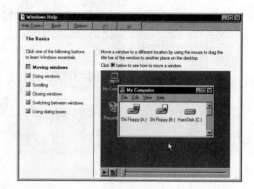

What's happening? → This window is divided into two sections, called *panes*. The left panc includesa list of activities. The right pane changes to reflect a demonstration of the activity that you chose from the left pane. The right pane, in addition to describing how to move a window, can demonstrate how it is done. At the bottom of the right pane is another example of a control, in this case, a slider bar.

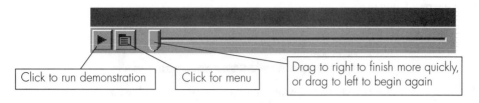

Click to run demonstration

Click for menu

Drag to right to finish more quickly, or drag to left to begin again

4 Click the **Menu** button on the control. Point at **View**.

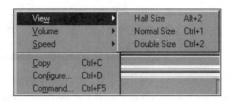

What's happening? You can control all aspects of this demonstration: View, Volume, and Speed. You can also use copy (Copy), adjust the video display (Configure), or run a program (Command) from this menu as well.

5 Click outside the menu to close it. Click the **Start** button to run the demonstration.

What's happening? You see a graphic demonstration with movement and sound that shows you how to move a window.

6 Click **Using dialog boxes** in the left pane.

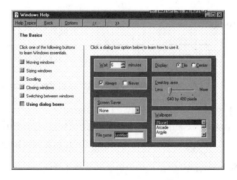

What's happening? In the right pane are examples of different types of dialog boxes.

7 Click the **Wait** dialog box.

Click the arrows to change the number.

What's happening? A pop-up window appears, telling you that to change the numbers, and you click the up or down arrow. This is an example of a spin box. Remember, you must click outside the pop-up description to close it.

8   Click the **Always** dialog box.

> Click the option(s) you want. You can select more than one.

$\rightarrow$ This is an example of a check box which may be set or unset (enabled or disabled). When check **What's happening?** boxes are available, you may select to set none, one, more than one, or all.

9   Click the **Screen Saver** dialog box.

> Click the arrow to see a list of options. Then click the option you want.

$\rightarrow$ This is an example of a drop-down list box. The default, or preferred choice, is in the box. Usually, **What's happening?** you must select an entry. You may not leave the list box blank. If you want to see or change your other options, you click on the down arrow to display other choices.

10   Click the **File name** dialog box.

> Type your selection in the box.

$\rightarrow$ This is an example of a text box. In a text box, you key in your choices. Sometimes your choice will **What's happening?** be limited to what already exists. For instance, if you are opening a file, you must key in a file that already exists. On the other hand, if you are saving a new file, you would key in a unique new name.

11   Click the **Display** dialog box.

> Click the option you want. You can only select one.

$\rightarrow$ This is an example of option buttons. The message reminds you that you may select only one **What's happening?** option when you are presented with option buttons. Option buttons provide mutually exclusive choices. You may do either one or the other, but not both.

12   Click the **Desktop area** dialog box.

> Slide the bar to make your selection.

$\rightarrow$ This is an example of a slider bar. To make a change, place your mouse on the slider, hold, and **What's happening?** slide.

13   Click the **Wallpaper** dialog box.

> Click the arrows to move through the list, and then click your selection.

This is an example of a list box. There are many choices in it, but there is no preferred choice. Often, in a list box, one of the choices is None, indicating that you do not want this option. Again, you click the up or down arrow to scroll through other choices. To make your choice, click it.

14 Close Windows Help.

You have returned to the desktop.

3.7   The Help Index

When you want help, you are often looking for a particular item. For instance, if you want help with printing, it would be easier to look up Printing than use the Contents sheet. If you used the Contents sheet, you would have to guess in which book the information you want is located. Using the Index tab allows you to key in a specific word or phrase. As in any index, you are limited to pre-defined words or terms.

3.8   Activity—Using the Index

1 Click **Start**. Click **Help**. Click the **Index** tab.

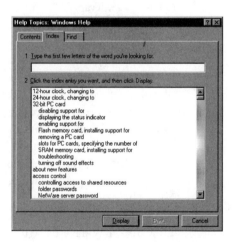

2 In the text box, key in the following: **s**

There are two parts to the dialog box: the text box and the list box. In the text box, you key in the information you seek. As you start to key in letters, the list of terms in the list box will begin scrolling to match what it is you are keying in.

As you keyed in the first letter, the list of terms moved to the first term that began with that letter s. As you continue to key in letters, you will move through the list.

3 Continue keying in the following: **ystem resources**

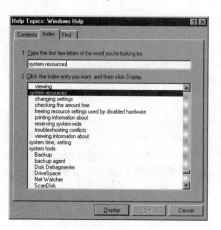

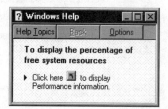

→ All of the topics associated with system resources are listed. System resources tell you about your computer system.

4 Double-click **checking the amount free** in the list box.

→ You are immediately taken to a window that tells you what to do. Furthermore, in this window is a shortcut button ⌐|. Remember, a shortcut is always indicated by the purple left curved arrow. The shortcut button will take you to the information you wish to see.

5 Click the shortcut button.

→ You see the System Properties property sheet. The Windows Help window remains open. The displayed page is Performance, which you asked to see. In the example, this computer has 16 MB of memory, and 93% of the resources are free. Your display will vary depending on the computer system you have.

Free system resources is an important concept. If you have many programs running, each program uses memory, disk space, video, and other features of your computer. In addition, Windows 95 has to manage the drawing of the screen, keep track of what memory is available, and other critical operating system tasks. These are the system resources that Windows 95 is managing. You may have 64 MB of memory, but if, for instance, you had only 12% free system resources, you could realistically run another program. You are not out of memory, but you are out of the resources that Windows 95 manages.

6   Click the **General** tab.

 The General property sheet tells you what operating system you are running (Windows 95) and the version number (4.00.950 or Windows 4.0). It states whom the product is registered to, what type of processor you have, and how much memory is installed on this computer. Your properties will vary.

7   Close the System Properties window.

8   In the **Windows Help** window, click the **Help Topics** command button.

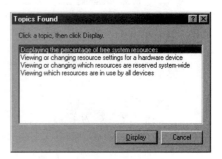 You have returned to the Index.

9   Double-click **viewing information about**.

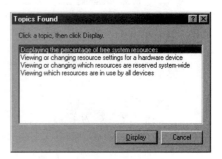

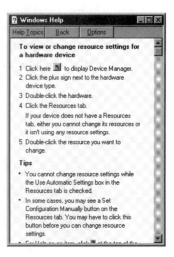 There are many topics related to viewing information about. Thus, a Topics Found dialog box opens, allowing you to choose the topic of your choice.

10   Double-click **Viewing or changing resource settings for a hardware device**.

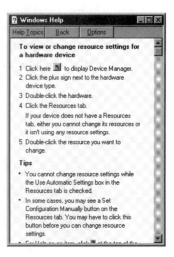

 You are taken to a new Help window. The previous Help window was closed. The new Help window contains information about resources that you access using the shortcut button.

11 Click the shortcut button.

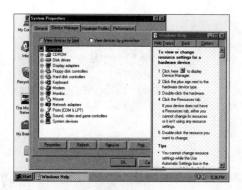

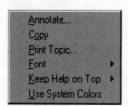

You are returned to the System Properties property sheet. This time, the Device Manager tab has been selected. This
lists all of your devices by type. If the
Windows Help window is obscuring the
display of the property sheet, you have
choices. You can move the window,
minimize it, or change it by using the
Options menu. The default option is to
keep the Windows Help window on top.
This allows you to refer to the help screen
as you do a task, but it also can get in the
way.

12 Click the **Options** command button in the
Windows Help window.

You opened the Options menu and can
see that one of the choices is Keep Help
on Top. A right triangular arrow indicates that Keep Help on Top has an additional menu.

13 Point to **Keep Help on Top**.

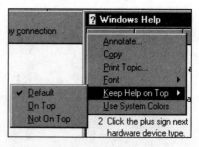

In this example, Default is the selected
choice, because it has a check mark next
to it. The default value of the Help window is that it is placed on top of all other
windows.

14 Click **Not On Top**. Click the **System Properties**
property sheet.

Now the System Properties property
sheet is the active window and is in the
foreground. The Windows Help window
retreats to the background. You may
make Windows Help the active window
by clicking it or clicking the button on
the taskbar.

15   Click the **Windows Help** window.

<table>
<tr><td>What's
happening?</td><td>→ The Windows Help window is now the
active window and is in the foreground.</td></tr>
</table>

16   Click the **Options** command button. Point to **Keep Help on Top**. Click **Default**.

17   Close all windows.

<table>
<tr><td>What's
happening?</td><td>→ You have returned to the desktop.</td></tr>
</table>

3.9   Using the Find Tab

When you use Contents, you must locate information by topic. When you use Index, you must locate information by a predetermined word or phrase. If you do not know what word or phrase you need, you can use Find. Find will search for words or phrases in the entire Help file. The first time you use Find, it builds a database listing all the words and phrases in the Help file. This may take a few minutes. Once the database is built, it need not be built again. Then, you may search for any word or phrase in the Help file.

3.10   Activity—Using the Find Tab

1   Click **Start**. Click **Help**. Click the **Find** tab.

<table>
<tr><td>What's
happening?</td><td>→ Since this is the first time that Find has been used, the Find Setup Wizard appears. A *wizard* is a series of screens that leads you through a series of steps.</td></tr>
</table>

2   Click **Next**.

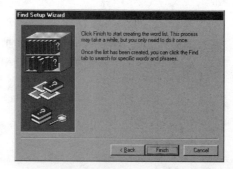

What's
happening? → You are warned that this process may take a few minutes. If this screen does not appear, then the Find database has already been created.

3   Click **Finish**.

What's
happening? → You see a message box that tells you the word list is being created.

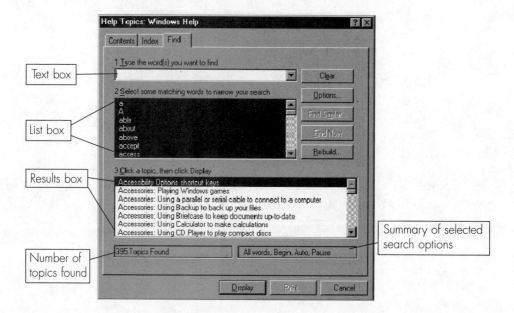

What's happening? Find is ready for you to enter data. This property sheet has a different focus. You key in the word or phrase you are looking for in the text box. You narrow your search by clicking the relevant word or phrase in the list box. Then you see, in the results list box, the topics that are germane. This property sheet will list the quantity of topics found as well as a summary of the options you have chosen.

4   Click the **Options** command button.

What's happening? The Find Options dialog box displays your selections. You may change any of these.

5   Click **Cancel**.

6   In the text box, key in the following: **system**

What's happening? In the list box, relevant phrases appear. The number of topics has been reduced to 27. By selecting a relevant topic in the list box, you continue to narrow your search.

7   Click **System** in the list box.

What's happening? You have further narrowed your topic selection to 10. If you have installed Microsoft Plus, you may have more topics.

8 Click in the text box. Press the $\boxed{\text{Shift}}$ and key in the following: **properties**

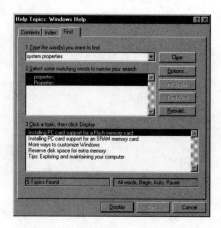

What's
happening? By combing phrases, you have limited your search to one topic. The ellipsis in front of each word in the list box indicates that there was a match for your first word (system). The list is words that match your second keyed in phrase.

9 Click **Properties**.

What's
happening? Now, you have only one topic. Again, if you installed Microsoft Plus, you may have more topics displayed. If you wanted to go to that topic, you would click the Display button. Clicking the Display button would close the Help Topics window and take you to the topic of interest.

10 Click the **Contents** tab.

11 Close Help.

What's
happening? You have returned to the desktop.

3.11 Annotating Help

One of the features of Help is the ability to write notes to yourself. As you continue to work with computers, one of the important ways to keep yourself up to date is to read different computer journals, such as *Windows, PC Magazine,* or *PC Week.* These journals will keep you current with new product reviews, articles about new technologies, and provide tips and tricks for using the computer. By talking to other users or experimenting, you can learn other ways to accomplish tasks. The best way to remember anything is to write it down. However, since you are in the computer world, you do not want pieces of paper floating around. An easy way to keep notes in a logical place is to use the Help annotation feature.

3.12 Activity—Creating Annotations

1 Click **Start**. Click **Help**. Click the **Index** tab.

2 Key in the following: **printing**

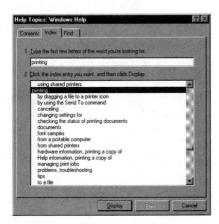

What's → You have found help about printing.
happening? Locate the phrase problems, troubleshooting.

3 Double-click **problems, troubleshooting**.

What's → Now you are going to create an annota-
happening? tion.

4 Click the **Options** command button. Click **Annotate**.

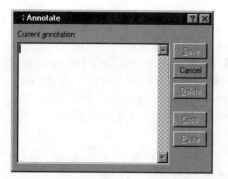

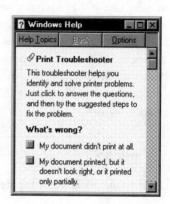

6 Click **Save**. *(Note:* If you are on a network, you may not be able to save.)

What's happening? You are presented with a blank screen in which you may key in information.

5 Key in the following: **Remember to check if the printer is both turned on and online.**

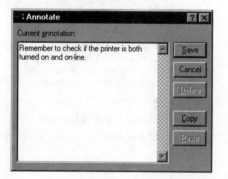

What's happening? You have keyed in a reminder to yourself. It is obvious to most people that a printer must have power before it can work, but there is another important facet to printing. Supplying power to the printer does not ensure that the printer will print. A printer must also be online. *Online* means that the computer knows that the printer is there. All printers have a Power button, and most printers have an Online button as well. To print, both must be on.

What's happening? This window has a paper clip next to its title, Print Troubleshooter. This paper clip represents your annotation (the note you wrote).

7 Click the paper clip.

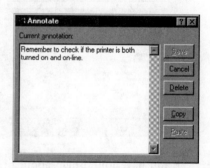

What's happening? Your annotation appears. You now may check the printer status. You may also eliminate an annotation.

8   Click the **Delete** button.

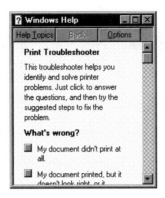

You are returned to the Windows Help dialog box. The paper clip indicating the annotation is
happening? gone.

9   Close all open windows.

You have returned to the desktop.

3.13 Using Help To Solve Problems

Although you can move about in Help to explore the various possibilities and to use the demonstrations to assist you, another aspect of Help is important. Help is designed to solve problems.

When you work with computers, both hardware and software, the chance that problems will
occur is high, no matter if you are a new or an experienced user. In fact, the only difference between a
beginner and an experienced user is that an experienced user can get into more trouble faster! A fact
of life in the computer world is getting into trouble and then getting out of trouble. Help is one tool
that can assist in solving your computer problems.

3.14 Activity—When Printing Does Not Work

Note 1:   If you are on a network and do not have a local printer, you will not be able to do this activity
completely. Skip Step 1 because you will not be able to turn off the printer.

Note 2:   Once you have performed this activity, you cannot redo it in this work session. It will not work
the same way, because, once you have solved a hardware problem in a work session, Windows 95
Help will not offer the same help again. Help tries to be smart. If you already completed the
steps, there is no point in repeating them.

1   If the printer is turned on, turn it off.

2   Place in drive A the Activities disk that came with the text.

3 Double-click **My Computer**. Double-click the **Drive A** icon.

You have "opened" the disk drive. *Opening a drive* means that you open the drive window to see what files and folders are on the disk. The items that look like folders are directories. They are shown first. The other icons are files in the root directory. If your window does not look like the above example, click View. Click Large Icons. Then click View. Point to Arrange. Click by Name.

4 Scroll through the window until you locate the file called **Dances**.

5 Double-click **Dances**.

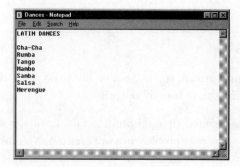

You have opened the document (file) called Dances. Whenever you open a document, you must first open the application program that created the document. In most cases, when you create a document with an application program, the application program has formatted the data in the document. This kind of formatting refers to information such as the size of the margins, the tab setting, the line spacing, or the size of the typeface. In order for the application program to display the document properly, the program places unique computer codes in the document for each formatting feature.

In this example, the program that created the Dances document is Notepad. Notepad is different from most other application programs because is a text editor. A text editor may also be called an *ASCII* editor. ASCII is a standard format for documents created in a text format. An ASCII file is one that has no embedded computer codes. The file is only text.

Although Notepad is an ASCII editor, it is still an application program. One of the features that all Windows application programs has in common is a menu bar. A menu bar has choices. File is usually the first choice, with Help being the last choice on the menu bar. One of the advantages of working with application programs in Windows 95 is that once you learn how to do a task in one program, the task is accomplished the same way in other application programs. As you begin working with Windows 95 application programs, you will begin to recognize these common elements.

6 Click **File**.

→ The File menu lists the common tasks you use to manipulate a data file. The data file, your document, is called Dances. It is actually called Dances.txt. The .txt file extension indicates the program that created the data. If Windows 95 knows the program, it will not display the .txt extension unless you request it. The Notepad program allows you to create a new file (New), open a previously created file (Open), save your file to disk (Save), save your file to a disk under a different name (Save As), change the way the document is laid out on the page (Page Setup), print a hard copy of the file (Print), and close the program (Exit). When you close the program, you close the file (document) as well.

7 Click outside the menu to close it.

8 On the taskbar click **Start**. Click **Help**.

9 Click the **Index** tab. In the text box, key in the following: **print**

→ The topic is print jobs. You are looking for help about printing.

10 Double-click **viewing**.

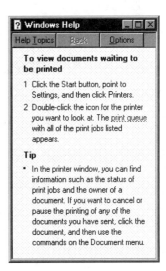

→ Help informs you that you may view the print jobs that are pending. The phrase *print queue* has a dotted underline. Whenever you see a dotted underline in a Help menu, it is a definition of a term.

11   When you move the mouse to **print queue**, the pointer becomes a hand. Click **print queue**.

> A print queue is a list of documents waiting to
> be printed on the printer. In the print queue,
> you can see information such as the size of
> the document, who sent the document, and
> status information for printing.

What's → A pop-up window appears defining print queue.
happening?

12   Click outside the pop-up window to close it. Close Help.

13   In the Notepad window, click **File**. Click **Print**. Look at the taskbar in the status area. (*Note:* If you are on a network with no local printer, the page will be printed on the network printer. Read the following steps, but do not do them.)

Dances - Notepad   11:35 AM

What's → The Taskbar button Dances - Notepad tells you which application is active. You may not see all
happening? of the title on the Taskbar button. If you hold the pointer over the button, the full title of the
application appears in a ToolTip. In addition, there is a printer icon indicating that something
is printing.

14   Wait until you see the following error message box. It may take a few minutes to appear.

Printers Folder
? There was an error writing to LPT1: for the printer (HP LaserJet
4/4M):
A printer timeout error occurred. To increase the timeout settings for
your printer,
open the Printers folder, click the icon for your printer, click the File
menu, and then click Properties.
To continue printing, click retry.
Windows will automatically retry after 5 seconds.

Retry   Cancel

What's → The Printers Folder message box indicates that there is an error. You cannot print.
happening?

15   Right-click the printer icon on the taskbar.

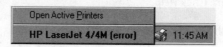

Open Active Printers
HP LaserJet 4/4M (error)   11:45 AM

What's → A shortcut menu appears with two choices. One choice is Open Active Printers. The other
happening? identifies the printer on this system. The identified printer has an error. If you look on the
taskbar, you will also see that the printer icon has a question mark in a red circle which is a
visual representation of a problem.

16 Click **Open Active Printers**.

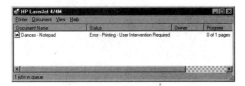

What's
happening? You open the active printer window where you find the name of the document and its status. The error message requires the user, you, to do something (User Intervention Required). If you cannot see the entire status, you may adjust the size of the Status column by dragging the right side of the Status button. Since this is a practice activity, you actually know the problem. But if you did not, you would use this process to discover the problem. The printer has no power.

17 Click **Printers** on the menu bar of the open window.

What's
happening? In this menu one of the choices is Purge Print Jobs. Purging a print job does not mean removing the document but only its place in the print lineup. Windows 95 lines up (*queues*) print jobs. Since printing is a slow process, Windows 95 manages the printing and feeds data to the printer, as the printer is available. The print management feature frees up the computer resources so that you may work on other tasks while Windows manages the printing.

18 Click **Purge Print Jobs**.

What's
happening? When you clicked Purge Print Jobs, the message states that Dances - Notepad is being deleted. You are not deleting the document, only its place in the print queue. Wait until the Printer window is empty which may take a few minutes. While you are waiting, you will see on the taskbar that the Printer Folders button is flashing. Here, again, is a visual alert to a problem.

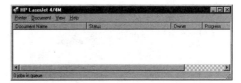

What's
happening? The Printer window is now empty.

19 Close the Printer window.

20 Click **Help** on the **Notepad** menu bar. Click **Help Topics**.

21 Double-click **Printing**. Double-click **Troubleshooting printer problems**.

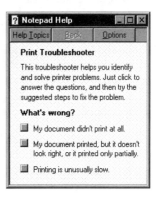

The Notepad Help Print Troubleshooter window helps you determine what is wrong. In this case, your document did not print.

22 Click the button in front of **My document didn't print at all.**

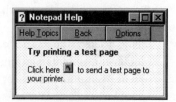

Notepad Help has a shortcut button that takes you to the place where you may print a test page.

23 Click the shortcut button.

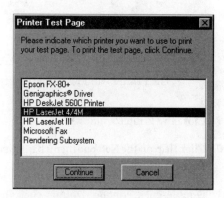

The Printer Test Page dialog box confirms your printer selection.

24 Click **Continue.**

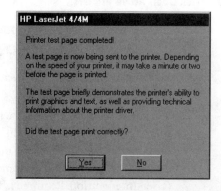

The dialog box for your printer brand appears, asking you if the test page printed. The page did not print.

25 Click **No**.

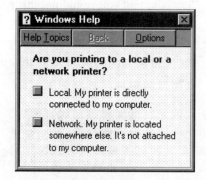

You are now in Windows Help. Printing is an operating system concern. The operating system needs to know to what device you are printing. Local and Network are the two defined choices. In the example, you are on a local printer. However, if you are on a network, your choice would be Network.

26 Click **Local**.

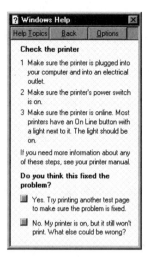

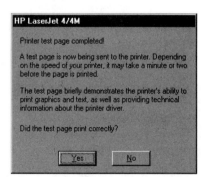

What's happening? Windows Help lists some items you should check. The first suggestion is to check if the printer plugged in. The second is whether or not your printer power switch is on. Your problem has been identified. The power switch in not on.

27 Turn the printer on.

28 Click **Yes** in **Windows Help**.

What's happening? The dialog asks you if the page printed correctly. Since you turned on the printer, you should have a printed page.

29 In the named printer dialog box, click **Yes**.

30 Close the **Help** window.

What's happening? You have solved your printer problem, and you can print in Notepad. When you are working with computers, you need to perform an analysis of why you are having a problem. A common problem beginning users have when running into a something that does not work is that they takes the same steps over and over again, which simply compounds the problem. In the above example, if you, as the user, continually clicked File, and then Print, you would not be solving the problem, but simply queuing up many print jobs and *never* getting a printed page. A good rule of thumb when having problems is that, if you take the same steps more than three times, you should stop and perform an analysis.

The first step in an analysis is to determine the problem. With computers, the cause of a problem is either hardware or software. By a process of elimination, try to determine which category the problem falls into. Here, Help tries to assist you. Check the obvious first. In our previous example, the steps were outlined for you in Help. Is the printer plugged in? Is it turned on? Will it print a test page? If all these items are true, it probably is not a hardware problem, but a software problem. In this case, it was a hardware problem that you solved.

31 Close Notepad.

32 Close all the open windows. Remember that holding down the $\boxed{\text{Shift}}$ key when clicking the **Close** button will close the child and parent windows in one step.

Chapter Summary

This chapter introduced you to installing Windows 95 components. You learned that the CD and floppy disk version are different, and you learned how to determine if you have missing components and how to add any them. You also learned how to remove the components you do not want.

In addition, you learned to use the Help feature available in Windows 95. To access Help, you may click Start, then click Help or you may press the F1 key. You found that there are three ways to access Help: the Contents tab, the Index tab, and the Find tab. Contents is arranged by topic. Index is arranged by key words or phrases. Find builds a database of all words in the Help file.

You found that Help, in addition to providing the necessary steps to accomplish a task, will often have a shortcut button that will take you to the window you need. You also learned that Help provided a What's This feature that, when activated, will provide definitions of new terms. Some Help offers animated demonstrations on how to accomplish a task.

You were introduced to the different types of dialog boxes and common controls in dialog boxes, and you learned about the controls that allow you to manipulate your actions. Common controls include list boxes, command buttons, option buttons, drop-down list boxes, text boxes, check boxes, spin boxes, combo drop-down list boxes, scroll bars, scroll boxes, and sample boxes. You also can create your own annotations to further help you.

You used Help to solve a problem, and you found that when you have a problem, you need to perform an analysis in order to solve the problem.

Key Terms

ASCII	Landscape mode	Sample box
Check box	List box	Scroll bar
Combo box	Online	Scroll box
Command button	Open scroll area	Shortcut button
Control	Opening a drive	Spin box
Drop-down combo box	Option buttons	Text box
Drop-down list box	Pane	Typing replaces
Ellipsis	Portrait printing	selection
Free system resources	Print queue	What's This?
Hypertext	Queues	Wizard

Discussion Questions

1. Describe how you could find out if you had any missing Windows 95 components.
2. List the steps to add or remove Windows 95 components.
3. Explain what is meant by online Help capabilities.
4. Help in Windows 95 is a hypertext utility. Explain.
5. What is the purpose and function of the Question Mark icon in a dialog box?
6. Compare and contrast the three ways Help is organized.
7. What is the purpose and function of an ellipsis?
8. Explain the purpose and functions of command buttons and option buttons.
9. Explain the purpose and function of a check box and a spin box.

10. What is the purpose and function of a text box?
11. Compare and contrast a list box and a drop-down list box.
12. Compare and contrast portrait printing with landscape printing.
13. What is a demonstration?
14. What are some of the limitations of using the Index sheet when seeking help?
15. What types of information can be found on the System property sheet?
16. What is a shortcut button in Help? How may it be used? What purpose does it serve?
17. Why is the concept of free system resources important?
18. What is the purpose and function of the annotation feature of Help?
19. What does it mean for a printer to be online?
20. What is a print queue?

True/False Questions

For each question, circle the letter T if the statement is true or the letter F if the statement is false.

T F 1. When you install Windows 95 and choose a Typical installation, all the components of Windows 95 will be installed.
T F 2. Help is a hypertext utility.
T F 3. When you see check boxes in a dialog box, more than one check box may be selected simultaneously.
T F 4. A shortcut button in a Help window will provide a brief description of an item in question.
T F 5. If you attempt to print and are unsuccessful, continue clicking the File and Print until your document prints.

Completion Questions

Write the correct answer in each blank space.

6. Windows 95 provides _____ Help, which minimizes the need for printed manuals.
7. If you click the _____ in a help dialog box and then click a word or phase, you will see a brief definition of the item.
8. When you click Start, and then Help, the three tabbed sheets that are available are _____, _____ , and _____ .
9. The symbol that means an annotation is present is a(n) _____.
10. The three dots that follow some menu selections are called a(n) _____.

Multiple Choice Questions

Circle the letter of the correct answer for each question.

11. When adding or removing Windows 95 components, you see a grayed check box with a check mark in it which means that
    a. the component you want is unavailable.
    b. all the components have been selected.
    c. some, but not all, of the components have been selected.
    d. none of the components have been selected.

12. If you click a phrase that has a dotted underline in a dialog box, you
    a. will open a menu.
    b. will open a pop-up window with a definition of the phrase.
    c. should note this item as extremely important.
    d. will open an annotation window.

13. If you knew the word or phrase you wanted help on, the fastest way to find what you need in Help is to choose the
    a. Index tab.
    b. Find tab.
    c. Search tab.
    d. Contents tab.

14. When Windows 95 is printing a document, a
    a. printer icon appears on the taskbar.
    b. menu appears on the taskbar with printing options.
    c. both a and b
    d. neither a nor b

15. Option buttons
    a. present choices that may be paired together.
    b. are available only in the Print menu.
    c. present mutually exclusive choices.
    d. are available in every dialog box.

Application Assignments

Problem Set I—At the Computer

Problem A

Click **Start**. Click **Help**. Click the **Contents** tab. Double-click **Introducing Windows**. Double-click **Welcome**. Double-click **A List of What's New**. Double-click **A new look and feel**.

1. What item *does not* appear on the list?
   a. Start buttons and taskbar.
   b. Properties.
   c. Printing.

In the list, click the **Close, Minimize,** and **Maximize** buttons.

2. Which icon(s) for a button(s) do you see in the window?
   a. Maximize button.
   b. Minimize button.
   c. Close button.
   d. all the buttons.

Close the What's New window. Click the **Options** command button in Windows Help.

3. Which menu choice will open further menus but not a dialog box?
   a. Print Topic.
   b. Font.
   c. Annotate.
   d. Use System Colors.

Close all open windows. Be sure Help is closed.

Problem B

Double-click **My Computer**. Double-click the **Printers** folder. Click your default printer so that it is selected. Do not double-click it. Right-click the printer. Click **Properties**. Click the **Details** tab. Click the **Spool Settings** command button.

4. **Spool print jobs so program finishes printing faster** is an example of a(n)
   a. option button.
   b. command button.
   c. check button.

Click the **Cancel** button.

5. **Print to the following port** is an example of a(n)
   a. list box.
   b. text box.
   c. drop-down list box.
   d. check box.

Click the **Port Settings** command button.

6. **Spool MS-DOS print jobs** is an example of a(n)
   a. list box.
   b. text box.
   c. drop-down list box.
   d. check box.

Click **Cancel** in the Port Settings dialog box. Click the **Question Mark** icon on the title bar and click **Not Selected** in the **Time-out Settings**.

7. Time is measured in
   a. hours.
   b. minutes.
   c. seconds.
   d. nanoseconds.

Close all dialog boxes and Windows Help. Close My Computer.

Problem C

Click **Start**. Click **Help**. Click the **Index** tab. In the Text box, key in the following: **saving** Double-click **desktop appearance schemes**.

8. The __| is an example of a(n)
   a. shortcut button.
   b. command button.
   c. option button.

Click the shortcut button.

9. You are taken to a(n)
   a. property sheet about Settings.
   b. property sheet about Appearance.
   c. Help dialog box.
   d. property sheet about Help.

Close all dialog boxes and open windows. Return to the desktop.

Problem D

Place the Activities disk that came with the text in Drive A. Double-click **My Computer**. Double-click **Drive A**. Locate the file called **February**. Right-click **February**. Click **Properties** on the menu.

10. The document, February.txt, is a
    a. Write file.
    b. Text Document.
    c. Word file.
    d. WordPerfect file.

11. Its size is
    a. 24 bytes.
    b. 54 bytes.
    c. 74 bytes.
    d. 94 bytes.

12. In **Attributes**, **Read-only** is an example of a
    a. text box.
    b. check box.
    c. list box.

Close the property sheet. Double-click **February**.

13. You have
    a. opened the file.
    b. printed the file.

On the menu bar, click **Help**. Click **Help Topics**. Double-click **Working with Text**. Double-click **Deleting, Cutting, Copying and Pasting Text**.

14. The window that you just opened has a title bar. Its title bar name is
    a. Windows Help.
    b. Windows 95 Help.
    c. Notepad Help.

15. To delete characters to the left of the insertion point, you must press the
    a. Minus key.
    b. Backspace key.
    c. Delete key.

Close Help. Close the document. Close all open windows and return to the desktop.

Problem E

Note: If all the Windows 95 components are not installed, you will not be able to use animated help.

Click **Start**. Click **Help**. Click the **Contents** tab. Double-click **Introducing Windows**. Double-click **Getting Your Work Done**. Double-click **Seeing what's on your computer**. Click to see the demonstration.

16. In the animated demonstration, which drive is selected to open?
    a. Drive A.
    b. Drive B.
    c. Drive C.
    d. Drive D.

17. In the animated demonstration, which folder is selected?
    a. Printers.
    b. To Do.
    c. Help.
    d. Control Panel.

Close all open windows. Close Windows Help.

Problem Set II—Brief Essay

For all essay questions, use Notepad to create your answer. Then print your answer.

1. You want to learn more about viewing the printing status. In Help, use the Contents tab, the Index tab and the Find tab to locate this information.
   a. You will find a tip. What is the tip? Did you find it useful?
   b. Compare and contrast the three methods you used to locate help on this topic.
   c. Which method did you prefer and why?

2. What steps would you use to locate the Windows 95 components installed on your system? How could you find out which components are missing? How do you install the missing components? If you could not load all the components because of limited disk space, what components would you choose to install and why? Which would you choose to uninstall and why?

Problem Set III—Scenario

A friend of yours just purchased a computer with Windows 95 installed on it. She does not understand the use of the dialog boxes and the controls that are in the dialog boxes. Using Notepad, write her a letter explaining the concepts of controls. Remember, controls are items like command buttons, option buttons, text boxes, and so forth. Then, give her some suggestions in using Help so she may locate more information about dialog boxes. Print the letter.

Chapter 4

Viewing Files and Folders in My Computer

Chapter Overview

In this chapter, you are introduced to program files and data files. You will also learn about the hierarchical structure of disks. You will find that locating files and folders is an important part of using Windows 95, and My Computer is one tool you use. You will learn how to manipulate the way your files and folders appear, and you will learn to differentiate between the program and docucentric approach. You will find that the Documents menu gives you easy access to your data files. You will be introduced to the Registry that allows Windows 95 to know which program is to open with which data file. You will learn to register your own file extensions.

Learning Objectives

1. Compare and contrast the purpose and function of program files and data files.
2. List and explain the file naming rules.
3. Explain the purpose and function of folders.
4. Describe the purpose of the hierarchical structure of disks.
5. Explain the purpose and function of My Computer.
6. Describe the different views in My Computer.
7. Explain the purpose and function of the Documents menu.
8. Compare and contrast the program and docucentric methods of accomplishing tasks.
9. Explain the purpose and function of the Registry.

Student Outcomes

1. Manipulate the way you view files in the My Computer window.
2. Alter the way you browse files and folders.
3. Clear the Documents menu.
4. Use Notepad to open a file.
5. Use the Documents menu to open a file.
6. Register a file extension with the Registry.
7. Unregister a file extension.

4.1   Files and Folders

Nearly all the work you do on a computer has do to with files. When you are working with a file, it is stored in temporary memory. When you are not working with a file, it is permanently stored on a disk. There are two major types of computer files: program files and data files. *Program files* are application programs that allow the user to solve some type of problem, such as a payroll program that lets the user create and maintain a payroll system for a company. Program files are step-by-step instructions that direct the computer to "do" something—the task that the user needs to resolve. Program files are also called *application packages*, *software packages*, *software*, or just *apps*.

Generally, you purchase programs so you can create data files. *Data files* are the files that contain information generated by the user, typically with an application program. Most often, only an application program can use data files directly. Data files are also called *documents* or *document files*.

You do not purchase a computer to run Windows 95. You purchase a computer to write letters, manage your checkbook, prepare your taxes, or create a budget. Before computers, many individuals or small businesses would employ someone else to do these tasks. Often, the individual or business could not support a full-time employee for each job. Therefore, an employment agency would be used to hire temporary employees on an as-needed basis: a secretary to write letters, a bookkeeper to manage checkbooks, and an accountant to prepare taxes.

In the computer world you have even greater flexibility. Instead of contracting temporary employees, you purchase application packages, the program files that help you do your work. These application packages fall into generic categories, such as word processing or spreadsheet programs, similar to categories of employees, such as secretaries or accountants. You might have a favorite employee at the agency, and instead of requesting a secretary, would specifically request Mr. Woo; or, instead of requesting an accountant, you would specifically request Ms. Brown. You do the same in the computer world. Instead of purchasing just any word processing or spreadsheet program, you would ask for WordPerfect for Windows (the secretary) and Peachtree (the accountant). There are many choices in the application world. To do word processing, you could choose WordPerfect for Windows, Word, or Ami Pro. Your favorite money management program might be Managing Your Money instead of Quicken for Windows. These application packages are the "temporary" employees because you call on them specifically when you need to perform tasks that only they can accomplish. The ones that suit your needs are your favorites.

In order for these application programs to do work, they must be placed in RAM, the workspace of the computer. When they are not working, they are stored on a disk as files. Windows 95 is like the temporary employment agency office manager. You tell Windows 95 what work you want to do, and Windows 95 will go to the disk to get the correct program file and place it in RAM. Windows 95 then lets the program do its job by *executing the program*.

Data files are the second part of the equation. Even though the secretary—Word for Windows—can create letters for anyone, you are interested only in the letters you create. Once you create the data, you want to keep it. Remember, all the work is occurring in RAM, which is volatile (temporary). In order to retain the information permanently, you direct Word for Windows to write (save) the information to disk as a data file. Word for Windows does not actually save the data; it turns this task over to Windows 95, which writes the file to disk. When you need to retrieve the data file, Word for Windows again turns to Windows 95, which then reads the disk to get the appropriate data file and delivers it to Word. The job of program files is to create and edit the data within the data file. The job of Windows 95 is to read and write program and data files to and from disk and memory.

A name must be assigned to each file so that Windows 95 can identify and locate it. Certain rules must be followed when you name files. First, a file name must be unique. Second, the name length must range from 1 to 256 characters. Third, the file name is broken into two parts: a *file name* and a *file extension*. The file name describes or identifies the file, and the file extension identifies the type of data.

Program files have predetermined names: Winword.exe for Word for Windows, Qw.exe for Quicken 5 for Windows, and Excel.exe for Excel. Data files, on the other hand, are named by the user. You may call the file anything you want, such as Letter to my sister, as long as you follow the naming conventions. You will find that, typically, a program such as Word will assign a file extension to your data file (document), so that the actual file name becomes Letter to my sister.doc. Now you, Word, and Windows 95 know what program created the data file.

Data files are generated by specific application programs, and the information or data in them can be altered or viewed only within the respective application program. You do not give your tax information to the secretary to make changes. You would give the tax data to your accountant. Data files may be used only in conjunction with an application program. Again, the job of Windows 95 is to fetch and carry both program and data files in and out of memory and to and from the disk (reading and writing).

To assist you in organizing your files, disks are divided into what are called folders. Folder is the Windows 95 name for a directory. *Folders* are containers for objects, typically files. The objects in a folder may be opened into windows. Folders may have *subfolders*. Folders allow you to group related objects such as program or data files so they will be easy to locate at a later date.

A primary directory (root) is automatically created when you prepare a disk to store information. It is named the root, but its symbol is \ (backslash). Under the root, you create additional folders and subfolders for storing related files. For example, all the program files related to a spreadsheet program such as Excel could be stored in a directory named Excel. You might then group any data files you created with Excel, such as Budget for 1996 and Budget for 1995, in another folder named Budgets, so that when you wanted to locate Budget for 1995, it would be in the directory called Budgets. Office personnel have been using a similar organization process for years; related documents are filed in labeled file folders and then stored inside filing cabinets.

4.2   The Hierarchical Structure—Files and Folders

My Computer, an icon on the desktop, is one way to locate files and folders on a disk. When you double-click the My Computer icon, a window opens displaying the disk drives on your computer, such as Drive A, Drive C, and Drive D. In addition, the My Computer folder has two folders labeled Printers and Control Panel. Each disk drive icon in My Computer may be opened into another window which displays the files or folders on that drive. Folders may hold files and/or other folders, which may, in turn, hold other files and other folders. The two folders, Printers and Control Panel, are almost always found on Drive C.

If you double-clicked the Drive C icon, you would open a window showing all the folders and files on Drive C. One of the folders is called Windows. If you double-clicked the Windows folder, you would open another window showing the operating system files and folders. Each folder you open is dependent on the folder above it. This multiple level structure forms a hierarchy. A *hierarchy* is a group of things ordered by rank; you begin at the top and work your way down through each subsequent level. In the Windows 95 hierarchy, you always begin at the root directory (the top level directory) and work your way down through all the levels.

In Chapter 2, when you were seeking Notepad, you clicked Start, pointed at Programs, pointed at Accessories, and then clicked Notepad. These steps were leading you through the hierarchical structure. The Start menu is actually a folder under the Windows folder. Programs is a folder under the Start Menu folder. Accessories is a folder under the Programs folder. You finally reached the object of interest, the program file called Notepad.exe. In Chapter 3, when you accessed Help, it was a program file called Windows.hlp. It was kept in a folder called Help, which was under the folder called Windows, which was under the root of C. The root (\ ) is *always* the top of the hierarchy. Figure 4.1 illustrates the hierarchy.

Figure 4.1   The Hierarchical Structure

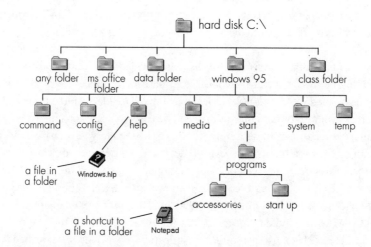

4.3   Viewing Files and Folders

You constantly use My Computer to locate disk drives, files, and folders. Windows 95 provides you with many ways to view them. When you first open My Computer, the default settings for viewing and browsing your files and folders are already selected, if you prefer not to set your own. The default settings for My Computer are the Status Bar on, the Toolbar off, and Large Icons arranged by Name. How you browse your folders is also preset. You can customize the view and browse settings. For instance, you can view the files as Large or Small Icons, as a List, or by file Details. You can choose to arrange your files by Name, Size, Date, or Type. You can arrange your icons. You can choose to browse the folders in different ways. In the next activity, you will learn to customize your settings.

4.4   Activity—Changing the Views

Note 1:   In order for the examples in this text to look and work the same, you must use the files and folders in the 95book directory. These practice files and folders are installed to the hard drive from the Activities disk that comes with this book.

Note 2:   **In a lab—**If you are in a lab environment, the 95book folder (directory) from the Activities disk probably has been been set up for you. You will need to find out on which drive the 95book folder has been installed. Check with your lab instructor for procedures in your lab environment.

Note 3:   **On your own computer—**If you are working on your own computer, you must first install the files from the Activities disk to the hard disk before proceeding. Instructions for installing 95book are located in Appendix A. You cannot copy the file from the disk to the hard disk; there is a special procedure you must follow.

1   Double-click **My Computer**. Click **View**. Click **Large Icons**. Click **View**.

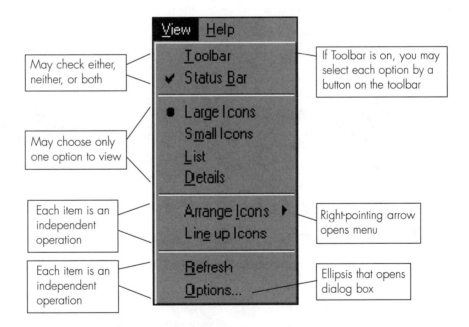

You have opened the View menu which is divided into sections. If there is a check mark, you may choose one option, both, or neither. If there is a dot, it is an option button and you may make only one choice in that section. Any item without a symbol is a command. You click it to activate it.

2 In the menu, click **Toolbar** to set it.

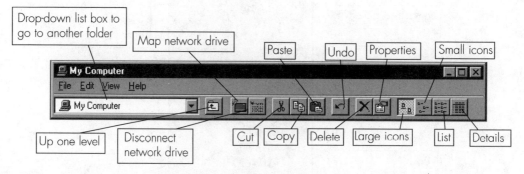 A toolbar appears. A *toolbar* contains shortcuts for entering menu commands. You make choices by clicking on a button in the toolbar rather than accessing the menu. In this example, the My Computer window is not large enough to let you see the entire toolbar.

3 Size the window so you can see the complete toolbar.

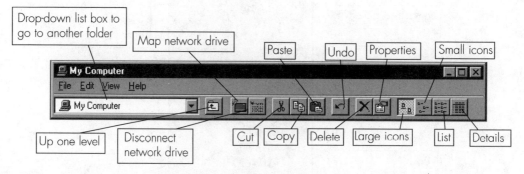 The toolbar makes it easy to customize the view.

4 Hold the pointer over the **Up One Level** toolbar button.

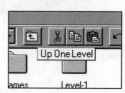

Whenever you need a description of a toolbar button, you may hold the pointer over the button and a ToolTip will appear for a few seconds.

5 Double-click the **Drive C** icon.

What's happening? → You have opened the Drive C window and are looking at the root directory, (C:\). You see the files and folders contained in the root directory. However, the toolbar is not visible. Windows 95 remembers the settings the way you last left the window.

6 Click **View**. Click **Toolbar**.

7 Double-click the **95book** folder.

8 Click **View**. Click **Toolbar**.

What's happening? → You have opened the 95book folder and can see its files and folders. Again, the toolbar may not be totally visible.

9 If you cannot see the complete toolbar, size the window so that you can. Click the **Small Icons** toolbar button.

What's happening? → You have changed your view of files and folders in the 95book folder window to small icons, in vertical columns, in alphabetical order from left to right.

10 Click the **List** toolbar button.

What's happening? → You have changed the view to a list which now appears in columns alphabetized from top to bottom.

11 Click the **Details** toolbar button.

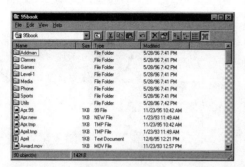

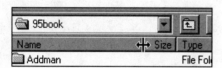

What's happening? → You now see the file details of the contents of the 95book folder under the root of C. The details view is displayed in a list with column headings. Name, Size, Type, and Modified are the details given for each file and folder. You can also adjust the width of columns.

12 Place the pointer between **Name** and **Size** on the column headings bar.

What's happening? → The cursor changed to a double-headed arrow.

13 Hold the left mouse button and drag the cursor to the right.

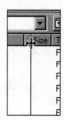

What's happening? → As you began to drag, a line appeared, indicating your adjustment to the column width.

14 Release the mouse button.

15 Place the pointer between **Type** and **Modified** on the column headings bar. When the cursor becomes a double-headed arrow, double-click.

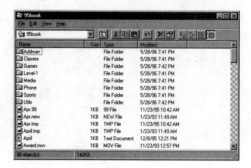

What's happening? → You have used two ways to adjust the column width.

16 Click the **Large Icons** toolbar button.

What's happening? → Your view now shows the icons in a large format, but the icons are bunched together. If Auto Arrange in the View/ Arrange Icons were set, the icons would automatically adjust to fit the window.

17 Click **View**. Point to **Arrange Icons**. Click **by Name**.

What's happening? → Now your icons are properly spaced.

18 Double-click the **Media** folder.

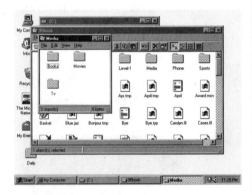

What's happening? → You are moving down the Drive C hierarchy. Media is under the 95book folder. The 95book folder is under the root of C. Media also has folders.

19 Double-click **Books**.

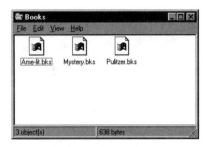

What's happening? → Books is a folder under Media, which is under 95book, which is under the root of C. The Books folder has only files, no folders.

20 In the Books window, click **View**. Click **Toolbar**. Size the window so that the toolbar is visible. Click the **Up One Level** toolbar button.

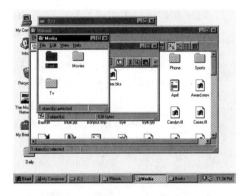

What's happening? → You made the Media window active. However, the Books window is still open. In fact, all the windows you opened are still open: My Computer, Drive A, Media, and Books. If you look at the taskbar, you will see a button for each open window.

21 Press the [**Backspace**] key.

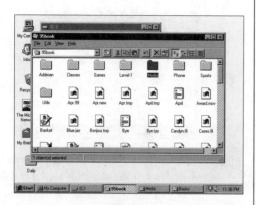

What's
happening? → Pressing the [**Backspace**] key is a key-board shortcut that takes you to the parent of a folder. The 95book folder is the parent of the Media folder. You have not closed a window; you have just made a different window active. Each time you double-click, you open a new folder window without closing the previous one. As you can see, the desktop becomes very cluttered with open windows.

22 Click in an empty spot in the **95book** window to deselect the **Media** folder. Hold the [**Ctrl**] key and double-click **Sports**.

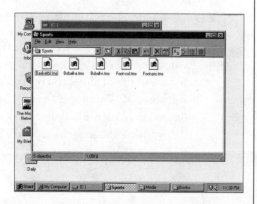

What's
happening? → Holding the [**Ctrl**] key when you click a folder is a keyboard shortcut to open a new window and close the previous window. If you look at the taskbar, you will not see a button for the 95book window.

Besides the visual clutter of many open windows, open windows require memory. Rather than remembering to hold the [**Ctrl**] key when you double-click a folder, you can change the default way that windows open in My Computer. There are two choices. Browse folders using a separate window for each folder is what you have been doing. The other choice is Browse folders by using a single window that changes as you open each folder, which will close one window before opening another.

23 Close all the open windows. Double-click **My Computer**. Click **View**. Click **Options**.

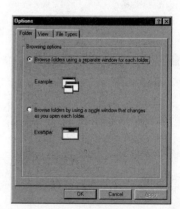

What's
happening? → You have opened the Options dialog box. Currently, Browse folders using a separate window for each folder is set. Its illustration

shows you that many windows will be opened.

24 Click the option button for **Browse folders by using a single window**.

 Choosing this option,

means that the previous window will close before another window opens.

25 Click **OK**.

26 Double-click the **Drive C** icon. Double-click the **95book** folder. Double-click the **Media** folder. Double-click the **Books** folder.

What's happening? As you opened a new window, the previous window closed, keeping your open windows to a minimum. Again, note the taskbar. Only one button appears.

27 Close the open window.

28 Double-click **My Computer**. Click **View**. Click **Options**. Click the **View** tab.

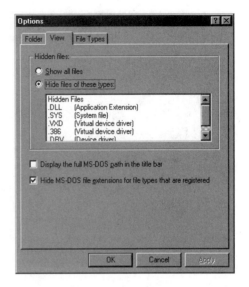

What's happening? You are looking at the View options. There are two option buttons: Show all files and Hide files of these types:. Hide files of these types: is set and is the default because you do not need to see these system files. In the two check boxes, Display the full MS-DOS path in the title bar is not set, but the Hide MS-DOS file extensions for file types that are registered is. These options are opposite to what most users want. You often need to see the entire file name, including its file extension (*file type*). The MS-DOS path name, when set, will display the structure of the disk so that you know where you are in the hierarchy. The *path name* is the statement that indicates precisely where a file is located on a disk.

29 Click to set **Display the full MS-DOS path in the title bar**.

30 Click to unset **Hide MS-DOS file extensions for file types that are registered**.

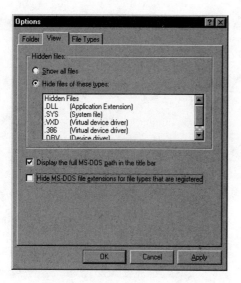

31 Click **OK**.

32 Double-click the **Drive C** icon. Double-click **95book**.

33 Scroll until you can see the **Dances** file.

What's happening? → In previous displays of this file, you saw only the file name Dances. Since you changed the View options, you will see the complete file name, Dances.txt.

34 Scroll up until you see the Media folder. Double-click **Media**. Double-click **Books**. Look at the title bar of the window.

What's happening? → You now see the hierarchical structure (path). Previously, the entry in the title bar was only Books. Setting the path name option for on allows you to see the structure.

35 Close all open windows.

What's happening? → You have returned to the desktop. The changes you made in Options will remain set. This text will assume these settings from now on. However, if you are on a network, your network may return the values to their defaults when you log off. You will need to alter them to the above settings each time you log on to your network.

4.5   The Documents Menu

Since Windows 95 is docucentric, one of the choices on the Start menu is the Documents menu. The Documents menu will display the last documents you worked on. This approach fits into the docucentric model for Windows 95. Prior to this model, the only way to view data was the program approach: open the program files and then search for the particular data files within. It worked the same way for every program and data file.

Using the older method, if you wanted to view the contents of a document called April.txt created in Notepad, you would have to take the following steps: click Start, point to Programs, then point to Accessories, and click Notepad. Then, in Notepad, you would have to click File, click Open, and locate April.txt. In the docucentric approach, you click Start, point at Documents, and click April.txt. Notepad will open automatically, displaying April.txt.

You may change the characteristics of the taskbar using the Taskbar Options property sheet. You can hide the taskbar, change the size of the icons in the Start menu, or control the clock display. The Taskbar Options property sheet contains all the options used to manipulate the Start and Documents menus.

4.6   Activity—Using the Documents Menu

1 Right-click the taskbar in an empty spot. Click **Properties**. Click the **Start Menu Programs** tab.

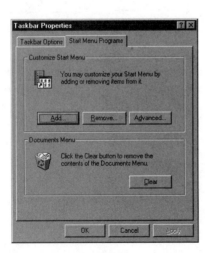

> **What's happening?** You have opened the property sheet that allows you to customize what appears on the Start menu. You can also clear the Documents menu. If the Clear button is dimmed, there are no documents in the Documents menu.

2 Click **Clear**.

> **What's happening?** The Clear button is dimmed, indicating that you have cleared the Documents menu.

3 Click **OK**.

4 Click **Start**. Point at **Documents**.

> **What's happening?** Since you clicked Clear, no documents are available. You see that the option Empty is dimmed.

5 Point at **Programs**. Point at **Accessories**. Click **Notepad**.

6 Click **File** on the **Notepad** menu bar. Click **Open**.

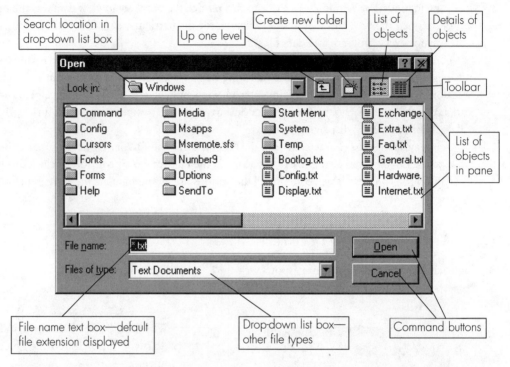

You have opened the File Open dialog box. This dialog box has a toolbar with a panel of controls. These controls provide quick access to options or commands. The drop-down list box indicates which folder you are looking in; here, it is the Windows folder. The dialog box also has icons that will perform an action when you click them. Since this dialog box contains a Question Mark icon, you may click the question mark and drag it to an item, click the item, and display its definition.

7 Click the **Question Mark** icon. Drag it to the **Up One Level** button. Click it.

What's happening? A pop-up definition tells you that if you clicked this icon, you could move up one level to the parent of the Windows folder, which is the root of Drive C. You are not going to do this.

8 Click the **Details** button on the toolbar.

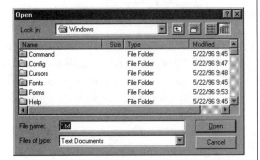

What's happening? The Details button displays information about the objects in the pane, including what the object is, its size, and the time and date it was last modified.

9 Click the **List** button on the toolbar. Click the down arrow in the **Look in** drop-down list box.

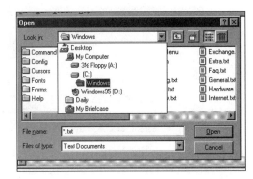

What's happening? You see the choices you can use to locate a file. Your display may be different. In this example, Windows is a folder under Drive C. You can choose to "look in" any disk drive or folder listed.

10 Click the **Drive C** icon in the drop-down list box.

What's happening? You see the files and folders on Drive C.

11   Double-click the **95book** folder. Click the **Details** button on the toolbar.

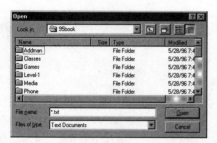

> **What's happening?** You see the details of the objects in the pane which are the files and folders in the 95book folder on Drive C.

12   Click the **List** button.

> **What's happening?** You see a list of the files and folders in 95book. All folders in 95book are listed, but only files with the .txt file extension are displayed. If you look at the File Name text box, you see .txt. If you look at the Files of Type drop-down list box, you see that Text Documents is the default. Notepad will automatically assign the extension of .txt to any document created, unless you state otherwise. Every time you install a program in Windows 95, the program file tells the Windows 95 Registry what file extensions the application program is claiming. The program "registers" the file extension, much like a person checking into a hotel. When you register at a hotel, you are "claiming" a room. The hotel knows which guest is in which room by looking at the register. The hotel also knows that it cannot rent rooms that are already occupied. In the same way, Windows 95 registers file extensions. The Notepad program has claimed the file extension .txt, and any time Windows 95 sees this extension, it recognizes the file as a Notepad file.

13   Click the down arrow in the **Files of type** drop-down list box.

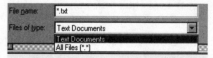

> **What's happening?** Your only other available choice is All Files (*.*). The *.*, called star, dot, star, indicates any file name with any file extension. The asterisk is a wildcard. Much like a card game where the joker may represent any card, the first asterisk may represent any file name; the last asterisk represents any file extension. The file name is separated from the file extension with a period (dot).

14   Click **All Files (*.*)**.

> **What's happening?** Your display now includes every file and folder in the 95book folder on Drive C.

15 Double-click **Apr.99**.

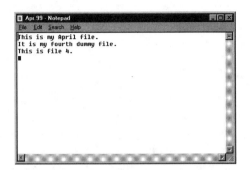

<u>What's happening?</u> → You are looking at the contents (the data) of the Apr.99 file.

16 Click **File**. Click **Open**.

<u>What's happening?</u> → You have again opened the File Open dialog box. It remembers the last settings you used (Drive C, 95book folder, all the files in a list format). The dialog box shows you every file and folder in 95book.

17 Double-click **April.txt**. If you cannot see it, scroll until you can.

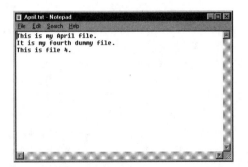

<u>What's happening?</u> → When you opened the document April.txt, you closed the document April.99. Since Notepad is a text editor, it can only open one document at a time. This procedure is the *program approach* to opening files, which means you must locate and execute the program file

before you locate and open the data file. There are many steps in the program approach. Windows 95 offers an easier way to access the last documents (data files) you worked on.

18 Close Notepad. Click **Start**. Point at **Documents**.

<u>What's happening?</u> → The file you last looked at, April.txt, is shown in the Documents menu.

19 Click **April.txt**.

<u>What's happening?</u> → You accessed your data file quickly. By using the Documents menu, you were able to open Notepad with the April.txt data file in one step. You did not need to take all of the steps required in the program approach.

20   Close Notepad.

 You have returned to the desktop. One thing to note is that when you opened the Documents menu, April.txt was listed but Apr.99 was not. In the next section you will learn how to register Apr.99.

4.7 Registering File Types With the Registry

The Registry is the mechanism that stores user information, application program information, and information about the specific computer you are using. The Registry centralizes and tracks all this information, including the data file extensions that an application program assigns, the icons that represent program or data files, and other file-oriented information. A special Windows program called the Registration Editor allows users to make changes directly to the files User.dat, System.dat, and Policy.pol. However, it is *very dangerous* to edit these files directly. Fortunately, you may register file extensions easily and without ever having to touch these important system files directly.

In order for a document to appear on the Documents menu, the file extension must be registered to an application program in the Registry. The *Registry* is a database program that keeps track of what data files belong to what application programs, based on the file extension (file type). When you install a program written for the Windows 95 interface, the program will register the extension it uses for its data files with the Registry.

4.8   Activity—Registering File Types

Note: Remember, you changed the settings in My Computer—the View options are set for Toolbar on, Large Icons arranged by Name. The Browse option is set to close the window before opening the next.

1   Double-click **My Computer**. Double-click the **Drive C** icon. Double-click the **95book** folder.

2   Double-click **Apr.99**.

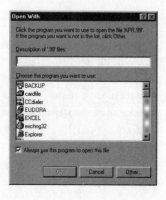

 The file called Apr.99 does not have a registered file extension. Windows 95 does not know what application program to open for a file with the extension of .99 and a dialog box appears, listing all of the programs installed on your computer system. The dialog box states that you are about to register the Apr.99 files, but you are only registering the file extension. The dialog box has an empty text box called Description of '.99' files: where you can add descriptive information when registering a file type (extension). Thus, you can create file extensions that mean specific things to you and clearly reflect your work.

3 In the **Description** text box, key in the following:

These are files for my Windows 95 class.

What's happening? Whenever you see a file with a .99 extension, you will have a generalized description of this type of file.

4 Scroll through the list box until you locate **Notepad**. Click **Notepad**.

What's happening? Notepad is the program that you wish to use with the .99 files. There is a check box in this dialog box labeled Always use this program to open this file. When this setting is checked, the specified program is *always* used to open any files with the selected extension. If you select OK when this box is checked, you will register the file. In this case, whenever Windows 95 sees a .99 file extension, it will open Notepad. If there were no check mark, you would open this file with Notepad this time only. No check mark means no entry in the Registry.

5 Be sure **Always use this program to open this file** check box has a check mark. Click **OK**.

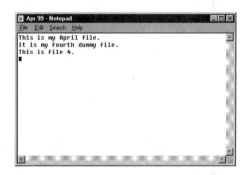

What's happening? Notepad opened, with Apr.99 as the data file.

6 Close Notepad.

 What's happening? In the C:\95BOOK window, the Apr.99 file now has the easily recognizable Notepad document icon. Figure 4.2 shows common document icons.

Figure 4.2 Common Document Icons

Apr.tmp

A generic document icon. Windows 95 does not know what program to use to open this file. If you double-click this icon, Windows 95 will present you with the Open With dialog box.

Apr.99

A user-registered document icon. Windows 95 knows that Notepad is the program to use to open any file with a .99 extension. When you double-click this icon, Windows 95 will open Notepad and display the Apr.99 document.

Bye.txt

A program registered document icon. Windows 95 knows that Notepad is the program to use to open any file with a .txt extension. When you create a file in Notepad, Notepad automatically assigns the .txt file extension. When you double-click this icon, Windows 95 will open Notepad and display the Bye.txt document.

7 Scroll until you see **Feb.99**.

What's happening? Since you registered the .99 file extension with Notepad in Windows 95, all files with a .99 file extension are registered. You may double-click any of them, and Notepad will open along with a .99 data file.

8 Double-click **Feb.99**.

What's happening? Since this is a registered file, Notepad opened it.

9 Close Notepad. Scroll until you can see the **Apr.99** icon.

10 Right-click **Apr.99**.

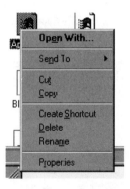

You have opened a shortcut menu that will help you manipulate the Apr.99 object. Each item on the menu describes an action you can take with the Apr.99 file; you can Open it, Copy it, or Delete it.

11 Click outside the menu to close it. Right-click **April.new**.

Since April.new is not a registered file, Windows 95 does not know what program to use to open the file, so instead of Open, your menu choice is Open With.

12 Click outside the menu to close it. Click **Apr.99**. Hold the **Shift** key and right-click **Apr.99**.

When a file is registered, it will *always* open the program that it is registered to. Sometimes you may have different programs that use the same file extension for their data files. To prevent confusion, Windows 95 permits only one registered extension per program. If a file extension is already registered to one program, it cannot be registered to another. For example, Word and WordPad which both assign the file extension, .doc, to their data files; however, .doc is registered only to Word. Any file with a .doc extension would automatically open Word, and only by holding the **Shift** key could you choose the Open With menu choice and select WordPad to open the file.

13 Click **Properties**.

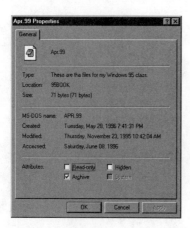

15 Click the **Start** button. Point at **Documents**.

What's happening? → You opened the property sheet for Apr.99. Not only does the property sheet tell you the name of this file and when it was created, but also why it was created. The only indication that Notepad created this file is its document icon. If you wanted to be more descriptive in your file type, you could have written your description as Notepad files for my Windows 95 class. Then you would know which application program created these files.

14 Click **Cancel**.

What's happening? → Now that you have registered the file extension, every registered file that you used is listed on the Documents menu. If you want, you can open any file on this list.

16 Click outside the **Start** menu. In the **95book** window on the menu bar, click **View**. Click **Options**. Click the **File Types** tab.

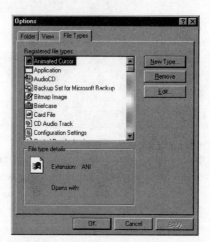

What's happening? → You may add or remove file types at any time by selecting the property sheet under Options from the View menu.

17 The list is alphabetically arranged. Scroll in the list window until you locate **These are my files for my Windows 95 class**. Click that line to select it.

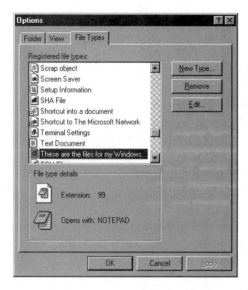

18 Click the **Remove** command button.

What's happening? You see an information message box warning you that once you remove a registered file type, you will no longer be able to double-click to open it easily. You may still open it, but you will have to use the program approach with its many steps.

19 Click **Yes**. Click **Close**.

What's happening? When you selected from the Registered File Types list box, the information in File type details at the bottom of the dialog box told you what the file extension is (.99) and the application program that opens it (Notepad). This is one way to identify which extensions are assigned to which programs.

What's happening? Apr.99 is no longer registered nor are any other .99 files. You can still open Apr.99 and any other .99 file to edit or print them. To open a .99 file, however, you will first need to open the application program, Notepad. Then you will use the File/Open command.

20 Hold the [Shift] key and click the **Close** button for the **95book** window.

What's
happening? ──▶ You have returned to the desktop.

Chapter Summary

In this chapter, you learned the difference between program files and data files. You learned that there is a hierarchical structure to a disk, and that every disk is structured around a root directory containing folders and files. You found that a file must have a unique file name of up to 256 characters plus a file extension.

You used the View menu in My Computer to alter how the files and folders are displayed. You found that you can place a toolbar on a window and use it to execute menu commands. You found that Windows 95 remembers the last way you left a window. You changed the view options, such as large icons, small icons, list, and details. Furthermore, you found that you can manipulate the way you browse folders, either continually opening windows or closing a window before opening the next window. You learned how to display the file extensions and the path in the title bar of the window.

You also found that the docu-centric approach of the Documents menu is an easy way to open a data file and the program it is registered to. However, a file must be registered before it will appear on the Documents menu. Files extensions are registered with the Registry when you install a program. The Registry is the database that Windows 95 uses to keep track of what file extensions belong to which files. You may also register file extensions manually.

Key Terms

Application packages	File extension	Program files
Apps	File name	Registry
Data files	File type	Software
Docucentric	Folders	Software packages
Document files	Hierarchy	Subfolders
Documents	Path name	Toolbar
Executing the program	Program approach	

Discussion Questions

1. What is the purpose and function of a program file?
2. What is the purpose and function of a data file?
3. What does it mean to "execute a program?"
4. Since all work done in RAM is volatile, what must be done to retain created data permanently?
5. What is the purpose and function of folders?
6. What is the hierarchical structure of a disk?
7. List and explain file naming rules.
8. Explain the difference between a file name and a file extension.
9. Who names data files? Program files? Why?
10. Why can data files only be used in conjunction with an application program?

11. How and why would you use the My Computer window?
12. What options can you change in the My Computer window?
13. Identify two changes you would make in the My Computer window and why.
14. Compare and contrast the toolbar and the menu in the My Computer window.
15. How can you quickly go to a parent of a folder?
16. What is the purpose and function of the Documents menu?
17. Explain the steps to open a file after you have opened Notepad.
18. Compare and contrast opening a file using the program approach versus using the docucentric approach.
19. Explain the purpose and function of the Registry.
20. How does the file extension play a key role in the Registry?

True/False Questions

For each question, circle the letter T if the statement is true or the letter F if the statement is false.

T   F   1. Application programs have user-selected names.
T   F   2. Data files are created by application programs.
T   F   3. The extension of a data file indicates what type of data is in the file.
T   F   4. The root directory is always the first directory on any disk.
T   F   5. If you double-click a registered document icon, Windows 95 will ask you which program you wish to open.

Completion Questions

Write the correct answer in each blank space.

6. The step-by-step instructions that direct the computer to perform the task that you require are called a _____ file.
7. A file name consists of two parts, the file _____ and the file _____.
8. One way to locate files and folders on a disk is to open the _____ window.
9. You may place a number of files in a subdirectory. Windows 95 calls this a _____.
10. The Start button's Documents menu can be emptied by choosing _____ from the Taskbar Properties sheet.

Multiple Choice Questions

Circle the letter of the correct answer for each question.

11. Folders are containers of objects. An object can be a
    a. a document or a program file.
    b. device or folder.
    c. both a and b
    d. neither a nor b

12. When you open Notepad, and click File, then Open, if the File Name text box has *.txt in it, then
    a. all files and folders will be listed.
    b. only files with a .txt extension will be listed.
    c. only folders will be listed.
    d. only files beginning with an asterisk (*) will be listed.

13. Directly using the Registration Editor to edit Windows 95 system files
    a. is the recommended method for changing file types.
    b. could cause extreme, even fatal, damage to Windows 95.
    c. is completely safe for any user.
    d. both a and c

14. You see the following icon in the My Computer window: . You know that this file
    Llreadme.txt
    a. was created with Notepad.
    b. cannot be opened.
    c. cannot be opened by double-clicking.
    d. is a program file.

15. On the My Computer toolbar, you see . Your view in the My Computer window is
    a. large icons.
    b. small icons.
    c. list.
    d. details.

Application Assignments

Problem Set I—At the Computer

Problem A

Click **Start**. Point at **Programs**. Point at **Accessories**. Many Accessories are listed.

1. One of the items listed is
   a. Paint.
   b. Paintshop.
   c. Painters.

2. The above item is a
   a. folder.
   b. program.

Open Notepad.

3. What item does *not* appear on the Notepad menu bar?
   a. File.   b. Edit.   c. Bookmark.   d. Search.   e. Help.

Key in your name and address. Close Notepad.

4. You are presented with a message box. It states
   a. Do you want to save the changes?
   b. Do you want to exit Notepad?
   c. Do you want to print your text?

Click **No**.

Problem B

Open My Computer. Open the Drive C window. Open the 95book folder. Maximize the window. Click **Small Icons**. Click **View**. Click **Arrange Icons**. Click **by Name**.

5. The folders and files are arranged in alphabetical order
   a. down the window.
   b. across the window.
   c. and show the file details.
   d. both a and c
   e. both b and c

Click **Details**.

6. The folders and files are now arranged in alphabetical order
   a. down the window.
   b. across the window.
   c. and are showing the file details.
   d. both a and c
   e. both b and c

Click **List**.

7. The folders and files are now arranged in alphabetical order
   a. down the window.
   b. across the window.
   c. and are showing the file details.
   d. both a and c
   e. both b and c

Restore the window. Click **Large Icons**. Click **View**. Point to **Arrange Icons**. Click **by Name**. Click **View**. Click **Options**. Be sure the View tab has Display... on and Hide MS-DOS... off. Double-click the **Addman** folder. Double-click the **Samples** folder.

8. The title bar of Samples states
   a. Samples.
   b. C:\Samples.
   c. C:\Addman\Samples.
   d. C:\95book\Addman\Samples.

9. Strings.usa is an example of a/an
   a. user registered document icon.
   b. generic document icon.
   c. program registered document icon.
   d. executable program.

Press the **Backspace** key twice.

10. You moved to the _____ window.
    a. C:\
    b. C:\95book
    c. C:\95book\Addman
    d. C:\95book\Addman\Sample
    e. My Computer

Scroll until you locate the **Chap01.wri** file.

11. The Chap01.wri file is an example of a data file that Windows 95 will
    a. be able to associate with an application program.
    b. not be able to associate with an application program.

Close all open windows.

Problem C

Clear the Documents menu. Open My Computer. Open the Drive C window. Open the 95book folder. Click **View**. Click **Large Icons**. Click **View**. Point at **Arrange Icons**. Click **by Name**. Locate the file called January.txt. Double-click it.

12. The following occurred:
    a. Notepad opened the file. Data appears in the window.
    b. Notepad opened with an empty screen. There is no data in the window.
    c. You were presented with the Open With dialog box.
    d. You were presented with an error message stating that Windows cannot open the requested file.

Close Notepad. Double-click the **Media** folder. Double-click the **Books** folder. Double-click **Mystery.bks**.

13. The following occurred:
    a. Notepad opened the file. Data appears in the window.
    b. Notepad opened with an empty screen. There is no data in the window.
    c. You were presented with the Open With dialog box.
    d. You were presented with an error message stating thatWindows cannot open the requested file.

Close all open windows and return to the desktop. Click **Start**. Point at **Documents**.

14. What file(s) appear on the Documents menu?
    a. January.txt
    b. Mystery.bks
    c. both January.txt and Mystery.bks
    d. No files appear on the Documents menu. It states (EMPTY).

Close the menu.

Problem Set II—Brief Essay

For all essay questions, use Notepad to create your answer. Then print your answer.

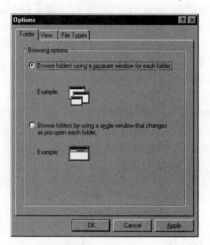 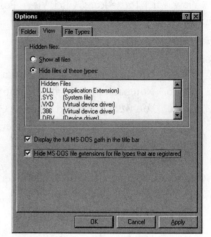

1. In the Options menu, the above views are set. Describe what would be displayed in any window you opened. Describe what would happen as you opened new windows. Would these be your choices? Why or why not? If they would not be your choices, describe your choices and explain what influenced your decision.
2. Compare and contrast the commands Open and Open With that appear on the shortcut menu when you right-click a document icon.

Problem Set III—Scenario

You have been asked to write an article for a Senior Citizens newsletter about aspects of My Computer in Windows 95. You have been using several view options, such as large icons, small icons, list, and details. You decide that you will differentiate among them and explain when each option might be useful. In addition, you want to discuss and describe the various types of icons that appear in the My Computer window. Create and print the article.

Chapter 5

Finding and Using
Files and Folders

Chapter Overview

In this chapter, you will learn that files and folders must follow specific naming rules. You will also see that there are strategies in naming files and folders so that you may locate them easily. You will learn that all files have properties that may be viewed using the property sheet. You will learn about the Find command, located on the Start menu, which will assist you in locating files and folders. You will discover that the Find dialog box allows you to locate files and folders by name, modification date, or a key word or phrase in the document.

You will discover that you can create shortcuts—pointers to objects—to files, folders, and devices. You will find that you can create a folder to keep your files and shortcuts in. You will also discover the convenience of dragging and dropping objects to the Recycle Bin to be eliminated.

Learning Objectives

1. Explain the function of file specifications.
2. Compare and contrast DOS and Windows 95 file naming rules.
3. Describe one file naming strategy.
4. Discuss the properties of a file.
5. Compare and contrast files and folders.
6. Explain the purpose and function of Find.
7. Describe the available features in the Find dialog box.
8. Explain the purpose and function of shortcuts.
9. Describe the steps to create a folder.
10. Explain the purpose and function of the Recycle Bin.

Student Outcomes

1. Name four rules for naming files in Windows 95.
2. View and manipulate the properties of a document.
3. Use Find to locate a file by name.
4. Use wildcards with the Find command.
5. Locate files with Find by file modification date.
6. Locate files with Find by key word.
7. Create shortcuts to devices, files, and folders.
8. Create a folder.
9. Use the Recycle Bin.

5.1   File and Folder Names

If everything to do with computers has to do with files and folders, it is a self-evident truth that all files and folders must be named. All operating systems have rules for how files and folders may be named. File and folder names follow the same rules. Actually, a folder is just a special type of file.

Prior to Windows 95, the rules fell under what is called the *FAT* (file allocation table) *file system*, or more commonly, the DOS 8.3 rule. Under the FAT file system, a file name is technically a *file specification*. The file specification is comprised of two parts, the file name and the file extension. When most people refer to the file name, they are referring to the entire name (file specification). The DOS rules are:

❑   The name of a file in a folder must be unique.
❑   No file name can be longer than eight characters.
❑   File extensions are optional, but an extension cannot be longer than three characters.
❑   A file name must be separated from its extension with a period, called a dot. The dot is an example of a delimiter. A *delimiter* is a punctuation mark that marks the end of one thing and the beginning of another. Delimiters are very specific; the dot (period) can only be placed between the file name and its extension. There are no spaces between the file name and its extension. If a file is called Myfile.txt, it cannot be keyed in as My file . txt.
❑   File names are not case-sensitive. MYFILE.TXT and myfile.txt signify the same file name.
❑   All alphanumeric characters can be used in the file specification *except* the following illegal characters:

   <Space>   . " / \ : ; [ ] | < > + = , * ?

❑   The maximum total length of a path and file name is limited to 80 characters.

Windows 95 introduced a major new feature provided by the *VFAT* (virtual file allocation table) *file system*. It is an extension of and compatible with the older FAT system, designed to maintain backward compatibility with DOS and Windows 3.1 programs still being used.

This new feature is the ability to handle long file names. *Long file names*, also referred to as *LFNs*, allow files (and folders) to have names up to 255 characters. In this scheme, every file has two names, the new long file name and the short file name that complies with the 8.3 rule. Nearly identical to the DOS rules, the Windows 95 rules are:

❑   The name of a file in a folder must be unique.
❑   No file name can be longer than 255 characters.
❑   File extensions are optional, but practically speaking, most files include a file extension (file type). As you saw, file types are heavily used by the Registry.
❑   Typically, a file name is separated from its extension with a period, called a dot. In the VFAT system, you may use the space and more than one dot. Thus, a file legally could be named MY FILE NAME.SECOND.TXT.

❑ File names are not case-sensitive. MYFILE.TXT and myfile.txt signify the same file name. However, Windows 95 will remember and display the file or folder names with the case you originally used.

❑ All alphanumeric characters, including spaces, can be used in the file specification *except* the following illegal characters:

   \ / : * ? " < > |

❑ The maximum total length of a path and file name is limited to 260 characters.

❑ The double quote (") is not a valid character but can be used to designate long file names.

❑ If you use long file names, the short file name is automatically created for you. To create this short file name, VFAT takes the first six characters of the long file name (ignoring spaces), adds ~1 (or a larger number), and then sets the file extension as the first three letters after the last period in the long file name. Thus, if you had two files, one called My file text document and a second called My file for handling taxes.document, Windows 95 would assign Myfile~1.doc to the first file and Myfile~2.doc to the second.

5.2   File Naming Strategies

Certain files must be named by the user. You do not name program files; these have predetermined names, such as Winword.exe for Word for Windows, Qw.exe for Quicken 5 for Windows, or Excel.exe for Excel. On the other hand, you do name data files.

If you are using application programs that were not designed to work with Windows 95, those application programs still follow the DOS file naming rules (the 8.3 rule). If you attempt to give a file a long name within an older application, the application will present an error message telling you that the file name is too long.

Even if you do have the new applications written for Windows 95 that support long file names, you have to think about what you are going to name your files. You are going to want to retrieve your files, and you should have a logical naming scheme to facilitate your search for them. If you name them randomly, locating them will become a problem. As the number of files increases, the likelihood of remembering all the names you have assigned becomes next to impossible.

For instance, if you are corresponding with Mr. Bob Wong, you could name one file Letter to Bob and another file Response to Mr. Wong's letter. These would both be valid file names, but when you wanted to locate all the correspondence with Mr. Wong, how would you find these files? Although the Start menu provides a Find command to locate files (that you will learn to use later in this chapter), you would have to look for each file individually. Locating similar files would be easier if you gave all the file names some element in common, such as the same file name prefixes in Wong.letter and Wong.response. When you wanted to find all the correspondence relating to Bob Wong, you would know they have an item in common.

Today, most application packages will assign a predetermined file extension to your data file unless you tell it otherwise. For example, Word for Windows assigns .doc. In the above example, if the data files were created with Word for Windows 95, the file names would actually be Wong.letter.doc and Wong.response.doc because Word would add the file extension .doc. Although the .doc extension is a common element, you would still have a problem locating files by .doc because every file you create with Word would have the .doc extension. You want a more distinctive way to locate files on a similar subject.

Whether or not a data file has an extension depends on the rules of the application program. Word, as mentioned, assigns .doc, PowerPoint assigns .ppt, and Excel assigns .xls by default. An application program may have more than one file extension registered. For instance, Access uses both .mdb and .ldb.

In Windows 95, a file name typically tells you about the file and the extension tells you about the data. For instance, if you had a data file called Sister letter.doc, the Sister letter would tell you that you wrote a letter to your sister and the .doc would tell you (and Windows 95) that the file was created with Word for Windows. In Windows 95, file extensions are referred to as file types. Programs can be identified because the file type .exe is reserved for programs, and Windows 95 recognizes it as a program file. The extension .exe stands for executable code. There are other "reserved" file types for programs, such as .dll for dynamic link libraries, or .sys for system files.

5.3   Activity—File Properties

Note :   The listed settings are assumed for each chapter. If you are working on your own computer, the changes you made in the default settings should be retained from one work session to the next. However, if you are working in a computer lab, you may have to change your settings each time you log into the network. The settings are as follows:

My Computer
❑   Toolbar and status bar on (in the View menu).
❑   Large icons arranged by name (in the View menu).
❑   Browse folders by using a single window that changes as you open each folder (View/Options/ Browse tab).
❑   Hide files of these types is set (View/Options/View tab).
❑   Display the full MS-DOS path in the title bar is set (View/Options/View tab).
❑ ˙   Hide MS-DOS file extensions for file types that are registered is not set (View/Options/View tab).

1   Double-click **My Computer**.

2   Double-click the **Drive C** icon. Double-click the **95book** folder.

3 Scroll until you see **Glossary.wri**.

What's happening? The document icon shown represents Write, the program that created this document. Since Hide MS-DOS file extensions for file types that are registered is not set, you can see the entire file name, Glossary.wri. You can always see the document's entire name if you look at its properties.

4 Right-click the icon for the document called **Glossary.wri**.

What's happening? You have opened the pop-up menu for this object. In this case, the object is a document. This menu lets you manipulate the document without changing the data it contains. From this menu you can initiate such object-oriented tasks as opening, deleting, copying, or printing the document (object).

All objects have properties, such as settings and parameters. Each object has a property sheet which displays a collection of information about the object. You can tell what the object is by looking at its properties.

5 Click **Properties**.

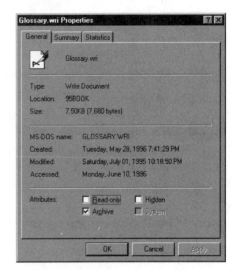

What's happening? By looking at the properties, you know the document's name is Glossary.wri. The Type statement tells you that Glossary.wri was created with the Write program and the Location of the file is in the 95book folder. You know the document's Size and its MS-DOS name. You also know when the document was created, modified, or accessed. Furthermore, check boxes indicate the file attributes. A file can have one of four attributes: it may be a Read-only file (which cannot be modified or deleted); an Archive file (which has changed since you last backed it up); a Hidden file (which doesn't display the file name); or a System file (which is a special file used by the operating system). System is unavailable for setting, but the others may be checked. Here, only Archive is set. This means that Glossary.wri has changed since the last time you backed up.

6   Click the **Cancel** command button to close the property sheet.

7   Right-click **Glossary.wri**. Click **Open**.

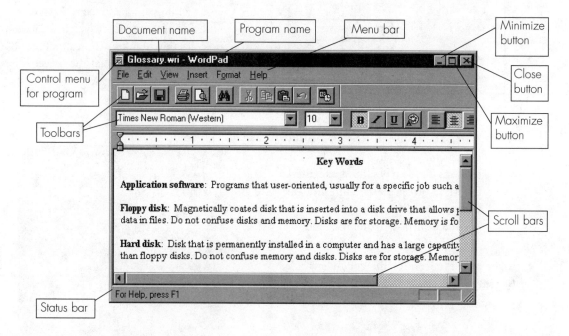

In order to see the data in the document, Glossary.wri, you had to open the application program. In this case, the WordPad program opened. The Write program was the program bundled with Windows 3.1. In Windows 95, WordPad has replaced Write as the word processor. Programs such as Windows 3.1 or Windows 95 come **bundled** with some software applications. These smaller programs, such as Write, WordPad, or Calculator, have been included with the larger program to make the larger program more attractive or functional. In Windows, these smaller programs are called **applets** because they are smaller, less powerful versions of application software.

WordPad opened as an application window with Glossary.wri as the document. In the Control menu, in the upper-left corner of the title bar, is the document icon for WordPad. You see the title bar of the application and document window. Since this application program was written for Windows 95, Glossary.wri, the filename, appears first and is followed by WordPad, the name of the application program that created it. This reflects the docucentric approach, where the document is more central than the application that created it.

Your screen might look different, depending on how WordPad is customized. However, you will have a window that you can size. You can minimize, maximize, or close the application. Most Windows applications also have a separate document window, so that you can open multiple document windows. Since WordPad is an applet, it does not have a separate document window. If you wanted to make changes to the data now, you would do so here in the application program.

8 Double-click the Control-menu icon on the title bar.

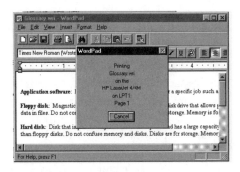

What's happening? → You now know two ways to close an application program, single-click the Close button ▣ or double-click the Control-menu icon ▯   . Since you opened this document by double-clicking its icon in the 95book window, you were returned to that window when you closed the program. If you wanted to print the document, you could do so by using the pop-up menu.

9 Be sure the printer is turned on.

10 Right-click **Glossary.wri**. Click **Print**.

What's happening? → You see WordPad quickly open. Then a message box appeared, telling you that WordPad is printing your document. You can print a document only from within an application. In other words, to print a document, you must first open the application program that created the document. By choosing Print on the shortcut menu, you automatically opened the program so that the document could be printed.

11 Close all open windows.

5.4   Folders

Folders are another tool to help you organize your files. A folder is a special type of file on a disk. The DOS name for a folder is a directory or subdirectory. Folder and directory are synonymous terms that can be and are used interchangeably. A *folder* is a container in which you can place related files. The only folder that is created for you on a disk is the root directory. Otherwise, either you create folders or they are created for you by the installation of a program.

When you install a program, it will usually create a folder or folders and place all of the files necessary to run the program within such folders. Application programs consist of many files. When you execute a program, more than likely it is not just one executable file. The program may be comprised of several, or even hundreds, of support files. These support files can include help files, font files, template files, and the .dll (dynamic link libraries) files. The .dll files are *code* (instructions to the computer) that several programs can use. The support files can vary from program to program, but all of a program's support files are needed to execute that program. These are the working program files. The program files are the tools you use to create your data, and you do not want to store your data files in the same place as your program files.

Before there were computers, you used tools like typewriters to create documents. When you used the typewriter to write a letter to Ms. Hall or a chapter in a book, you would not file both documents under T for typewriter. In the computer world, the same logic applies. If your tool is Word for Windows, a folder called Winword contains all the program files that make Word work. You do not want to store the Hall letter and the Chapter 1 document in the Winword folder.

Therefore, you would want to create your own folders. Chapter 1 and the Hall letter are not related documents. You want to place these documents in their own folders. You might have a folder called Book in which you place the Chapter 1 file, and you might have another folder called Letters in which you place the Hall document. When you need to locate either of these documents, you can go directly to the appropriate folder and know that the related documents are in the folder.

The Windows 95 docucentric paradigm assumes that you are interested in your own documents, not the tool that created them. It is much more efficient to create folders for different topics than to search for documents among the program files. Besides helping you locate the document you need, folders allow you to easily back up your data and manipulate your files.

5.5   Finding Documents

As you work, you will create many documents. This is no different than working in any office environment, although in offices of the past, you used paper, filing cabinets, and tools such as typewriters. In the computer age, your tool is the software application package, and you store your files electronically. Your tasks, however, are the same.

In the old office environment, people realized that they had to organize information in some fashion so that they could store and retrieve it. They used filing cabinets to store documents. They placed documents in folders and arranged them in some sort of order, such as numerical or alphabetical. They might place several files in a larger folder, grouping related information together. For instance, instead of filing the electric bill and gas bill under Electric and Gas, they might put them in a folder called Utilities that would hold both documents. To find anything, they needed to search their memory and recall where it had been filed.

Windows 95 has a Find feature you can use to search your disks (electronic filing cabinets) for the files and folders you need.

5.6   Activity—Using Find

1   Click **Start**. Point at **Find**.

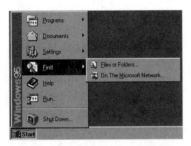

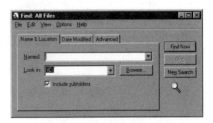 The Find menu opens the submenu. It asks you if you want to look for folders or files. If you are on a network, you will have another choice (Computer...). When you are on a network, you have access to the files and folders on your own computer as well as the files and folders on all the other computers that the network connects. In order to find an object for you, Find first asks the name of the computer in which you wish to look. If you have signed up with the Microsoft Network, you will also have this additional choice. The Microsoft Network is an online information search that lets you search around the world for information. You must have a modem and you must sign up with MSN for this choice to be available to you.

2   Click **Files or Folders**. Click the **Name & Location** tab.

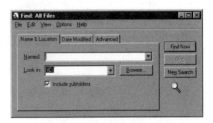

You are presented with the Find All Files dialog box. You have three places for information—the Named drop-down list box, the Look In drop-down list box, and the Include Subfolders check box.

3   Click the down arrow in the **Named** drop-down list box.

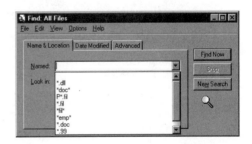

The Named drop-down list box keeps a list of your previous searches for a file. You can choose from this list.

4   Click outside the list box to close it.

5 Click the down arrow in the **Look in** drop-down list box.

What's happening? → The Look In drop-down list box is asking you to name the drive in which you wish to look. In this example, (C:) is the default choice. In addition, the default for the check box, Include subfolders, is set. A *default* is a setting that the program applies to documents in the absence of any specific instructions from the user. A computer must always have instructions. As the user, you take advantage of defaults. Instead of having to key in the drive letter, it has defaulted to Drive C. Your default drive could be different. Find will look through all the directories on the disk.

6 Click in the **Named** text box. Key in the following: **Computer.xls**

7 Click the **Browse** button.

What's happening? → The Browse for Folder dialog box opens. Searching even one hard drive for a file can take a long time. Find will search the entire hard drive literally from top to bottom. If you can narrow your search

to a folder, you will decrease the search time. My Computer is the default selection. My Computer will search for your file on every drive attached to your computer (all hard drives, all floppy drives, any CD-ROM drives, and if you are on a network, every network drive. This can take a long time!)

8 Double-click **(C:)**. Click the **95book** folder. Click **OK**.

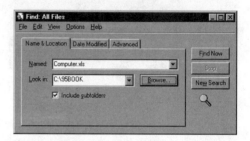

What's happening? → In this example, you know both the name of the file you will be looking for and its approximate location. You have entered the information in each text box.

9 Click the **Find Now** command button.

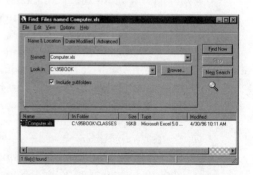

What's happening? → The file, Computer.xls, was found in Drive C in the 95book folder in the Classes folder. This document was created with Excel. You can also see the Size, the Type, and date and time the file was last Modified. If you cannot see all the information, you can alter the size of this dialog box. Now that you have located the file, you can manipulate it. If you have the Excel program, you can double-click the file to open it, or you can right-click it to see the pop-up menu.

10   Right-click the **Computer.xls** document icon.

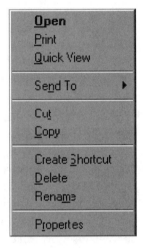

What's happening? → You have opened the shortcut menu that reflects what you can do with the Computer.xls file. This file was easy to locate because you knew its file specification and its approximate folder location.

As you work, you will create many documents. Remembering what you called every document becomes problematic. You can search the disks with less than the full name.

11   Click outside the menu to close it.

12   In the Named text box, drag the mouse over **Computer.xls** to select it.

13   In the **Named** text box, key in the following: **c**

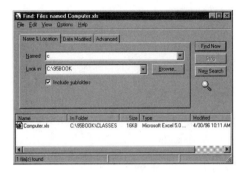

What's happening? → When you highlight a word or phrase and then key in another word, you replace what was there with what you keyed in. You are looking in Drive C in the 95book folder for a file that begins with the letter c.

14   Click the **Find Now** command button.

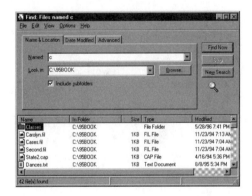

What's happening? → The letter c was extremely vague. The display shows any file that has the letter c anywhere in its name, not just the files that begin with c. You got the folder Classes, but also Dancer.txt. You need to be more specific. Since you know that this document was created with Excel, you should know that data files in Excel have an .xls file extension. But if all you can remember about the file name is that it begins with c, you may use a wildcard, *, to look for an unknown group of characters. There are two wildcards: the question mark (?) is used to represent a single character and the asterisk (*) is used to represent any string of characters. The asterisk is most commonly used.

15 In the **Named** text box, key in the following: **c*.xls**

16 Click **Find Now**.

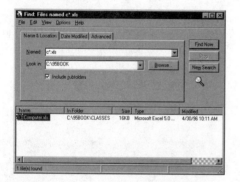

What's happening? This approach worked. You asked to see every file that begins with the letter c, has any number of characters following the c, and has an extension of .xls. (c*.xls). You used the * to represent all the characters you did not know.

17 In the **Named** text box, key in the following: ***fil***

18 Click the **Find Now** command button.

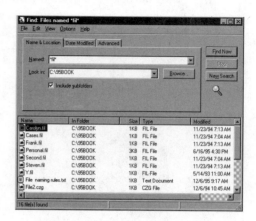

What's happening? You asked for a file that had fil somewhere in its name. As you see, sixteen files were found. These found files include files that have the extension .fil and files that begin with fil. This is one of the reasons that, when you name files that are subject related, you like their names to contain an element in common.

19 In the Named text box, key in the following: ***.fil**

20 Click the **Find Now** command button.

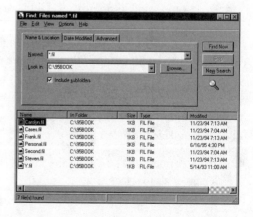

What's happening? In this case, your "in common" feature was the file type, .fil. When you keyed in your query, you asked for any file name (*) but only files that had the extension of fil (.fil). You included the *.fil for a very specific reason.

21 In the **Named** text box, key in the following: **.fil** **Enter**

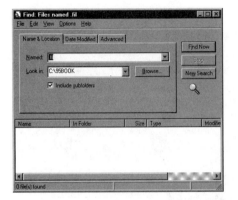

What's
happening? → Pressing **Enter** serves the same purpose as clicking the Find Now command button. Notice that no files were found. This is because you asked for a file with no file name, but only the extension of .fil. A file must have a name; it cannot have an extension only. Remember when you asked for *fil*, you found all the files with fil anywhere in their name. Each time you have asked for different information and have found different answers.

22 In the Named text box, key in the following: **ca*.fil** **Enter**

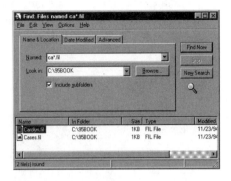

What's
happening? → You found two files that began with ca and had a file extension of .fil. You can further refine your search.

23 In the **Named** text box, key in the following: **CA*LYN.FIL** **Enter**

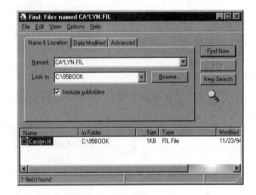

What's
happening? → In this case, you asked to locate every file that began with CA, ended with LYN, had characters in the middle, and had a file extension of .FIL. Case did not matter. You used uppercase letters, but the search results would have been the same if you had used lowercase letters.

24 Close the Find dialog box.

5.7   Other Features of Find

Find has three ways to find files: Name & Location, Date Modified, and Advanced. You have used the first, Name & Location. The second, Modified, has to do with file dates. Every time you modify a file, the current system date and time are stamped on the file folder. If you know when you created or modified a document, you can search by different date criteria. See Figure 5.1.

Figure 5.1   Finding Files by Date Criteria

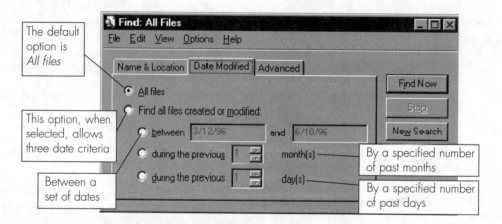

Advanced allows you to look for files by type, size, or a word or phrase within a document. The default is All Files and Folders. See Figure 5.2.

Figure 5.2   Finding Files Using the Advanced tab

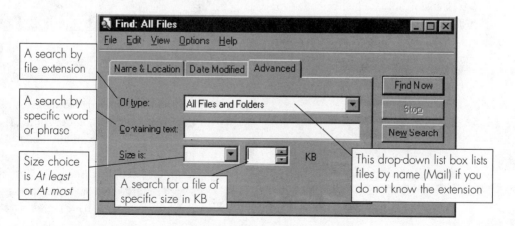

You may set criteria in all three sheets. For instance, you could specify a search for a file named Myfile.txt located in C:\95book folder in the Name & Location sheet. Then specify that it was created last month in the Date Modified sheet. Then specify that the file can be no larger than 4800 KB. When you enter these options, they must all be true in order to locate the file. If a file was found that met all other criteria except that it was 4900 KB, the file would not be found. It must meet all the criteria.

Finding files is easiest when you have a plan on how you named them. For instance, if you worked in a law office, you could have a naming scheme that all pleadings would start with Pl. If you were looking for the documentation of a pleading from the previous month concerning your client Panezich, you could specify a search for all files that begin with Pl, were created last month, and have Panezich as a key word.

5.8   Activity—Using Other Find Options

1 Click **Start**. Point at **Find**. Click **Files or Folders**.

2 Click **Browse**. Double-click **(C:)**. Click **95book**. Click **OK**.

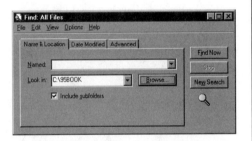

> **What's happening?** You have limited your search to the 95book folder and all the folders beneath it.

3 Click the **Date Modified** tab.

4 Click the **between** option button.

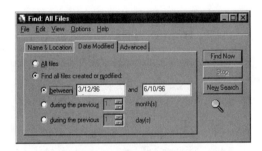

> **What's happening?** When you selected between, you also selected Find all files created or modified. There are more choices available. You can search among files created between a range of dates. You can look during a past month or days, specifying how far back in the past you want the search to go. You can alter the number of days or months by using the spin box.

5 Key in the following in the **between** text boxes:
7/1/95   7/15/95

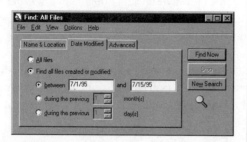

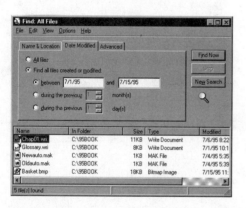

What's **→** You have selected your search criteria.
happening? You want to locate any files created between 7/1/95 and 7/15/95 that are in the
95book folder on Drive C.

6 Click the **Find Now** command button.

What's **→** Five files met your criteria. Now you
happening? want to locate specific text within a
document. Thus, if you remember some
phrase or word in a document, you can
key it in.

7 Click the **Advanced** tab.

8 In the **Containing** text dialog box, key in the
following: **Tuttle**

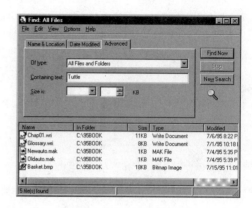

What's **→** You are ready for your search.
happening?

9 Click the **Find Now** command button.

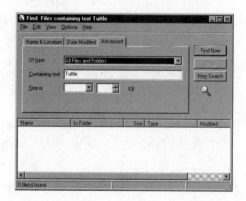

What's **→** It seems that no file met your criteria.
happening?

10 Click the **Date Modified** tab.

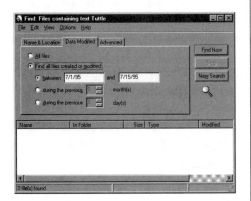

What's
happening? Because you did not clear the dates, you asked to find a file with Tuttle in it, but only in a file created between 7/1/95 and 7/15/95.

11 Click the **All files** option button. Click the **Advanced** tab. Click **Find Now**.

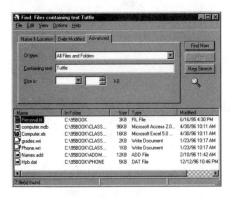

What's
happening? Seven documents on this disk, in the 95book folder, have the word Tuttle in them. In order to see the data in the documents, you must have the programs that created the documents. If you

double-clicked Computer.xls and did not have Excel, you would not be able to see the document. Since you do have WordPad, you can open the document called Grades.wri.

12 Double-click **Grades.wri**. Maximize the window.

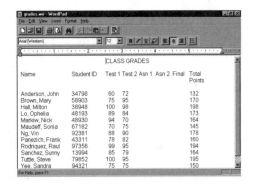

What's
happening? You were interested in the document called Grades.wri, which was created with WordPad, so you opened WordPad. Indeed, the word Tuttle appears at the end of the document.

13 Restore the **WordPad** window.

14 Close WordPad.

15 Close the Find dialog box.

What's
happening? The problem with looking for text in a document is that it is very time-consuming. You were only looking in one folder on the hard drive. If you were looking on a 2-GB hard disk or on a network disk, the search for text could take minutes, even hours. This is not the most efficient way to locate files.

5.9   Finding Folders

One advantage to grouping your files in folders is the ability to limit your searches for these files later. When first using an application package to create documents, many people have no idea where their data files are being saved. Most application packages will set a default folder where all data files will be stored. As you continue to create new files, however, this folder grows at a rapid pace, making it increasingly harder to locate a specific file. An easier method to organize your files is to create folders that will hold similar files. If you are writing a mystery book, you could create a folder called Mystery Book and keep all your chapters in that folder. As you will see in the next activity, if you know the folder name, it is easier to locate files. In this activity, the folders were created for you. You will learn how to create your own folders later.

5.10   Activity—Using Find To Find Folders

1   Click **Start**. Point to **Find**. Click **Files or Folders**.

2   Click the **Browse** button. Double-click **Drive C**. Click **95book**. Click **OK**.

3   In the Named text box, key in the following: **Classes**

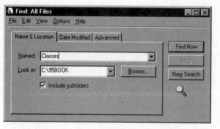

> **What's happening?** You are looking for the folder called Classes. Classes was a folder that was created for you in the 95book directory. A folder called Classes would logically store any files that deal with classes. When Find searches the 95book folder, it is looking for either files or folders named Classes. Find does not distinguish between files and folders. If you remember, a folder is just a special type of file.

4   Click **Find Now**.

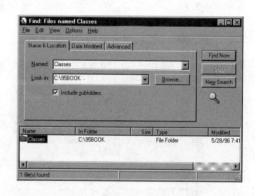

> **What's happening?** You found the Classes folder under the 95book folder. What is in the folder?

5 Double-click the **Classes** folder in the list box.

→ Your window size and shape may vary. You can size it to see all the files. There are six files in the folder.

What's happening? → Your window size and shape may vary. You can size it to see all the files. There are six files in the folder.

6 Close the open window. Close the Find dialog box.

What's happening? → You have returned to the desktop.

7 Double-click **My Computer**. Double-click the **Drive C** icon. Double-click the **95book** folder.

What's happening? → An icon helps you differentiate between a folder and a file. A folder icon looks like an actual folder. If the folders are not visible, scroll up until they are.

8 Double-click the **Classes** folder.

What's happening? → You are looking in the container (folder or directory) called Classes. In Classes are six documents (data files) that deal with classes. You can see that although Find is useful in helping you locate files, it is faster and more efficient to have an organizational scheme that allows you to access files quickly. It is easier to remember a folder name than to remember all the individual file names and use Find.

No organizational scheme is perfect. As you work with computers, you will create more files, and it is inevitable that you will "lose" files. They are not really lost, just misplaced somewhere on a drive. If you name like files with similar names, and if you place like files in a folder that has a meaningful name, you have a much better chance of locating the needed document.

9   Close the Classes window.

What's →   You have closed all the open windows.
happening?

5.11 Introducing Shortcuts and Drag and Drop

Windows 95 offers a feature called a shortcut. A *shortcut* is a way to place commonly used objects on the desktop (or in other convenient locations) for easy access. A shortcut can be a file, folder, program, or even a device. For instance, if you had an address book and needed to look up telephone numbers constantly, it would be most productive to have the address book on the desk instead of filed away in a filing cabinet. However, the address book takes up space on the desk. One solution to the problem would be to place the address book in the filing cabinet but to have a string on the desktop that you could pull to grab the address book quickly when you needed it. This is somewhat like a shortcut. A shortcut is a *pointer* to the actual object. The shortcut appears on the desktop. It points to the object so that you can access it quickly. The desktop is not the only location where you can place a shortcut. Since one of the most common tasks users want to perform is printing a document, having the printer available to you quickly would be convenient. Therefore, you can create a printer shortcut.

With the *drag and drop* feature, you select an object, drag it with the mouse, and reposition it somewhere else (drop it). In essence, when you moved windows across the desktop, that is what you were doing. Drag and drop has some powerful components and can simplify many tasks in Windows 95. If you drag a document and drop it on a printer icon, you are issuing a command to open the application program and print the document.

5.12   Activity—Creating and Using a Shortcut

1   Double-click **My Computer**. Double-click the **Printers** folder.

Figure 5.3   The Default Printer

> → You have opened the Printers folder. The
> *What's happening?* window displays all the printers available on your system. If you are using your own computer, there is probably only one printer icon. If you are on a network, you may have many choices. Only one printer is the default printer. If you have more than one printer icon and do not know which is the default, right-click each printer icon. The default printer is indicated by a check mark, as shown in Figure 5.3.

2   Click your default printer to select it.

3   Hold the right mouse button down and begin to drag the icon out of the **Printers** folder onto the desktop.

HP LaserJet
4/4M

> → As you begin to drag the icon across the
> *What's happening?* open window, the icon acquires the international symbol for No, a circle with a line through it. This tells you that you cannot move the printer.

4 Continue to drag the printer icon onto the desktop.

HP LaserJet
4/4M

What's happening? → As you drag the object onto the desktop, a shortcut symbol appears. This shortcut symbol is different from the shortcut button used in Help. You remember that that symbol was a left-bent purple arrow ⌐. The shortcut icon has a right bent-black arrow on top of the object's normal icon:

aserJet
4/4M

This helps distinguish it from the normal icon and indicates that it is a pointer to the object.

5 Release the mouse button.

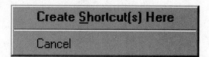

Create Shortcut(s) Here

Cancel

What's happening? → A pop-up menu appears, giving you the choice to create a shortcut or to cancel the operation.

6 Click **Create Shortcut(s) Here**.

7 Close all open windows.

8 Drag the shortcut icon to the left of the screen, so that it is arranged with the other desktop icons.

9 Click somewhere on the desktop to deselect the shortcut icon. A deselected item is no longer highlighted.

Shortcut to HP
LaserJet 4-4M

What's happening? → On the desktop is a shortcut to the printer. The icon represents the printer, and the shortcut has both the shortcut symbol and the words "Shortcut to."

10 Double-click **My Computer**. Double-click the **Drive C** icon. Double-click the **95book** folder.

11 Scroll through the window until you locate **Glossary.wri**. Click it.

What's happening? → You should be able to see both Glossary.wri and the shortcut to the printer. If you cannot, move the window until you can.

12 Be sure the printer is on. Right-drag **Glossary.wri** out of the **95book** folder and position it on top of the shortcut to the printer icon.

What's happening? → When Glossary.wri is poised over the printer shortcut, you see that the document acquires a plus symbol.

13 Drop **Glossary.wri** onto the shortcut to the printer icon.

What's happening? → You see WordPad being loaded quickly, and a message box informs you that the document is being printed. You then receive a hard copy of the document.

What happens to the document depends on where you drop it. If you had released the mouse button (dropping the document) on the desktop, you would have opened the shortcut menu. See Figure 5.4.

Figure 5.4   The Right-Drag Shortcut Menu

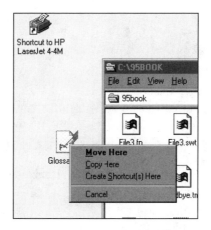

On the same drive, the default operation is Move Here. If you had left-dragged, you would have moved the Glossary.wri file to the desktop folder. The difference between a left-drag and a right-drag is that a left-drag will perform the default operation, and a right-drag will open a menu containing other choices before it completes the operation. The Copy Here choice places another copy of Glossary.wri on the desktop while retaining the file in the 95book folder. The Create Shortcut(s) Here choice maintains the one copy of Glossary.wri in the 95book folder and places a pointer to it on the desktop. A plus sign indicates a copy operation; absence of the plus sign indicates a move operation. A left bent arrow indicates a shortcut operation.

14 Close all open windows.

What's happening? → You have returned to the desktop.

5.13 Creating Shortcuts for Documents and Folders

Shortcuts are not limited to devices. You can create shortcuts for program files, data files, and even folders. You can place shortcuts on the desktop or in folders, but the actual file will not move from its original location. When you create a shortcut for a file, you are creating a pointer that indicates where the file is located, giving you quick access to frequently used documents or programs. You might think of a shortcut as an alias for the actual file. As your work changes, you can add new shortcuts or delete shortcuts that you are no longer using.

5.14 Activity—Creating Shortcuts for Documents and Folders

1   Double-click **My Computer**. Double-click the **Drive C** icon. Double-click the **95book** folder.

2   Double-click the **Classes** folder.

3   Right-click and drag **Grades.wri** onto the desktop. Release the right mouse button.

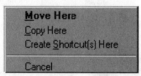

What's happening? → Since you right-dragged the document icon, the pop-up (shortcut) menu appears. Moving and copying an object are much different than creating a shortcut. If you selected Move Here, you would be removing the document from the 95book folder and placing it in Drive C in an actual folder (directory) called Desktop. If you selected Copy Here, you would have two copies of Grades.wri, one in the 95book folder, and one in the Desktop folder. The problem with having two copies is that if you added or changed data in Grades.wri on the desk-

top, you would not change the data in Grades.wri in the 95book folder. If you create a shortcut, however, there is only one Grades.wri file, the one in the 95book folder.

4   Click **Create Shortcut(s) Here**.

What's happening? → You now have a shortcut to your document.

5   Close the **Classes** window.

6   Double-click **Shortcut to grades.wri**.

What's happening? → You have quickly opened the WordPad program, which opened your document, Grades.wri. You can also create a shortcut for a folder.

7   Close WordPad.

8   Double-click **My Computer**. Double-click the **Drive C** icon. Double-click the **95book** folder.

9 Right-click and drag the **Classes** folder onto the desktop. Release the right mouse button.

Since you used the right mouse button to drag the folder icon, the pop-up menu appeared. Again, you could move or copy the folder with all the documents in it, but you only want one version of the folder.

10 Click **Create Shortcut(s) Here**.

11 Close all open windows.

You now have shortcuts to both the document called Grades.wri and the folder called Classes.

12 Double-click the Classes shortcut.

You now have immediate access to the Classes folder. When you boot Windows 95, you can immediately access the Classes folder, which contains all your class-related documents. Look carefully at the document icons. There are no shortcut icons. These are the actual files in the C:\Classes\95book folder. You created a shortcut to the folder, not a shortcut to the documents in the folder.

13 Close the **Classes** window.

5.15 Creating Folders

A convenient method to quickly access the files and folders you use daily is to create a folder on the desktop. In this folder, you place shortcuts to the programs and files you use most often. You can then quickly access what you need, enabling you to by-pass the Start menu and My Computer. Since you place shortcuts in this folder, you can alter what is in the folder as your work needs change.

5.16 Activity—Creating Folders on the Desktop

1 Right-click the desktop. Point to **New**.

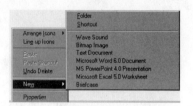

What's happening? ➔ The New menu has appeared. You can now create a new folder, shortcut, or document. The programs on your system will be shown here. You may select the program you want to use to create a new document. Your options will vary, depending on what programs you have on your system. In this case, you are going to create a new folder.

2 Click **Folder**.

What's happening? ➔ You have just created a new folder. The cursor is blinking where you can key in your folder name.

3 Key in the following: **EVERY DAY**

4 Click outside the text box.

What's happening? ➔ You have named your folder.

5 Double-click the **EVERY DAY** icon.

What's happening? ➔ It is an empty folder.

6 Left-drag and drop all your shortcuts into the **EVERY DAY** window. This includes the shortcut to Classes, Grades.wri, and the printer.

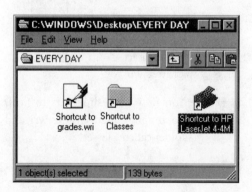

What's happening? ➔ You have placed all the shortcuts into a folder on the desktop. In this case, you are not creating new shortcuts, but moving them from the desktop to the folder called EVERY DAY. When you left-drag on the same drive, the default operation is to move objects, rather than copying them.

7 In the **EVERY DAY** folder, click **View**. Click **Arrange Icons**. Click **Auto Arrange** if it does not have a check mark in front of it.

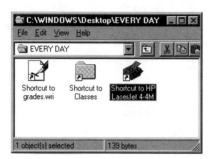

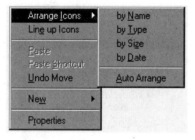

Because you have used the Auto Arrange feature, the icons will automatically be arranged each time you open the EVERY DAY folder.

8 Close the **EVERY DAY** folder.

The objects on your desktop are not arranged in any particular order.

9 Right-click the desktop. Point at **Arrange Icons**.

You have the same choices to arrange your icons on the desktop as in any folder—by Name, by Type (file extension), by Size, or by Date. The desktop is just a special folder. In this example, Auto Arrange is not set. If you have a check mark in front of Auto Arrange, remove it by clicking it.

10 Click **by Date**.

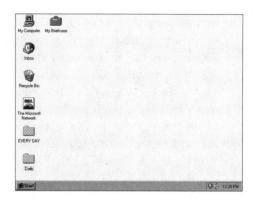

The folders and documents are arranged by date. You could confirm this by right-clicking on each object and clicking Properties to confirm the date. You will notice that when you arrange icons on the desktop, objects such as My Computer or Network Neighborhood do not move. (If you are not on a network, you will not have the Network Neighborhood icon.) Only document icons, folder icons, and shortcuts are rearranged.

11 Right-click the desktop. Point at **Arrange Icons**. Click **by Name**.

You have now your icons by name. If your icons were already arranged, you will see no change on the desktop.

5.17 The Recycle Bin

One of the advantages of Windows 95 is its flexibility. As you work, your priorities change. You may work on one project for a week and then a new project the next week. You could create a shortcut for each new project. But, as you can imagine, your desktop could become very cluttered with shortcuts. You may want to eliminate old shortcuts. When you delete a shortcut, you are not deleting the object, document, or folder, only the pointer to the object, document, or folder.

In Windows 95, an easy way to eliminate objects is to send them to the Recycle Bin. The advantage of the Recycle Bin is that items do not get permanently deleted until you tell the Recycle Bin to empty. It is much like putting items in a wastebasket. If you need an item back, you can go through your wastepaper basket and recover what you need.. Once you take your wastepaper basket to the trash bin and trucks haul the trash away, however, you cannot recover a document. The same is true with the Recycle Bin.

5.18 Activity—Using the Recycle Bin

1 Right-click the **Recycle Bin** icon. Click **Properties**.

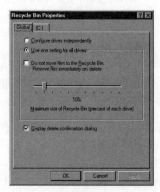

> **What's happening?** The Recycle Bin is an object and has properties. The default size of the Recycle Bin is 10 percent of your disk drive. If you have more than one hard drive, you may have different settings on each (configure drives independently). If you do not want the ability to recover deleted files, folders, and shortcuts, you would set the check box Do not move files to the Recycle Bin. Remove files immediately on delete. If you do not want every deletion confirmed, you would unset the Display delete confirmation dialog box.

2 Click **Cancel**.

3 Double-click **EVERY DAY**. Drag the **Shortcut to grades.wri** to the Recycle Bin. Drop it onto the Recycle Bin.

> **What's happening?** The shortcut to the Grades.wri is no longer in the EVERY DAY folder.

4 Double-click the **Recycle Bin** icon.

> **What's happening?** You opened the Recycle Bin window and can see your shortcut inside. You may have more items in the Recycle Bin window if you previously deleted other files. You can take your shortcut out of the Recycle Bin.

5 Drag the **Shortcut to grades.wri** to the desktop.

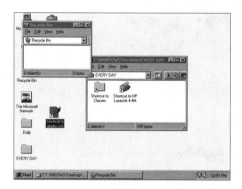

What's happening? If you had no other files in the Recycle Bin window, it should be empty. The shortcut has been retrieved and is on the desktop.

6 Drag and drop the **Shortcut to grades.wri** back to the Recycle Bin window.

7 Close the EVERY DAY folder. Drag and drop the **EVERY DAY** folder to the Recycle Bin.

What's happening? The three items in the Recycle Bin are the shortcuts you created. The name of the folder EVERY DAY does not appear. The contents of the EVERY DAY folder are placed in the Recycle Bin. You have thrown your shortcuts into the trash. Now you want to take out the trash.

8 Click **File** on the Recycle Bin menu bar.

What's happening? You have dropped down the menu. One of the choices is Empty Recycle Bin. When you choose this menu item, you delete everything in the window. You may also use the closed Recycle Bin icon. If you right-click the icon, one menu choice is Empty Recycle Bin.

9 Click **Empty Recycle Bin**.

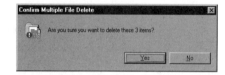

What's happening? Since the Display delete confirmation dialog was set, a message gives you one more chance to save what is in the Recycle Bin. Remember, when you delete shortcuts, you are not deleting the objects, only the pointers to these objects. However, if you had placed a file in the Recycle Bin, you would be deleting the data. In this case, you do want to empty it.

10   Click **Yes**.

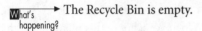 → The Recycle Bin is empty.

11   Close the **Recycle Bin** window.

Chapter Summary

You learned that files and folders follow specific naming rules. You also learned that although Windows 95 allows long file names (LFNs) of up to 255 characters, there are shortcomings in using long file names. You learned that folders are created by application programs or by the user. Folders typically contain files, other folders, or shortcuts.

You learned how to locate the properties of files using the shortcut menu. You found that the Find command allows you many ways to locate files. The Find dialog box provides three tabbed sheets, Name & Location, Date Modified, and Advanced, that allow you to search for files by different search criteria.

You learned that if you drag an object from one location to another on the same drive, the default operation is a move. You learned that if you right-dragged an object, you will see a shortcut menu that allows you to choose whether you want to move, copy, or create a shortcut for an object. You created shortcuts for a device, a file, and a folder. You found that a shortcut is a pointer to an object. You created a folder on the desktop. You used the Recycle Bin to delete the shortcuts you created, and you found that you could retrieve items from the Recycle Bin, if you had not emptied it.

Key Terms

Applets	Drag and drop	Long file names (LFNs)
Bundled	FAT file system	Pointer
Code	File specification	Shortcut
Default	Folder	VFAT file system
Delimiter		

Discussion Questions

1. List four file naming rules in Windows 95.
2. Describe how Windows 95 creates a short file name. Discuss why Windows 95 gives both a long and short file name to each file.
3. What can you learn about an object by looking at its properties?
4. Explain the purpose and function of folders.
5. Who may create folders? Why?
6. Why would you not put data files in the same folder as program files?
7. How can you differentiate between a folder and a document?
8. Explain the purpose and function of Find.
9. Name two ways Find lets you locate files and folders.
10. What is a wildcard? How may it be useful in locating a file?
11. What is a shortcut?
12. Explain the purpose and function of shortcuts.
13. Why would you want to place a shortcut on the desktop?
14. How can you identify the icon for a shortcut?
15. When dragging a document on the desktop, what happens to the document depends on where you drop it. Explain.
16. Compare and contrast moving, copying, and creating a shortcut.
17. Identify two ways icons may be arranged on the desktop.
18. Explain the purpose and function of the Recycle Bin.
19. What features may you set for the Recycle Bin? Where may you set them?
20. What is an advantage of using the Recycle Bin in eliminating objects?

True/False Questions

For each question, circle the letter T if the statement is true or the letter F if the statement is false.

T   F   1. Both Windows 95 and DOS have identical file naming rules.
T   F   2. Data files and program files should be placed in the same folder for easy access.
T   F   3. A property sheet is a collection of information about an object.
T   F   4. In order to use Find, you must know the exact file name and folder location to locate the file.
T   F   5. Shortcuts may be placed only on the desktop.

Completion Questions

Write the correct answer in the blank space provided.

6. A file specification is composed of the file _____ and the file _____.
7. A collection of information about an object is located in the object's _____.
8. A file that cannot be modified has its _____ attribute set.
9. A right-bent arrow over the usual object icon signifies that the object is a(n) _____.
10. Deleting a document shortcut does not delete the document, but only the _____ to the object.

Multiple Choice Questions

Circle the letter of the correct answer for each question.

11. Dragging a document and dropping it on a shortcut to a printer will
    a. result in an error message.
    b. print the document.
    c. open a shortcut menu.
    d. create a shortcut that prints the document when double-clicked.

12. The Find dialog box has three tabbed sheets in which you may enter information. They are
    a. Contents, Index, and Folder.
    b. Name & Location, Contents, and Advanced.
    c. Name & Location, Date Modified, and Advanced.
    d. Name & Location, Associated Application, and Advanced.

13. You may create shortcuts for
    a. devices.
    b. data files.
    c. folders.
    d. all the above

14. Which of the following search criteria may you use in Find?
    a   by file specification.
    b. by file extension.
    c. both a and b
    d. neither a nor b

15. In Windows 95, a shortcut
    a. is a pointer to an object.
    b. is a copy of an object.
    c. cannot be used with devices.
    d. can be placed only in a folder.

Application Assignments

Problem Set I—At the Computer

Problem A

Double-click **My Computer**. Double-click the **Drive C** icon. Double-click the **95book** folder. Scroll until you locate the document called **Chap01.wri**. Open the property sheet for the file.

1. What is the entire name of the document?
   a. Chapter 1 document
   b. Chapter01.doc
   c. Chap01.wri
   d. Chapter 01 write

2. What is the size of the document?
   a. 11,264 bytes.   b. 22,485 bytes.   c. 35,994 bytes.

3. The type of file is a
   a. Microsoft Word 6.0 Document.
   b. Write Document.
   c. WordPad Document.
   d. text document.

Close any open windows.

Problem B

Create a shortcut to the printer. Locate the file called **File naming rules** in the **95book** folder. Locate and use the property sheet for this file.

4. What is the Windows 95 file name for this file?
   a. File naming rules
   b. Filenamingrules
   c. File naming rules.txt
   d. Filena~1.txt
   e. Filename.txt

5. What is the MS-DOS file name for this file?
   a. File naming rules
   b. Filenamingrules
   c. File naming rules.txt
   d. Filena~1.txt
   e. Filename.txt

Be sure the printer is on. Drag and drop this file onto the printer shortcut. (Be sure you drop the file on the shortcut to the printer and not on the desktop.) Read the document.

6. Spaces are allowed in file names
   a. only in DOS or applications written for DOS.
   b. only in Windows 95 or applications written for Windows 95.
   c. in both DOS and Windows 95 applications.

Close any open windows.

Problem C

Use Find to locate the file called **Jan.99** in the **95book** folder.

7. In the Find dialog box, in the Size column, what file size is displayed for this file?
   a. 1 Byte.   b. 1 KB.   c. 1 MB.

8. In the Find dialog box, in the list box, what date is displayed for this file in the Modified column?
   a. 11/23/95.   b. 12/23/95.   c. 11/23/94.   d. 12/23/94.

Begin a new search. In the **95book** folder, including all subfolders, locate all the files that have 99 as their file extension.

9. How many files did you locate?
   a. 1 file.   b. 2 files.   c. 3 files.   d. 4 files.

Begin a new search. Clear the **Named** text box. Use the **Date Modified** tab. In the **95book** folder, including all subfolders, find all the files that were created or modified between 5/14/94 and 10/12/94.

10. Among the files found,
    a. only Blue.jaz is listed.
    b. only Bye.typ is listed.
    c. both Blue.jaz and Bye.typ are listed.
    d. neither Blue.jaz nor Bye.typ are listed.

Click the **All Files** option button in the **Date Modified** tab. Begin a new search. Use the **Advanced** tab. In the **95book** folder, including all subfolders, find any file that has **Westlake** in its contents.

11. The word Westlake was found in
    a. the Computer.xls file.
    b. the Mystery.bks file.
    c. both the Computer.xls and Mystery.bks files.
    d. neither the Computer.xls nor Mystery.bks file.

Close all dialog boxes and windows.

Problem D

Double-click **My Computer**. Double-click the **Drive C** icon. Double-click the **95book** folder. Double-click the **Media** folder.

12. Does the Media folder display any document icons?
    a. Yes   b. No

Double-click the **Movies** folder in the **Media** window.

13. Does the Movies folder display any document icons?
    a. Yes   b. No

14. Does the Movies folder display any folder icons?
    a. Yes   b. No

Close all open windows.

Problem E

Create a new folder called **Today** on the desktop. Double-click **My Computer**. Remember to right-drag the folder or file and choose **Create Shortcut(s) Here**. In the **Today** folder, create a shortcut to the **Level-1** folder in the **95book** folder. In the **95book** folder, there is a file called **April.txt**. Create a shortcut to this file and place the shortcut in the **Today** folder on the desktop. Close My Computer. In the **Today** folder, open the Level-1 shortcut.

15. How many document icons are in the Level-1 shortcut?
    a. one   b. two   c. three

16. How many folder icons are in the Level-1 shortcut?
    a. one   b. two   c. three

Remember to right-drag the folder or file and choose **Create Shortcut(s) Here**. Create a shortcut on the desktop to the **Hello.txt** file in the **Level-1** shortcut folder.

17. Is there still a document icon for Hello.txt in the Level-1 folder?
    a. Yes.   b. No.

Close all open windows.

Problem F

Drag and drop the shortcut to **Hello.txt** on the desktop onto the Recycle Bin. Drag and drop the shortcut to the printer onto the Recycle Bin. Drag and drop the **Today** folder onto the Recycle Bin. Open the Recycle Bin. Click **View**. Click **Details**. Locate the **Size** column. If you cannot see it, scroll until you can.

18. What size are the shortcuts?
    a. 1 byte.   b. 1 KB.   c. 1 MB.

Click **View**. Click **Large Icons**. Click **Shortcut to Hello.txt** in the **Recycle Bin** window. Click **File**. Click **Delete**.

19. What is the name (title) of the message box?
    a. Empty Recycle Bin.   b. Confirm File Delete.   c. Confirm Multiple File Delete.

Click **Yes**. Empty the Recycle Bin. Close all open Windows.

Problem Set II—Brief Essay

For all essay questions, use Notepad to create your answer. Then print your answer.

1. On your computer, you have two folders. One is named Letters, and the other is named Business Letters. You want to locate the following files:

   > **Modern Electric Company.doc.**
   > **Mortgage.txt.**
   > **Mom.letter.doc**
   > **Mom.doc.**
   > **Mom.birthday.txt**

   ❑ If you used Find, describe what strategies and search criteria you used to locate all the business letters.

   ❑ If you used Find, describe what strategies and search criteria you used to locate all the letters to your mother.

   ❑ If you used Find, describe any strategy and search criteria you used to locate all the files at one time.

   ❑ If you did not use Find, describe the other ways you used to locate the files.

2. DOS follows the 8.3 file naming rules. Windows 95 allows the use of LFNs. Compare and contrast these two sets of rules. Which set of rules do you prefer? Is there any reason to continue to use the 8.3 rules? Explain your answer.

Problem Set III—Scenario

For the next week, you will be writing and printing letters and resumes to help your brother with his job search. Your brother's documents are in a folder called Brother. In addition, you are writing a research paper for your history class, Civil war.doc, located in a folder called History. You decide that the easiest way to access these documents will be to create shortcuts to files, folders, and the printer. Describe what shortcuts you would create, how you would create them, and where you would place them. At the end of the week, you will want to remove these shortcuts. Describe what steps you will need to take to eliminate the shortcuts.

Chapter 6

Using Explorer

Chapter Overview

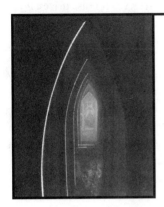

In this chapter, you will further examine the hierarchical structure of the folders and file system in Windows 95. You will discover the importance of the path in locating a file or folder. You will learn to move around in the Explorer window. You will find that opening multiple windows assists you in locating and manipulating files and folders, and you will discover the differences between a logical view and a physical view of your computer system. You will find that My Computer is typically a logical view, whereas Explorer is a physical view. You will learn to determine which view best suits your needs. You will find that you can alter menus, but only if you locate the correct folders once you locate the file.

You will learn how to copy a disk, and you will find that when you prepare a disk for use, you are setting up the way Windows 95 manages information on a disk. Formatting creates a directory, FAT, and data sectors on a disk so that files and folders can be located efficiently.

Learning Objectives

1. Describe the hierarchical structure of a disk.
2. Explain the purpose and function of Explorer.
3. Identify the parts of an Explorer Window and explain the purpose and function of each part.
4. Compare and contrast logical and physical views that are presented in Windows 95.
5. Explain the purpose and function of copying disks.
6. Explain the purpose and function of the boot record, FAT, and the root directory.

Student Outcomes

1. Use Explorer to see the hierarchical structure of folders and files on your disks.
2. Use Explorer to explore different aspects of files and folders.
3. Use Windows 95's multitasking ability to open multiple Explorer and My Computer windows.
4. Discern between logical and physical views presented to you in Windows 95.
5. Add and remove a printer from the Send To menu.
6. Make a copy of a disk.
7. Format a disk.

6.1   A Disk's Hierarchical Structure

As you have seen, all files are stored on and retrieved from disk. A disk can be a floppy disk in Drive A or Drive B, a hard disk such as Drive C, or a network disk drive such as Drive Y. A hard disk or network disk has a much larger capacity to store files than any floppy disk. CD-ROM disks also have a large capacity to store files. Unless you have an exceedingly expensive CD-ROM drive, though, you usually can only retrieve, or "read" files from CD-ROM disks. You cannot save files to CD-ROM disks. Drives are assigned letters in order for Windows 95 to differentiate among drives so that you to know which disk stores your files. Letters of the alphabet followed by a colon (A:, B:, C:) are reserved for disk drives. If you do not tell your program on which drive to save a file, it will assume the default drive. There is always a default drive because the program has to look to a disk to retrieve or store files.

So that you may manage your files easily, you may also organize a disk with folders. The DOS name for folders is directories. Folder and directory are synonymous terms and can be used interchangeably. Every disk has a hierarchical, tree-shaped structure. The tree begins with what is called the root directory, which is created when any disk is formatted. The root (\ ) is the top of structure. Then, like a tree growing more roots, other folders branch out from the root. Each of these folders can have folders of its own. Within folders are files (documents or programs). You can start at the root and "burrow" down the tree to a folder or subfolder, or you can start at the last subfolder and burrow your way up to the root. Remember, it is all connected. You cannot jump from folder to folder. You have to follow the path to the file. See Figure 6.1.

Figure 6.1   The Tree-shaped Hierarchical Directory Structure

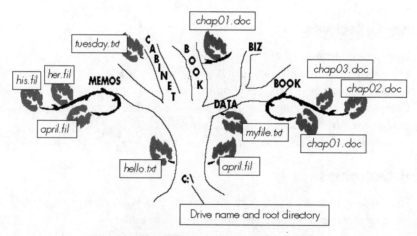

Folder (directory) names appear in regular text
File names appear in italic

A file is saved or retrieved from a specific location on a disk. Although a file can be saved to the root directory, it is best saved to a folder. To locate the file later, you need to know the name of the drive and the folder where the file is stored. The path specifies the drive and the folder in which the file is located.

If you had a file called Myfile.txt on the disk in Drive C and in the folder called Data, the "path" to the file would be C:\Data. If you were using an application program and wanted to retrieve the file, the application program would present you with a dialog box in which you would key in the file name. You would need to key in C:\Data\Myfile.txt. The second backslash is a delimiter that separates one folder or file name from another. The first \ indicates the root directory; the second \ is used to separate the folder name from the file name. A backslash may never be used as a part of a file name. If you look at Figure 6.1, you see a file called Tuesday.txt in the Cabinet directory on Drive C. If you key in the name as \Cabinet\Tuesday\txt, you are asking to locate a file called Txt in a folder called Tuesday in a folder called Cabinet that is under the root.

File and folder names must be unique so that the correct file may be identified. Thus, in Figure 6.1, C:\April.fil is clearly identified as a different file from C:\Memos\April.fil. Each can be identified because of the path. The same would hold true for C:\Book\Chap01.doc and C:\Data\Book\Chap01.doc. Although the folder and file names appear identical, they are not because each follows another path in the tree.

As you begin to create files and add new programs, a tool called Windows Explorer (referred to as Explorer) allows you to browse your drives to locate files and folders. Although you have learned to use Find, Find is most useful when you already know the names of your files or folders. Another drawback of Find is that it requires you to search the entire disk or an entire directory structure.

If you have organized your files and folders, you can use Explorer to quickly find the drive and folder you want. Explorer also gives you the option to browse a folder to see what files it contains. This option is useful when you want to evaluate which files or folders are candidates for deletion or backup. You may even find that you wish to reorganize your files and folders for easier access. You cannot do any of this from the Find menu. With Explorer, you are not only able to locate and browse folders and files, but also to launch application programs.

6.2   The Explorer Window

When you open Explorer, you will find that Explorer looks nearly identical to My Computer in List view. The major difference between the My Computer and Explorer windows is that the Explorer window is divided into panes. The left pane is the hierarchical structure of the selected disk. The right pane displays the contents of the default drive or folder from the left pane. In fact, the right pane is exactly like My Computer. Figure 6.2 shows a sample Explorer window with the new items identified. In this case, you are looking at Drive C.

Figure 6.2   The Explorer Window

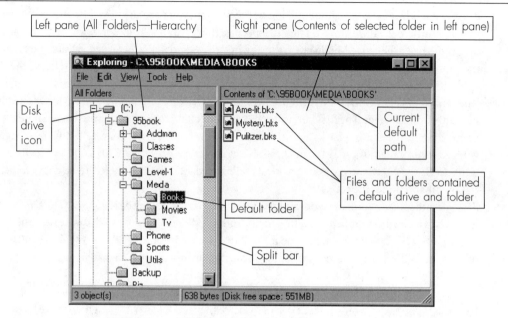

The following new elements appear in an Explorer window:

All Folders pane	The hierarchical tree of folders, also called the tree pane.
Contents pane	The files and folders currently in the selected default drive and folder.
Current default path	The files and folders in the current default drive and directory.
Disk drive icon	Represents a drive on your computer system. The drive letter follows each icon.
Default folder	The location of the current folder that appears in the title bar of the window. Every disk has one root folder, the \. The folders branch from the root and are located under the root.
Split bar	A line between the left and right panes of the Explorer window that change the pane's dimensions. You use the mouse to drag the *split bar*.

6.3   Activity—Moving Around in the Explorer Window

Note: The listed settings are assumed for each chapter. If you are working on your own computer, the changes you made in the default settings should be retained from one work session to the next. However, if you are working in a computer lab, you may have to change your settings each time you log into the network. The settings are as follows:

My Computer
- ❏ Toolbar and status bar on (in the View menu).
- ❏ Large icons arranged by name (in the View menu).
- ❏ Browse folders by using a single window that changes as you open each folder (View/Options/ Browse tab).

❏ Hide file of these types is set (View/Options/View tab).
❏ Display the full MS-DOS path in the title bar is set (View/Options/View tab).
❏ Hide MS-DOS file extensions for file types that are registered is not set (View/Options/View tab).

1   Click **Start**. Point to **Programs**. Click **Windows Explorer**.

2   Click **View**.

What's happening? ➡ The default settings for Explorer are Status Bar on in List view, with the Toolbar that you used in My Computer turned off. You will find that the toolbar is a useful feature in Explorer.

3   Click **Toolbar** to set it.

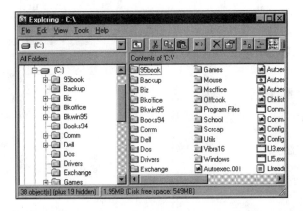

What's happening? ➡ Your display will be different, depending on the hardware, software, folders, and files on your computer system. This is the Explorer window. The left pane is the physical structure of the hard drive. In this example, you are looking at Drive C. The left pane is also called the tree. If you are on a network, you could be looking at another drive. In the right pane, you see the contents of the currently selected Drive C, consisting of files and folders. The right pane looks exactly like the My Computer window. My Computer and Explorer use the same engine (program), but Explorer displays two panes and includes the hierarchical structure and My Computer displays only the right pane with no hierarchical structure.

4   Click **95book** in the **All Folders** pane. It may be necessary to double-click the drive on which the **95book** folder is located. If you cannot see the **95book** folder, scroll until you can. (*Hint:* Click the folder name, **95book**, not the plus or minus sign.)

 You are looking at the List view of folders and files in the right pane and the hierarchical structure in the left pane. Look in the drop-down list box. It now shows 95book as the *default folder*. The Contents pane also tells you that you are looking at Contents of 'C:\95book'.

5   Click **View**. Click **Options**.

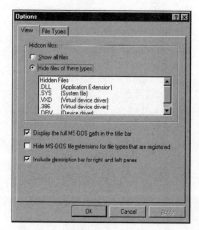

 You are looking at the Options dialog box. It has two option buttons and three check boxes. Again, it is similar to the Options

dialog box in My Computer. The settings that you set in My Computer are retained. The additional check box is Include description bar for right and left panes. The default is on. This choice is not available in the My Computer dialog box because there is only one pane, not two. If it is not on, set it on now.

Another difference between the two dialog boxes is that there are only two tabs in the Explorer dialog box (View and File Types), while there are three tabs in the My Computer dialog box (Folder, View, and File Types). If you want to change your browse options (Folder), you must use the options in My Computer.

6   Click **Cancel**.

7   Click the **Details** button on the toolbar.

8   Click **Apr.99** in the Contents pane.

 If you look for the sizes of the folders, you will see none shown. Unlike files, a folder is a container and has no specific size of its own. The file, Apr.99, appears to be 1 KB in size. But it seems that all the subsequent files are also 1 KB. Can all these files be the same size? It is possible, but unlikely. Explorer rounds off the size and shows it in kilobytes. If you want to know the actual size of a specific file, you need to look its properties.

9 Right-click **Apr.99**. On the pop-up menu, click **Properties**.

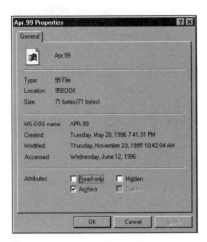

What's happening? Apr.99 is only 71 bytes in size. When files are small, Explorer rounds them off to 1 KB. In addition to the actual file size, the property sheet gives you full information about the file.

10 Click **Cancel**.

11 Press the letter **g**.

What's happening? You arrive at the first file that begins with the letter g. Pressing a letter on the keyboard will move you to the first file that begins with that letter. In this case, Glossary.wri is shown as being 8 KB.

12 Right-click **Glossary.wri**. Click **Properties**.

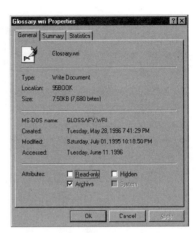

What's happening? The file is actually 7.5 KB, which Explorer rounded up to 8 KB.

13 Click **Cancel**.

14 Make sure **NumLock** is off. Press the **Home** key.

What's happening? Pressing the **Home** key is a quick way to move to the top of a document or window. If you look at the 95book All Folders pane (the left pane), you will see a **+** sign by the 95book folder. This indicates that there are folders beneath the current folder and that the 95book folder can be expanded.

15 Double-click the folder name, **95book** in the **All Folders** pane.

When you double-clicked the 95book folder, it expanded to show you the folders beneath it. The 95book folder now has a – sign in front of it. The minus sign serves two purposes. The first is to show you that the 95book folder can be collapsed, and the second is to indicate that there are no folders hiding beneath it. In the list of folders beneath 95book, three folders have plus signs, indicating that they also have subfolders.

16 Double-click the folder name, **Level-1**, in the tree pane.

Both the left and right panes have changed. The hierarchical tree shows that Level-1 has the Level-2 folder beneath it. Since Level-2 has a plus sign, it can be expanded. The right side of the pane shows that the Level-1 folder contains one file (Hello.txt) and one folder (Level-2).

17 Double-click the folder name, **Level-2**, in the hierarchical tree (left pane).

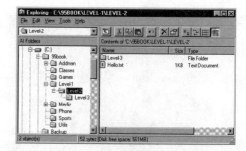

Both the left and right panes have changed. The hierarchical tree shows that Level-2 has the Level-3 folder beneath it. Since Level-3 has no plus sign, it cannot be expanded any further. The right pane shows that the Level-2 folder contains one file (Hello.txt) and one folder (Level-3).

18 Click the **Up One Level** button on the toolbar.

You moved to the parent of Level-2, which is Level-1. Thus, Level-2 is a child folder to Level-1 and a parent folder to Level-3. It is helpful to remember that a parent can have many children, but a child can have only one parent.

19 Click the **Up One Level** button on the toolbar.

What's happening? You moved to the parent of Level-1, which is 95book. Level-1 is a child folder to 95book, but a parent folder to the Level-2 folder. A folder can be a child to a folder, but have children of its own. This parent/child analogy shows the hierarchical nature of the directory tree. Notice that as you moved up the tree in the left pane, the right pane also changed to show the contents of the default (currently selected) folder.

20 Double-click the folder name, **Level-1**, in the left pane.

What's happening? By double-clicking, you collapsed all the children of Level-1.

21 Double-click the folder name, **95book**, in the left pane. Click the **List** button on the toolbar.

What's happening? You collapsed 95book to its highest level. The 95book folder is a child to the root directory. You also changed the view of the right pane to Explorer's default, List.

22 Press the ⊞ key on the numeric keypad.

What's happening? Pressing the ⊞ key on the numeric keypad is a keyboard shortcut for expanding the hierarchical tree. You can see all the branches to the 95book folder.

23 Press the ⊟ key on the numeric keypad.

 Pressing the $\boxed{-}$ key is a keyboard shortcut for collapsing a branch to its highest level.

24   Close **Explorer**.

6.4   Opening More than One Folder Window

One of the advantages of using a graphical interface to manage files and folders is that you can see more than one file and folder at a time. This allows you to compare the contents of different folders on the same disk drive or different disk drives, to analyze your organizational scheme, or to manipulate files and folders from one directory window to another. In Windows 95, one way to see more than one folder with its files is to launch multiple copies of Explorer. You can then tile or cascade the open windows.

6.5   Activity—Using Multiple Copies of Explorer

1   Click **Start**. Point to **Programs**. Click **Windows Explorer**.

2   Double-click **95book**. Double-click **Media** in the left pane.

3   Click **Movies** in the left pane.

 You are looking at the documents located in the Movies folder, which is under the Media folder, which is under the 95book folder, which is under the root of Drive C. An easier way to state that is to look at the path name. To describe that scenario, you would say that the path is C:\95BOOK\MEDIA\MOVIES. If you want to look at the files in the Book folder, you can open another copy of Explorer.

4   Click **Start**. Point to **Programs**. Click **Windows Explorer**.

5   Double-click **95book**. Double-click **Media** in the left pane.

6 Click **Books** in the left pane.

7 Right-click in an empty spot on the taskbar. Click **Tile Horizontally**.

  Now you can compare what files you have in the Books folder and what files you have in the Movies folder.

8 Right-click the taskbar. Click **Cascade**.

  Now your Explorer windows are cascaded, or stacked upon one another. You are not limited to opening two folder windows. You can keep adding copies of Explorer. However, this would mean that you were running several copies of a program. Each program takes up room in memory and uses system resources. If you do not have a lot of memory or system resources, you could reach a point where you were unable to open another program. You would get an out of memory warning. Out of memory messages can be confusing to you. You might have 32 MB of memory installed on your system and cannot understand how you could possibly be out of memory. Most often, you are not. A Windows 95 out of memory error can mean that you are out of system resources.

The term *system resources* does not refer exactly to how much memory you have installed on your computer system. System resources are what Windows 95 uses for critical system tasks, such as drawing the windows on the screen, using fonts, or running many applications. Windows 95 maintains 32-bit regions of memory, which are called *heaps*. Graphic device interfaces (GDIs) and user system components use these memory heaps. The amount of space available in the heaps is identified as a percentage of free system resources. Thus, your system could report that it was out of memory, even though the amount of free memory shown would still be high. Windows 95 tries to manage system resources effectively so this does not occur. You can check what system resources you have left.

9   Click **Help** on the **Explorer** menu bar. Click **About Windows 95**.

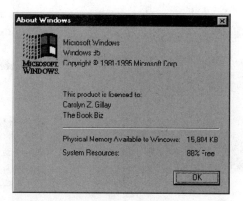

 In this example, 15,804 KB (referred to as 16 MB) of physical memory is installed on this system. Eighty-eight percent of system resources is free. Remember, this percentage is not referring to the 16 KB of physical memory, but the resources that Windows 95 needs. With this amount of free resources, you should have no problem running programs or opening more windows. If you drop to 50 percent or less of system resources, you could receive an out of memory message. You would then have to close programs or open windows to reduce the load on the system resources.

10   Click **OK**.

11   Close all the open **Explorer** windows.

6.6   Logical and Physical Views

Windows 95 presents a logical rather than a physical view of your computer. The desktop is a *logical view* of your computer system. On the desktop are objects that you need, represented by icons. This logical view adheres to the docucentric paradigm. As the user, you are interested in your documents, not the programs that created them. But without the program, you cannot create, edit, or view a document. So, Windows 95 places My Computer (and Network Neighborhood if you are on a network) on the desktop.

My Computer is another example of a logical view of your computer system. My Computer shows what drives you have and what folders and files are on those drives by displaying them as document or program icons. Explorer, for the most part, affords a *physical view* of what files and folders are on your system and where they are located. If you opened My Computer, double-clicked the 95book folder, and double-clicked the Media folder, you would see the files and folders. If you opened Explorer, 95book, and Media, you would see the hierarchical structure and the path name (C:\95book\Media). Explorer provides a map to the physical locations of folders and files.

To understand the difference between a physical and logical view of objects, consider the way you use the telephone. You know that there are physical telephone lines that connect your phone with all the other telephones in the world. When you want to call your mother, though, you simply dial the number. You probably realize that there is not just one telephone line that directly connects your phone to your mother's phone, but you do not really care. You are using the telephone logically.

If, however, your telephone does not work or you want to add another telephone line, you have to call the telephone repair person. When the telephone repair person arrives at your home, he needs a map that shows where the telephone line comes into your house and where the telephone line goes. He is actually going to track the telephone wires and may need the map of telephone lines for your neighborhood or your city to do this. This is the physical view of your telephone.

Both logical and physical views are important and necessary, and for this reason Windows 95 gives you the logical view, My Computer, and the physical view, Explorer. The view you use depends on what task you are trying to accomplish. But these view are not absolute. Although Explorer, for the most part, shows you the physical view of your computer and its resources, it also displays a logical view. See Figure 6.3.

Figure 6.3   Explorer in a Logical View

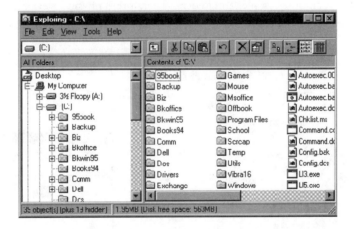

This hierarchical view shows the Desktop folder at the top of the hierarchy, with My Computer branching off, and the drive branching off from there. In reality, each drive is a separate physical device with its own hierarchical structure. The Desktop folder, shown at the top of the hierarchy, is physically located under the Windows folder. See Figure 6.4.

Figure 6.4 Explorer in a Physical View

When you want to accomplish certain tasks, you cannot use a logical view. When you want to change the Start menu, add something to pop-up menu, or copy or move files and folders, you must know the physical location of files and folders. Therefore, a physical view is appropriate for making these changes.

6.7   Activity—Comparing My Computer and Explorer

1   Double-click **My Computer**.

2   Click **View**. Point to **Arrange Icons**.

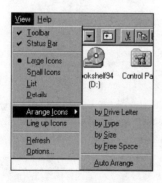

> **What's happening?**   Since you are using the logical view to look at your computer system, you have different choices in arrangement than you did when you were arranging files and folders. You can now arrange your window by Drive Letter, by Type, by Size, or by Free Space.

3   Click **by Type**.

> **What's happening?**   Your display will be different, depending on the devices on your system. If your arrangement did not change on your system, it was already arranged by Type. Any drive attached externally to your system

is listed first (Floppy Drive A and CD-ROM Drive D). In this example, the CD-ROM drive has a label, Bookshelf94. Whenever you see a label, you know that there is a CD-ROM disc in the CD-ROM drive. On this system, there is no external Drive B, but drive letter B is always reserved for the future addition of a floppy drive. Listed next are any internal hard drives. If you had more than one internal hard drive, they would all be listed here. The folders come last.

4　Click **View**. Point to **Arrange Icons**. Click **by Drive Letter**.

What's happening?　Now the window is arranged by drive letters in alphabetical order, followed by the folders.

5　Click **View**. Click **Options**. Click the **Folder** tab. Set **Browse folders using a separate window for each folder**. Click **OK**.

6　Double-click the **Drive C** icon. If necessary, move the **Drive C** window so you can see both the **My Computer** window and the **C:** window.

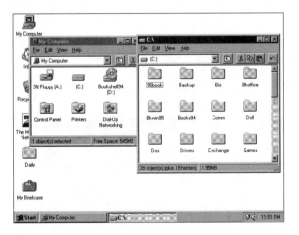

What's happening?　Notice that unlike Explorer, you do not see the drive's hierarchical structure in this window. You view only the contents side, or right pane, of Explorer. The logical view is an easy way to locate a file or folder.

7 Double-click the **95book** folder. If you are not in large icon view, click **View**. Click **Large Icons**. If necessary, move the **95book** window so that you can see all three open windows.

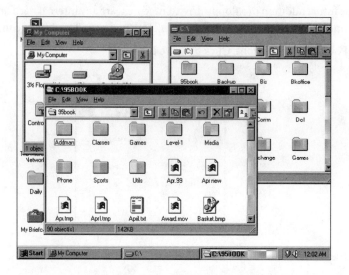

 When you opened the window for the 95book folder, the Drive C window and the My Computer window did not close, although the hierarchy shows that the 95book window is a child to the Drive C. The only way to know that is by looking at the title bar. The logical view works very well, though. If you wanted to open a document that you kept in the 95book folder, you could do so easily. The hierarchical structure is not important to you in this case.

8 Hold the [Shift] key and click the **Close** button on the **95book** window.

9 Double-click **My Computer**. Click **View**. Click **Options**. Set **Browse folders by using a single window that changes as you open each folder**. Click **OK**.

10 Double-click the **Drive C** icon. Double-click the **95book** folder.

 Only the 95book window is open. Notice that the logical view is easy to use when you want to open a file or folder.

11   Close the **95book** window.

12   Double-click **My Computer**.

13   Click the **Drive C** icon.

14   Hold the **Shift** key. Double-click the **Drive C** icon.

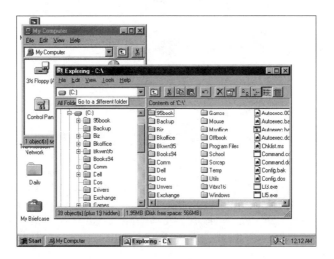

 The My Computer window stayed open, and the Drive C window opened Explorer. Whenever you hold the **Shift** key and double-click a drive icon in My Computer, you open Explorer.

15   Close all open windows.

16   Click on the desktop to deselect **My Computer**.

17   Hold the **Shift** key and double-click **My Computer**.

 Indeed, you opened Explorer, not My Computer. When you look at this window, it appears as if the Desktop folder is at the top of the hierarchical tree, with My Computer as its child and Drive C as a child to My Computer. This logical view of your system is misleading. In reality, the desktop is a subfolder (directory) in the folder (directory) that holds the Windows 95 program files. My Computer is more like a program. Somewhat analogous to File Manager in Windows 3.1, it is the window that shows you the devices and system folders on your system.

18   Click **Desktop**.

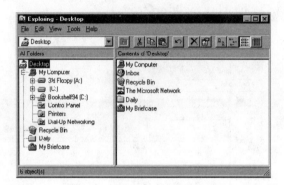

 The left pane is the hierarchical structure. You see the Recycle Bin, My Briefcase, and Daily icons. These icons represent folders that are located under the root of C. Only Daily (created by this computer) has a folder icon. The Recycle Bin and My Briefcase do not have folder icons, but they are folders. The right pane is a logical view of the Desktop folder and displays the objects located on your desktop. You want the physical view of the Desktop folder that will show you the files located there.

19   Double-click the **Drive C** icon. Press **w**.

 You should be at, or near, the Windows folder. It may be called Windows, Win95, Windows 95, or a similar name. This text will use Windows to refer to the folder that holds the Windows 95 programs. You will use whatever folder name your system uses for the Windows folder.

20 Double-click on the **Windows** folder (or whatever your Windows folder is called).

 The left pane shows all the files and folders that make up Windows 95. The Desktop folder does not appear to be here, however.

21 Click **View**. Click **Options**. In the **View** property sheet, click **Show all files**. Click **OK**.

 The Desktop is a hidden directory. By choosing Show all files, you will see anything that was hidden. The Desktop folder, under the Windows folder, has a ⊞ sign, so it may be expanded.

22 Double-click the **Desktop** folder in the left pane (tree).

  Any document, folder, or program that you or the system placed on the desktop appears. Note that icons such as My Computer or MSN do not appear. My Computer is a virtual container that contains everything about your computer system. Anything that is *virtual* is not real, but the computer representation of what is real. Thus, if you right-click My Computer and click Properties, you are taken to the System Properties property sheets. The System property sheets are real and allow you to view and manipulate every device on your system. If you have MSN installed, it is a program that typically is kept in the Windows\System directory. If you are signed up with MSN or a service like CompuServe or America Online, double-clicking the MSN icon will connect you to the Microsoft Network.

23 Double-click the **Desktop** folder in the tree to collapse it to its highest level.

24 Double-click the **Start Menu** folder in the left pane.

  You see the Programs folder on the Start menu.

25 Double-click the **Programs** folder in the left pane.

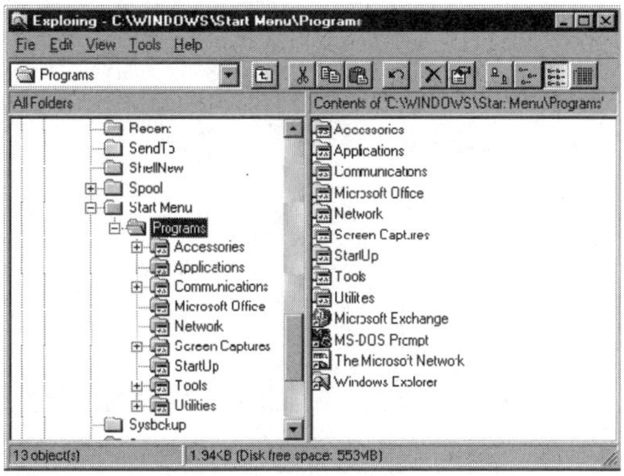

What's happening? If you look at the left pane, any folders on the Start menu are listed here. If you look at the right pane, programs on the Start menu are listed as well as the folders. Remember, the left pane shows the hierarchical structure of a folder and the right pane shows its contents.

26 Double-click the **Accessories** folder on the tree.

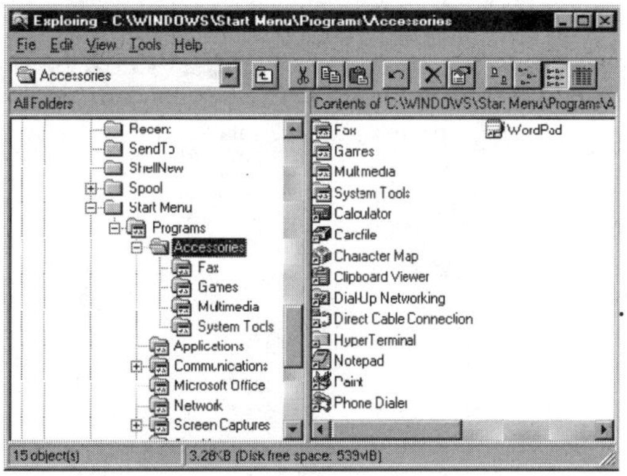

What's happening? If you look at the left pane, all folders on the Accessories menu are listed here. If you look at the right pane, programs on the Accessories menu are listed as well as the folders. Notice that the programs in the right pane are the shortcuts to the program files, not the actual program files.

27 Click the **Games** folder.

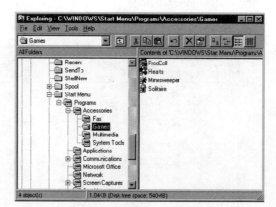

 These are the games you see when you click the Start button, then point at Programs, then Accessories, then Games. All of these objects in the Games folder are shortcuts to the program files.

28 On the tree, double-click **Accessories**. Double-click **Programs**. Double-click **Start Menu**. Double-click **Windows**.

You have collapsed the Windows folder to its highest level.

29 Double-click the **Recycle Bin**.

 The Recycle Bin is a folder on the tree side under the root of C:. In this example, you can see in the right pane that there is one file in the Recycle Bin directory that is ready to be retrieved or deleted. Your pane may be empty or have more files in it.

30 Click **View**. Click **Options**. Click the **View** tab. Click **Hide files of these types:**. Click **OK**.

31 Close the **Explorer** window.

 You have reset the default settings and returned to the desktop.

6.8   Manipulating Windows

Now that you know where to locate the physical files and folders, you can manipulate items. You can add programs, files, and folders to the Start menu or to any of the program folders, or you can remove programs, files, and folders from these areas. You may also add items to or delete items from pop-up menus.

6.9   Activity—Using My Computer and Explorer To Add a Printer to a Menu

1 Right-click the **Start** button.

 When you right-click the Start button, you open a shortcut menu that allows you to perform three critical tasks: you can open a program, open Explorer, or open the Find dialog box.

2   Click **Explore**.

You are taken to Explorer. But instead of being at the top of the hierarchy, you are in the current default drive and directory, which is Windows. You could have been taken elsewhere. Some systems have users with separate identities. In that case, you would have arrived at the Start menu of the user who is logged in. Whenever this happens, the Start menu is in a directory called Profiles. See Figure 6.5.

Figure 6.5 A System with Profiles

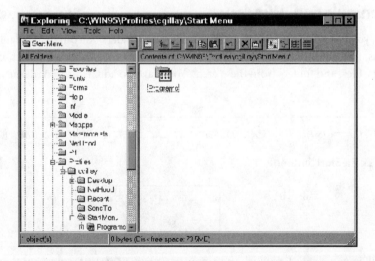

Each user has a profile. In this example, the user is cgillay. If you do not have separate logins for different users, you will not see this menu. The advantage to *user profiles* is that each user can customize his or her system, Start menu, and so forth. Windows 95 will keep track of each user's preferences. If you have a Profiles folder on the tree side, double-click it to collapse it to its highest level.

3 Scroll up the tree side until you locate the **95book** folder. Double-click the **95book** folder.

4 Right-click **April.txt** in the Contents (right) pane. Point to **Send To**.

 You have selected a file. You may send (copy) a file to a floppy disk, an electronic mail program, a fax machine, a mailbox, or My Briefcase. The choices that appear on this menu depend on what programs have been installed on the system. You would like to be able to send a file to the printer, but that choice is not listed here. You want to add a printer shortcut to this menu. You do this by locating the Send To directory and dragging the printer shortcut to this folder.

5 On the tree side, double-click **95book** to collapse it to its highest level.

6 Double-click the **Windows** folder.

7 Locate the **SendTo** folder under the **Windows** folder. On the tree side, click the **SendTo** folder.

 You can see all the objects in the SendTo folder on the contents side. The one that is missing is the printer shortcut.

8 You may need to move the **Explorer** window to see the **My Computer** icon on the desktop. On the desktop, double-click **My Computer**. Double-click the **Printers** folder.

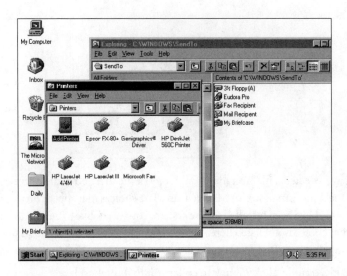

 You see the printers your system.

9 Right-drag your default printer into the **SendTo** window of **Explorer**. Release the right mouse button.

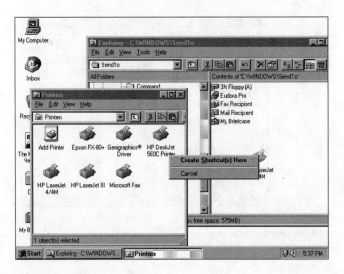

 Because you right-dragged and dropped, you are asked if you want to create a shortcut.

10 Click **Create Shortcut(s) Here**.

11 Close the **Printers** folder. Click the **Explorer** window to make it active.

 You now have a shortcut to your printer in the SendTo folder.

12 On the tree side, double-click the **Windows** folder to collapse it to its highest level.

13 On the tree side of the **Explorer** window, scroll until you see the **95book** folder. Double-click it.

14 In the Contents pane, right-click **Apr.txt**. Point to **Send To**.

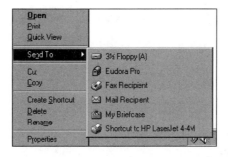

 You have added a shortcut to the Send To menu. By right-clicking, you can print your document. Although you added a shortcut to a device in this case, you can add shortcuts to another drive, a folder, or wherever you might want to send an item. The one tricky task is placing a shortcut to a folder on the Send To menu. If you later used this shortcut to send a file to the folder, you would be moving it from one location to another. You can also remove items from the Send To menu by reversing the process you followed when you added the printer shortcut.

15 On the tree side, locate the **Windows** folder. Double-click the **Windows** folder.

16 Locate and click the **SendTo** folder.

 You see the printer shortcut object.

17 Drag the **Printer** shortcut and drop it on the **Recycle Bin** on the desktop.

 You have eliminated the printer shortcut. By performing this task, you have also removed it from the Send To menu.

18 On the tree, double-click the **Windows** folder to collapse it to its highest level.

19 On the tree, scroll up until you locate the **95book** folder. On the tree, click the **95book** folder.

20 Right-click **April.txt**. Point to **Send To**.

What's happening?   You have removed the printer from the Send To menu.

21   Double-click **95book** folder to collapse to its highest level.

22   Close **Explorer**. Close any open windows.

What's happening?   You have returned to the desktop.

6.10 Managing Disks with Explorer

You have been using Explorer and My Computer to search for files, look at different details about files and folders, and manipulate folders. As you have seen, you may use either Explorer or My Computer to accomplish tasks. The tool you use will be the one that works best for you. Both My Computer and Explorer let you perform operating system functions, such as copying floppy disks and preparing a disk for use. Although you perform file-related tasks most often, you still need to know how to perform disk-related tasks.

6.11 Copying Floppy Disks

Although you will work primarily on and with the hard disk, this does not mean you never use the floppy disk drive and floppy disks. One of the purposes of the floppy disk drive is to load (copy) application program files from the floppy disks that come with application software. Floppy disk drives and floppy disks have another important functions, such as making a disk copy. You can make backup copies of your application disks or any data disks you create. Often, computer software manufacturers will instruct you to make copies of the disks that you purchase and then to install from the copies. This protects you; if something happens to the original disk, you have another copy. If you purchased your programs on a CD-ROM, you will not be able to make a copy right now. As CD-ROM technology advances and prices come down, however, you will be able to make copies of CD-ROM discs as well as floppy disks.

You can copy floppy disks, not hard disks. You will learn how to copy files from a hard disk to a floppy disk, but this is not the same as copying the actual disk. When you copy one floppy disk to another floppy disk, the disk media must be identical. For instance, if you have a 3½-inch high-density disk, you must have a blank 3½-inch high-density disk. You cannot copy a 5¼-inch disk to a 3½-inch disk. You can copy the files from one disk media type to another, but you must copy the files individually, not as an entire disk.

You will make a copy of the Activities disk to practice backing up a floppy disk. You could copy the folders and files from the hard disk to a floppy disk, but this would take much longer than making a disk copy.

6.12 Activity—Making a Copy of the Activities Disk

1 Place the Activities disk that came with the text in Drive A.

2 Click **Start**. Point to **Programs**. Click **Windows Explorer**. If you cannot see the **Drive A** icon, scroll until you can. Click the **Drive A** icon.

 The left All Folders pane shows you the floppy disk drives on your computer system. The right Contents pane shows you the files and folders that are located in the disk's root directory in drive A.

3 Right-click the **Drive A** icon.

 The pop-up menu appears listing the tasks you can accomplish with this object—the disk in Drive A. Explore is the current choice. In this case, Explore means showing you what files and folders are on the disk in Drive A. If you select Open, you will open a Drive A window. If you are on a network, you will see another choice, Sharing. Sharing allows you to determine whether or not you will allow anyone else access to your files and folders.

4   Click **Open**.

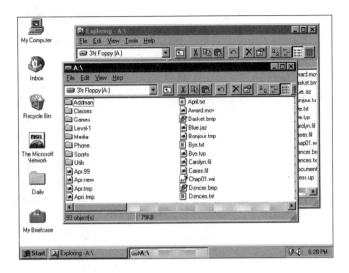

What's
happening? This window is the same display you would have gotten if you had double-clicked My Computer and then double-clicked the Drive A icon.

5   Close this window. Right-click the **Drive A** icon in the tree. Click **Properties**.

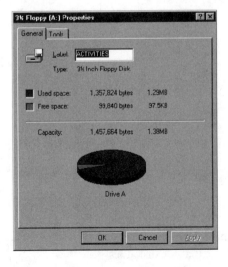

What's
happening? If you had double-clicked My Computer, right-clicked the Drive A icon, and chosen Properties, you would have seen the same property sheet. You are looking at the properties of the disk in Drive A. Windows 95 gives you a graphical view of how much free space there is on a drive. As you can see, there is very little free space on this disk for files and folders. Notice that Label is high-

lighted. This is an internal rather than an external label that you place on a disk. An internal label helps you identify what is on a disk. This property sheet also tells you that this is a 3½-inch disk. When you see a capacity of 1,457,664 bytes, you know that this is a high-density disk. There are two tabs on the top of this property sheet, General and Tools. The Tools include the abilities to back up your disk and improve its performance. You will learn more about the Tools later. If you are on a network, you will also see the Sharing tab. If you installed DriveSpace, you will see the Compression tab. Compression allows you to double the disk's storage space.

6   Click the **Cancel** button.

7   Right-click the **Drive C** icon. Click **Properties**.

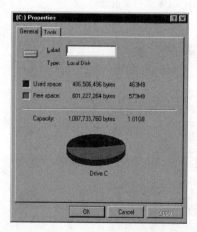

 You are looking at the amount of space available on the hard drive. This disk is about half full. Note that the disk does not have a label.

8   Click **Cancel**.

9   Right-click the **Drive A** icon. Click **Copy Disk**.

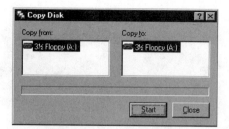

 You have opened the Copy Disk dialog box. Both the Copy from and the Copy to panes indicate Drive A as the default source and destination. If Drive A and Drive B were both the same type of disk, you could disk-copy from Drive A to Drive B. The disk you want to copy is in Drive A, so you can begin.

10   Click **Start**.

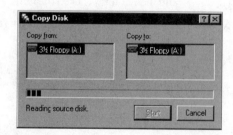

 At the bottom of the dialog box, you see the progress bar indicator, also known as a *progress bar control*. A progress indicator usually appears when you are doing an operation that can be lengthy. It gives you some idea where you are in the task. You also see the message, Reading source disk. When you copy a disk, the contents of the disk are being copied to RAM (memory), which is called reading. When the task is complete, you see the following informational message box:

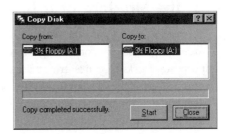

What's happening? This message says you need to remove your original disk and insert the disk to which you want the information copied. When you copy a disk, whatever was on the destination disk will be overwritten with the information in memory.

11　Use a new disk or a disk whose information you no longer want. If neither of these options is suitable, you may use the disk you formatted in Chapter 2 labeled Data disk.

12　Remove the Activities disk from Drive A and place the Data disk in Drive A. Click **OK**.

What's happening? What was in RAM (memory) is being copied, or written, to the disk in Drive A. When the copy is complete, you see the following message in the Copy Disk dialog box:

What's happening? The message in the dialog box, Copy completed successfully, states that your operation succeeded.

13　Click **Close**.

14　Right-click the **Drive A** icon. Click **Open**.

What's happening? The contents of this disk are identical to those of the Activities disk. You now have a copy of the disk as well as the original disk.

15　Close all open windows.

What's happening? You have returned to the desktop.

6.13　Preparing a Disk

You have seen how to use disk-copy. In addition to doing this, you also want to be able to copy certain files and folders from a floppy disk, hard disk, or network disk to other floppy disks. To do so, a disk must be prepared, or formatted. You formatted a floppy disk in Chapter 2. As you saw, the process of formatting a disk is simple. Now you are going to learn what formatting actually does.

6.14 The Structure of a Disk

Formatting a disk consists of two parts: *low-level* or *physical formatting* and *high-level* or *logical formatting*. Low-level formatting creates and sequentially numbers tracks and sectors for identification purposes. *Tracks* are concentric circles on a disk. Each track is divided into smaller units called sectors. A *sector*, which is the smallest unit on a disk, is always 512 bytes. The number of tracks and sectors varies depending on the type of disk. When data needs to be written to or read from the disk, the identification number of the tracks and sector tells the read/write head where to position itself. This process accounts for every space on the disk. It is similar to assigning every house a unique address so that it can be instantly identifiable. However, even after a disk is physically prepared to hold data, it is not ready for use. In the second part of formatting, high-level or logical formatting, Windows 95 builds the disk's structure so it can keep track of where files are located. When you format a floppy disk, both the physical and logical formatting process occur.

A hard disk needs only logical formatting. The low-level formatting of a hard disk usually is done in the manufacturing process or by the computer system vendor. Most commonly, when you purchase a computer system, the high-level and low-level formatting of the hard disk is done.

Logical formatting determines how Windows 95 uses disks, both hard and floppy. The logical format process builds a way for Windows 95 to manage files on a disk so that files can be saved and retrieved easily. You accomplish this process by using the Format command. When you execute the Format command, it first checks for any bad spots on the disk. If bad spots are found, they are marked as unusable. Then three critical elements are created: the boot record, the file allocation table, and the root directory. These elements occupy the first portion of the disk and only take up 1 to 2 percent of the disk space. The remainder of the disk is used for file storage. See Figure 6.6.

Figure 6.6   Logical Structure of a Disk

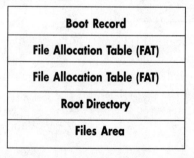

The order of the sections is always the same. The boot record, two copies of the FAT, and the root directory table are always located in the first sectors. These elements control how the files are stored on a disk and how Windows 95 saves and retrieves files. The data sectors are where the data or files are actually stored.

6.14.1   Boot Record

The first part of a disk is the ***boot record.*** The boot record contains a short program, called the bootstrap loader, that begins loading Windows 95, or copying the necessary system files, from the disk into memory. If the disk the system is trying to boot from is not a system disk, you see a message:

Non-System disk or disk error

Replace the disk and press any key when ready

Even if a disk is not a system disk (one capable of booting the system), it still has a boot record. This boot record contains information about the physical characteristics of the disk: the number of tracks per disk, the number of bytes per sector, the number of sectors per track, which version of the operating system was used to format the disk, the size of the FAT and the root directory, the volume serial number, and so forth. This allows Windows 95 to identify the type of disk, distinguishing between a hard disk, a 720 KB floppy disk, and so on.

6.14.2   File Allocation Table (FAT)

Windows 95 needs to monitor the status of all of a disk's data sectors so it can answer critical questions. Does a sector already have information in it, or is it damaged? In either case, it cannot be used. Is it an empty sector, available for data storage? Since there can be so many sectors on a disk, particularly on a hard disk, it would be too time-consuming for Windows 95 to manage them one sector at a time. Instead, it combines one or more sectors into logical units called ***clusters***. When Windows 95 writes a file to a disk, it copies the file's contents to unused clusters in the data sectors. The smallest unit that Windows 95 works with when reading or writing to disk is a cluster, also referred to as an ***allocation unit***, since this unit allocates disk space. To be able to read and write files to a disk, Windows 95 tracks the location in the ***file allocation table (FAT)***. A map of the disk's data clusters, the FAT is made up of entries that correspond to every cluster on the disk. The number of clusters varies from one type of disk to another. Table 6.1 indicates the cluster size for common disk types.

Table 6.1 Common Cluster Size

Disk	Cluster Size
3½-inch 2.88 MB disk	2 sectors make a cluster (1024 bytes)
3½-inch 1.44 MB disk	1 sector makes a cluster (512 bytes)
3½-inch 720 KB disk	2 sectors make a cluster (1024 bytes)
5.¼-inch 1.2 MB disk	1 sector makes a cluster (512 bytes)
5.¼-inch 360 KB disk	2 sectors make a cluster (1024 bytes)
Hard disk—varies	4 sectors make a cluster (2048 bytes) 8 sectors make a cluster (4096 bytes) 16 sectors make a cluster (8192 bytes)

Since the smallest unit Windows 95 will deal with is a cluster, a file of only 100 bytes would occupy a full cluster, or 8192 bytes of storage space, on a hard disk with sixteen sectors per cluster. As you can imagine, a data file will hardly ever be exactly one cluster in size. Nor will it necessarily be an even number. In order to manage the data, each entry in the FAT is a number indicating the cluster's status. A 0 in the FAT means the cluster is empty and available for use. Certain numbers indicate that a cluster is reserved or bad and should not be used. Any other number indicates that a cluster is in use.

6.14.3   Root Directory

The *root directory* is a table that records information about each file on the disk. When you use Explorer or My Computer, the information displayed on the screen comes from this root directory table.

In order to make Windows 95 compatible with older Windows and DOS programs, some changes had to be made in the root directory table. The DOS directory structure only recognizes the 8.3 file name. Windows 95 needed to allow long file names while still letting users use DOS or Windows 3.1 or 3.11 programs with the 8.3 file name limitation. The DOS root directory stores information in a table about every file on a disk and includes the file name, the file extension, the size of the file in bytes, the date and time the file was last modified, and the file attributes. The Windows 95 root directory table still includes this information, but it also uses previously unused spots in the table, particularly the file attributes. In addition to the file attributes you have learned about, Windows 95 uses a special combination of attributes to signal that an entry is the first of a series of directory entries. This allows a series of directory entries to be chained together so that long file names can be used.

To maintain compatibility with DOS or Windows 3.1 or 3.11 programs, Windows 95 gives every file name with both a long file name and a short file name. The short file name is based on the long file name and is stored in the first directory entry using the DOS 8.3 name.

Another critical entry in the root directory table is the starting cluster number. This number indicates which cluster holds the first portion of the file, or the first FAT address. In this way, the root directory tells Window 95 what is on the disk, and the FAT tells Windows 95 where data is on the disk.

6.14.4   The Fat and the Root Directory

Imagine a book on computers with a table of contents. Like the root directory, the table of contents tells you what is in the book. One chapter could be called *The Hard Disk*, with page number 30 following the chapter title. This page number is the "pointer" (or starting page) to where you must go to find the information about the hard disk. The page number is similar to the FAT.

You must turn to page 30 to begin reading about the hard disk. However, the information about the hard disk is not located only on page 30. You must read page 31, then page 32, and so on, until you have all the information about the hard disk. The pages are "linked," or have a trail. If a book were like a disk, the table of contents (root directory) would be followed by a chart (the FAT) instructing you to begin on page 30, then go to page 31, then to page 32, and so on. The number in the FAT is a pointer to the next cluster that holds data in the file, enabling the system to follow the trail of a file longer than one cluster. A special entry in the FAT, called an *EOF* (*end of file*) marker, indicates that there is no more data in the file. See Figure 6.7.

Figure 6.7   The Root Directory and the FAT

Root Directory

Description			
File name	Myfile	Your	This
File extension	Txt	File	One
Date	11/23/95	11/25/95	12/13/95
Time	1:45 A.M.	2:13 P.M.	3:11 P.M.
Other info			
Starting cluster number	1	5	9

FAT

Clusters	Pointers	Data
1	2	Myfile.txt
2	3	Myfile.txt
3	4	Myfile.txt
4	EOF	Myfile.txt
5	6	Your.fil
6	7	Your.fil
7	EOF	Your.fil
8	9	This.one
9	10	This.one
10	EOF	This.one
11	0	
12	0	

The FAT works in conjunction with the root directory table. The FAT can occupy as many sectors as it needs to map out the disk.

6.14.5   Data Portion or Files Area

The rest of the disk, which is the largest part, is used for storing files or data. As far as Windows 95 is concerned, all files, programs, and data are chains of bytes laid out in sequence. Space is allocated to files on an as-needed basis, one cluster at a time. When a file is written to a disk, Windows 95 begins writing to the first available cluster. It writes in adjacent, or *contiguous*, clusters if possible, but if any adjacent sectors are already in use (allocated by FAT), Windows 95 skips to the next available (unallocated) space. Thus, a file can be *noncontiguous*, or physically scattered over the disk.

6.14.6 Understanding the FAT and the Root Directory Table

To understand how the root directory table and the FAT work, imagine that you want to create a file called Myfile.txt, which will occupy three clusters on a disk. Assume that clusters 3, 4, and 6 are free. The first thing Windows 95 does is create an entry in the root directory table and fill in the file information (file name, file extension, date, time, etc.). In the first free cluster, Windows 95 places the number 3 as the starting cluster number in the root directory table. Windows 95 knows it will need three clusters and must link or chain them. It does this by placing a 4 (pointer) in the number 3 cluster, pointing to the next available cluster. When it gets to cluster 4, it places a 6 (another pointer) pointing to the next available cluster. When the FAT gets to cluster 6, it places an end of file marker, a "note" indicating that the file ends here.

To use an analogy, imagine a self-storage facility comprised of storage bins that hold things (data). The managers of the self-storage facility do not care what is in the bins. They only have to know how many bins there are, where they are located, and if anything is in them. The managers have a map of all the numbered storage bins (FAT) and a list (root directory) of assigned or unassigned bins. If a new customer walks in and wants to rent space (write a file to disk), the managers look in the list (directory) to see if there are any available slots. If there are, they can assign a space to the newcomer.

If the managers have rented out the space, they can retrieve the things in the bins for the customer. A customer named Elvira Gonzales walks in. Elvira says that she wants all the boxes stored for Gonzales. The managers look up Gonzales in the list (directory) to be sure that her boxes have been stored there. They find the name Gonzales, so they know that Elvira has rented at least one bin. Next to her name, the directory instructs them to go to the map (FAT), starting with bin 3. After consulting the map, (FAT), the managers see that storage bin 3 is linked to storage bin 4, which is linked to storage bin 6. Storage bin 6 has no links. Now the managers know that Gonzales has bins 3, 4, and 6, and can send someone (the operating system will rotate the disk) to bins 3, 4, and 6 to retrieve her boxes (data). To look at this process graphically, see Figure 6.8.

Figure 6.8 Storing Files

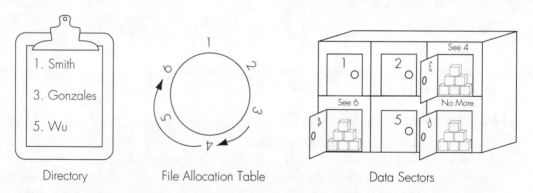

Directory   File Allocation Table   Data Sectors

This analogy gives you some of the basic information you need in order to understand the structure of a disk. Now when you format a disk, you know what is happening.

6.15 Activity—Formatting a Disk

1 Place the disk labeled Data disk in Drive A.

2 Click **Start**. Point to **Programs**. Click **Windows Explorer**. Click the **Drive A** icon.

You do not need the information on this disk any more.

3 Right-click the **Drive A** icon. Click **Format**.

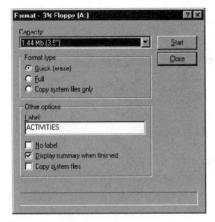

 The Format dialog box appears. The media type is highlighted. The default media type for this disk drive is a 1.44- MB 3½-inch disk. You also have three option buttons in this dialog box: Quick (erase), which is the default choice, Full, and Copy system files only. The Quick format choice can only be used on a disk that has already been formatted. It is "quick" because the formatting process erases the record of the file from the root directory table and the FAT. The data on the floppy disk is still there and can be recovered if you immediately realize you have formatted the wrong disk. The minute you write data to the disk, however, you cannot unformat it. The Full format choice is an unconditional format, which means no data can be recovered. This process not only initializes the root directory table and the FAT, but overwrites everything in the files area of the disk so that there is no data on the disk.

When you choose Copy system files, you are able to copy system files to a disk that is already formatted without erasing any other files already on the disk. If something goes wrong with your hard drive and you cannot boot, you have no way to see if you can fix any of the problems. If you make a bootable floppy disk with the proper system files on it, you can always boot from Drive A should an emergency arise. This choice also allows you to copy hidden system files.

The Label text box has Activities in it. This is the electronic label that lets you quickly identify what is on the disk. You may change this label or have no label. The first check box gives you the choice of No Label. In addition, you can display summary information about the disk you format.

4 Click the **Start** button.

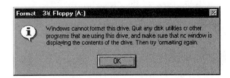

 You get a message telling you that you cannot format this drive. Since the Drive A window is open, you cannot get rid of the information on it.

5 Click **OK**. Click **Cancel** for the **Format** dialog box. Click the **Drive C** drive icon in the **Exploring** window.

6 Right-click the **Drive A** icon. Be sure the **Quick (erase)** option button is set.

7 Replace **Activities** with **Data** disk.

8   Click **Format**. Click the **Start** command button.

 As you saw, Quick format was quick. The message box tells you how many bytes were available and formatted (1,457,664 bytes), that no bytes were used for system files, and that there are no bad sectors on this disk. It also tells you that a cluster on a 3½-inch disk is one sector (512 bytes in each allocation unit). If you multiplied the total number of allocation units times the number of bytes in each sector (2847 × 512), you would have 1,457,664 bytes. This tells you how much space you have on the disk.

The serial number identifies each disk uniquely. If you remove a floppy disk during some procedure, Windows 95 knows that you replaced it and will ask for the correct disk.

9   Click **Close**. Click **Close** again.

10   Close all open windows.

 The disk has been formatted. There no longer are any files on it. You have returned to the desktop.

Chapter Summary

In this chapter, you learned more details about the hierarchical structure of folders and files. You found that you can identify the location of a file by its path. You found that My Computer presents a logical view of your system and Explorer presents both a logical and a physical view. You learned that the difference between the two is that My Computer opens only one pane, the Contents side, whereas Explorer presents two panes, the hierarchical as well as the Contents pane.

You will discover that when you want to accomplish tasks such as adding an item to a menu, you need to know the physical location of a file or folder in order to make changes.

You found that copying a disk requires the two disks to be identical media types, and that when you format a disk, you are establishing the way Windows 95 manages the storage and retrieval of files and folders on that disk. You found that the directory tells Windows 95 what files and folders are on a disk, whereas the FAT tells Windows 95 where the files and folders are located. The majority of the disk is comprised of sectors where the data is stored, but the directory and FAT allow Windows 95 to locate what you need.

Key Terms

All Folders pane	High-level formatting	Sector
Allocation unit	Logical view	Split bar
Boot record	Logical formatting	System resources
Clusters	Low-level formatting	Tracks
Contiguous	Noncontiguous	User profiles
Default folder	Physical formatting	Virtual
EOF (end of file)	Physical view	
File allocation table (FAT)	Progress bar control	
Heaps	Root directory	

Discussion Questions

1. Explain the purpose and function of the root directory.
2. Explain the purpose and function of a path.
3. Compare and contrast the left and right panes of an Explorer window.
4. When you are looking at an All Folders hierarchical tree, why is the size of the folder not given?
5. What is the purpose and function of the ✚ key on the numeric keypad when in Explorer?
6. Explain the purpose and function of system resources.
7. Compare and contrast the physical and logical views of objects.
8. How are My Computer and Explorer similar?
9. What is one advantage of using Explorer over My Computer?
10. Why must you use the physical view rather then the logical view to change items on the Start menu?
11. The desktop is a hidden directory; how can you display this directory?
12. What purpose does a user profile serve?
13. List and explain two uses of floppy disks.
14. Explain the purpose and function of low-level (physical) formatting.
15. Explain the purpose and function of high-level (logical) formatting.
16. Explain the purpose and function of the boot record.
17. Explain the purpose and function of the FAT.
18. Explain the purpose and function of the root directory.
19. Explain the purpose and function of clusters.
20. What kinds of information does Windows 95 track in the root directory table? the FAT?

True/False Questions

For each question, circle the letter T if the statement is true or the letter F if the statement is false.

T F 1. System resources refers to how much memory has been installed on the computer.

T F 2. Explorer presents objects in a physical rather than a logical fashion.

T F 3. Every hierarchical tree begins with the root directory.

T F 4. If you want to change your browse options, you must use the View/Options in My Computer.

T F 5. Clusters are made up of one or more sectors.

Completion Questions

Write the correct answer in the blank space provided.

6. When using Explorer, the left pane displays the _____ structure of a disk.
7. If you hold the [**Shift**] key and double-click My Computer, you will open _____.
8. To know the actual size of a specific file, you should view the _____ of the file.
9. When copying floppy disks, both disks must be the _____ media type.
10. The _____ records information about each file, such as its name and size.

Multiple Choice Questions

Circle the letter of the correct answer for each question.

11. When using My Computer, you double-click on the Next folder. Inside the Next folder is the One folder.
    a. Next is the child of One.
    b. One is the child of Next.
    c. One is the parent of Next.
    d. none of the above

12. One advantage of opening more than one copy of Explorer is that you may
    a. compare the contents of two folders.
    b. minimize the use of system resources.
    c. both a and b

13. When you first open Explorer, it shows the desktop at the top of the hierarchy because
    a. the desktop is the top of the hierarchy.
    b. the desktop is the most important folder in the tree.
    c. Explorer is presenting a logical view of your system.
    d. none of the above

14. You have opened Explorer. The Contents pane is active. You press the letter N. The following occurs:
    a. all files and folders beginning with N are selected.
    b. all files and folders are arranged by name.
    c. the first file or folder beginning with N is selected.
    d. the cursor moves to the next file or folder.

15. When you make a copy of a disk, the newly copied disk
    a. retains any files that were on the disk and includes all the new files.
    b. is blank.
    c. is identical to the original disk.
    d. none of the above

Application Assignments

Problem Set I—At the Computer

Problem A

Open **Explorer**. Double-click the **95book** folder on the all folders side.

1. The 95book folder has _____ folders displayed beneath it on the tree side.
   a. no
   b. two
   c. four
   d. six
   e. eight

Collapse the **95book** folder to its highest level in the tree pane.

2. The 95book folder has _____ folders displayed beneath it on the tree side.
   a. no
   b. two
   c. four
   d. six
   e. eight

3. If you wish to use the keyboard, you must first click in the Contents pane. The first file on the contents side that begins with C is
   a. Carol.fil
   b. Carolyn.fil
   c. Cases.fil

Close **Explorer**.

Problem B

Open **Explorer**. Double-click the **95book** folder on the all folders side. Click **View**. Point to **Arrange Icons**. Click **by Name**. Click the **Details** button.

4. The file called Bye.typ has a last modification date of
   a. 11/23/92.
   b. 8/1/93.
   c. 10/12/94.

5. Is the file called Bye.typ a system file?
  a. Yes.
  b. No.

Click **View**. Point to **Arrange Icons**. Click **by Type**.

6. Which file (not folder) appears first?
  a. Apr.99
  b. Bye.txt
  c. Carolyn.fil
  d. Y.fil

Click **View**. Point to **Arrange Icons**. Click **by Date**.

7. Which file (not folder) appears first?
  a. Apr.99
  b. April.txt
  c. Carolyn.fil
  d. Y.fil

Click **View**. Point to **Arrange Icons**. Click **by Name**. Click the **List** button. In the tree pane, double-click the **Addman** folder. In the tree pane, click the **Samples** folder.

8. The Samples folder is a _____ to the Addman folder.
  a. parent folder
  b. child folder

9. The 95book folder is a _____ to the Addman folder.
  a. parent folder
  b. child folder

Click the – by the Addman folder to collapse it. Double-click the **95book** folder to collapse it to its highest level. Close Explorer.

Problem C

Open **Explorer**. Open the **95book** folder so you can see the subfolders. Place the Activities disk in Drive A. Open another copy of **Explorer**. Locate Drive A on the new copy of **Explorer**. Double-click it. Tile the windows horizontally. In the **C:\95book** window, click the **Games** folder on the tree side. In the **Drive A:** window, click the **Games** folder on the tree side. Look at the status bar for both windows.

10. Both Explorer windows have the same number of objects in them.
    a. True.
    b. False.

In the **Drive C:\95book** window, right-click the **Hatch.bmp** file on the Contents side. Click **Properties**.

11. The Hatch.bmp file type is
    a. Games.
    b. Bitmap Image.
    c. Microsoft Word 6 Document.

Click **Cancel**. In the **C:\95book folder**, click 95book. In the **Drive C:\95book** window, right-click **April.txt** on the Contents side. Point to **Send To**.

12. You may send April.txt to
    a. Floppy A.
    b. Printer.
    c. 95book folder.
    d. all the above

Right-click the taskbar. Click **Undo Tile**. Collapse **95book** to its highest level in each window. Close both **Explorer** windows.

Problem D

Remove the Activities disk from Drive A. Insert the Data disk into Drive A. Open **Explorer**. Right-click the **Drive A** icon. Click **Properties**.

13. In what color is Free Space Available shown?
    a. Pink.
    b. Blue.
    c. Green.

Close the property sheet. Open the **Format** dialog box for the disk in Drive A. Change the label from **Data** disk to **Class** in the **Label** text box. Click the **No Label** check box to place a check mark in it.

14. What happened in the label text box?
    a. Class is still visible in the Label text box.
    b. Data disk is now shown as the label in the Label text box.
    c. The Label text box is empty of any data.

Click the **No Label** check box to remove the check mark.

15. What happened in the Label text box?
    a. Class is still visible in the Label text box.
    b. Data disk is now shown as the label in the Label text box.
    c. The Label text box is empty of any data.

Change the label to **Data** followed by your initials, i.e. **Data-czg**. Format the disk. After the disk is formatted, close all open windows.

Problem Set II—Brief Essay

For all essay questions, use Notepad to create your answer. Print your answer.

1. Compare and contrast My Computer and Explorer. Give examples and reasons for when you might use each.
2. The following is an open Explorer window. Identify and explain the purpose of each labeled item.

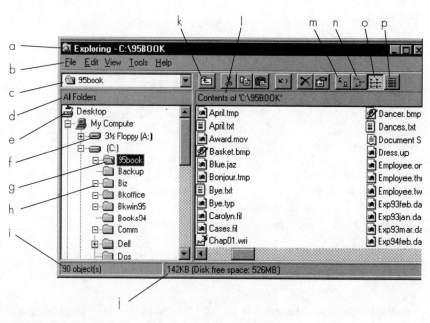

Problem Set III—Scenario

You have just taught a friend how to format a disk, and she is happy to find that the process is simple. However, she doesn't understand why she must format a disk and what is happening when it is formatted. Briefly answer her questions. Include an explanation of the purpose of the boot record, the directory table, the FAT, and the data sectors.

Chapter 7

Managing Files

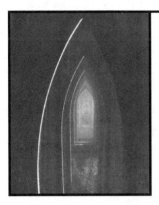

Chapter Overview

You have been using Explorer and My Computer to search for files and look at different details about files and folders. Another function of these tools is the ability to launch programs. Not all files in a program folder are programs; many are support files that allow the program to be executed.

You can perform similar tasks in Explorer and My Computer. Only Explorer, however, allows you to see the entire structure of all your disks. Both My Computer and Explorer let you perform operating system functions, such as creating directories, removing directories, copying files, moving files, renaming files, and deleting files. You manage your files and folders with Explorer and My Computer.

Learning Objectives

1. Determine if a file is a program or support file.
2. Explain the purpose of program and support files.
3. Explain the purpose of file management commands.
4. List and explain two methods to copy files and folders.
5. List and explain two methods to move and rename files and folders.
6. List and explain two methods to delete files and folders.

Student Outcomes

1. Launch a program from Explorer.
2. Copy files and folders.
3. Move files and folders.
4. Rename files and folders.
5. Remove files and folders.

7.1 Program Files

As you continue to use your computer, you will find yourself accumulating programs for different purposes. It is important to remember that programs are files. Not all your programs appear on the Start/Programs menu. In fact, you do not want all of your programs to appear on the Start/Programs menu. If you keep the Programs menu small, it is more efficient to use. It is easy to decide which progams to put on the Start/Programs menu, since you do not use all programs with the same frequency. For instance, you probably use your word processor daily, so you will want this program on the Start/ Programs menu. If you have a program to design your own greeting cards, on the other hand, you probably only use it occasionally. Having this program on the Start/Programs menu is not efficient. It would be better to access this program from My Computer or Explorer when you need to use it. To do this, you need to be able to recognize a program file from a data file as well as understand what other files belong to a program. You can use either My Computer or Explorer to launch applications programs.

7.2   Activity—Using My Computer To Launch a Program

Note: The listed settings are assumed for each chapter. If you are working on your own computer, the changes you made in the default settings should be retained from one work session to the next. However, if you are working in a computer lab, you may have to change your settings each time you log into the network. The settings are as follows:

My Computer
❑   Toolbar and status bar on (in View menu).
❑   Large icons arranged by name (in View menu).
❑   Browse folders by using a single window that changes as you open each folder (View/Options/ Browse tab).
❑   Hide file of these types is set (View/Options/View tab).
❑   Display the full MS-DOS path in the title bar is set (View/Options/View tab).
❑   Hide MS-DOS file extensions for file types that are registered is not set (View/Options/View tab).

Explorer
❑   Toolbar and status bar on (in View menu).
❑   List view arranged by name (in View menu).
❑   Include description bar for left and right panes is on (View/Options/View tab).

1   Double-click **My Computer**. Double-click the **Drive C** icon.

2   Double-click the **95book** folder. Double-click the **Games** folder.

The name of this folder indicates that it contains games. The window shows the objects in the Games folder. (If you cannot see all the objects, size or maximize the window.) Each file name has an icon. Not all of these files are games. What, then, are these objects, and how you can tell which is a program (a game to play) and what the other icons are? Sometimes you can recognize a program by its icon. There are four games in this window: Cipher20.exe, Mlshut.exe, Tp.exe, and Winspidr.exe. You know which ones are programs because they also have the .exe file extension. The extension .exe stands for executable and always indicates a program file. Mlshut.exe is a game written for DOS, but it can still be run under Windows 95. The other games were written for Windows 3.1, but can also be played in Windows 95. Remember, Windows 95 is backwards compatible, which means you do not have to purchase new Windows 95 versions of programs. You may run older programs under Windows 95.

In this window, you also see several files with the .hlp extension. As you have probably guessed, these are the help files for the games. But what are the other files? Are they candidates for deletion? They are not. The .hlp files and the other nonprogram files are support files. Remember, support files can vary from program to program but are needed to execute a program properly.

3 Double-click the **Bridge.tp** icon.

Windows 95 does not know what to do with this file. The extension is not registered to a program. Windows 95 presents the Open With dialog box, which lists all the programs on your system. Windows 95 is hoping that you know what program it should open for a .tp file and helps you by providing a list of programs. But the .tp file is neither a program nor a document.

4 Click **Cancel**.

5 Double-click the **Tp.exe** icon. If it is not visible, scroll down until you locate **Tp.exe**.

6 If the background is not a solid color, click **Background**. Click **Solid**.

 You have opened (executed) the game called Taipei, which is a variation on mahjongg. Taipei is *shareware*, a trial version of a program that is not distributed through commercial channels, saving the programmer the costs of marketing and distribution. You may try out shareware and see if you like it. If you wish to keep the program and use it, you pay a registration fee to the programmer (or company) that owns it. If you do not like the program or do not use it, you delete the program files from your disk and do not owe anyone anything. As you will see with Taipei, executable programs are usually not just a single file such as Tp.exe. Programs have support files. This program, Taipei, also has support files.

7 Click **File**. Click **Load Layout**.

 You may choose the variation of Taipei you wish to play. These .tp files do not have to be registered with Windows 95 because the Taipei program knows what to do with them. You want to use the Bridge.tp, which you tried to open before. Now you can use it.

8 Scroll until you see **Bridge.tp**. Click **Bridge.tp**. Click **Open**.

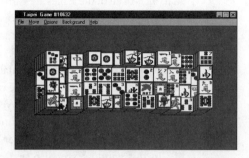

 This is the bridge layout. If you wanted to know how to play this game, you would choose Help from the menu bar. You can try another layout.

9 Click **File**. Click **Load Layout**. Click **Cube.tp**. Click **Open**.

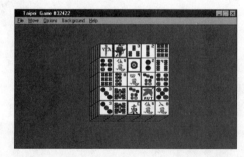

 This is a variation on the game. Now you can see how support files are used with programs. If you deleted the .tp files, you would not be able to play the games. Like the executable program (.exe), nearly all programs will have a multitude of files to support them. If it were a word processing program, the support files could include a spell checker, different fonts, or templates (samples of documents). The support files vary from program to program, but they are critical to being able to use the program.

10 Click the **Close** button on the title bar.

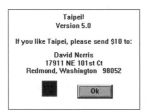

David Norris is asking a $10.00 registration fee if you like his game and want to keep it. He supplies his name and address. When you are finished with this class, if you would like to keep this game, please send him your fee.

11 Click **OK**.

You have returned to the Games window. You can arrange these icons in more convenient ways. In this window, it would be nice if all the executables were together. *Executables* is another way to refer to programs that run.

12 Click **View**. Click **Arrange Icons**. Click **by Type**.

All your executable programs are now at the top of the window so that you may easily access them.

13 Click **View**. Point at **Arrange Icons**. Click **by Name**.

If you look at the status bar, you see that you have twenty-three objects (plus one hidden). To see the hidden files, you need to change your view options.

14 Click **View**. Click **Options**. Click the **View** tab. Click **Show all files**. Click **OK**.

You changed your view. By choosing to show all files, you can see the support files that help run programs. The status bar has changed and now shows twenty-four objects with no hidden files. The hidden file was Wincards.dll.

15 Click **View**. Click **Options**. Click the **View** tab. Click the **Hide Files of this type** option button to set it. Click **OK**.

What's
happening? → You have reset the option.

16 Close the **My Computer** window.

What's
happening? → You have returned to the desktop.

7.3   Creating Shortcuts

One of the advantages to Windows 95 is the ability to customize the desktop to meet your needs. You have created shortcuts for devices, files, and folders. You can also create a shortcut for a program. When you create a shortcut for a program, you must know where the .exe file is physically located. You must be careful when creating a shortcut for a program, and be sure not to move or copy the program by mistake. As you have seen, support files are necessary to executing a program. If you moved a program, instead of creating a shortcut, you would need to move all the support files, including the hidden ones.

7.4   Activity—Creating a Shortcut for Explorer

1 Right-click the **Start** button.

2 Click **Explore**.

4 Click **Windows** on the tree side. (Remember, on your system, the **Windows 95** folder could have a different name.)

What's
happening? → When you chose Explore, you open a copy of the Explorer program. Since you were at Start, you were taken to Start in the hierarchical tree.

3 Scroll up the tree and locate the **Windows** folder.

What's
happening? → You will be using Explorer a great deal in the next activities. Rather than having to go through several steps to reach Explorer, why not put it on your desktop with a shortcut that is easily accessible? In order to do this, you must locate the program file called Explorer.exe. Since this program file is a Windows 95 program, it will be located in the Windows folder.

5 Click the contents side of the pane. Press the letter **E** on the keyboard.

Image depicting Windows Explorer window

What's happening? You will be taken to the first object that begins with the letter E.

6 If you cannot see **Explorer.exe**, scroll until you can. Click it.

What's happening? You should see the Explorer.exe object. It does not have a shortcut arrow on its icon, so you know that this is the program file. It is located in the Windows folder.

7 Right-click and drag the **Explorer** object to the desktop. Release the right mouse button.

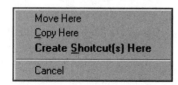

What's happening? You are presented with a pop-up menu that gives you choices. You can move, copy, or create a shortcut. Because pro-

gram files often have support files that they must access, moving program files to a different location can cause them to malfunction. Copying a program file such as Explorer is also undesirable because having two copies of the program would take up disk space. Creating a shortcut is ideal in this situation, which is why it is the default choice.

8 Click **Create Shortcut(s) Here**.

9 Close all open windows.

10 Right-click the desktop. Point to **Arrange Icons**. Set **Auto Arrange**.

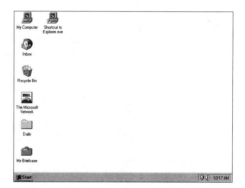

What's happening? Now Explorer is readily available on the desktop as a shortcut that points to the program file's location in the Windows folder. You have also set Auto Arrange so that your icons line up on your desktop.

7.5 Manipulating Files with Explorer

Some of the most common tasks Explorer handles are file management tasks. Explorer enables you to copy, rename, delete, or move files and folders. These are tasks you perform on a daily basis. Typically, most of your time is spent manipulating your data files. You are constantly working with your files to maintain control over your hard disk. You will want backup copies of your current data files. You want to delete out-of-date files to free space on your hard drive and create new folders as your work changes. Except for backing up files, most of your file management occurs on the hard disk. You will now practice file management on a floppy disk. This will allow you to learn how to use the commands and yet preserve the integrity of your hard drive.

7.6 Activity—Copying Files with Explorer

1 Place the Data disk in Drive A. (This disk was formatted in Chapter 6.)

2 Double-click **Shortcut to Explorer**.

3 Double-click the **Drive C** icon. Double-click the **95book** folder. Click the contents side of the pane. Press the **G** key twice.

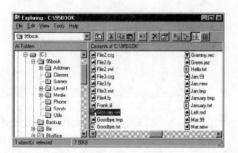

 By making the contents side active and pressing the G key twice, you moved first to the Games folder and second to Glossary.wri, the first document that began with the letter G. You might want to copy Glossary.wri from the hard disk to the floppy disk, either because you are transporting the file from one computer to another, or because you want a backup copy of this file.

4 Right-click **Glossary.wri**. Point to **Send To**.

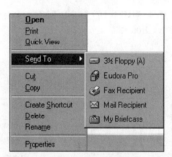

 When you select Send To, you given a list choices for where you may send the file. When you use Send To, you are making a copy of the file.

5 Click **3½ Floppy (A)** icon.

 You see a message box. A progress indicator tells you that you are copying the file called Glossary.wri from the 95book folder to the root of A (A:\).

6 When the task has been completed, click the **3½ Floppy (A:)** icon in the **All Folders** (left) pane.

What's happening? You can see that the file was successfully copied from C:\95book to A:\. If you wish to copy more than one file, you might find it tedious to copy the files one at a time. You can copy, delete, or move a group of files at the same time by selecting them. Whether you are in My Computer or Explorer, you select multiple files the same way. You will find some interesting features when you select multiple files.

7 On Drive C, click the **95book** folder in the **All Folders** pane.

8 Click the **Apr.new** document. Hold the **Shift** and click the **Apr.tmp** document.

What's happening? When you click an object, hold the **Shift** key, and click another object, you are selecting *contiguous*, or adjacent objects. The

status bar at the bottom of the window tells you that you have two objects selected. You may still use the Send To command with a group of objects.

9 Click **Apr.new**. Hold the **Shift** key and right-click **April.tmp**.

What's happening? Once again, you selected contiguous objects. When you click an object, then hold the **Shift** key and click another object, you select all objects between the first and second click. When you right-clicked on the last object while holding the **Shift** key, you not only selected contiguous objects, but you opened the pop-up menu at the same time.

10 Point to **Send To**. Click the **3½ Floppy (A)** icon.

What's happening? As each file is copied, you see the Copying message box.

11 When the copying is complete, click the **3½ Floppy (A:)** icon in the tree side (left pane).

  As you can see, you now have copies of these files on the Data disk. Selecting contiguous files with the **Shift** key seems fairly straightforward. However, depending on where you click and what view you are in, the contiguous files may not be what you expected.

12 Click the **95book** folder on the tree side. Click the **Large Icons** view.

13 Size the **Exploring - C:\95book** window so that it looks like the window below. When it is sized, click **View**. Point to **Arrange Icons**. Click **by Name**.

  You have sized your window and changed your view.

14 Scroll on the contents side until your window looks like the one below.

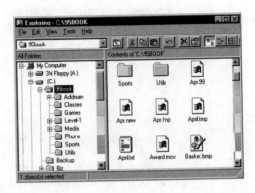

15 Click **Apr.99**. Hold the **Shift** key and click **April.tmp**.

  In this case, contiguous means stacked vertically, like a column. When you were in list view, clicking an object, holding the s key, and clicking another object selected the files between the two clicks. In Large Icons view, this procedure still selects contiguous objects, but the objects are selected in columns rather than side by side.

16 Click the **Sports** folder. Hold the Shift key and click **Apr.tmp**.

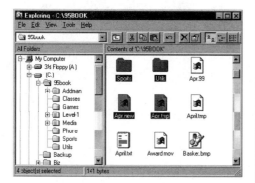

  As you can see, your selection begins with your first click (Sports), ends with your Shift click (Apr.tmp), and the between is selected in columns. Thus, you also selected the Utils folder and the Apr.new file, but not the Apr.99 or April.tmp file. There is another technique to selecting objects. You may *lasso* them. You can use the mouse to draw an imaginary lasso around the objects. The lasso appears as a dotted line. You may lasso in the large icons view only.

17 Click the **95book** folder in the tree (left) pane. Scroll in the contents side (right pane) until you can see both the April.txt file and the Bonjour.tmp file. Your screen will look as follows:

18 Place the mouse pointer just above the **April.txt** file, not on the file. Hold down the left mouse button and drag in a downward direction.

  You see a dotted line, which is your lasso. The lasso must be rectangular. Drag the dotted line down until **Bonjour.tmp** and **April.txt** are selected. Keep holding the mouse button.

You see the lasso and the selected files, which are in an inverse color (highlighted). Whenever you have lassoed the files you want, release the mouse button.

19 Release the left mouse button.

You have lassoed these four objects. They are contiguous by column. Once you have selected objects, you can manipulate them, either copying, moving, or deleting them, or by performing other types of file maintenance tasks.

20 Right-click one of the highlighted icons. Point to **Send To**. Click the **3½ Floppy (A)** icon.

A message box indicates that you are copying these files to the Data disk. You may also select files that are not contiguous by holding the **Ctrl** key when you click the file.

21 Click **April.txt**. Hold the **Ctrl** key and click **Carolyn.fil**.

You have selected two files by clicking them and using the **Ctrl** key. This technique for selecting noncontiguous files works in all views. If you hold the **Ctrl** key and right-click a file, you will also open the pop-up menu.

22 Click **April.txt**. Hold the [Ctrl] key and right-click **Carolyn.fil**. Point at **Send To**.

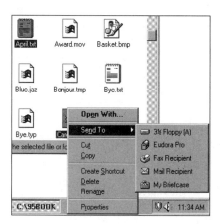

 You selected two noncontiguous files and opened the shortcut menu.

23 Click the **3½ Floppy (A)** icon.

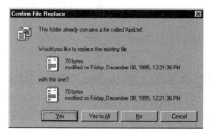

 Windows 95 knows that you have a file on Drive A called April.txt. When you attempt to copy a file from one location to another and the file already exists in the new location, you will overwrite the existing file. When you *overwrite* a file, you replace what was there with new information. The old information will no longer exist. Normally, you want to overwrite files because you want to have the most current information in your file. However, because you may not have known that you had a certain file,

Windows 95 confirms your intentions before it overwrites. This prevents you from destroying data accidentally. You have several command buttons, Yes, Yes to All, No, and Cancel. If you choose Yes, you are giving permission to overwrite only this specific file and will be queried for any other duplicate files. If you choose Yes to All, Windows 95 will overwrite any files that have duplicate names. Choosing No would prevent the computer from copying this specific file, but it would continue to copy any files that did not have a duplicate name. Cancel allows you to change your mind and copy no files.

24 Click **Yes to All**.

 Your files are being copied.

25 Click the **3½ Floppy (A:)** icon on the tree side.

 You can see that your files have been copied.

26 Click the **List View** button on the toolbar.

27 Click the **(C:)** icon on the tree side. Double-click **95book** to collapse it to its highest level.

28 Close all open windows.

 You have returned to the desktop.

7.7   Other Ways To Copy Files

As you can see, you can select files in a variety of ways. There are many ways to copy files as well. You may want to copy many files to the Data disk, perhaps because you are transporting data from a home computer to a computer at work or school. Instead of merely selecting and using the Send To pop-up menu, you want to see both your source (what you are copying) and your destination (the place to which your copying items). A Drive A shortcut on your desktop will be the easiest way to accomplish these goals.

7.8 Activity—More Techniques for Copying Files

1 Double-click **My Computer**. Click **View**. Point to **Arrange Icons**. Set **Auto Arrange**.

2 In the **My Computer** window, right drag the **Drive A** icon onto the desktop. Release the right mouse button.

3 Click **Create Shortcut(s) Here**. Close the **My Computer** window.

> What's happening? You have created a Drive A shortcut.

4 Double-click the **Drive A** shortcut. Double-click the **Explorer** shortcut.

5 On an empty spot on the taskbar, right-click the taskbar. Click **Tile Horizontally**.

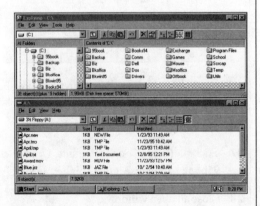

> What's happening? In this example, the Explorer window is open on the top with the Drive A window open on the bottom.

6 In the **Drive A** window, click the **Large Icons** button.

7 In the **Explorer** window on the tree side, double-click the **95book** folder icon to expand it to its fullest level.

8 Scroll on the contents side until you can see the file, **Award.mov**. Begin to left-drag **Award.mov** to the **Drive A** window.

> What's happening?   As you drag the file Award.mov out of the Explorer window and into the Drive A window, you see an outline of the document with a plus sign box. Whenever you see a plus sign as you drag an object, it indicates that you are doing a copy operation. When you left-drag files across drives, as you are doing now, the default operation is to copy.

9   Drop the **Award.mov** icon into the **Drive A** window.

    Before Windows 95 completes the copy, it displays the Confirm File Replace dialog box. Since you already have a file on Drive A called Award.mov, Windows 95 is telling you that you are about to replace it with a file from Drive C also called Award.mov.

10   Click **Yes**.

    The file from Drive C was copied, replacing the file on Drive A.

11   Locate the file called **Cases.fil** on the contents side of the **Explorer** window. Left-drag and drop it into the **Drive A** window.

    You saw the Copying message box rather than a pop-up menu offering choices. Remember, you are copying from one drive to another, so the default operation is to copy.

12   Right-drag **Blue.jaz** from the **Explorer** window to the **Drive A** window. Release the right mouse button.

    When you right-drag an object across drives, copy is the default and is highlighted on the pop-up menu.

13   Click **Copy Here**.

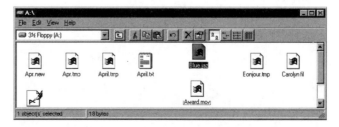

    After the Copying message box appears, you have copied Blue.jaz from the 95book folder on Drive C to the root of Drive A, where Blue.jaz is already. You will get another message about overwriting.

14 In the contents side of the **Explorer** window, locate the file called **Bye.txt** and click it. Locate the file called **Dances.txt**. Hold the $\boxed{\textbf{Ctrl}}$ key and click it. Holding the $\boxed{\textbf{Ctrl}}$ key, locate and click the file called **Employee.one**. Release the $\boxed{\textbf{Ctrl}}$ key.

 Remember, when you hold the $\boxed{\textbf{Ctrl}}$ key and click, you can select noncontiguous files. You could right-drag or left-drag the selected files to copy them to the floppy disk in Drive A, but there is also another method—you may use the drop-down menus.

15 Click the **Edit** menu on the **Explorer** menu bar.

 You have dropped down the Edit menu. The Undo Copy choice is available. If you wanted to "undo" the last copy, you could make this selection. If Undo Copy were dimmed, it would be unavailable. Since you have neither cut nor copied anything, the Paste and Paste Shortcut choices are dimmed. Notice that there are keyboard shortcuts next to the menu choices. If you wanted to cut an object, you would need to select it and press the $\boxed{\textbf{Ctrl}}$ key plus the letter X. If you wanted to copy an object, you could use the keyboard shortcut $\boxed{\textbf{Ctrl}}$ key plus the letter C. You will find these keyboard shortcuts almost universal, not only in Windows 95, but also in the application program world. The menu has a Select All choice, which is self-explanatory. But what is the Invert Selection choice?

16 Click **Invert Selection**.

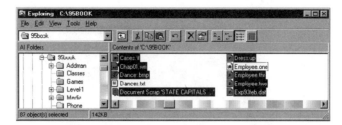

 When you chose Invert Selection, that choice reversed your selection. Now every object is selected *except* the ones you originally selected. This is a quick way to select files when there are few files you do not want to manipulate. It saves you the trouble of holding the **Ctrl** key and clicking many files.

17 Click **Edit** on the **Explorer** menu. Click **Invert Selection**.

 Now your Exploring - C:\95book window shows the files that you originally selected.

18 Click the **Edit** menu on the **Explorer - C:\95BOOK** menu bar. Click **Copy**.

19 Click the **Edit** menu on the **Drive A** window menu bar.

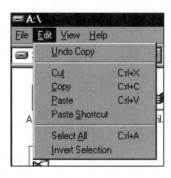

 Both the Paste and Paste Shortcut options are available because you have copied something to the Clipboard. If you selected Paste Shortcut, the actual files would not be copied from Drive C to Drive A. Instead, there would only be a pointer to the files on Drive C. Because you want to take this floppy disk back and forth between two computers, having a pointer to Drive C would do you no good. You need copies of the files, not a pointer to the files.

20   Click **Paste**.

   Now you see the message box indicating the progress of the files being copied.

21   Right-click the taskbar. Click **Undo Tile**.

22   Close all open windows.

   You have returned to the desktop.

7.9   Folders and Files

You can select files in a variety of ways. You can use these same techniques to select folders. Once a folder is selected, you can copy it, move it, delete it, or use any of the other file manipulation commands. However, be aware that when you manipulate a folder, you are also dealing with all the files and subfolders in that folder. For example, if you copy a folder to a different drive or directory (folder), you are recreating the folder and the files in it in the new location. As with files, you can select contiguous and noncontiguous folders. You may drag and drop with files and folders and use the menu commands to copy and paste.

7.10 Activity—Copying Folders and Files

1   Double-click the **Drive A** shortcut. Double-click the **Explorer** shortcut.

2   On an empty spot on the taskbar, right-click the taskbar. Click **Tile Horizontally**.

3   In the **Explorer** window, double-click the **95book** folder.

4   In the **Exploring - C:\95book** window, in the tree pane, left-drag and drop the **Level-1** folder to the Drive A window.

   Because you left-dragged across drives, no pop-up menu appeared. Copying occurred as the default operation. As you read the Copying message box, you see that not only folders are being copied, but files as well.

5 Click the **Level-1** icon on the tree side of the **Exploring - C:\95book** window. Then press the key on the numeric keypad.

6 Click the **Level-1** folder in the **Drive A** window. Hold the **Shift** key and double-click the **Level-1** folder in the **Drive A** window.

 Pressing the ✱ key is a keyboard shortcut for expanding a branch of the tree, as you did in the Explorer window. If necessary, move the A:\Level-1 window so that you can see the tree structure of the Exploring - C:\95book window. You can see that when you dragged the Level-1 folder from 95book on Drive C to Drive A, you recreated the hierarchical structure with folders and files on Drive A. Your options in View are set so that when you open one window, you close the previous window. Sometimes you may want to leave the current window open and open another window. Rather than having to go back to the Options/View property sheet, you can use the keyboard shortcut of holding the **Shift** key when you double-click a folder. This leaves the previous window open and opens another window.

7 Close the **A:\Level-1** window.

8 In the **Exploring-C:\95book\Level-1** window, click the **Level-1** folder icon in the tree (left) pane. Press the ⊟ key on the numeric keypad.

You used the keyboard shortcut to collapse the Level-1 folder to its highest level.

9   In the tree pane of the **Exploring** window, scroll up and double-click the **95book** folder to collapse it to its highest level.

10   In the tree pane of the **Exploring** window, scroll up to the **Drive A** icon. Double-click this icon. Click the **Level-1** folder in the tree pane. Press the [✱] key on the numeric keypad.

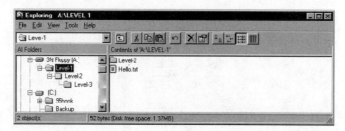

> **What's happening?**   The Exploring - A:\Level-1 window indicates that the entire Level-1 folder with its subfolders and files was copied to the disk in Drive A.

11   In the **Exploring - A:\Level-1** window, click the **Level-1** folder on the tree. Press the [−] key on the numeric keypad. Double-click the **Drive A** icon to collapse it to its highest level.

12   Right-click in an empty area of the **A:** window. Point to **Arrange Icons**. Click **by Name**.

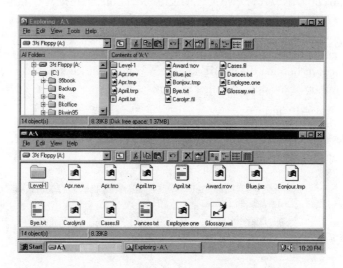

> **What's happening?**   You have collapsed the Drive A icon to its highest level in the Exploring window. In the Drive A window, you have arranged your icons by name.

13   Right-click the taskbar in an empty spot. Click **Undo Tile**.

14 Close all open windows.

 If you do not Undo Tile, the next time you open an Explorer or My Computer window, each will retain the current tiling shape. In this case, Windows 95 would have "remembered" that each window occupied half the screen the last time the program was accessed. Another way to eliminate the Tile Horizontal shape is to right-click the taskbar and click Cascade.

7.11 Copying and Moving

When you drag and drop files from one drive to another, the default operation is always a copy. If, however, you are on the same drive and use drag-and-drop, your default operation becomes a move. Remember, when you copy a file, you are leaving the original where it was and creating a duplicate. A move operation, on the other hand, removes the file from one location and places it in another. You start with one file and end with one file.

When you use the Copy and Paste choices in the Edit menu, you are copying the file. When you use the Cut and Paste choices in the Edit menu, you are moving the file.

As you continue copying and moving files, you must remember that every file in a folder (directory) must have a unique name. If you have two files on Drive A called Myfile.txt, with one located in the Data directory and the other in the root directory, the file names are unique. The "real" file names are A:\Myfile.txt and A:\Data\Myfile.txt. The path makes these names unique. Windows 95 will allow you to have duplicate file names in different folders. If you tried to copy A:\Data\Myfile.txt to A:\Myfile.txt, Windows 95 will give the second file the name of Copy of A:\Myfile.txt, enforcing the unique file name rule.

7.12 Activity—Copying and Moving Files on the Same Drive

1 Double-click the **Explorer** shortcut on the desktop. Locate the **Drive A** icon on the tree. Double-click it.

 You have opened the Exploring - A:\ window. You have also expanded the tree. One advantage to using Explorer instead of My Computer is that you can see the disk's structure. You can drag a file from the Contents pane to the tree pane without having to open multiple windows.

2   Begin to drag **Bye.txt** from the contents side to the tree side over the **Level-1 folder** under the **Drive A** icon.

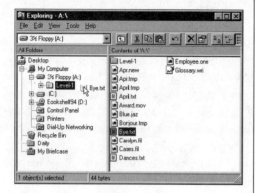

What's happening?   As the file icon passes over the border between the two windows, you see the outline of the file. If you dragged the file over the Drive C icon, you would see a plus sign, indicating a copy. But since you were over the Drive A icon, you did not see the ✚ sign. This means that you are moving, not a copying.

3   Drop the **Bye.txt** icon onto the **Level-1** folder, under the **Drive A** icon on the tree side.

What's happening?   Notice that the message box now says Moving. It is important to read the titles of the message boxes so you know what you accomplished. You removed the file from the root of Drive A and placed it in the Level-1 folder.

What's happening?   The file Bye.txt is no longer located in the root of Drive A.

4   Double-click the **Level-1** folder on the contents side.

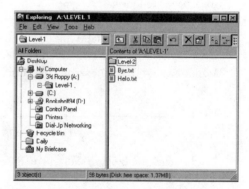

What's happening?   The file is now located in the Level-1 folder. Its name is now A:\Level-1\Bye.txt instead of A:\Bye.txt.

5 On the contents side, right-drag **Bye.txt** to the **3½ Floppy (A:)** icon on the tree side. Release the right mouse button.

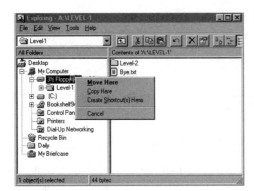

 You see a pop-up menu, but now the default choice is Move Here. Since you are on the same drive, when you drag and drop, the default is a move operation.

6 Click **Move Here**.

7 Click the **Up One Level** button on the toolbar. Click the Contents pane to make it active.

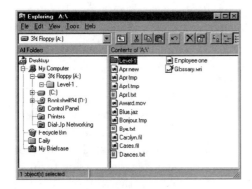

You have moved the file Bye.txt back to the root directory of A.

8 Left-drag **Bye.txt** from the Contents pane to the tree pane and drop it on the **3½ Floppy (A:)** icon in the tree pane.

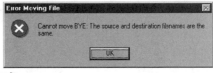

You get an error message. You cannot move a file to the same location.

9 Click **OK**.

10 Right-drag **Bye.txt** from the Contents pane to the tree pane and drop it on the **3½ Floppy (A:)** icon in the tree pane.

11 On the **shortcut** menu, click **Copy Here**.

You were allowed to copy the file, but Windows 95 gave it a new name, Copy of Bye.txt. Remember, files must have unique names if they are in same drive and folder.

12 In the Contents pane, click **Bye.txt**. Click **Edit**. Click **Copy**.

13 Click **Edit**. Click **Paste**.

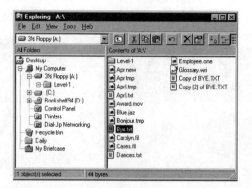

 Once again, you were allowed to copy the file Bye.txt to the same drive and folder, but Windows 95 assigned the file a different name, Copy (2) of Bye.txt. You can never have duplicate file names.

14 Close the window.

 You have returned to the desktop.

7.13 Making Folders and Other File Management Commands

There are many commands that you can use in Explorer or in My Computer. You have been copying and moving files and folders from one drive to another and on the same drive. Other commands enable you to rename files and folders and create folders so you can store similar files in one location.

When working with your computer, you will work primarily on the hard disk. You are going to learn to accomplish tasks using the floppy disk rather than the hard disk. Since you are in a learning environment, this will allow you to learn and practice without harming files or folders on your hard disk.

7.14 Activity—Creating Folders and Copying Files

1 Double-click the shortcut to **Explorer**. Double-click the **Drive A** icon on the tree side.

2 Right-click an empty spot on the contents side. Point to **New**.

 You have opened the cascading menu for the New command. If you select one of the top two commands, Folder or Shortcut, you can create a new folder or shortcut on the contents side. In this case, the folder or shortcut would be located in the root of A (the default). Below Folder and Shortcut the list of programs will vary, depending on what programs are installed on your system. At the very least, Text Document will appear as a choice. If you choose that option, you will open the application program, Notepad. You wish to create a folder to hold files.

3 Click **Folder**.

> **What's happening?** You see a folder icon with a dotted line around the words New Folder. This is where you key in the name of the folder.

4 Key in the following: **TEST** Enter

> **What's happening?** You have a new folder called Test with no files in it. Although you used uppercase letters (TEST), Windows 95 changed the case so that the folder name reads Test. You now decide that you would like a more descriptive name. You may rename files and folders any time.

5 Right-click on the **Test** icon. Click **Rename**.

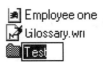

> **What's happening?** The box appears around Test. You can directly key in your new name.

6 Key in the following: **MY TEST FILES** Enter

> **What's happening?** You have renamed your folder. Since you renamed it, Windows 95 retained your capitalization of MY TEST FILES instead of creating a new folder. You can rename files just as easily with the same technique. You can also use the following technique.

7 Click **Award.mov**.

> **What's happening?** You have selected a file.

8   Click **Award.mov** again.

What's happening?   Now Award.mov has a box around it where you can key in the new file name.

9   Key in the following: **ACADEMY AWARD MOVIES** **Enter**

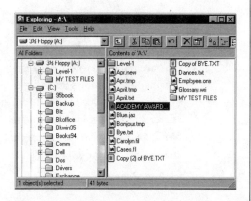

What's happening?   You renamed a file, and again Windows 95 maintained your capitalization. But you cannot see the entire file name.

10   Click the **Large Icons** button on the toolbar.

11   Click **View**. Point to **Arrange Icons**. Click **by Name**.

What's happening?   You can see the entire file name. Windows 95 also *wrapped* (created additional lines for text) your file name. This makes it easier to read than if ACADEMY AWARD MOVIES appeared on one line.

12   Click the **List** button on the toolbar.

What's happening?   When you changed your view back to a list view, Windows 95 adjusted the window so you could see the entire file name.

13   In the tree pane, if the **3½ Floppy (A:)** is not fully expanded, double-click it so it is.

14 In the tree pane, double-click the **95book** folder. Click the **Utils** folder.

What's happening? You can see the Utils folder under 95book. You want to copy it, and its files, to the MY TEST FILES folder on Drive A.

15 Right-click **Utils**. Point to **Send To**. Click **3½ Floppy (A:)**.

16 On the tree side, click the **3½ Floppy (A:)** icon.

What's happening? The Send To command only allows you to send files or folders to a drive. The folder was sent to the root of A:\. Using the Send To menu, the only way to send files or folders to a folder on a floppy disk is to add a folder name to the menu.

17 On the contents side, drag and drop **Utils** on top of the **MY TEST FILES** folder.

What's happening? Because you are on the same drive, you moved Utils from the root of A to the folder MY TEST FILES.

18 On the tree side, double-click **MY TEST FILES**.

What's happening? You moved the folder and files.

19 Double-click the **Utils** folder on the contents side.

20 Right-drag and drop **Timekard.exe** to the **3½ Floppy (A:)** icon on the tree side. Release the right mouse button.

 Even though you were dragging within the same drive, the default choice is Create Shortcut(s) Here. You could, in fact, see this when you were dragging because you saw the bent shortcut arrow on the icon. Timekard.exe is a shareware program. It is a personal time manager, designed to provide you with an accurate figure of how much time you spend working and playing with your computer. If you have ever wondered how much time you spend playing Solitaire, you can find out by using this program. Timekard can also monitor your computer while you are away from it, so that you know what your friends, family, or co-workers are using your computer for.

21   Click **Create Shortcut(s) Here**.

22   Click the **3½ Floppy (A:)** icon on the tree side.

 You can see your shortcut.

23   On the tree side, double-click the **MY TEST FILES** folder to collapse it. Double-click the **3½ Floppy (A:)** icon to collapse it to its highest level.

24   Double-click the **95book** folder to collapse it to its highest level.

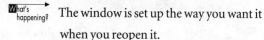 The window is set up the way you want it when you reopen it.

25   Close all open windows.

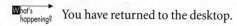 You have returned to the desktop.

7.15 Removing Files and Folders

One of the most important tasks handled by My Computer and Explorer is deleting files and folders you no longer need. Keeping these files on a disk is problematic because you use up valuable disk space and it is more difficult to find the files you want. It becomes time-consuming to search all the files you no longer want along with those you do want.

There is a difference between deleting files on a hard disk and a floppy disk. When you delete files on a hard disk, they are not really deleted. They are copied to the Recycle Bin instead, so you can retrieve them in case you change your mind. If the Recycle Bin directory gets too full, Windows 95 begins deleting files with the oldest files being deleted first. When you delete a file or folder, most of the time you do want to get rid of it. If you delete files from a floppy disk, however, they do not get copied to the Recycle Bin. They are deleted, and you cannot recover them.

You will find that deleting files one at a time is laborious. You previously used the Find command from the Start menu to locate folders that you wanted to copy, move, or delete. In a lab environment you do not want to delete files from the hard disk. You are going to delete files and folders from the Data disk. If you are on a network, you may not have delete privileges.

7.16 Activity—Deleting Files and Folders

1   Open **Explorer**. Double-click the **3½ Floppy (A:)** on the tree side.

2   Press **Alt** + **Enter**.

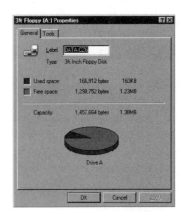

 You are looking at the files and folders on the Data disk. You want to see how much available space is on the disk. You could right-click the disk drive icon on the tree side, but there is a keyboard shortcut to reach the property sheet.

 Whenever an object is selected, pressing **Alt** plus **Enter** will bring up the property sheet. This disk has a large amount of unused space, but let's assume you need more space. You want to delete files and folders you no longer need.

3 Click **Cancel** on the property sheet.

4 Left-drag **Copy of Bye.txt** to the **Recycle Bin** on the desktop.

 You get an information box confirming that you want to delete this file. Notice that the message does not say it is sending the file to the Recycle Bin.

5 Click **Yes**.

 It appears as if the file is being sent to the Recycle Bin.

6 Double-click the **Recycle Bin** on the desktop.

 The Recycle Bin window is empty. (Note that if you had dragged other files there, there could be some entries, but Copy of Bye.txt will not be in this window). The Copy of Bye.txt file was deleted. It did not go to the Recycle Bin. When you delete files from a floppy disk, dragging them to the Recycle Bin on the hard disk does

not keep a copy of the file. This can be advantageous, since files in the Recycle Bin take up disk space. If you know you want to delete a file without sending it to the Recycle Bin, you can use a keyboard shortcut. Hold down the **Shift** key while pressing the **Delete** key. This will bypass sending the file to the Recycle Bin. When you delete a file and it does go to the Recycle Bin, you have to empty the Recycle Bin, resulting in two steps to delete a file. If you always want files to bypass the Recycle Bin, you can unset the option to Display delete confirmation dialog in the Recycle Bin property sheet.

7 Close the **Recycle Bin** window.

8 Click **Copy (2) of Bye.txt** on the contents side of the **Explorer** window to select it.

9 Hold the **Shift** key and press the **Delete** key.

 The Confirm File Deletion message appears.

10 Click **Yes**.

 The file is gone. You do not see an additional message box showing the file being copied to the Recycle Bin. Typically, you want to delete many files. Selecting and deleting each file one at a time is very labor-intensive. You can delete many files simultaneously. A quick way to do this is to use Find from the Start menu.

11 Press **F3**.

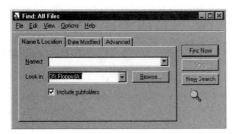

What's
happening?
Pressing **F3** is a keyboard shortcut to the Find dialog box. Because you were in Drive A, the Look In drop-down list box reflects that drive. The Look in text box used the default drive and directory.

12 In the **Named** text box, key in the following: **time*.***

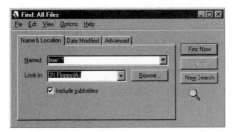

What's
happening?
You are asking Find to find all the files that have file names beginning with time and are located in Drive A.

13 Click **Find Now**.

What's
happening?
Find Now has located all the files that begin with time in any folder on the Data disk. The status bar tells you that five files were found.

14 If you cannot see all five files, scroll to the end of the list of files. Hold down the **Shift** key and click on the last file name.

What's
happening?
You have selected all the files in the Find list box.

15 Press the **Delete** key.

What's
happening?
The Confirm Multiple File Delete message window tells you five items will be deleted.

16 Click **Yes**.

What's
happening?
Another information box tells you that when you delete a program, you will no longer be able to use it or edit documents. You have more command buttons than usual. If you click Yes, you will be queried each time Windows 95 finds a program during this find operation. If you click Yes to All, you answer that you want to delete everything and do not want to be queried each time Windows 95 runs across a program during this operation.

17 Click **Yes to All**.

18 Close the **Find** box after the files are deleted.

19 Double-click the **MY TEST FILES** on the tree side.

20 Click the **Utils** folder on the tree side.

What's happening? You no longer see "time" files, but some files remain. You decide that you want to get rid of the MY TEST FILES folder, the Utils folder, and any files in them. The fastest way to do this is to delete the MY TEST FILES folder. When you delete a folder, you delete all the files in it as well as any folders that are beneath it.

21 Right-click **MY TEST FILES** on tree side. Click **Delete**.

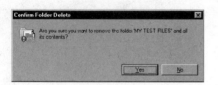

What's happening? The Confirm Folder Delete message appears, warning you that are about to delete the folder and all its contents.

22 Click **Yes**.

23 Click **Yes** in the dialog box to delete the **Setup.exe** file.

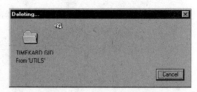

What's happening? The Deleting progress message box shows each file name as it is being deleted. These files are not going to the Recycle Bin. The MY TEST FILES folder and all its files are gone.

24 Double-click the **3½ Floppy (A:)** icon to collapse it.

25 Close all open windows.

What's happening? You have returned to the desktop.

Chapter Summary

In this chapter, you learned that many files comprise a program. Although you launch an executable, programs also need support files such as .hlp files. You can execute a program by locating it and double-clicking the file name.

You found that you can copy and move files across drives and within the same drive by using such techniques as drag and drop, copy and paste, or the Send To option on the pop-up menu. You learned that all files must have a unique name. You learned that when you drag a file on the same drive, the default operation is a move, but if you drag a file to a different drive, the default operation is a copy.

You found that you can create a new folder by right-clicking the desktop and choosing New. You name your folder by keying in its name in the selected box. You may rename files and folders at any time by using the shortcut menus or selecting the file and keying in the new name. You can eliminate files and folders by pressing the **Delete** key, dragging them to the Recycle Bin, or using the shortcut menu. When you delete files on a floppy disk, they are not kept in the Recycle Bin.

Key Terms

Contiguous
Executables
Lasso
Overwrite
Shareware
Wrapped

Discussion Questions

1. Explain the purpose of a support file.
2. List two ways to launch a program.
3. What would be the purpose of creating a desktop shortcut to Explorer? To a drive?
4. What is the purpose and function of file management commands?
5. List three tasks that can be accomplished with file management commands.
6. Describe one way to select contiguous objects, and one way to select noncontiguous objects.
7. Explain what it means to lasso objects.
8. What does it mean to overwrite a file?
9. Why would you want to overwrite a file?
10. Describe two ways that files and folders can be copied.
11. What is the difference between copying and moving a file or folder?
12. Describe the purpose of the Invert Selection menu choice.
13. Compare and contrast dragging and dropping files from one drive to another and on the same drive.
14. When using the Edit menu, differentiate what happens when you use Copy and Paste and Cut and Paste?
15. What happens if you try to copy a file to a folder that already contains a file by that name?
16. How can you create a folder?
17. List two ways to rename a file or folder.
18. List two ways to delete a file or folder.
19. Why is it important to be able to delete files and folders?
20. If you drag a file from a floppy disk to the Recycle Bin, what happens?

True/False Questions

For each question, circle the letter T if the statement is true or the letter F if the statement is false.

T   F   1. Support files can be deleted because they take up valuable space.
T   F   2. Moving a file brings about the same results as creating a shortcut.
T   F   3. When you drag a file from one drive to another, the default operation is a copy.
T   F   4. Only contiguous files and folders can be selected at one time.
T   F   5. To bypass sending a file to the Recycle Bin, hold down the **Shift** key when you press the **Delete** key.

Completion Questions

Write the correct answer in each blank space provided.

6. The extension .exe stands for _____ and always indicates that the file is a program file.
7. A trial version of a program that is not distributed through commercial channels is called _____.
8. The default action when dragging an object between folders on the same drive is a(n) _____ operation.
9. If you hold down the left mouse button and drag it, you create a rectangle of dotted lines. This box is called a _____.
10. Copying over an existing file is called _____.

Multiple Choice Questions

Circle the letter of the correct answer for each question.

11. To create a folder, right-click the desktop and choose
    a. New.
    b. Properties.
    c. Create folder.
    d. Create file.

12. If you drag a file from one drive to another and see a plus sign, you know that
    a. this is a program type of file.
    b. there is already a copy of this file on the new drive.
    c. this file will be copied.
    d. none of the above

13. To select contiguous files, hold the _____ key when you select the files.
    a. Ctrl
    b. Shift
    c. Alt
    d. Delete

14. Is it possible to have a file called First.one in the Apps folder and another file named First.one in the Files folder?
    a. Yes, file names do not have to be unique.
    b. No, files must have unique names, and these names are not unique.
    c. Yes, these files have unique names because of the path.
    d. No, First.one is not a valid file name.

15. You move a file to a new location on the same drive by
    a. left-drag and drop.
    b. right-drag and drop.
    c. clicking Copy. Then clicking Paste from the Edit menu.
    d. either a or b

Application Assignments

Problem Set I—At the Computer

Problem A

Open the **95book** folder so you can see the subfolders. Click the **Games** folder in the tree pane. Open **Cipher**. Click **About** on the menu bar.

1. The author of the program is
    a. John A. Junod.
    b. Dave Norris.
    c. Brad Trupp.

2. He lives in
   a. Canada.
   b. Great Britain.
   c. United States.

3. Cipher is a
   a. maze game.
   b. solitaire card game.
   c. word puzzle game.

Click **OK** to close **About**. Close **Cipher**. Open **Winspidr**. Click **OK** to the **User Info** dialog box. Click **Help** on the menu bar. Click **About**.

4. The author of the program is
   a. John A. Junod.
   b. Dave Norris.
   c. Brad Trupp.

Click **OK**.

5. Winspidr is a
   a. maze game.
   b. solitaire card game.
   c. word puzzle game.

Close **Winspidr**. Click the **List** view button on the toolbar. Double-click the **95book** folder on the tree side to collapse it to its highest level.

Problem B

If you do not have a shortcut to Explorer on the desktop, create it now. Double-click the **Explorer** shortcut. Double-click the **Drive C** icon. Double-click the **95book** folder on the tree side. Click the **Utils** folder on the tree side. Click the **Large Icons** button on the toolbar.

On the Contents side, you also see this icon:

Timekard

6. This icon represents a(n)
   a. data file type.
   b. program file type.
   c. unknown file type.

On the Contents side, you also see this icon:

Timekard.dat

7. This icon represents a(n)
   a. data file type.
   b. program file type.
   c. unknown file type.

Click the **List** view button on the toolbar. Click the **95book** folder on the tree side. Close **Explorer**.

Problem C

Open **Explorer**. Double-click the **95book** folder to expand it. Click the **Large Icon** button on the toobar. Locate **Dress.up** on the Contents side of the window. Size the window if necessary so that **Employee.one** and **Employee.thr** are next to **Dress.up**. You may nccd click **View/Arrange Icons/by Name**. The files will be displayed as follows:

Document   Dress.up   Employee.one   Employee.thr
Scrap 'STATE
CAPITALS ...'

Click **Dress.up**.

You also wish to select **Employee.one** and **Employee.thr**.

8. The quickest way to select all three adjacent (contiguous) files was to hold the _____ key when you clicked Employee.thr.
   a. Shift
   b. Ctrl
   c. Alt

Copy the selected files to the root of the Data disk. Overwrite any existing files.

9. You may copy the selected files by
    a. using the Send To command.
    b. dragging the files to the Drive A shortcut.
    c. either a or b

Click in the contents side to deselect the files. Select the files **Left.red**, **March.txt**, **Stated.Txt**, and **Steven.fil**.

10. To select these noncontiguous files, you had to hold the _____ key when you clicked each file.
    a. **Shift**
    b. **Ctrl**
    c. **Alt**

Copy the selected files to the root directory of the Data disk. Select the **Media** folder and copy it to the Data disk. Select the **Sports** folder and copy it to the Data disk. Use **Explorer** to open the **Drive A** window.

11. Media and Sports appears as _____ icons in the Drive A window.
    a. file
    b. folder

Double-click the **Drive A** icon on the tree side of the **Explorer** window to expand it. Double-click the **Media** folder on the tree side of the **Explorer** window to expand it.

12. Media has _____ subfolders.
    a. no
    b. one
    c. two
    d. three

Double-click the **Media** folder on the tree of the **Explorer** window to collapse it to its highest level. Double-click the **Sports** folder on the tree side of the **Explorer** window to expand it.

13. Sports has _____ subfolders.
    a. no
    b. one
    c. two
    d. three

Double-click the **Sports** icon on the tree side of the **Explorer** window to collapse it to its highest level. Double-click the **Drive A** icon on the tree side of the **Explorer** window to collapse it to its highest level. Click the **Exploring - C:\95book** window to make it active. Double-click the **95book** folder in the **C:\95book** **Explorer** window on the tree side to expand it. Horizontally tile the two open **Explorer** windows. In the **Exploring - C:\95book** window, click the **Games** folder once to select it. Click **Edit**. Click **Copy**. Click the **Drive A** window. Click **Edit** in the **Drive A** window.

14. Is Paste available to use?
   a. Yes.
   b. No.

Paste **Games** into the **Drive A** window. Right-click the contents side of the **Drive A** window. Point to **Arrange Icons**. Choose **by Type**.

15. What folder appears first?
   a. Media.
   b. Games.
   c. Level-1.
   d. Sports.

Click the **Exploring - C:\95book** window to make it active. Click the **List** view button on the toolbar. In the **Exploring - C:\95book** tree pane, double-click **95book** to collapse it to its highest level. Right-click the taskbar. Click **Undo Tile**. Close all open windows and return to the desktop.

Problem D

Double-click the **Explorer** shortcut. Double-click the **Drive A** icon on the tree side so you may see the structure. Make the contents side active. In the root, create a folder called **Demonstration files**. Click **View**. Point to **Arrange Icons**. Click **by name**. Move the **March.txt** file and the shortcut to **Timekard.exe** in the root to the **Demonstration files** folder so you do not see a pop-up (shortcut) menu.

16. To move these items without the pop-up menu, you had to
   a. left-drag the items.
   b. right-drag the items.

17. What is the MS-DOS name of the Demonstration files folder?
   a. Demonstration~1
   b. Demon~1
   c. Demon~1.txt

Rename the **Demonstration files** folder to **Samples**.

18. What is the MS-DOS name of the Samples folder?
    a. Samples
    b. Samples~1
    c. Samples~1.txt

In the Contents pane, open the **Samples** folder on the Data disk. Select the file **March.txt**. Hold the [Ctrl] key and drag it to the **Drive A** icon on the tree side. Before you release the left mouse button, look for any symbols.

19. Did any symbol appear?
    a. Yes, the bent arrow appeared.
    b. Yes, the + symbol appeared.
    c. No, no symbol appeared.

Release the left mouse button while on top of the **Drive A** icon on the tree side.

20. The file was _____ to the root directory of A.
    a. copied.
    b. moved.

Delete the **Samples** folder.

21. What is the message box title?
    a. Confirm Folder Delete.
    b. Confirm File Delete.

Delete the **Games** folder.

22. Does a Confirm File Delete message box appear?
    a. Yes.
    b. No.

Click **Yes** or **Yes to All** in any dialog box. Open the **Sports** folder on the Data disk. Double-click the **Foot-col.tms** file icon.

23. What dialog box opened?
    a. Open With.
    b. Save As.
    c. no dialog box opened.

If any dialog box opened, close it. Change the name of the **Foot-col.tms** to **College football teams.txt**. Double-click the **College football teams.txt** file.

24. What is the nickname of the Michigan team?
    a. Bruins.
    b. Tigers.
    c. Wolverines.

Close the file. On the tree side, double-click the **3½ Floppy (A:)** icon to collapse it to its highest level. Close any open windows. Delete the **Explorer** and **Drive A** shortcuts on the desktop. Empty the Recycle Bin.

Problem Set II—Brief Essay

For all essay questions, use Notepad to create your answer. Then print your answer.

1. Compare and contrast moving and copying files and folders. Explain when you would choose to copy files and folders and when you would choose to move files and folders.
2. Deleting files and folders can have serious consequences. Agree or disagree with this statement, and explain your answer. In addition, describe the differences between deleting files and folders from a hard disk and from a floppy disk.

Problem Set III—Scenario

You see the following display:

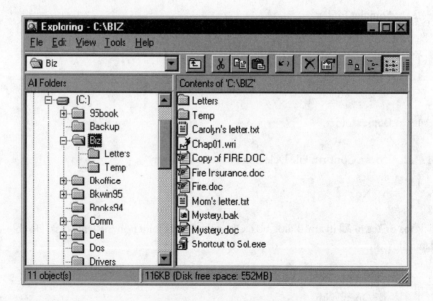

You do not want any files in the root of the Biz directory. Describe what folders you would create or rename. Explain your rationale. Are there any files that you feel you could delete? Explain your rationale. Describe the steps you would take to move, copy, and/or delete any files or folders.

Chapter 8

Organizing Your Disk

Chapter Overview

You do not purchase a computer exclusively to use Windows 95. You purchase a computer to help you be more efficient in doing your work. Work on a computer is comprised of two aspects—the applications programs that perform the work and the data files that you create to store your information. As you work with a computer, you accumulate many program and data files. If you are going to be an efficient user, you must have a way to manage these files. An operating system such as Windows 95 helps you manage those files. You have already used several tools to help you locate files and folders such as Explorer, My Computer, and Find.

As you have learned, folders allow you to group files together in a logical manner. The root directory, created when a disk is formatted, is limited in the number of entries it can contain. Folders that you create can contain any number of entries, limited only by the available disk space. You may add, delete, or rename folders as your needs change. These steps help in managing a large number of files efficiently, but it is best if you have an organizational scheme when manipulating files and folders.

In this chapter you will learn about strategies for organizing your disk as well as common pitfalls you should avoid. You will continue to work with Explorer and My Computer as well as learn about a new tool, Quick View.

Learning Objectives

1. Compare and contrast program files with data files.
2. Explain how Windows 95 can be used to manage program and data files.
3. Explain the importance of having an organizational scheme for a disk.
4. List and explain criteria that should be considered when organizing a hard disk.
5. Explain how to view the contents of a document in a program other than the one that created it.

Student Outcomes

1. Use Windows 95 to load program and data files and view the contents of files.
2. Copy and move data and program files, and create folders for files.
3. Use Explorer to organize the Data disk.
4. Use Quick View to view the contents of a document.

8.1 Revisiting Program and Data Files

You use your computer primarily to create and modify data files. Application programs enable you to make these editing changes. Looking at two application programs, Notepad and Address Manager, will help you understand why you want to organize your disk. Notepad is an application program written specifically for the Windows 95 environment, whereas your version of Address Manager was written for the Windows 3.1 environment. This is typical for most users. You will use programs written for Windows 95 and Windows 3.1.

Notepad, as you have learned, is an applet that comes with Windows 95. Notepad can be accessed from the Start menu (Start/Programs/Accessories/Notepad). The supplied version of Address Manager in the 95book\Addman folder is a shareware program that was written for Windows 3.1. It can be used, even though the operating system is now Windows 95. The Address Manager files were not installed on your system, but copied there. This is why the Address Manager program does not appear on any menu. The purpose of using these programs is to provide an example of how you work with Windows 95 in common business situations. You are going to use Windows 95 to load the program and data files.

A program file (application program) is a file that you load from a disk into memory. It provides the computer with instructions to the system. Windows 95 is the means by which a program is loaded into memory. Windows 95 then turns control over to the application program, but steps in again when the application program needs to interface with the hardware. For instance, when the program wants to write a character to the screen, it tells Windows 95 what to write and Windows 95 does the task of writing to the screen.

An application program is not sufficient unto itself; you also want to produce results, or data. Data, like the program that created it, is stored in files. A special relationship exists between the data and program files since a data file can typically be used only by the application program that created it. You may ask yourself, how does Windows 95 fit into the picture? Remember, the work you do takes place in memory. Windows 95 is the means by which the application program gets loaded into memory and also assists in loading the data file into memory so that the application program can use the data. This cooperative effort between Windows 95, the application program, and the data files is managed by Windows 95. An operating system takes care of all these tedious but necessary tasks. As the user, you do not directly interface with Windows 95 at this level. You will use Notepad and Address Manager to help you understand this process.

8.2   Activity—Using Notepad and Address Manager

Note: The following are the assumed settings:

My Computer
❑   Toolbar and status bar on (in the View menu).
❑   Large icons arranged by name (in the View menu).
❑   Browse folders by using a single window that changes as you open each folder (View/Options/Browse tab).
❑   Hide file of these types is set (View/Options/View tab).
❑   Display the full MS-DOS path in the title bar is set (View/Options/View tab).
❑   Hide MS-DOS file extensions for file types that are registered is not set (View/Options/View tab).

Explorer
❑   Toolbar and status bar on (in the View menu).
❑   List view arranged by name (in the View menu).
❑   Include description bar for left and right panes is on (in View/Options/View tab).

1 Click **Start**. Point at **Programs**. Point at **Accessories**. Click **Notepad**.

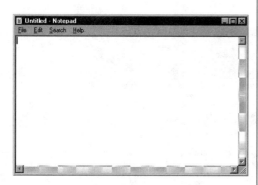

 You have opened the application program Notepad. Now you want to open a data file.

2 Click **File**. Click **Open**.

3 In the **File Name** text box, key in the following: **C:\95book\Stated.txt** **Enter**

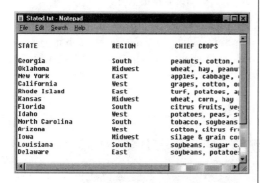

 You have opened a data file. Its content is a list of states, their geographic region, and their chief agricultural products. You have just used Windows 95 to load a program and a data file.

4 Close **Notepad**.

5 Click **Start** on the taskbar. Point at **Programs**.

 Depending on what programs were installed on your system, you will have more or fewer programs on the Programs menu than are displayed here. When you purchase a new program, you install it on your hard disk from a floppy disk. One of the steps in this process is to place the name of the newly installed application on the Start/Programs menu. Address Manager is not listed here, however. Why not? Its files were copied to the hard disk, not installed on the hard disk.

You may wonder why this program was not installed. As you work with your computer, you will accumulate more programs. You will not use all these programs with the same regularity. For instance, if you have a program that lets you generate birthday cards, you may only use it three or four times a year. If you have thirty programs that you use infrequently, having them on the Programs menu is not efficient. If a program is not listed on the Programs menu, this does not mean you cannot use the program; you just access it in a different way.

6   Open **Explorer**. Double-click the **95book** on the tree side (All Folders).

7   Click the **Addman** folder on the tree side.

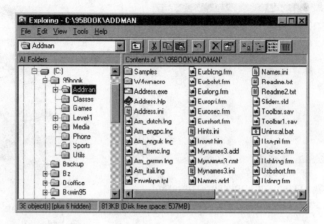

 You see that the Addman folder contains two subfolders, Samples and W4wmacro. The Contents side also contains many files. How do you know which is the application program and which are the data files? In this window there are two data files, Myname3.add and Names.add. The other files are support files. At this point, the only reason you know that there are two data files is because you were told. You can usually identify a program by its icon.

When you see an icon like this,   , it is probably a program icon, an executable. Programmers try to create an icon that represents what the program does, but icons are not always clearly identifiable. Another way to identify a program is by its extension. Address.exe is the program.

8   Double-click **Address.exe**. Click **I Agree**.

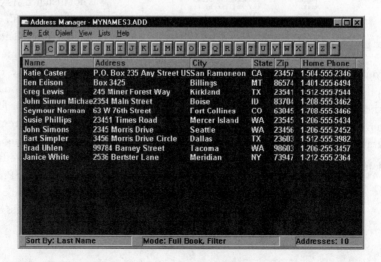

You had to click I Agree to acknowledge the conditions for using this shareware program. You are looking at the program called Address Manager. Address Manager, when loaded, automatically opened a data file called Mynames3.add. The title bar displays the program and data file names. As the program name implies, its purpose is to store addresses. If you have a Hint window on top, close it. If you see only one name instead of a list of names, click the [★] button on the alphabet toolbar.

The program is in a window with a menu bar. To use this program, you would need to learn the commands. However, there are some things you already know. You have menus that will be common to all Windows programs, such as a File menu and an Edit menu. You will find that certain commands are always located in the same menu. For instance, if you wanted to print, you know that Print would be found in the File menu; if you wanted to cut or copy information, you would know to go to the Edit menu. An advantage to using Windows 95 is that once you learn how to do something, you can apply those skills to the next program. The title bar reads Address Manager (the program), followed by Mynames3.add (the data file). The names and addresses listed are the data. If you want to view different data, you can open another data file.

9   Click **File**. Click **Open**.

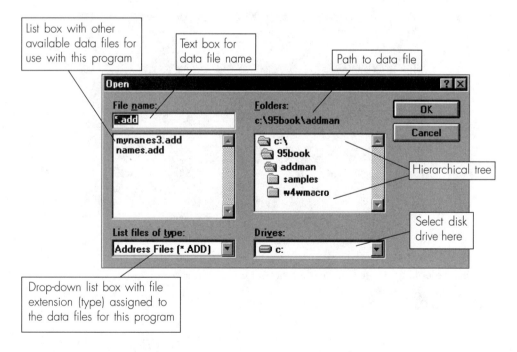

This is the File Open dialog box. It is the "old" way of looking for data files. The new File/Open box, as seen in Notepad, may look different but the elements are the same. You want to know on what drive and in what directory (folder) the data file is located.

10   Click **names.add** in the **list** box.

You have selected the file called names.add on Drive C in the subdirectory called Addman, which is beneath the subdirectory called 95book, which is beneath the root of C. The path name to the file would be written as C:\95book\Addman\Names.add. Case is immaterial.

11   Click **OK**.

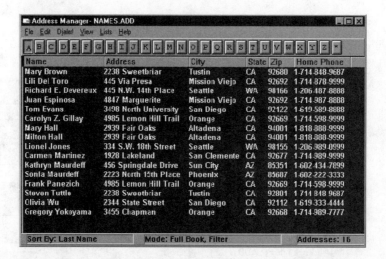

You are looking at data from a different file but with the same program.

12   Click **File**. Click **Open**. Click **Mynames3.add**. Click **OK**.

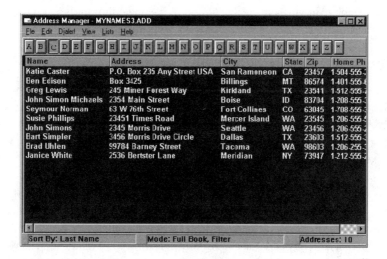

 You are viewing the data file you looked at originally. You have now looked at program files and data files.

13 Close **Address Manager**.

14 On the tree side, double-click **95book** to collapse it to its highest level. Close **Explorer**.

 You have returned to the desktop.

8.3   Getting Organized

In the last activity, you used two programs and three data files. This is just the beginning. You will accumulate many programs, and with each program you usually generate more data files. What you have is an information explosion. You need to manage these programs and data files so that you can locate what you need quickly.

As an example of this problem, imagine that you own 10 books. By reading each title, you can quickly peruse the authors and titles and locate the book you wish to read. Suppose your library grows and you now have 100 books. You do not want to have to read each author and title looking for a specific book, so you classify the information. A common classification scheme is to arrange the books alphabetically by the author's last name. If you want a book by Gillay, you quickly go to G. You may have more than one book by an author whose name begins with G, but by going to the letter G, you have narrowed your search. Now imagine you have 10,000 books. Organizing them alphabetically by author is not good enough. You may have 200 books by authors whose last names begin with G. So you further classify your books. You first divide them into categories like Computer or Fiction. Then, within the category, you arrange them alphabetically by last name. So if you wanted a computer book by Gillay, you would first go to the computer section, then to the letter G. If you wanted a novel by Greenleaf, you would first go to the fiction section and then the letter G. As you can see, you are classifying and categorizing information so that you can find it more quickly.

This is exactly what you want to do with files. Remember, you have many program and data files. You want to be able to locate them quickly. Grouping files logically is the best way to organize them. With Windows 95, you create folders (subdirectories) for storing related files.

8.4   Organizing a Hard Disk

Most people are inclined to place program and data files into the root directory of their hard disk, no matter what its size. When they purchase new programs, users either copy files from the floppy disks to the hard disk, use the standard setup, or install programs to place application programs on the hard disk. These programs create a folder for each application program and then copy the files from the floppy disks (or CD-ROM) to the named folder on the hard disk.

When you use Explorer or My Computer to view your files and folders, the file and folder names in the root directory seem to be endless. Even if you manage to load your program, you still need to locate your data files. It becomes difficult to know what files are on the hard disk and where they are located. You will spend your time looking for data files instead of working with them.

Since the root directory table has a finite limit, folders become mandatory. If every file were located in the root directory, you would ultimately get a message that the disk is full. The root directory table is what would actually be full. When you create a folder it counts as one entry in the root directory table, although the folder may hold hundreds of files or other folders. Your limitation then becomes the physical size of your hard disk.

When users discover folders, the norm is to create "lump" folders by dividing the disk into major applications, such as a word processing folder, a spreadsheet folder, and a database folder. The installation programs encourage this tendency. For example, when you install a program such as Word for Windows with the setup program, a folder called Winword is created to store all the Word program and support files.

You probably have more than one program on your computer system. The programs may have come with the computer when you purchased it, or you may have purchased additional programs. For instance, you might have a word processing program (Word for Windows), a spreadsheet program (Lotus 1-2-3), a database program (Access), a checkbook management program (Quicken for Windows), and your operating system, Windows 95. Figure 8.1 shows what your hard disk might look like.

In the figure, the ellipsis (...) represents the rest of the files. The installation program would create a folder for each application and place the program and support files that belong to the application program in the proper subdirectory. Some programs, like Quicken, will automatically create a separate folder for data files.

The point is, you want to use the programs to do work. As an example, say you are a salesperson selling widgets and bangles. You use Word to write letters to clients and make proposals, Lotus to do budget projections, Quicken to manage expenses, Access to manage client names and addresses in a database, and Windows 95 to manage your files and disks. You understand that you do not want the data files such as report.doc or clients.mdb in the root directory. To begin the organization of your disk, you could move the Report.doc file to the Word folder and the Clients.mdb file to the Msaccess folder.

Placing the data files in the program folders is not a good organizational technique for several reasons. Program files do not change, while data files change as often as you add or delete information.

Figure 8.1 A Typical Hard Disk Organization

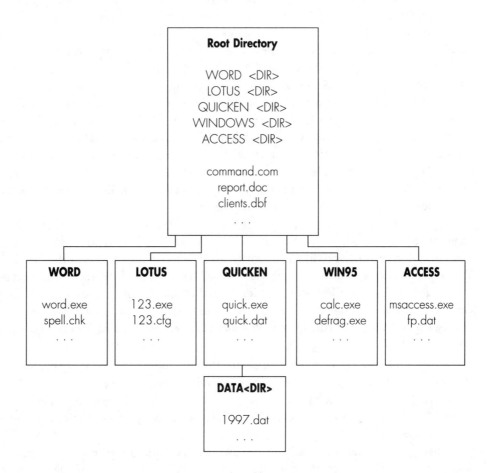

Within this process you are also adding and deleting files. You will want to back up your files from the hard disk to a floppy disk or tape to insure you do not lose your data. If you have placed your data files in the program folders, you will have to sort through many program and support files to back up your data. Furthermore, part of the rationale for folders is to categorize information; data files are information.

Part of a good organizational scheme is creating meaningful names for your data files so you may identify what they contain at a later date. Remember, naming data files requires more thought than most beginning users realize. Because Windows 95 allows up to 255 characters for a file name, it might seem easy to create meaningful names. The availability of long file names can actually be problematic, however. Certainly, if you are using older programs, you must still use the old 8.3 file naming rule. As you remember, Windows 95 creates an MS-DOS alias for a long file name. Thus, when using long file names, you will find it is helpful to know the 8.3 file name in older applications. You encounter another problem, however, if you named one file Status report for January and another file Status report for February. If you tried to open these files in an older application program, your choices would be Status~1.doc and Status~2.doc in the File Open dialog box. If you had named the files Jan status report.doc and Feb status report.doc, your aliases becomes much easier to read: Jansta~1.doc and Febsta~1.doc. In addition, many utility programs will not work with long file names. Utility programs include such types of programs as virus scanning programs or disk repair utilities. Many of these types of programs rely on the FAT, not the VFAT, and will not work with long file names.

Long file names may pose a problem in Windows 95 as well. Although the file name can be up to 255 characters in length, the full path name cannot be more than 260 characters. Thus, if you had a 250-character file name and tried to move it to a different folder, you may exceed the maximum number of characters allowed since the folder name is part of the file name. Furthermore, file names that are too long make browsing a list of files in Explorer very difficult. Remember, also, that for older application programs, you will only be able to give the documents long file names in Explorer or My Computer. The application program will not let you save a long file name.

An added difficulty in creating meaningful names is that you often have similar file names. As an example, let's say you are a salesperson who sells two products, widgets and bangles. You could track your clients for the bangles product line in a database and save the information in a file called Clients for the Bangles product line (Client~1.mdb). This is a good, definitive name. When you create a client list for the Widgets product line, Clients for the Widgets product line (Client~2.mdb) is a good name for that file. An efficient way to distinguish one file from another is to create two folders, Bangles and Widgets, and to place each client file in the appropriate folder. Figure 8.2 shows a hard disk organizational scheme with folders for data.

Although this organizational scheme is better than placing the data files in the root directory or in the program folders, it is still very inefficient. There are too many repeated folder names. In addition, every time you wanted to use a data file, you would have to remember what application was used to created the file and where the appropriate data file was located. You would have to key in long path names such as C:\Word\Widgets\Report.doc.

You can use data files in conjunction with different application programs. For instance, you could use Access to generate a mailing list from your client~1.mdb file and use the same file with Word to send out a form letter. When you begin doing this, you end up with data in two places: the word processing folder and the database folder. When you purchased a new program, you would need to add a new folder for that program and further folders for your products, bangles and widgets. What if you picked up a new product line, such as beads? Now you would have to create a Beads folder under each application program. Finding out where the files are located and deciding what data files to keep would be a logistical nightmare.

The real problem with this typical organizational scheme is the logic behind it. Remember, programs are tools. In the past, when you used tools such as a pencil, calculator, or typewriter, did you file documents according to the name of the tool you used? When you wrote a letter using a typewriter, did you file it in a folder labeled Typewriter? Of course not. But in the above organizational scheme, that is exactly what you have been doing.

It makes much more sense to organize a hard disk by the way you work rather than by the application package (tool). An efficient organizational scheme makes it easier to save, locate, back up,

Figure 8.2 Organizing a Disk by Software Application Package

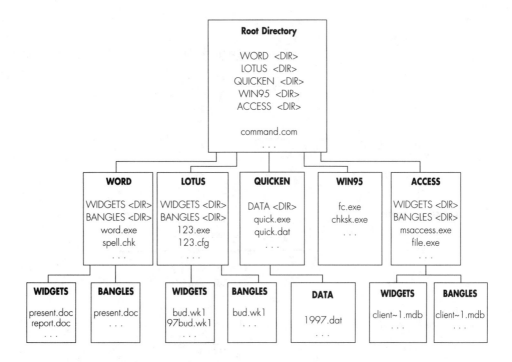

add, and delete data files, as well as to add and delete program files. The following section will recommend some guidelines to assist you in organizing your hard disk. You must keep in mind, however, that what is a good organizational scheme for one user may not work for another.

8.5   Methods of Organizing a Hard Disk

The following criteria can give a hard disk an efficient and logical organization:

❑   The root directory should be a map to the rest of the disk. Look at the root directory as the index or table of contents to your entire hard disk. Ideally, when you execute Explorer, you should be able to see all the folders and files on Drive C without scrolling.

❑   Plan the organization of your hard disk.

❑   Create as many folders and subfolders as you need *before* copying files into folders and subfolders.

❑   Keep folder names short but descriptive. Try to stay away from vague folder names such as Data.

❑   Do not place data files in the same folder as program files.

❑   Create folders that are shallow and wide instead of compact and deep. This means that you would have several folders branching from the root directory, rather than having one folder, with a subfolder beneath it, and another subfolder beneath that, and so on. This makes it easier for you to find files. If you create folders that are compact and deep, you will have buried files several levels down. See Figure 8.3.

Figure 8.3   *Shallow and Wide versus Compact and Deep*

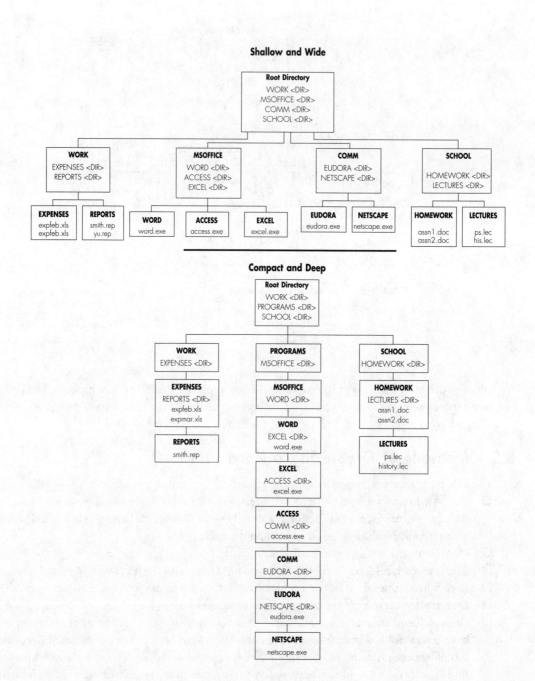

❑ Many small folders with a few files in each are better than a large folder with many files. If you begin to get too many files in a folder, think about breaking the folder into two or more subfolders. On the other hand, if a folder has only one or two files, think about placing those files in another folder.

❑ Create a separate folder containing all the application software you will be using. This program subdirectory will be a map to all the software application programs on the disk.

❑ Learn how to use the application package and how the application package works.

❑ Analyze the way you work. If you always use an application program's default data directory when you save and retrieve files, then you might want to create data directories. Figure 8.4 shows another way to organize your hard disk.

Figure 8.4 Another Organizational Scheme

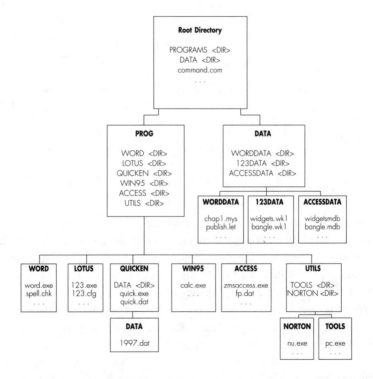

❑ Analyze your environment. If, for instance, you are in an educational environment, organizing your disk by application package is logical.

An organizational scheme following the project logic and based on our salesperson scenario could look something like Figure 8.5.

Figure 8.5   Organization by Project

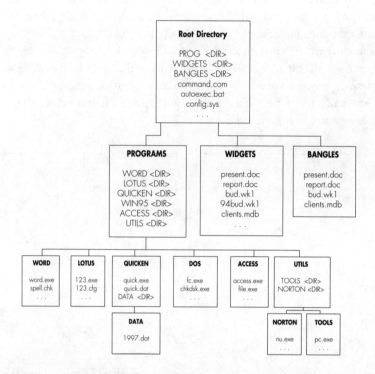

This organizational scheme has many advantages. You know where all your software application programs are located. In addition, it is much easier to add a new software package or to update an existing software package because all the program files are located in one place. For instance, if you wanted to add a presentation software application program such as Harvard Graphics, you would create a folder called C:\Programs\Hg. All the files would be installed in that location. Since this scheme is organized by project, it is also easy to add a new project or delete an old one. If, for example, you are now selling beads, you create a folder called C:\Beads. If you no longer are selling widgets, you eliminate the Widgets folder entirely. This scheme makes it easy to tell which data files belong to which project. You can also tell what data file belongs to which program by virtue of the file extension. In this example, if you look at the subdirectory called Widgets, you know that the data files Present.doc and Report.doc were created with Word, that the data files Bud.wk1 and 94bud.wk1 were created with Lotus, and that Clients.mdb was created with Access. The same is true for the Bangles folder. This example also shows leaving the Data subdirectory in Quicken, because that is where the Quicken program prefers the data.

This, of course, is not the only way to organize a hard disk. You can organize your hard disk any way you wish, but there should be some logic to your organization. Although it may take some time in the beginning, organization will ultimately make more effective use of the hard disk and of your time. The two major considerations for any organizational scheme are, How do *you* work? and How do the *application programs* work?

8.6   Organizing Programs

When working with your computer in an office environment, you will work primarily on the hard disk. But since you are in a learning situation, you are going to learn to accomplish tasks using the floppy disk rather than the hard disk. In this way, you will not harm files or folders on your hard disk as you learn and practice. You are using the Data disk instead of the hard disk, but the techniques you learn are the same.

You want to organize the Data disk so that files and folders are logically organized. You want to be able to quickly see what is on the disk. As you know, there are many commands to help you with these tasks in Explorer or My Computer. You can create folders and copy or move files from one location to another easily. In order to exemplify the process, you are going to work with both program and data files.

8.7   Activity—Creating Folders and Copying Files

1 Place the Data disk in Drive A.

2 Open **Explorer**. Double-click the **Drive A** icon in the tree side.

3 Right-click on the Contents side. Point to **New**. Click **Folder**.

4 Key in the following: **Addman Enter**

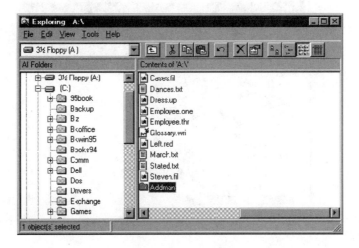

 You have a new folder called Addman with no files in it. You decide you would like a more descriptive name. You may rename files and folders any time.

5   Press the F2 key.

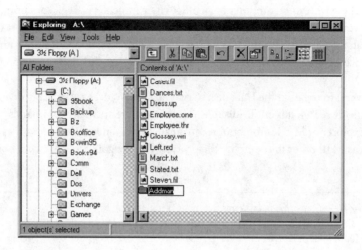

 What's happening?   Pressing the F2 key is a keyboard shortcut to renaming files and folders. The box appears around Addman. You can directly key in your new name.

6   Key in the following: **ADDRESS MANAGER** Enter

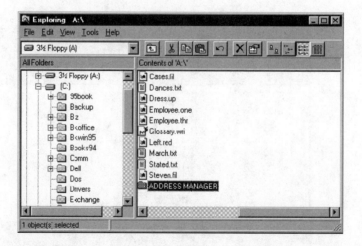

What's happening?   You have renamed your folder without creating a new folder. Since you renamed it, Windows 95 retained your capitalization of ADDRESS MANAGER.

7   Click **View**. Point to **Arrange Icons**. Click **by Name**. If necessary, scroll so your window looks as follows:

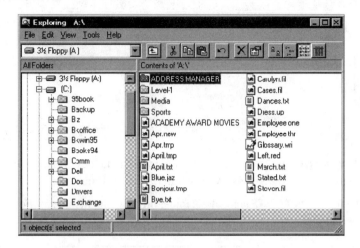

8   Open another copy of **Explorer**. Double-click **Drive C**. Double-click **95book** in the **Exploring - C:** window in the left pane. Double-click **Addman** in the **Exploring - C:\95book** window in the left pane. Right-click the taskbar. Click **Tile Horizontally**.

9   In the **Exploring - C:\95book\Addman** window, click **View**, then click **Options**. Click the **View** tab. Click the **Show all files** command button. Click **OK**.

10   In the **Exploring - C:\95book\Addman** window, hold down the Ctrl key and select the following files. (*Note:* You will need to scroll to select all the files.)

Address.exe	**Mynames3.add**	**Toolbar.sav**
Address.hlp	**Mynames3.cmt**	**Toolbar1.sav**
Address.ini	**Mynames3.ini**	**Wwwdbms.dll**
Ctl3dv2.dll	**Names.add**	**Wwwddec.dll**
Hints.ini	**Names.ini**	**Wwwinsrt.dll**
Insert.bin	**Sliders.sld**	**Wwwtoys.dll**
Instlstr.dll		

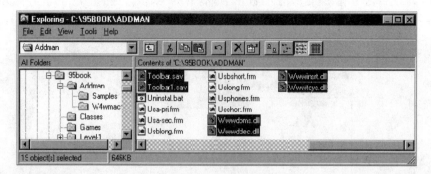

 You have selected program files, support files, and data files. You have selected the files you are going to drag into the Address Manager folder on the Data disk.

11 Left-drag the files to the **ADDRESS MANAGER** folder on the Contents side of the **Exploring - A:** window. It is already expanded.

 As you begin to drag them across the window border, you see the outline of all the files you are copying. You also see the + sign, which denotes a copy operation.

12 When you are over the **ADDRESS MANAGER** folder in the **Exploring - A:** window, release the left mouse button.

 The Copying information box tells you the progress of the copy.

13 Right-click the taskbar. Click **Undo Tile**. Close the **Exploring - C:\95book\Addman** window.

14 Click the **Exploring A:** window to make it active. Double-click the **3½ Floppy (A:)** on the tree side to expand it.

 You dragged and dropped files from the hard disk to the Data disk to the ADDRESS MANAGER folder. You have two copies of all these files—a complete set on the hard disk and another set on the floppy disk. Now you want to organize this disk so it is most convenient for you.

15 Right-click in the Contents side. Point to **New**. Click **Folder**. Key in the following: **MY APRIL PROJECT** [Enter]

16 Click **View**. Point to **Arrange Icons**. Click **by Name**.

17 Scroll so that you may see your folders.

18 Select all the **April** files. Drag them into the **MY APRIL PROJECT** folder.

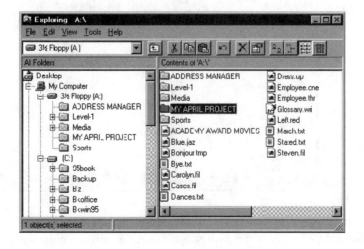

When you left-dragged the April files into MY APRIL PROJECT folder, the default was a move. Already your disk is a little easier to read because there are less files in the root directory. If you left-drag within the same drive, the default is to move the files.

19   Double-click the **Media** folder on the tree side to expand it. Click the **3½ Floppy (A:)** to select it.

 You have expanded the tree. You want to move the ACADEMY AWARD MOVIES and the Dances.txt files to the Movies folder, which is under the Media folder.

20   Select those two files on the Contents side and drag them to the **Media** folder on the tree side.

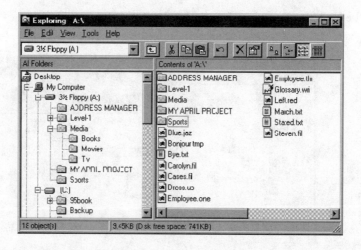

 You are moving your data files from one location to another. Although you can move data files from one location to another with ease and safety, moving program files is another story. If you want to move an installed program to another location, many problems can occur. First and foremost is the possibility that the program will not be able to locate all its support files and will not work. Second, if the program was installed (as opposed to copied), the Registry will not be updated and the program will not run.

21 Double-click the **ADDRESS MANAGER** folder on the tree side. Select **Address.exe** and right-drag it to the **3½ Floppy (A:)** icon on the tree side.

> **What's happening?** The default choice is Create Shortcut(s) Here. You want to choose Move Here.

22 Click **Move Here**. Click the **3½ Floppy (A:)** icon on the tree side.

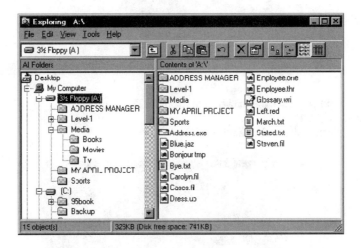

> **What's happening?** You moved a program file. There is only one copy of it on the Data disk, in the root directory folder.

23 Double-click **Address.exe** on the Contents side.

> **What's happening?** Indeed, the program will not run. You cannot move program files easily, but you can move data files.

24 Right-drag **Address.exe** back to the **ADDRESS MANAGER** folder.

25 In the root directory of A, create a new folder called **Clients**.

26 Click **View**. Point to **Arrange Icons**. Click **by Name**. Click the **ADDRESS MANAGER** folder on the tree side.

27 Click on the **Mynames3.add** file. Hold the Shift key and click **Names.ini**.

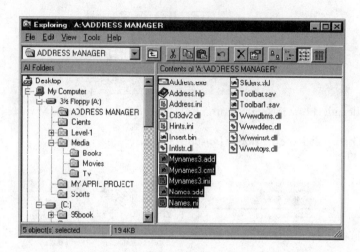

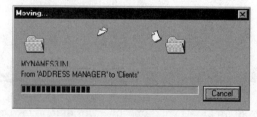

You are going to move the data files to the new Clients directory.

28 Left-drag the selected files to the **Clients** folder.

You have moved the files. You use the address program every day. You are going to create a folder for your daily events.

29 In the root of A, create a new folder called **Daily**. Arrange your folders by name. Click the **ADDRESS MANAGER** folder. Drag **Address.exe** into **Daily**. Open **Daily**.

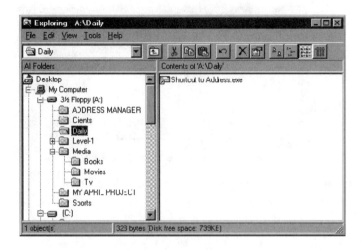

 You have created a shortcut to the Address program. You did not move it.

30 Double-click **Shortcut to Address.exe**. Click **I Agree**. Click **File**. Click **Open**.

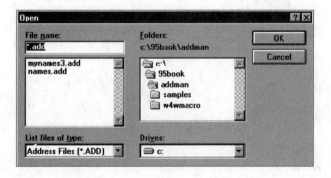

Address Manager remembers the last place you opened a data file: on Drive C, in the 95book folder, in the Addman subfolder. You want Address Manager to look on Drive A, in Clients.

31   In the **Drives** drop-down list box click **a**. Double-click **Clients** in the **Folders** list box. Click **Mynames3.add** in the **File name** list box.

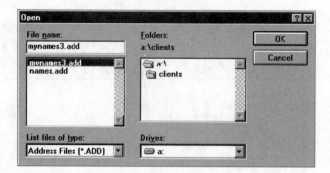

 You are telling Address Manager where to find the file of interest.

32   Click **OK**.

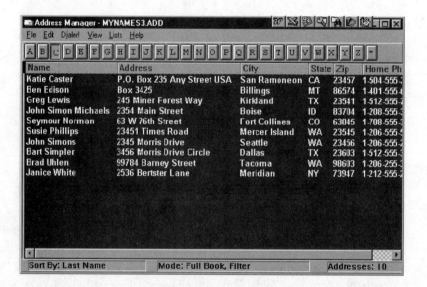

 You are now looking at this copy of the Mynames3.add file in the Clients folder.

33 Close **Address Manager**. Double-click the **Clients** folder on the tree side.

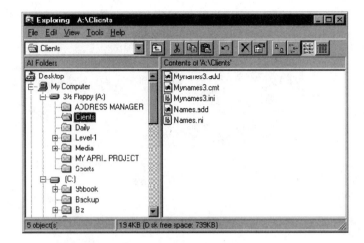

> What's happening?   You decide that these file names are not sufficiently descriptive, so you want to give them more distinctive names.

34 Select **Names.add** and press F2.

35 Key in the following: **NAMES OF ALL MY FRIENDS.ADD** Enter

36 Select **Mynames3.add** and press F2.

37 Key in the following: **NAMES OF ALL MY CLIENTS.ADD** Enter

38 Click the **Large Icons** view button.

39 Click the **List** view button. **Arrange by Name**.

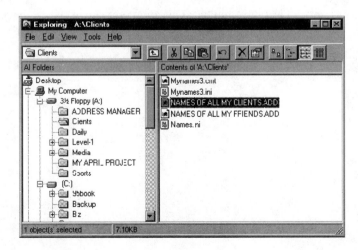

You now have more distinctive names. You rearranged the view so that you could see the full file names.

40 Click **Daily** on the tree side. Double-click **Shortcut to Address Manager**. Click **I Agree**.

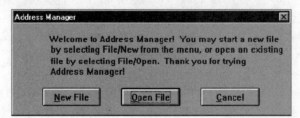

 Since you changed the file name, Address Manager can no longer find the file.

41 Click **Open File**.

42 Double-click the **a:** icon in the **Folders** window. Double-click the **Clients** folder.

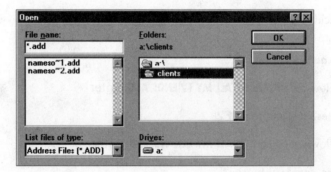

 You have a long file name. Although Address Manager will work in Windows 95, it cannot recognize long file names. The File/Open box is looking for files with the .add extension in the clients directory. You now see the truncated file names, nameso~1.add and namcso~2.add. You may still use either file, but within the application program, it is hard to identify which file is which.

43 Click **nameso~1.add**. Click **OK**.

 The data file opened and the data is the same as it was under the old file name. If you look at the title bar, you see that the name of the program appears first (Address Manager), followed by the 8.3 character file name (NAMESO~1.ADD). Thus, using long file names will be problematic until older application programs are updated to the Windows 95 way of naming files. Even when programs are updated to reflect long file names, you should not give your files just any name. You should develop a naming scheme that allows you to retrieve all the files that deal with the same topic.

44   Click **File**. Click **Open**. Click **nameso~2.add**. Click **OK**.

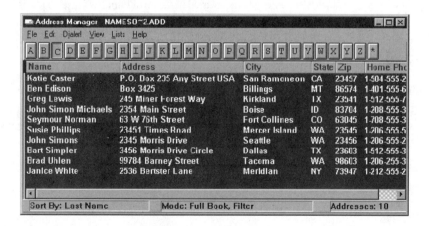

 You have opened the other data file.

45   Close **Address Manager**.

46   On the tree side, click the **Drive A** icon to select it. Press the ⊟ key on the numeric keypad to collapse it to its highest level.

47 Click **View**. Click **Options**. Click **Hide files of these types**. Click **OK**.

48 Close all open windows.

  You have returned to the desktop.

8.8   Previewing Documents

The ability to identify what is contained in data documents helps you to organize your files. Once you know what is in a document, you can determine what to do with the document (move, delete, or copy it). In order to look at the contents of a document, you must first open the application program that created the document, either by double-clicking the document icon (if it is a registered file type) or by opening the application program and then using the File/Open command on the menu bar. It can take anywhere from a few seconds to a few minutes to open an application program. The time it takes to open an application program depends on your hardware (processor speed and disk drive speed) as well as the application program's inherent speed of opening.

Windows 95 provides a feature called Quick View. After you select a document, Quick View is available on the File menu of Explorer or My Computer or on the pop-up menu when you right-click. This feature gives you a fast look at the contents of a file. You cannot change or modify the data in Quick View. To do this, you must use the application program that created the data, and you must, therefore, own the application program.

To use Quick View, Windows 95 must be able to recognize the object's type. The file must have a registered file extension, assigned either by you or the application program. Quick View is not installed by default when you install Windows 95. You must choose to install this option. You can add this feature at any time by using Add/Remove Programs, located in Control Panel. If Quick View is not available on a menu, it means that either you did not install Quick View or there is no support in Quick View for that file type. The Quick View feature can show you the contents of many types of files, even files created in applications that you do not own.

As an example of how you might use Quick View to assist you in organizing your hard disk, you will view some documents in the 95book directory to find out what they contain. Even if you do not own the application program that created the document, you will be able to look at the document's contents. When you know what is in a document, you can then decide what to do with it.

8.9 Activity—Using Quick View

1 Open **Explorer**. Double-click the **95book** folder on the tree side.

2 On the Contents side, right-click **Apr.99**.

  A pop-up menu appears. Since the .99 file extension is not a registered file type, Windows 95 does not know what program created the data. Quick View is not an option on the pop-up menu.

3 Click **File** on the menu bar.

  This is the other way to access the Quick View choice. Because Quick View does not recognize the file type, it still is not an available option.

4 Click on the desktop to deselect **Apr.99**.

5 Locate **April.txt** in the **Contents** window of the **Exploring - C:\95book** window. Right-click **April.txt**.

  Since .txt is a registered file extension (the default extension for Notepad documents), Windows 95 knows it can open it. A pop-up menu appears with Quick View on it.

6 Click **Quick View**.

7 Click **View**. If **Toolbar** and **Status Bar** are not set, click each one to set these options.

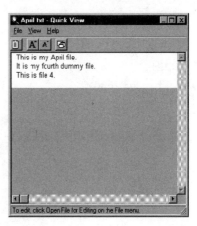

  You can see the data in the document. The message at the bottom of the Quick View window tells you that you can open this file for editing from this window. Some, but not all, file types allow this option in Quick View. You may open this document either by using the File/Open File for Editing choice or by using the Open File for Editing button on the toolbar.

8   Hold the mouse over the first icon on the toolbar.

 A ToolTip pops up, indicating that you can edit this file. To edit the file, you will open the application that created the data. The two A icons on the toolbar allow you to increase or decrease the size of the font.

9   Click the large **A** icon five times.

 Now the text is easier to read. This changes the font size only in Quick View, not in the document.

10   Click **View** on the menu bar.

 You have dropped down the View menu. The Toolbar is set, as is the Status Bar. Replace Window is not set, which means that if you right-click documents and choose Quick View, a new Quick View window will open for each document. If you set Replace Window, one window will remain open and each time you right-click a document and choose Quick View, the new document will replace the previous one. Another choice on the menu is Page View. With this option, you can look at the document as it would appear on a printed page.

11   Click **Page View**.

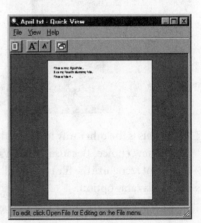

 You can see a print preview of this document. Since the Quick View window is open, you can drag other documents (files) into it. If you cannot see the Explorer window, move the Quick View window so you can.

12 Click **View** on the **Quick View** window menu bar. Unset **Page View** by removing the check mark.

13 Drag and drop **Award.mov** from the **Explorer** window into the **Quick View** window.

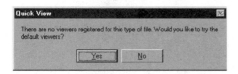

  The .mov extension is not registered, but Quick View will try and help you. It will see if it can open the file with the its default viewers. These viewers are data files created with popular Windows-based programs.

14 Click **Yes**.

  Since this is a text file, the default viewer could open it and show you the contents.

15 Drag and drop **Basket.bmp** from the **Explorer** window into the **Quick View** window.

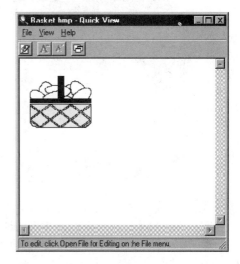

  The .bmp file extension is registered to the Paint program, so Quick View could open this file and show you the graphic. Note that because there are no fonts in this document, you do not have font choices available on the toolbar.

16 Click **View** on the menu bar of the **Quick View** window.

  Since this is a graphic (picture), Font is not available on the menu but Rotate is.

17 Click **Rotate**.

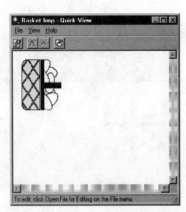

You rotated the object and placed it on its side. You are not changing the actual picture, only the view of it in Quick View.

18 Click the first button on the toolbar, **Open File for Editing**.

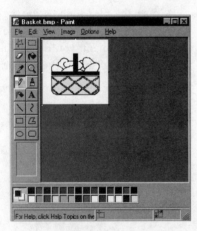

You opened the application program Paint, which allows you to add to the drawing, change colors, or make other changes. Note that the picture is not rotated in the application program; you only rotated the view, not the picture. Since you opened the program that created the data, Quick View is no longer open.

19 Click the **Close** button for **Paint**.

20 Click the **Classes** folder in the tree pane of the **C:\95book** folder.

21 Right-click **Computer.xls** in the Contents side of the window.

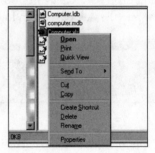

Even if you do not own the Excel program, Excel is a registered file type that Quick View recognizes. If you own Excel, you may edit the document. If you do not own Excel, you may view the document with Quick View but cannot edit it.

22 Click **Quick View**.

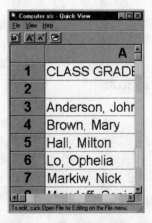

You are looking at the file called Computer.xls. Notice the large font size. The Quick View window remembers the last option you set.

23   Click the **Decrease Font Size** button five times on the **Quick View** menu bar.

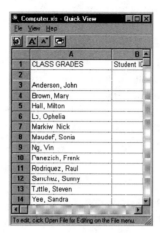

 You have returned the font to the default size. The next time you open a document in Quick View, it will be in this font size.

24   Close the **Quick View** window.

25   Close all open windows.

 You have returned to the desktop.

Chapter Summary

In this chapter you learned that all disks should be organized. Program and data files should not reside in the same directory. Many users organize their disks by application programs, focusing on the tools rather than the data. In general, it is best to focus on your data files. Once organized, it is then easier to move, copy, save, back up, and accomplish the other necessary data management tasks.

You also learned that part of an organizational scheme is naming your files. If you will be working with older programs that use the 8.3 file naming rule, you must be cautious in using long file names. Even if your application program recognizes long file names, you should still plan how you will name your files so that you may locate them easily. You learned that Quick View is a tool that will assist you in identifying what is in a file so that you may best decide what to do with it.

Discussion Questions

1. Explain the relationship between application programs and data files.
2. Why would a user copy program files to the hard disk rather than install the program?
3. Why would it be important to group your files in a logical manner?
4. Explain why it is important to organize a disk.
5. Why is it mandatory to use folders?

6. Why is it important to avoid placing data files in program folders?
7. Why should file and folder names be chosen with care?
8. Identify two advantages in using long file names.
9. Identify two disadvantages in using long file names.
10. Explain how having the root directory serve as a map to the rest of your disk would be helpful in organizing your disk.
11. List and explain five criteria that should be considered when organizing your disk.
12. What happens to long file names in a program that does not recognize them?
13. Identify two ways to view the contents of a document.
14. Explain the purpose and function of Quick View.
15. How could you use Quick View to help you organize a disk?

True/False Questions

For each question, circle the letter T if the statement is true or the letter F if the statement is false.

T   F   1. A folder in the root directory can contain an infinite number of files limited only by the size of the disk.

T   F   2. There is no difference between copying program files to a hard disk and installing a program to the hard disk.

T   F   3. It is not wise to place data files in program folders as data files are constantly changing while program files rarely change.

T   F   4. Many small folders with few files is a better organizational scheme than one large folder with many files.

T   F   5. Quick View can be used to edit information in a file.

Completion Questions

Write the correct answer in each blank space provided.

6. A file name can have up to _____ characters in its name.
7. A good rule of thumb to use when naming folders is to make the folder name _____ and descriptive.
8. When organizing your disk, _____ files are safe to move.
9. A file is called My budget files for 1995.doc. The short file name would be _____.
10. A tool to assist you in looking at a data file's contents is _____.

Multiple Choice Questions

Circle the letter of the correct answer for each question.

11. If you have a file called Run.exe and right-drag the file to a different folder on the same drive, the default action will be
    a. a move.
    b. a copy.
    c. a shortcut.
    d. none of the above

12. Which of the following types of files should not moved?
   a. Program files.
   b. Data files.
   c. Shortcuts.
   d. all the above

13. Copying program files to the hard disk is different from installing the program because
   a. installing the program will register the program's data file type.
   b. installing a program will create an entry for it under the Start menu.
   c. both a and b
   d. neither a nor b

14. To rename a folder or file, after you select the object, you may press _____ to rename it.
   a. **Alt** + R
   b. **F2**
   c. **Ctrl** + N
   d. none of the above

15. If you right-click a file and the Quick View option is not shown, what could be wrong?
   a. Quick View is not installed.
   b. There is no support in Quick View for that type of file.
   c. both a and b
   d. neither a nor b

Application Assignments

Problem Set I—At the Computer

Problem A

Place the Data disk in Drive A. Open **Explorer**. Create a folder on the root of the Data disk called **Expenses**. Use Find to locate all the files that begin with **Exp** and have **.dat** as a file extension in the **95book** folder. *Hint:* Remember wildcards. Copy them to the newly created **Expenses** folder on the Data disk.

1. How many files were copied?
   a. three files.
   b. six files.
   c. nine files.
   d. twelve files.

On the Data disk, in the **Expenses** folder, rename **Exp93jan.dat** to **Expenses for January, 1993.txt**. On the Data disk, in the **Expenses** folder, rename **Exp93feb.dat** to **Expenses for February, 1993.txt**.

2. What is the MS-DOS name for Expenses for February, 1993.dat?
   a. Expens~1.txt
   b. Expens~2.txt
   c. Expenses1.txt
   d. Expenses2.txt

Close any open dialog boxes. Use **Notepad** to open **Expenses for February, 1993.dat**.

3. The title bar of Notepad states
   a. Expenses for February, 1993.txt - Notepad
   b. Notepad - Expenses for February, 1993.txt

4. Notepad
   a. supports long file names.
   b. does not support long file names.
   c. will let you choose whether to use the long file name or the MS-DOS file name.
   d. both a and c

Close **Notepad**. Close **Explorer**.

Problem B

Open an **Explorer** window. Double-click the **95book** folder on the tree side. Click the Contents side. Press the **G** key.

5. You quickly moved to the
   a. Games folder.
   b. Glossry.wri file.

Locate the file called **Grammy.rec** in the **95book** folder. Right-click it.

6. Is Quick View available for this file?
   a. Yes.
   b. No.

Locate the file called **Timekard.doc** in the **Utils** folder in the **95book** folder. Right-click it.

7. Is Quick View available for this file?
   a. Yes.
   b. No.

Close **Explorer**.

Problem C

In the **95book** folder, locate the file called **Stated.txt**. Use **Quick View**. Use the Font buttons to increase or decrease the size of the fonts and size the screen so that you can see three columns, **State**, **Region**, and **Chief Crops**.

8. A chief crop of Georgia is
   a. citrus fruit.
   b. corn.
   c. hay.

Leave the **Quick View** window open. Locate the file called **Grammy.rec** and drag it into the **Quick View** window.

9. In 1992, what artist won a Grammy for *Tears in Heaven*?
   a. Bette Midler.
   b. Paul Simon.
   c. Eric Clapton.

Leave the **Quick View** window open. Locate the file called **Plane.bmp** and drag it into the **Quick View** window.

10. What color is the plane?
    a. Red.
    b. Blue.
    c. Green.

Close **Quick View**. Close **Explorer**.

Problem Set II—Brief Essay

For all essay questions, use Notepad to create your answer. Then print your answer.
1. List five criteria that can be used for organizing a hard disk. Explain the rationale for each.
2. One way to organize a hard disk is by project. Another way is to organize it by application program. Which way do you prefer? What advantages/disadvantages do you see to each method? Explain your answer.

Problem Set III—Scenario

You are currently enrolled in college. You are taking Political Science, History, and Windows 95. You have been using your computer for your lecture notes, assignments, and other classroom requirements. You have created the following files:

File name	Purpose of file
PS - Lecture 1.txt	Notes for first week's lectures in political science.
Lecture 2 - PS.txt	Notes for second week's lectures in political science.
History lecture	Notes for first week's lectures in history.
2ndHlec.txt	Notes for second week's lectures in history.
Win951.doc	Notes for first week's lectures in the Windows 95 class.
95-2.txt	Notes for second week's lectures in the Windows 95 class.
history.rep	Beginning of a history research paper.
Assn1.win95	First assignment for the Windows 95 class.
Assn1 for history.doc	First assignment for the history class.

You decide you need to organize your information efficiently. You need to create folders. You may rename your files in this plan. You may use long file names for any or all of your files, if you choose. Write a brief paper discussing your organizational scheme. Include the following information in your report:

1. A drawing showing your folder structure.
2. The purpose of each folder.
3. The location of each file and why you placed it there.
4. If you rename a file, the old name and the new name.
5. If you use a long file name, your rationale for the new name.
6. A file naming scheme for the new files that you anticipate creating for your classes. Describe your reasons for your file naming plan.

Chapter 9

Customizing Your System

Chapter Overview

In this chapter, you will begin to appreciate the Windows 95 options that allow you to customize your computer based on your needs. You will be able to save time by setting features so that they behave the way you want. You can personalize the computer by setting up user profiles. You can see what fonts are installed on your system and arrange them by similarities. Depending on your hardware, you will be able to alter your monitor's resolution. You can set fonts, colors, patterns, and wallpaper for your desktop. You will learn about screen savers and how they help to protect your monitor. If you have a sound card, you can assign sounds to computer events. You can adjust your mouse or keyboard to better meet your needs. You will be able to customize the Start menu by adding or removing programs and files.

Learning Objectives

1. Explain the purpose and function of Control Panel.
2. Discuss user profiles and passwords.
3. Describe the purpose of system date and system time.
4. Identify regional settings that can be altered.
5. List the types of fonts and describe their purposes.
6. Explain the purpose and function of screen resolutions.
7. Explain how to customize your desktop by using color schemes, patterns, and wallpaper.
8. Explain the purpose and function of screen savers.
9. List reasons for and ways of customizing the mouse and keyboard.
10. Describe the steps to add items to or remove items from the Start menu.
11. Describe an event and explain why sounds are assigned to it.

Student Outcomes

1. Use Control Panel to customize and adjust screen elements and to set a password.
2. Set and display the date and time.
3. View and alter regional settings.
4. Use the Fonts folder to view and arrange fonts.
5. Identify the resolution and colors availability of the monitor.
6. Use wallpaper, patterns, and color to customize your desktop.
7. Use and customize a screen saver. Set a password for a screen saver.

8. Alter the functions of the mouse and keyboard.

9. Add items to and remove items from the Start menu.

10. Add a sound to an event, but only if a sound card is available.

9.1   Introducing Control Panel

When Windows 95 was installed on your computer, it gave you a standard configuration for your desktop, keyboard, and mouse. The setup program chose standard colors, screen resolution, button and icon sizes, and icon locations. The way the keyboard and mouse operate is also established by the setup program.

You are not limited to these default choices. Control Panel allows you to make changes to these default settings. You can change the appearance and behavior of different elements of your workspace. For instance, you can control how much information fits on the screen by changing the resolution of your monitor (depending on the kind of monitor and video card you have). You can change the colors, add wallpaper, and change the size of the font for icons, toolbars, or any other fonts that appear on your screen. You can also speed up or slow down the movement of your mouse or keyboard. If you have the correct software, you can select larger, smaller, or animated pointers.

Besides changing some of the features of your system, Control Panel provides ways for you to maintain your system. Maintaining your system means adding or removing hardware or programs. Through Control Panel you can support networks, modems, and multimedia devices. Windows 95 also provides special support to physically challenged individuals so that they can have better control of their computer.

The contents of Control Panel depend on the choices that were made when Windows 95 was installed and if Microsoft Plus! was installed. Microsoft Plus! is a purchased add-on to Windows 95. An *add-on* is an accessory or utility program designed to work with, extend, and increase the capabilities of an original product. To install Microsoft Plus!, you must have at least a 486 processor, 8 MB of memory, and a monitor/video card capable of displaying a minimum of 256 colors. Microsoft Plus! expands the number of desktop backgrounds, provides visual enhancements, additional sounds, Internet tools, and more games. One invaluable utility provided by Microsoft Plus! is the improved version of the disk compression program DriveSpace 3.

The following is list of the options available in Control Panel:

Accessibility
Options

If an individual is hearing, visually, or mobility challenged, this option presents choices that make Windows 95 easier to use. You can alter the display, mouse, and keyboard settings and utilize sound to improve your ease of use.

Add New
Hardware

Windows 95 will detect and install new hardware by using this option.

Add/Remove
Programs

You may add or remove Windows 95 components and programs with this option.

Date/Time

Use this to change the system date or time.

Display

Use this option to alter nearly every setting for your desktop. It also controls the type of monitor and monitor-related settings.

Fonts

Use this folder icon to see what fonts you have on your system and to add or remove fonts.

Joystick

A joystick is a popular pointing device primarily used for playing computer games. If you have this device installed, you can control its settings.

Keyboard

Use this Keyboard icon to change keyboard settings such as the cursor blink rate or the repeat rate of a key (how quickly characters repeat when you hold down a key).

Mail and Fax

If you installed Microsoft Exchange for electronic mail and facsimiles, you use this icon to send and receive e-mail and faxes.

Microsoft Mail Postoffice

If you are using the Microsoft Client/Server network to exchange messages, this icon is used by the administrator to set up new mailboxes, add new users, or delete old users.

Modems

Use this icon to identify the properties of your modem or to install a new *modem* (a device to transmit data over phone lines).

Mouse

Use this icon to alter the characteristics of your mouse. You can alter settings such as the speed of the mouse as you drag it or the double-click speed.

Multimedia

The Multimedia icon controls any audio or visual devices attached to your system, such as a CD-ROM or microphone.

Network

The Network icon will be displayed if there is a network. Use this icon to control what network software you are using as well as who may access your devices. You will not be able to manipulate any settings unless you are the System Administrator or have the permissions, or rights, of the System Administrator.

ODBC

Use this icon to add, delete, or configure data sources (the data a user wants to access and the information needed to get to that data). It also allows you to install new Open Database Connectivity (ODBC) drivers on your computer. A *device driver* is a special piece of software that drives, or controls, another device. It can also control a data translation. You will rarely use this option.

Passwords

Use the Passwords icon if you wish to be queried for a password before you can use Windows 95. A *password* is a security measure used to restrict access to files and programs. It is a unique string of characters that a user keys in as an identification code. You also use this icon to change your password.

Printers

Use the Printers icon to add or delete a printer, choose paper size, and manipulate other printer-related tasks.

Regional
Settings

The Regional Settings icon accommodates use of Windows when used in different countries. You can, for instance, change currency symbols or the date format.

Sounds

Use this icon to enable or disable the beeping the computer that informs you of errors. If you have a sound card, you may assign prerecorded sound files to keyboard or mouse actions. For instance, you could have the computer make a chime sound every time you open a file.

System

The System icon provides information about all your system resources such as the CPU and your disk drives. The controls for all these devices are also located here.

9.2   User Profiles

User profiles allow two or more people to use the same computer and still maintain their own customized settings. These settings include colors, backgrounds, Start menu items, open windows, the arrangement of the icons, and what shortcuts have been created. Each time someone logs onto a computer that has user profiles set up, Windows 95 will restore the individualized working environment that was in place when that user logged off. You may want to set up individual user profiles for each person who uses the same computer. User profiles are created in Control Panel.

If you are on a network, however, Windows 95 may already be set up with specific user profiles that the network administrator determines. In that case, you may customize your system as much or as little as the network administrator allows in that working environment.

9.3   Activity—Using Passwords

Note: The following are the assumed settings:

My Computer

❑   Toolbar and status bar on (in the View menu).

❑   Large icons arranged by name (in the View menu).

❑   Browse folders by using a single window that changes as you open each folder (View/Options/ Browse tab).

❑   Hide files of these types is set (View/Options/View tab).

❑   Display the full MS-DOS path in the title bar is set (View/Options/View tab).

❑   Hide MS-DOS file extensions for file types that are registered is not set (View/Options/View tab).

Explorer

❑   Toolbar and status bar on (in the View menu).

❑   List view arranged by name (in the View menu).

❑   Include description bar for left and right panes is on (in View/Options/View tab).

1   Click **Start**. Point at **Settings**. Click **Control Panel**.

2   Click **View**. Click **List**.

What's
happening?   → These are the objects in Control Panel. All of these objects control some aspect of your system.

3   Double-click **Passwords**.

Note: If you are in a classroom or lab environment, be sure you make no changes in the password dialog boxes.

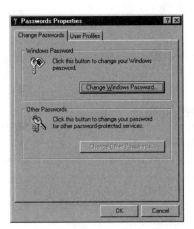

The Passwords Properties property sheet appears. If you are on a network, you will have one more tab, labeled Remote Administration.

4   Click the **User Profiles** tab.

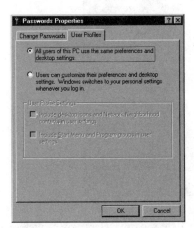

In order to maintain a user's customized features, the User can customize their preferences... option button (second button from the top) must be set. In order

to maximize customization, both check boxes must be set. Once these options are set, the next time you turn on your computer, you will see the dialog box shown in Figure 9.1. At that time, you will enter your user name. You will then be asked for a password. If you do not want to have a password, click OK.

Figure 9.1   User Profiles

5   Click the **Change Passwords** tab.

6   Click **Change Windows Password**.

Here is where you can change your password, but you must know your old password in order to do so. You key in your old password, then your new password. You are asked to key in your new password again. Entering your new password the second time confirms it.

7   Click **Cancel**. Click **Cancel**. Close **Control Panel**.

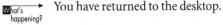

You have returned to the desktop.

9.4   Date/Time and Regional Settings

Your computer has a clock that indicates the current date and time, called the *system date* and *system time*. All programs use the system date and system time. Whenever you save a new file, the logged date and time of the file come from the system date and system time.

The date and time are set to the geographic area in which you live. How they are displayed relates to the country in which you live. Many programs support international settings. When you alter regional settings, you may affect the way programs display and sort dates, times, currency, and numbers. For instance, in the United States, dates are displayed in the format of mm/dd/yy. The long form of the date is written as August 1, 1996, and the short form appears as 8/1/96. Many other countries use the format of dd/mm/yy, so that the long form of the date would be written as 1 August 1996, and the short form would appear as 1/8/96. Currency symbols also vary. In the United States, the $ sign is used. In Great Britain, the £ sign is used. With Control Panel, you can customize the way the date, time, currency, and numbers are displayed, based on either a country's setting or your preferences. Since Windows 95 sets the regional preferences appropriate for your country, you will rarely need to change your settings.

9.5   Activity—Using Date/Time and Regional Settings

1   Double-click **My Computer**. Double-click **Control Panel**.

2   Double-click the **Date/Time** object.

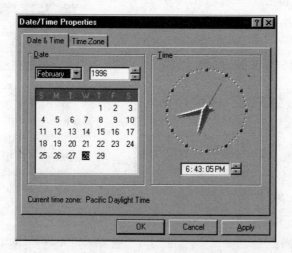

You have opened the property sheet for the system date and time. Here, you can reference and, if needed, correct the date and time. If you look at the bottom of the property sheet, you see that the time zone for this computer is Pacific Daylight Time. You can also see an image of the time zone.

3   Click the **Time Zone** tab.

 You see a graphic image of the time zone. In the list box, you see GMT-8.00. This tells you that Pacific Time is Greenwich Mean Time less 8 hours. The check box for Automatically adjust clock for daylight saving is set. Although this works correctly in most cases, there are exceptions. Arizona, for instance, does not participate in Daylight Saving Time. If you lived in Arizona, you would not check the daylight saving box. If you are in a network environment, you too might not want to check this box, as most file servers adjust for Daylight Saving Time. If you did check it under these circumstances, you would get a two hour adjustment instead of the one hour change that was needed.

4   Click **Cancel**.

5   Double-click the **Regional Settings** object.

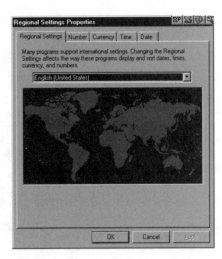

 Regional Settings is the top property page. The default setting is English (United States).

6   Click the arrow in the drop-down list box.

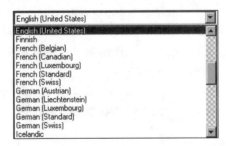

As you can see, there are hundreds of countries to pick from. If you selected one of these countries, Windows 95 would inform you that it needed to restart in order to install all the components for that country.

7 Click **Cancel**. Click the **Date** tab.

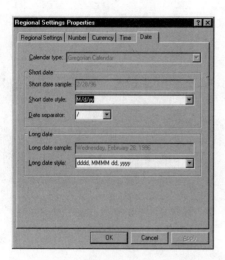

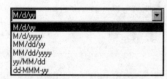 Although the United States setting is the default, you still have options about the way the date is displayed in both short and long forms. Currently, in the Short date sample, the date is dimly displayed as 2/28/96. You can alter that in the drop-down list box, but not in the sample.

8 Click the down arrow in the **Short date style** drop-down list box.

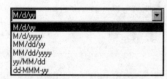 Currently, the selected format is M/d/yy. You want to change the format.

9 Click **MM/dd/yyyy**.

10 Click the **Apply** command button.

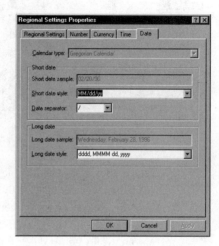

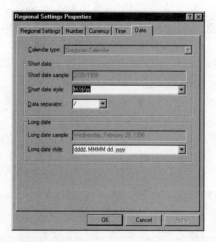 Now the sample reads 02/28/1996. Your date now displays in a different way.

11 Click the down arrow in the **Short date style** drop-down list box.

12 Click **M/d/yy**.

13 Click the **Apply** command button.

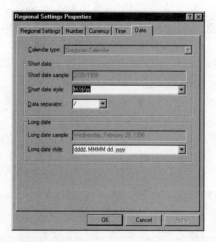

 You have reset the date format.

14 Click **Cancel**.

15 Close **Control Panel**.

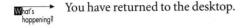 You have returned to the desktop.

9.6   Fonts

Any text that appears on the screen or is printed on paper appears in a font. A *font* is a set of characters with a specific typeface. A *typeface* is a design for a specific set of characters. Each typeface has an assigned name, such as Times New Roman or Courier. A font is one specific size of a specific typeface, such as 12-point Arial or 10-point Times New Roman. A font can also refer to a specific style (such as italic) or a thickness, called a *stroke weight* (such as bold). Font refers to all the characters available in a particular size, style, and weight for any type design. Typeface refers to the design itself. Most computer users apply the term font to both font and typeface.

Windows 95 uses fonts to display and print characters. Fonts can be scaled (made bigger or smaller). In the days of the typewriter, type sizes were measured in characters per inch. Thus, a measurement such as 10 CPI means that ten characters would fit horizontally into one inch. These days, you typically work with fonts that are measured vertically in points, with one point equaling 1/72 of an inch. Typefaces, also referred to as fonts, are either monospaced or proportional. Monospaced typefaces give all characters the same width. Courier is an example of a monospaced font. Proportional typefaces vary the space given to each character so that, for instance, an M will take more space than an I. An example of a proportional font is Times New Roman. In a typical word processing environment, proportional fonts are used because these fonts are read easily.

Fonts are divided into two main categories, serif and sans serif. *Serif fonts* have a small line at the end of each main line of a character, called a serif. Serif fonts, like proportional fonts, are used for most word processing activities. *Sans serif fonts* (sans in French means without) have no small lines. Sans serif fonts are used primarily for emphasis in headings, titles, and subtitles. Figures 9.2 and 9.3 give examples of different serif and sans serif fonts.

Figure 9.2   Serif Typefaces

Pappl Laudatio 10 point

Baskerville 10 point

Times New Roman 10 point

Times New Roman 12 point

Figure 9.3 Sans Serif Typefaces

Arial 12 point

Arial 14 point

Futura 12 point

Futura 16 point

The technology that places text on a computer screen differs from the technology that prints the characters on a printer. Your computer and your printer each have fonts, appropriately called *screen fonts* and *printer fonts*.

Windows 95 uses different ways to display fonts on your screen. A font provided by Windows 95 is a *bitmapped font*, which uses a pattern of dots to create characters. These dots are called pixels (picture elements). A *pixel* is the smallest point of light that can be displayed on a monitor. You cannot scale bitmapped fonts because they come in predetermined sizes. The size of each font must be stored separately on the disk. Windows 95 provides Courier, MS Sans Serif, Serif, Small Fonts, and Symbol bitmapped fonts in the predetermined sizes of 8, 10, 12, 14, 18, and 24 points. These fonts are used for Windows 95 menus and icon labels.

With bitmapped fonts, what you see on your screen may not exactly match what is printed on your printer. The variance between screen fonts and printer fonts can have a tremendous impact on your documents. You may format your document in a particular fashion, decide that it looks perfect on the screen, and print it—only to find that the printed copy looks nothing like what appeared on the screen.

To solve this problem, Windows introduced TrueType fonts. *TrueType fonts* are designed so that the screen and printer fonts are the same. A TrueType font is designed to be a *WYSIWYG* (pronounced wissiwig)—what you see is what you get. TrueType fonts are outline fonts because the shapes of the characters are defined in terms of mathematically generated lines and curves rather than a pattern of dots. These fonts can then be scaled to any size and are mathematically calculated for the point size you select. Instead of storing an entire set of fonts, only one outline of each character is stored. The character outlines generate both the screen and printer fonts. You can identify TrueType fonts by their symbol:

Five TrueType fonts are included with Windows 95: Arial, Courier, Times New Roman, Symbol, and WingDings.

Printer fonts give directions to your brand of printer. When you install a printer, you are installing the correct printer driver for that printer. A *printer driver* is a software program designed to enable application programs to work with a printer without concern for the specifics of the printer's hardware and internal "language." Different printers require different codes and commands to operate properly. You communicate with your printer by installing the correct printer driver to manage all the subtleties of that printer.

Printers come with ***built-in fonts***, sometimes called ***resident fonts***. If you use a printer's built-in font in your application, Windows 95 will try to match that font on the screen as close as it can with one of its bitmapped screen fonts. If the match is not exact, your printed document will be different from the on-screen display. TrueType fonts are scaleable, viewable fonts and resolve the inconsistency between screen and printer. There are other manufacturers of scaleable, viewable fonts such as Bitstream, Postscript, and Speeedo. These fonts are also supported by Windows 95 and will have their own file type icons, ensuring that what is displayed on the screen is identical to what is printed by your printer.

9.7   Activity—Looking at Fonts

1   Double-click **My Computer**. Double-click **Control Panel**. Double-click the **Fonts** folder.

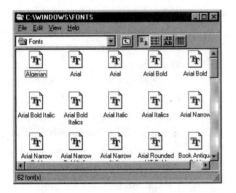

 You have opened the Fonts window that displays the fonts on your system. Each font is contained in a separate file and is represented by its own icon. The icon for bitmap fonts is represented by a red A:

Courier
10,12,15

The TrueType fonts have a blue TT symbol:

Colonna MT

2   Double-click the **Arial** font icon.

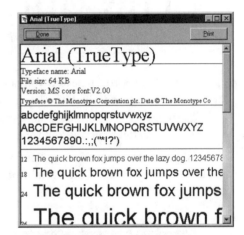

 You see a screen displayed with information about and samples of the font.

3   Scroll until you see the last point size.

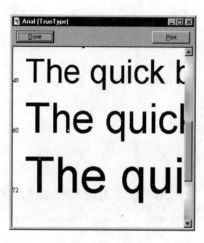

Since this is a TrueType font, you can see how sharp and clear the letters are formed. If you wanted a hard copy sample of this font, you could print it.

4   Click **Done**. Locate the **MS Sans Serif** icon. Double-click it. Scroll to the bottom of the window.

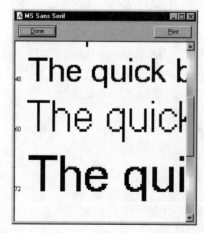

Since MS Sans Serif is a bitmapped font, you see the "jaggities." Unlike TrueType fonts, the edges of the characters cannot be rounded because bitmapped characters are formed with pixels.

5   Click **Done**. Click **File** on the menu bar.

If you purchased additional fonts, here is where you can install them. You may also delete fonts from this menu; be very cautious, however, because you do not want to delete a font that Windows 95 relies on, such MS Sans Serif. Some fonts are similar in appearance, and at times it can be difficult to distinguish among them. In this situation, the Fonts windows will assist you. Many fonts have what is called a PANOSE file, which supplies information about the fonts. Windows 95 can compare fonts that have PANOSE files and list the similar ones. If a font has no PANOSE file, Windows 95 cannot compare it to other fonts.

6   Touch the **Esc** key to close the **File** menu.

7 Press **Ctrl** + **Home**. Click **View**. Click **List Fonts by Similarity**.

 You see a list of fonts. They are listed by similarity to Arial. You also see that all styles of Arial are listed such as Bold and Bold Italic.

8 Click **View**. Click **Hide Variations (Bold, Italic, Etc.)** to set it.

 By hiding the variations, it is easier to see what fonts are similar others. In this example, you can see that Arial and Century Schoolbook are not alike.

9 In the **Lists fonts by similarity to** drop-down list box, click the down arrow. Locate and click **Times New Roman**.

 Now you are comparing fonts that are similar to Times New Roman.

10 Scroll to the end of the window.

 You see that the bitmapped fonts have no PANOSE information and therefore cannot be compared.

11 Click **View**. Click **Large Icons**.

12 Click **View**. Click **Hide Variations (Bold, Italic, Etc.)** to unset it.

13 Press **Ctrl** + **Home**. Close the **Fonts** window.

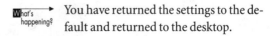 You have returned the settings to the default and returned to the desktop.

9.8   Screen Resolution

Standard VGA, the default screen configuration, has a grid that is 640 pixels horizontally × 480 pixels vertically, along with a 16-color palette. The 640 × 480 configuration (pixels is understood) is the resolution of your screen. When Windows 95 was installed, the Setup program determined what type of monitor and video adapter your computer uses, and it made the appropriate settings. Often, Windows 95 will choose standard VGA, although your video card and monitor can be set to higher resolutions.

Today, most people have monitors and video cards that support higher resolutions. The most common are 800 × 600 and 1024 × 768. If you choose to use higher resolutions, you gain more workspace on the desktop. Since higher resolutions require more pixels, your display will be sharper but much smaller. In fact, icons on the display may become so small that you cannot identify them in high resolution. However, you can change the size of the fonts to make the descriptions of the icons larger.

Depending on your monitor and video card, you may also change how many colors you can display. A 256-color setting permits you to see certain images that you would not see in a 16-color setting. A true color setting, involving 16.7 million colors, will make your screen display as clear as a high-quality color slide.

There are drawbacks to increasing the resolution and number of colors. With a higher resolution, your system has to work much harder to manage the display because there are more pixels to process. This is also true when you choose a higher number of colors.

Both your monitor and video card limit the resolution and color settings of your system. Once you know your hardware limitations, you can decide what works best for you. If you work with multimedia applications, you will probably want the highest resolution and the most colors your system supports. On the other hand, if your primary work is done with a word processing or spreadsheet program, you do not need the highest resolution and the most colors. In fact, using high resolution and many colors in these applications will slow down your work.

9.9   Activity—Viewing Your Resolution

1   Right-click the desktop. Click **Properties**.

You have accessed the Display Properties property sheet by right-clicking the desktop and choosing Properties.

2 Click the **Settings** tab.

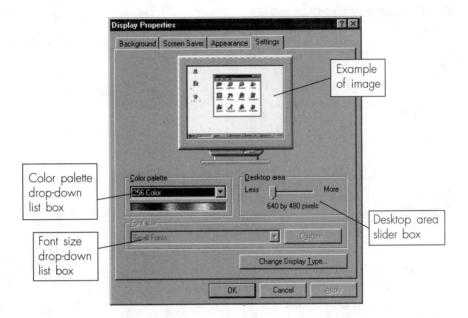

Example of image

Color palette drop-down list box

Font size drop-down list box

Desktop area slider box

 Each item on the property page controls your display. The ways you alter your display will depend on the choices your hardware supports. This system is currently set to 640 × 480 resolution. If you have a standard VGA monitor and adapter card, you will not have additional choices and will not be able to do the following steps.

3 If you can, slide the slider box to the right to 800 × 600 pixels. Look at the example of the desktop.

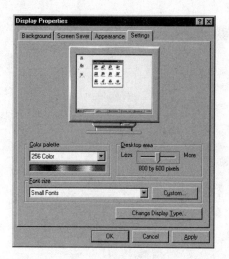

4 Click the down arrow in the **Font size** drop-down list box.

What's happening? The current setting is Small Fonts. If you wanted to use Large Fonts, you would select it and then click OK. Windows 95 would need to restart for your changes to take effect.

5 Click outside the drop-down list box to cancel it.

6 Click the **Custom** button.

What's happening? In the example, you have more desktop area available because the resolution was raised. You can usually click OK and make the resolution change without having to restart Windows 95. However, if you attempt to change the color palette and the resolution, you will have to restart Windows 95.

What's happening? You can scale your fonts to sizes more specific than large or small fonts.

7 Click **Cancel**.

8 Click **Cancel**.

What's happening? You have returned to the desktop.

9.10 Patterns and Wallpaper

You can customize your system by changing the background of your desktop. You may choose a pattern or a wallpaper. A *pattern* is a small grid of dots that repeats to fill the screen. A *wallpaper* is a graphic image, which is stored as a bitmapped graphics file in the standard .bmp (bitmapped) format. Windows 95 comes with several wallpapers, which are stored in the Windows folder. You can also create your own wallpaper with a graphics program such as Paint. You can scan in an image and modify it, or you can modify an existing wallpaper. You can purchase different wallpaper files as well.

Most users select either a wallpaper or a pattern. If you have selected a pattern, a wallpaper will typically cover the pattern. A pattern is like paint on a wall—you can put wallpaper over the paint so that the paint is no longer visible. Both patterns and wallpapers use memory, but patterns consume less memory than wallpapers. If you begin to run out of memory, one way to conserve it is to have no pattern or wallpaper covering the desktop.

9.11   Activity—Using Patterns and Wallpapers

1   Double-click **My Computer**. Double-click **Control Panel**. Double-click **Display**.

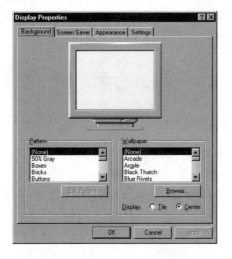

 You can access this dialog box either by right-clicking and choosing Properties or by going to the Control Panel and choosing Display. The Background tab is active.

2   Click the down arrow in the drop-down list box for **Pattern**. Choose **Thatches**. Click **OK**.

What's
happening? →   You have a cross-hatched pattern as the background of your desktop.

3   Open the **Control Panel** window. Double-click **Display**. Click the **Edit Patterns** command button.

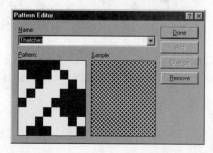

What's
happening? →   You can edit this pattern but only with a mouse. Every time you click, you reverse the color of a block.

4   Click a few blocks in the pattern area.

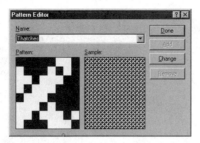

 Each time you clicked, you reversed the color.
happening?

5   Click **Done**.

 The message box is telling you that you have changed the Thatches pattern. You can choose
happening? whether or not to save your changes.

6   Click **No**.

7   In the **Wallpaper** drop-down list box, locate **Forest**. Click **Center**. Click **OK**.

 When a wallpaper image is centered, only one copy of the image appears. You may have to move
happening? the Control Panel window out of the way to see the image.

8   Double-click **Display**. Click **Tile**. Click **OK**.

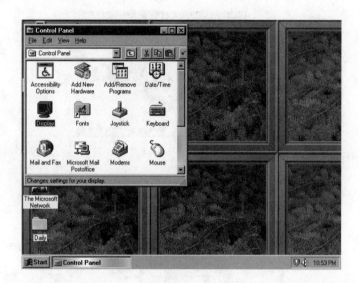

 Tiling an image repeats the image until the desktop is covered. Your pattern is no longer visible on the desktop. For this reason, one usually picks a pattern or a wallpaper, not both. The pattern or wallpaper you select may be so busy that you cannot see your desktop icons. Simplicity is best.

9   Double-click the **Display** icon. Click **None** for both **Pattern** and **Wallpaper**. Click **OK**.

10   Close the **Control Panel** window.

 You have returned to the desktop.

9.12 Changing the Appearance of the Desktop

In addition to wallpapers and patterns, the desktop may be further customized. You may choose a color scheme for your desktop or select specific colors for elements of the desktop. You can use different fonts in different styles for icons and alter icon spacing. All these changes can be made in the Appearance page in the Display Properties property sheet.

9.13   Activity—Customizing the Desktop

1   Right-click the desktop. Click **Properties**. Click the **Appearance** tab.

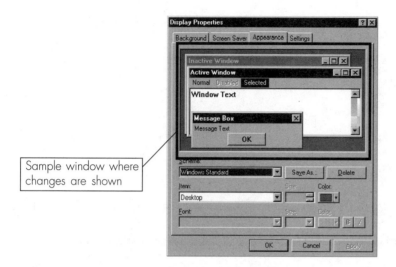

Sample window where
changes are shown

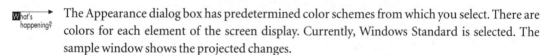

What's
happening?   The Appearance dialog box has predetermined color schemes from which you select. There are colors for each element of the screen display. Currently, Windows Standard is selected. The sample window shows the projected changes.

2   Click the down arrow in the **Schemes** drop-down list box. Click **Desert**. Click **OK**.

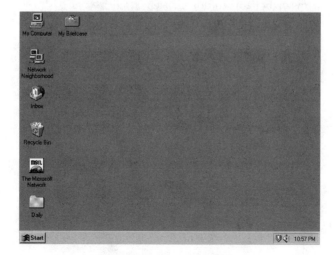

   Your changed your desktop color scheme to desert tones.

3   Right-click the desktop. Click **Properties**. Click the **Appearance** tab.

4   Click the down arrow in the **Schemes** drop-down list box. Click **Windows Standard (Extra Large)**. Click **OK**.

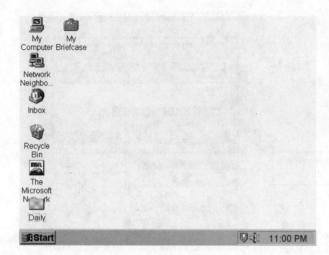

You have restored the standard color scheme, but as you can see, your taskbar and icons have larger fonts that are easier to read.

5   Right-click the desktop. Click **Properties**. Click the **Appearance** tab.

6   Click the down arrow in the **Schemes** drop-down list box. Click **Windows Standard**.

7   Click the down arrow in the **Item** drop-down list box. Click **Menu**.

The item you selected, Menu, has a size of 18 points, which is its size in pixels. Since the menu object has a size, you may make the menu larger or smaller. The Font drop-down list box also has a size, so you may alter the point size for the text for the menu. The currently selected font for menus is MS Sans Serif at 8 points. You can alter individual items on the desktop, but in this case you are only going to alter the font's point size for menu text.

8   Click the down arrow on the **Font** drop-down list box. Select **Times New Roman**.

9   In the font **Size** box for the menu, select **14** points.

You have retained the standard color scheme but changed the font and font size from MS San Serif 8 points to Times New Roman 14 points.

10   Click **OK**.

11   Right-click the desktop.

Only the menu font has changed. The other items on the desktop remained the same.

12   Click **Properties**. Click the **Appearance** tab.

13   Click the down arrow in the **Item** drop-down list box. Click **Menu**.

14   Click the down arrow in the **Font** drop-down list box. Select **MS Sans Serif**.

15   In the font **Size** box for the menu, select **8** points. Click **OK**.

You have restored the default values for the desktop. You can alter other elements, such as the spacing between icons.

16   Right-click the desktop. Click **Properties**. Click the **Appearance** tab.

17   Click the down arrow in the **Item** drop-down list box.

18   Click **Icon Spacing (Vertical)**. Make a note of the number.

19 Change the number to **100** in the item **Size** spin box.

 ➤ You are adjusting the vertical space between icons, which is measured in pixels.

20 Click **OK**.

21 Right-click the desktop. Point to **Arrange Icons**. Click **by Name**.

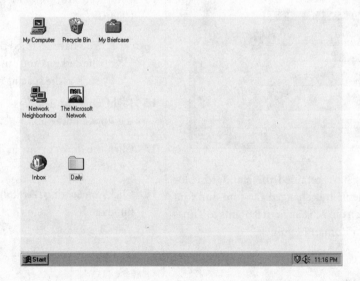

 ➤ Now the icons are much farther apart on your desktop.

22 Right-click the desktop. Click **Properties**. Click the **Appearance** tab.

23 Click the down arrow in the **Item** drop-down list box.

24 Click **Icon Spacing (Vertical)**.

25 Change the number to its former value in the item **Size** spin box. Click **OK**.

26 Right-click the desktop. Point to **Arrange Icons**. Click **by Name**.

 Your icons are now returned to their default spacing.

9.14 Screen Savers

There has always been a debate among computer people about whether or not you should turn your computer off when you finish working. Some schools of thought believe that you should turn off the computer and monitor to save energy and wear and tear on the electronic components. Others feel that the energy savings are minimal compared with the risk of turning the computer on and off. The items most likely to break on a computer are the mechanical parts, such as the switch. Furthermore, when you turn on the power, there is a slightly higher power surge that could damage electronic components. If you are in a lab or work environment, there is probably a policy for whether computers should be turned off after each work session. If you are in charge of your own computer, it is up to you. Most people decide that if they are going to be gone a short while—an hour or two—they will leave the computer on. If they are going to be gone for a longer period of time, however, they will turn off the computer.

One point on which everyone agrees is the importance of caring for the monitor. In the early days of monitor technology, if a monitor were left displaying the same image, the image could "burn in," and a ghostly shadow would remain on the screen forever. *Screen savers* were developed to prevent this. Early screen savers were actually blank screens. When a user did not have any keyboard or mouse activity, the screen would go blank until the user reactivated the system by pressing a key or using a mouse. Since blank screens are rather boring, people developed screen savers comprised of constantly moving images.

In today's monitor technology, burn-in is not usually a problem, and screen savers are more for fun than for practical purposes. They do provide some password security so that if you leave your computer for a time, no one can see your work. In addition to all the commercial screen savers available, Windows 95 comes with a choice of screen savers. You can locate screen savers with the same techniques you have been using.

9.15 Activity—Using Screen Savers

1   Right-click the desktop. Click **Properties**. Click the **Screen Saver** tab.

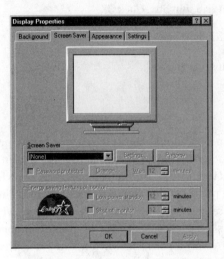

 You have opened the Screen Saver property page in the Display Properties sheet. The number of screen savers available to you depends on the software you have installed.

2   Click the down arrow in the **Screen Saver** drop-down list box.

3   Click **Curves and Colors**.

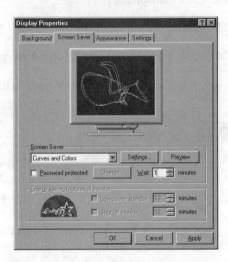

 In the sample screen, you see a preview of what the screen saver will look like. In the Wait spin box, you can choose how much time elapses before the screen saver goes into effect. In this example, it is set to 1 minute, which means that if there is no activity within one minute, the screen saver will be activated.

4   Click the **Preview** command button.

 You see a full-screen view of your choice.

5 Click the **Settings** command button.

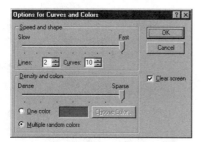

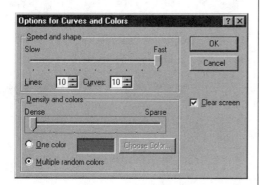

→ *What's happening?*   You can customize this screen setting by altering the number of lines, the speed, the density, and the colors.

6 In the **Lines** spin box, change the number to **10**.

7 Move the slider so that it is under **Dense** in **Density and colors**.

→ *What's happening?*   You have altered the way the screen saver will look.

8 Click **OK**.

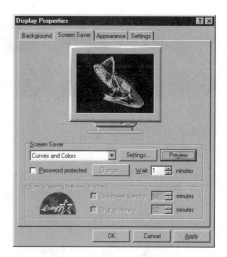

→ *What's happening?*   Now your image has more lines and is much thicker in the display preview. You can also password protect your computer using the screen saver. Be particularly careful in the following steps because if you key in your password incorrectly, you will lock yourself out of the computer.

9 Click the **Password protected** check box to set it. Click the **Change** command button.

→ *What's happening?*   The dialog box is asking you for a password. When you key in a password, it will not see be displayed. In order to verify your password, you will be asked to key it in a second time.

10 In the **New password** text box, key in the following: **CZG**

11 Press the Tab key.

12 In the **Confirm new password** text box, key in the following: **CZG**

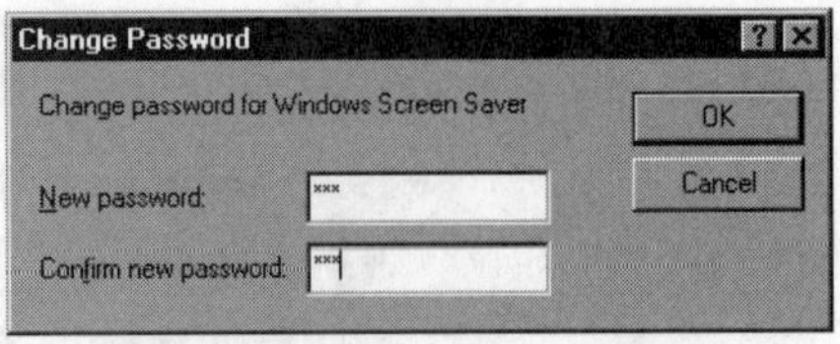

What's happening? All you see are asterisks, which represent your hidden password.

13 Click **OK**.

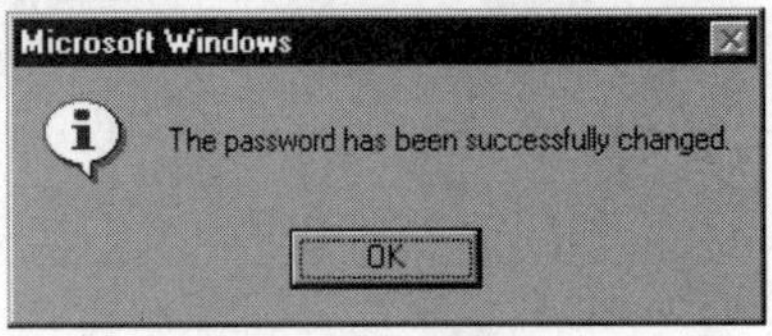

What's happening? An information message box informs you that you have been successful in changing the password.

14 Click **OK**.

15 Click the **Apply** command button.

16 Click the **Preview** command button.

17 Press **Enter**.

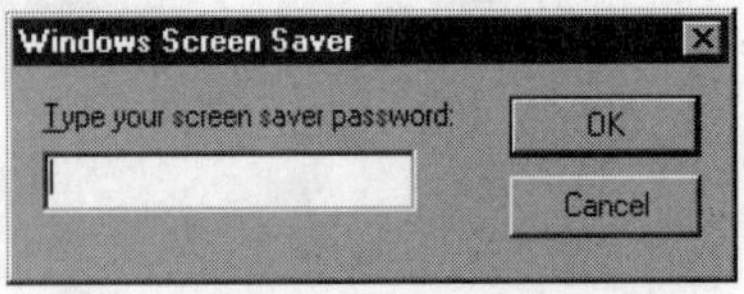

What's happening? You cannot return to your screen until you key in the correct password.

18 Key in the following: **CZG Enter**

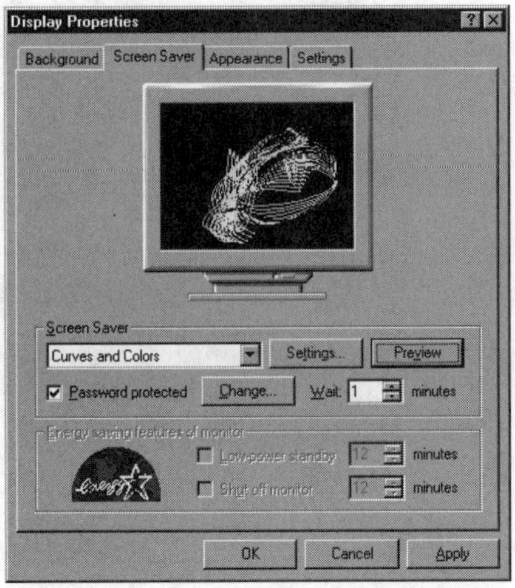

What's happening? With the correct password, you have returned to the Display Properties sheet. You may also remove a password.

19 Click the **Change** command button.

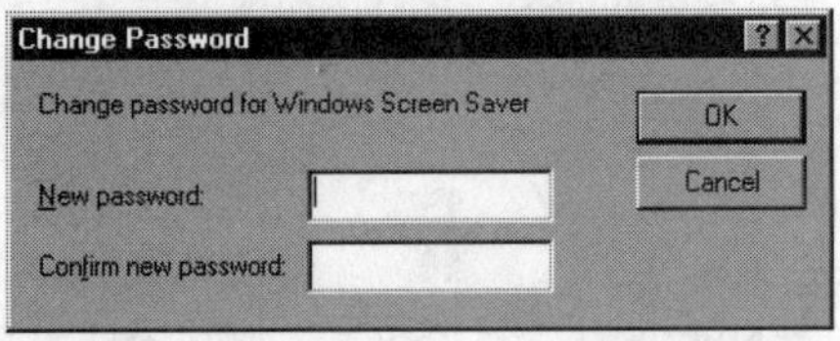

What's happening? To have no password, you leave both text boxes empty.

20 Click **OK**.

21 Click the check box for **Password protected** to unset it.

22 Click the **Settings** command button.

23 In the **Lines** spin box, change the number to **2**.

24 Move the slider so it is under **Sparse** in **Density and colors**.

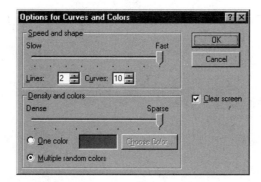

   You have returned to the default values.

25 Click **OK**.

26 In the **Screen Saver** list box, choose **(None)**. Click **OK**.

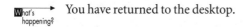   You have returned to the desktop.

9.16 The Mouse and the Keyboard

You can also customize the mouse and the keyboard. You adjust such mouse-related items as the double-click speed, the pointer movement, the pointer size, and the *tracking speed*, which is the rate at which the pointer moves across the screen. You can also enable *mouse trails*, which leave images tracking the mouse's path. This feature is particularly useful on notebook computers or any computer with a monochrome monitor where the pointer is difficult to see. You can switch the left and right mouse buttons, which is useful for left-handed users.

The keyboard can be adjusted as well. Your keyboard has a typematic feature, which repeats a character after you have held a key down for a period of time. You can also adjust the rate at which the cursor blinks. You can install keyboard support for different languages, but you must have your original Windows 95 CD-ROM discs in order to do so. When you install Windows 95, it only installs one language.

9.17 Activity—Customizing the Mouse and the Keyboard

1 Double-click **My Computer**. Double-click **Control Panel**.

2 Double-click the **Mouse** object.

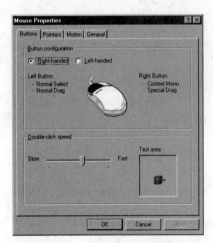

What's happening?

You have opened the controls for the mouse. The left mouse button is for normal dragging and dropping, whereas the right mouse button is used for right-clicking. Right-clicking opens a pop-up menu, also called a *context menu*, which you used when you right-clicked the desktop and chose Properties. There is a slider bar that sets the speed for the amount of time it takes to double-click.

3 Double-click in the **Test area**.

What's happening?

When you successfully double-clicked, the jack in the box popped up in the Test area. If you were dissatisfied with the double-click speed, you could drag the slider to the left for a slower speed and to the right for a faster one.

4 Click the **Pointers** tab.

What's happening?

Here, you see each pointer symbol and its meaning. Your choices may be different, depending on what pointers were installed on your system.

5 Scroll until you see the **Unavailable** pointer symbol.

You see the symbol , indicating that the desired task is not available. For instance, you cannot drag and drop the printer icon onto a program; if you tried, you would see the unavailable symbol.

6 Click the down arrow in the **Scheme** drop-down list box.

The choice, 3D Pointers (three-dimensional), gives pointers more perspective. The Animated Hourglasses choice will display the pointer as an hourglass that turns as it fills whenever the computer is busy performing a function, such as saving a file. If you do not like the size of your pointers, you can change the size.

7 Click **Windows Standard (extra large)**.

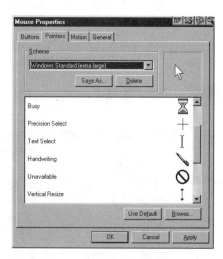

Your pointers are now larger.

8 Click the down arrow in the **Scheme** drop-down list box. Click **Windows Standard**.

9 Click the **Motion** tab.

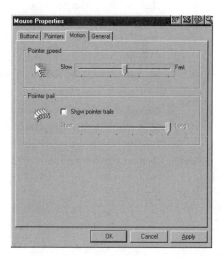

Here you can adjust the tracking speed of your pointer. You also have a check box where you can set Show pointer trails.

10   Set **Show pointer trails** by clicking the check box.

 As you drag the mouse, you should see a trail of pointers.

11   Unset **Show pointer trails** by clicking the check box.

12   Click the **General** tab.

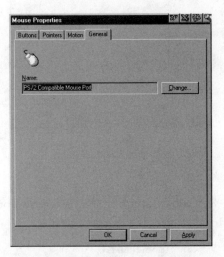

 This property page tells you what brand of mouse you have and where it is connected. If you get a new mouse, you could tell Windows 95 what brand it is by using this page. Depending on what mouse drivers are installed, you might also have more choices about your pointer. To refresh your memory, a driver is a program that tells a device how it should work.

13   Click the **Change** button.

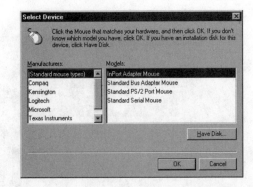

 In this example, the installed mouse is a generic one, not a specific brand. If you can choose to install a specific brand of mouse, you may be asked for the disk that contains the driver for that mouse. A specific mouse driver usually includes special features. The process to install a specific mouse driver would follow along the lines of the scenario presented in Figure 9.4. *Note:* Read, but do not execute, the steps to Installing a Mouse Driver.

14   Click **Microsoft**.

Figure 9.4   Installing a Mouse Driver

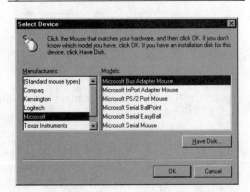

 You see the selections for the type of mouse connection. This computer has a special port (plug) for connecting the mouse to the system.

15 Click **Microsoft InPort Adapter Mouse**.

 Windows 95 needs to install the driver for the mouse. Windows 95 has the correct driver, but in order to install the driver you need the original Windows 95 installation CD-ROM.

16 Place the disc in the CD-ROM drive and click **OK**.

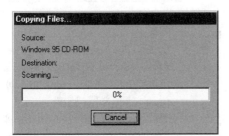

 When the necessary mouse driver files are copied, you are returned to the General tab

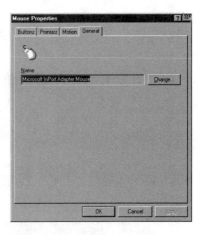

 Although you have installed the correct driver, it is not yet activated.

17 Click **Apply**.

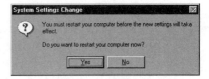

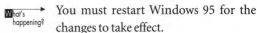

 You must restart Windows 95 for the changes to take effect.

18 Restart **Windows**. Open **Control Panel**. Double-click the **Mouse** icon. Click the **General** tab. Click the **Options** command button.

 Along with the mouse driver, you may also have additional software for managing the mouse. If so, it may have features similar to those shown above that allow you to change the size and color of the pointer.

19 Click **Cancel**. Close the **Mouse** dialog box.

20 Double-click the **Keyboard** object in **Control Panel**.

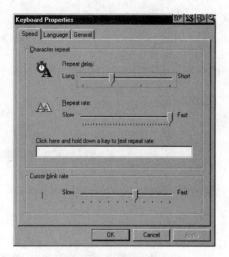

The Keyboard property sheet has three tabs, Speed, Language, and General. Speed controls the *repeat rate*, which is how fast a key repeats when held down, and the *repeat delay*, which is the length of time that Windows 95 waits before it repeats. You can also adjust the cursor blink rate. The second tab allows you to change the language of your keyboard.

21 Click the **Language** tab.

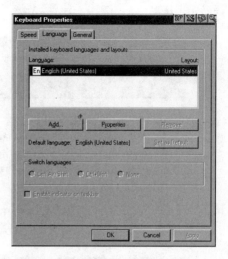

The selected language is English (United States). The keyboard is comprised of two parts—the physical keyboard and the driver that tells the computer, when you press a key, what letter should be used. Thus, on the English keyboard, when you press the letter p, you see the letter p on the screen and in your printed documents.

If you use another language, such as French, you can purchase a French keyboard. The French keyboard will have keys that are labeled with the necessary French accents, such as the accent grave (è). Having the French keyboard is not enough, however. You must install the driver for the French keyboard so that when you press the labeled grave key, the accent mark will appear on your screen and in your documents. To install another keyboard driver, you would need your Windows 95 disks to retrieve the keyboard driver.

22 Click the **General** tab.

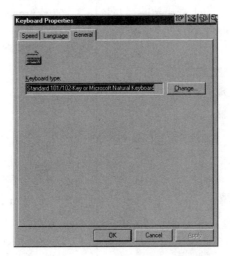

    If you purchased a new-style keyboard, such as the Microsoft Natural Keyboard, you could inform Windows 95 of this fact in the Keyboard Properties dialog box. Since the Microsoft Natural Keyboard is split at an angle to be more ergonomically correct, it helps to prevent carpel tunnel syndrome. In addition, it has special Windows 95 keys that will, when pressed, pop up menus. If you purchase and connect a new keyboard, you will need the proper keyboard driver.

23 Close the **Keyboard** dialog box. Close **Control Panel**.

    You have returned to the desktop.

9.18 Customizing the Start Menu

You can alter two sections of the Start menu—the top of the Start menu and the cascading Programs menu. In these two places, you may place, rearrange, or remove whatever folders, programs, or documents you wish. By adding a frequently used item to the Start menu, you can avoid the extra step of using the cascading menus. If there are, you can remove programs that you seldom use from the Start or Programs menus.

9.19   Activity—Altering the Start Menu

1   Right-click the taskbar. Click **Properties**. Click the **Start Menu Programs** tab.

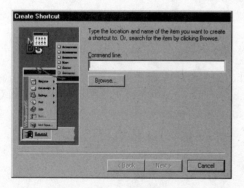

3   Click **Browse**.

What's happening?   You are looking at the structure of Drive C.

4   Double-click **95book**. Double-click the **Addman** folder. Click **Address.exe**.

What's happening?   Now that you have located the program, you can proceed.

What's happening?   The easiest way to add a program is to use the Wizard. A *wizard* is a program that leads you through the steps you need to take to accomplish your desired end.

2   Click the **Add** button.

What's happening?   An item on the Programs menu is usually a shortcut to a program. To create a shortcut, you must know the name and location of the program. You are looking for a program called Address.exe, which is located in the Addman folder under the 95book folder.

5   Click **Open**.

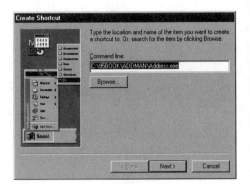

 The Command line text box displays the entire path name.

6   Click **Next**.

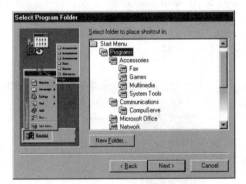

 You see the hierarchical structure of the Start menu. You may place a program anywhere in the structure, but if you want immediate access to the program, you place it on the Start menu itself.

7   Click **Start Menu**. Click **Next**.

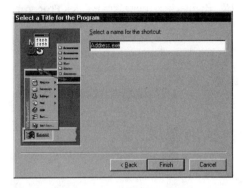

 You may choose any name you wish for the shortcut.

8   Key in the following: **ADDRESS MANAGER**

9   Click **Finish**. Click **OK**.

10   Click the **Start** button.

 Because you placed ADDRESS MANAGER in the Start Menu folder, it appears at the top of the Start menu. What if you wanted it to appear in the cascading menu? You must first remove it from its current location and then place it where you want.

11 Touch the $\boxed{\text{Esc}}$ key to close the **Start** menu.

12 Right-click the taskbar. Click **Properties**. Click the **Start Menu Programs** tab.

13 Click the **Remove** button.

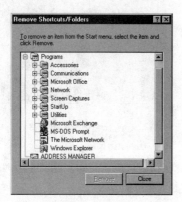

What's happening? → You must locate ADDRESS MANAGER. In this case, it is at the bottom of the list.

14 If it is not visible, scroll until you locate **ADDRESS MANAGER** and click it.

What's happening? → Now that you have selected it, you can remove it.

15 Click **Remove**.

16 Click **Close**. Close the window.

17 Click **Start**.

What's happening? → ADDRESS MANAGER is no longer on the Start menu.

18 Click on the desktop to close the **Start** menu.

19 Right-click the taskbar. Click **Properties**. Click the **Start Menu Programs** tab. Click **Add**.

20 In the **Command line** text box, key in the following: **C:\95book\Addman\Address.exe**

21 Click **Next**.

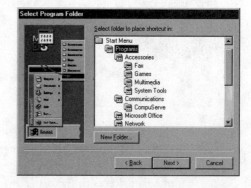

What's happening? → You can rearrange any item on this menu. You can move items from one folder to another or create new folders and move items there. You could place this program under the Programs folder, but you are going to create a new folder under Programs to store the shortcut to Address Manager.

22 Click **New Folder**.

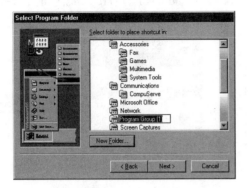

 Windows 95 assigns a name to the folder, Program Group (1). You can give the folder any name you wish.

23 Key in the following: **Other** [Enter]

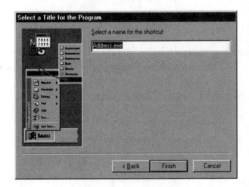

 You are given the opportunity to name the program.

24 Key in the following: **ADDRESS MANAGER**

25 Click **Finish**.

 You have returned to the Taskbar Properties dialog box. In addition to placing programs on menus, you can also place documents on the Start menu in any folder you wish. You are going to add a document to the Other folder.

26 Click **Add**.

27 Click **Browse**. Double-click **95book**.

 Browse is looking only for programs. You want to see all of the files.

28 Click the down arrow in the drop-down list box for **Files of type**. Click **All Files**. If you cannot see **April.txt**, scroll until you can. Click **April.txt**. Click **Open**. Click **Next**.

 You want to place this file in the Other folder.

29 Locate and double-click the **Other** folder.

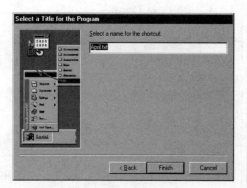

 Again, you may give any name you want to this shortcut to a file.

30 Key in the following: **MY APRIL FILE**

31 Click **Finish**. Close the **Taskbar Properties** dialog box.

 You may also drag and drop items to the Start menu. If you do, however, your only choice is to add the object to the Start menu, not a subfolder.

32 Double-click **My Computer**. Double-click the **Drive C** icon. Double-click the **95book** folder. Locate **Dances.txt**. Drag and drop it to the **Start Menu** button.

33 Close the **C:\95book** window.

34 Click **Start**. Point to **Programs**. Point to **Other**.

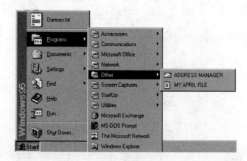

 You have accomplished several goals. You dragged and dropped Dances.txt to Start menu. You also created a cascading menu, in which you placed a program and a data file. Now you can access these choices from the menus.

35 Click outside the menu to close it.

36 Right-click the taskbar. Click **Properties**. Click the **Start Menu Programs** tab. Click **Remove**.

37 Locate the **Other** folder. Click it.

 Now that you have located and selected the folder, you can remove it and all the objects in it.

38 Click **Remove**.

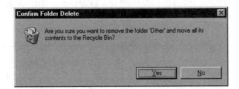

 A message appears asking you to confirm that you really want to delete Other.

39 Click **Yes**.

40 Click **Dances.txt** (at or near the bottom of the list). Click **Remove**.

41 Close the **Taskbar Properties** dialog box.

42 Click **Start**. Point at **Programs**.

 You have removed the Other folder and Dances.txt from the Start menu.

43 Click outside the menus to close them.

 You have returned to the desktop.

9.20 Sound

Windows 95 provides many sounds for you. These sounds are related to certain events. An event is an action performed by you or a program that your computer can notify you about. For example, your computer will beep when you press an incorrect key. There are sounds assigned to many events, such as when you start or exit Windows 95 or when you empty the Recycle Bin. If you have a sound card, you can change the sounds assigned to events or add a sound to an event that does not have one. You can also choose to have no sounds at all. Windows 95 provides sound schemes, much like the color schemes you saw in Desktop Appearances. Sound schemes are entire collections of sounds grouped together under a specific name. Sound files have a .wav file extension. If you do not have a sound card, you will not be able to do the next activity,. but you should read through the steps to gain an understanding of how sounds are assigned.

9.21 Activity—Using Sound

1 Double-click **My Computer**. Double-click **Control Panel**. Double-click the **Sounds** object.

2 Click **Exit Windows** in the list box.

In the Schemes drop-down list box, Windows Default is the selection. You are looking at the sound assigned to the event of exiting Windows 95. In the Name drop-down list box, the file name Tada.wav appears. You can preview this sound.

3 In the **Preview** box, click the **Play** button.

You should have heard the sound.

4 Click **Close program** in the **Events** list box.

In the list box, the Close Program event has no assigned sound. You can tell because there is no sound icon next to its name. In the Name drop-down list box (None) is stated.

5 Click the down arrow in the **Name** drop-down list box.

You see a list of the sound files available on your system. Again, your list will vary based on what is installed on your system.

6 Click **Chimes.wav** (if that is not available, select another sound). Preview the sound.

7 Close the **Sounds** dialog box.

 When you closed the **Sound** dialog box, you heard the sound you selected.

8 Double-click **Sounds** in **Control Panel**.

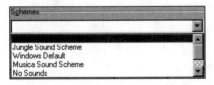 In the Schemes text box, no scheme is listed. When you assigned a sound to the Close program event, you changed the sound scheme. Once it is altered, it is no longer the default.

9 Click the down arrow in the **Schemes** drop-down list box.

The schemes that are available to you depend on what was installed with Windows 95 and if you installed any add-ons.

10 Click **Windows Default**.

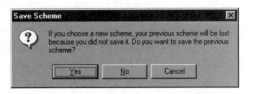

You created a scheme based on the Windows default. If you do not save it, you cannot choose it as an option. In this case, you do not want to save it.

11 Click **No**.

Now Close programs has no sound associated with it.

12 Click **OK**.

13 Close **Control Panel**.

You have returned to the desktop.

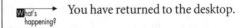

Chapter Summary

In this chapter you learned about user profiles. You can set up user profiles that will preserve settings for each computer user on the system. You looked at the system date and time by accessing the Date/Time object in Control Panel. You learned about Regional Settings and how to change them. You discovered that there are screen and printer fonts. You learned that the technology to display fonts on the screen differs from the technology required to print fonts. You learned that TrueType fonts provide fonts for computer system that print the same as they appear on the screen. You also learned about the different resolutions and colors available on your system. You looked at the different color schemes you could use when you select the Display properties. You learned to access the Display property either from the Control Panel or by right-clicking the desktop. Display provides many options for altering the screen including using a wallpaper, using a pattern, using a screen saver, changing color schemes, or adjusting elements of the desktop. You can alter the keyboard and mouse to meet your needs with the Keyboard and Mouse objects. You can customize the Start menu by using the Taskbar Properties dialog box. You can add or remove programs and documents from the Start menu according to your needs. You can drag and drop programs and documents to the Start menu. By accessing the Sound object, you can assign or remove sounds to computer events.

Key Terms

Add-on	Pattern	Screen savers
Bitmapped font	Pixel	Serif fonts
Built-in fonts	Points	Stroke weight
Context menu	Printer driver	System date
Device driver	Printer fonts	System time
Event	Proportional typefaces	Tracking speed
Font	Repeat delay	TrueType fonts
Modem	Repeat rate	Typeface
Monospaced typefaces	Resident fonts	User profiles
Mouse trails	Sans serif fonts	Wallpaper
PANOSE file	Scaled	Wizard
Password	Screen fonts	WYSIWIG

Discussion Questions

1. Explain the purpose and function of Control Panel.
2. Explain the purpose and function of an add-on.
3. What options does Microsoft Plus! Give the user?
4. Explain the purpose and function of user profiles.
5. Explain the purpose and function of the system date and system time.
6. What impact does a regional setting have on system date and time?
7. Compare and contrast the long and short form for displaying the date.
8. Compare and contrast font and typeface.
9. Compare and contrast a screen font and a printer font.

10. What is a bitmapped font?
11. What advantages do TrueType fonts offer?
12. What tasks can you accomplish in the Fonts folder?
13. Describe VGA.
14. What is a pixel?
15. What are some of the advantages and disadvantages of using a higher resolution setting for your monitor?
16. What factors must you take into account to determine what resolution you can use?
17. What are the advantages and disadvantages of having more colors displayed on your monitor?
18. What is a pattern? A wallpaper?
19. Explain how you would use a pattern or a wallpaper.
20. Compare and contrast tiling and centering wallpaper.
21. What is a color scheme? How can you use it?
22. Describe the steps to change the font of icons or menus.
23. Explain the purpose and function of a screen saver.
24. Why would you use a password with a screen saver?
25. List reasons for and ways of customizing the mouse and keyboard.
26. What is a mouse trail? Why would you want to enable this feature?
27. Explain the terms repeat rate and repeat delay.
28. List and explain the purpose and function of the Start menu.
29. Describe two ways to add a document to the Start menu.
30. What is an event? How may a sound be assigned to an event?

True/False Questions

For each question, circle the letter T if the statement is true or the letter F if the statement is false.

T F 1. Control Panel includes an object to add new hardware.
T F 2. In the computer world, the terms font and typeface are used interchangeably.
T F 3. Both a wallpaper and a pattern use memory, but a wallpaper uses less memory than a pattern.
T F 4. Screen savers can provide password security.
T F 5. You may add programs only to the Start menu.

Completion Questions

Write the correct answer in each blank space.

6. If two users share the same computer, they can preserve their preferred settings by creating _____.
7. The smallest point of light that can be displayed on the screen is called a(n) _____.
8. A _____ font creates characters by a pattern of dots.
9. When you use the Appearance tab in the Display property sheet, Windows Standard, Rainy Day, Desert, and Windows Standard are all examples of _____.
10. Sound files used by Windows 95 will have the extension of _____.

Multiple Choice Questions

Circle the letter of the correct answer for each question.

11. Characters appearing in 12-point Times New Roman are examples of a
    a. font.
    b. bitmapped graphic.
    c. both a and b
    d. neither a nor b

12. You can set all of the following in Regional Settings Control Panel *except*
    a. automatically adjusting the clock for daylight saving time.
    b. the way the date is displayed.
    c. the way the time is displayed.
    d. the currency symbol used.

13. The main factor(s) in determining the monitor resolution you can use is the
    a. version of Windows 95 you are using.
    b. monitor you have.
    c. video card you have installed.
    d. both b and c

14. A program that leads you through the steps of a task is a
    a. task manager.
    b. wizard.
    c. helper program.
    d. none of the above

15. The Programs folder within the Start menu folder
    a. contains all the programs available on your computer.
    b. contains all shortcuts and folders found on the Programs submenus.
    c. contains programs that require a password.
    d. cannot be modified.

Application Assignments

Problem Set I—At the Computer

Problem A

Open **Control Panel**. Open the **Passwords** object. Click the **Change Password** tab.

1. Which definition suggests that you have only one password to remember? (*Hint*: Remember What's This?)
   a. Windows Password.
   b. Other Passwords.

Close the **Passwords Properties** property sheet. Open the **Date/Time** object. Click the **Date & Time** tab. Click the down arrow in the **Date** spin box until you reach the earliest year that Windows 95 recognizes.

2. The earliest year that Windows 95 recognizes is
   a. 1900.
   b. 1950.
   c. 1980.
   d. 1990.

Change the year to the current year. Click the **Time Zone** tab. Click the down arrow on the drop-down list box. Drag the scroll box to the end of the list. You should see **Wellington, Auckland**.

3. The number of hours past Greenwich Mean Time (GMT + x) for Wellington, Auckland, New Zealand is
   a. 4:00.
   b. 8:00.
   c. 12:00.
   d. 16.00.

Be sure your correct time zone is selected. Click **Cancel**. Close the **Time/Date** dialog box. Open **Regional Settings**. Click the **Date** tab. In the **Long Date** format style, note the style. Then, in the **Long Date** drop-down list box, select the **dd, MMMM, yyyy** format. Click **Apply**. Your month, date, and year will vary. The format will be one of the answers below.

4. The long date sample appears as
   a. October 1, 1995.
   b. October 01, 1995.
   c. 1 October, 1995.
   d. 01 October, 1995.

Return the **Long Date** format style to the default settings. Close **Regional Settings**. Close **Control Panel**.

Problem B

Open **Fonts** in **Control Panel**. Double-click **Courier New**.

5. Courier New is _____ KB in size.
   a. 97
   b. 197
   c. 299
   d. 300

Close the window. Click **List Fonts by Similarity**. In the drop-down **List fonts by similarity to**, choose **Courier New**. In the **Name** list box, locate **Arial**.

6. Arial
   a. is similar to Courier New.
   b. is not similar to Courier New.
   c. has no PANOSE information.

Click **View**. Click **Large Icons**. Close the **Fonts** window.

Problem C

Open **Control Panel**. Open the **Display** object. Choose the **Appearance** tab. Choose **Lilac** in the **Scheme** drop-down list box.

7. In the Sample box, the Inactive Window title bar has what background color?
   a. Lilac.
   b. Gray.
   c. White.

Choose **Rose** in the **Scheme** drop-down list box.

8. In the Sample box, the term Window Text appears in what color?
   a. Rose.
   b. Gray.
   c. White.
   d. Black.

Locate **ToolTip** in the drop-down **Item** list box. Click it.
9. Does ToolTip have a font and a font size assigned to it?
   a. Yes.
   b. No.
   c. ToolTip is not listed.

Click **Cancel**. Close **Control Panel**.

Problem D

Open the **Display** property sheet. Click the **Background** tab. Choose the **Triangles** pattern. Click **Edit**.

10. Which drawing is the **Triangles** pattern?

   a.

   b.

Click **Done**. Select **(None)** for **Patterns**. In the drop-down list box for **Wallpaper,** select **Setup**. Be sure **Tile** is set. Click **Apply**. Close the **Display Properties**. If the **Control Panel** window is open, close it.

11. The wallpaper on the desktop has many pictures in it. One of the pictures is a
   a. monitor.
   b. keyboard.
   c. mouse.
   d. both b and c

12. If you choose to use a wallpaper, you will
   a. use more memory.
   b. use less memory.
   c. have no affect on memory.

Open the **Display** property sheet. Choose **(None)** for Wallpaper. Click **Apply**. Close **Display Properties** sheet.

Problem E

Open the **Display** property sheet. Click the **Screen Saver** tab. Choose the **Flying Windows** screen saver. Preview it.

13. What appears is/are
   a. pictures of files.
   b. pictures of the Windows 95 logo.
   c. a blank screen.

Choose the **Flying Through Space** screen saver. (It may be called **Stars**.) Click the **Settings** button.

14. In the Starfield density, the number of stars can range from
    a. 0–100.
    b. 10–100.
    c. 10–200.
    d. 100–200.

Click **Cancel**. Close the **Display** property sheet.

Problem F

Open **Control Panel**. Open the **Mouse** object. Click the **Motion** tab.

15. In order to set or unset Show pointer trails, you must
    a. click the Show pointer trails check box.
    b. click the Show pointer trails command button.

Close the **Mouse** properties sheet. Open the **Keyboard** object. Click the **question mark** on the title bar. Drag it to the **clock** icon and click.

16. Which tip appears?

    a. Adjusts the speed at which a character repeats when you hold down a key.

    b. Adjusts the amount of time that elapses before a character begins repeating when you hold down a key.

Close the **Keyboard Properties** sheet. Close **Control Panel**.

Problem G

Open **Control Panel**. Open the **Sounds** object. **Windows Default** should be the sound scheme. Locate **Maximize** in the **Events** list.

17. Does it have a sound associated with it?
    a. yes.
    b. no.

Locate **Default Sound** in the **Events** list. Click it.

18. In the drop-down list Name box, there is a file name. What is it?
    a. Chimes.wav
    b. Ding.wav
    c. Tada.wav

Close the **Sounds** properties dialog box. Close **Control Panel**.

Problem Set II—Brief Essay

For all essay questions, use Notepad to create your answer. Then print your answer.

1. Why do you think Windows 95 provides multiple options for changing fonts, colors, the desktop background, and other display options for screen elements? Discuss the advantages and disadvantages of these multiple options.
2. Compare and contrast fonts and typefaces. Identify the major category of fonts that Windows 95 uses. Include in your discussion what the fonts are and how and why they are necessary. Describe the purpose and function of TrueType fonts.

Problem Set III—Scenario

When you click the Start button, you see the following:

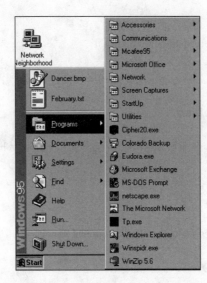

Colorado Backup is a tape backup utility and WinZip is a utility program that allows you to compress files. Mcafee95 is a set of utility programs that checks your computer for viruses. Eudora and Netscape are programs that allow you to receive electronic mail and to surf (wander about) the Internet. Dances.bmp and February.txt are document files that you use occasionally.

Create a plan to alter this menu scheme so that it assists you in working more efficiently. List the steps you would take to alter these menus. Include in your answer the folders you would create, if any, and what items you would remove, if any. State which items you would move and where you would move them. Discuss your rationale.

Chapter 10

Windows 95 Accessories— Calculator, Notepad, WordPad, and Character Map

Chapter Overview

Windows 95 provides some convenient tools to use with its desktop accessories. You can access them through the Start/Programs/Accessories menus when you need them. You have already worked with one of these tools, a text editing application called Notepad. You have used Notepad to look at text files. You are now going to learn how to use Notepad to create text files. Another accessory you will learn more about in this chapter is WordPad, a simple word processor. WordPad offers formatting capabilities that Notepad does not. A third tool you will work with in this chapter is Calculator, which performs basic mathematical calculations as if it were a calculator on your desk. The last tool that you will encounter is Character Map, which is a collection of special symbols, such as ™, ®, ¼, or ½, that you can insert into documents.

Learning Objectives

1. Explain the purpose and function of Calculator.
2. List the ways in which Calculator can be operated.
3. Explain the purpose and function of Notepad.
4. Explain how to open, save, print, and close files in Notepad.
5. Explain the purpose and function of WordPad.
6. Explain how to open, save, print, and close files in WordPad.
7. Compare and contrast WordPad and Notepad.
8. Explain the purpose and function of Character Map.
9. Explain how to move special characters from Character Map to another application.

Student Outcomes

1. Use Calculator.
2. Use Notepad to create, save, and print files.
3. Create, edit, save, and print documents in WordPad.
4. Insert special characters into WordPad using Character Map.

10.1 Calculator

The Calculator tool is an arithmetic and scientific calculator. An arithmetic calculator provides basic mathematical functions, such as addition, subtraction, and division. A scientific calculator provides additional mathematical functions, such as calculating the sine and cosine of numbers or converting decimal numbers into binary, hexadecimal, or octal numbers. Calculator does not provide any business functions such as calculating interest rates, rate of return, or future values.

10.2 Activity—Using Calculator

1 Click **Start**. Point at **Programs**. Point at **Accessories**. Click **Calculator**.

 You opened Calculator, which, by default, is in its standard arithmetic mode.

2 Click **View**.

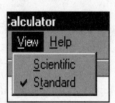

 You dropped down the View menu, which provides two choices: Standard or Scientific. The check mark identifies Standard as the current view.

3 Click **Scientific**.

 You are now looking at the scientific mode of the calculator. In the scientific mode, you can perform a number of scientific functions, such as squaring a number, identifying the reciprocal of a number, and establishing logarithm exponents.

4 Click **View**. Click **Standard**.

 You have returned to the standard arithmetic calculator. Using the calculator is simple. You may use the mouse to click on any button on the calculator. You may also use the numeric keypad on the far right of the keyboard. The numeric keypad has numbers as well as direction symbols on it. When the **NumLock** is off, pressing the keys marked with arrows will move the cursor in different directions. If you wish to use the numeric functions, you must turn them on by pressing the **NumLock** key. When the **NumLock** is on, its keyboard light is on; when the **NumLock** is off, its light is off. The sign used to indicate multiplication is an asterisk (*). The sign for division is a forward slash (/).

5 Click **7**. Click *****. Click **5**. Click **=**.

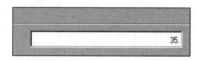

You have stored the results of your calculation in the calculator's memory. The letter M in the calculator's smaller window indicates that there is something in memory.

10 Click **C**. Click **20**. Click *****. Click **10**. Click **=**. Click **+**. Click **MR**. Click **=**.

You multiplied 7 by 5 and the answer is 35.

6 Click **View**. Click **Scientific**.

The 35 is displayed in decimal form in the scientific calculator display window. You can convert this number to its binary equivalent.

7 Click the **Bin** option button.

The decimal number 35 was converted to its binary equivalent. The binary number system uses only two digits, the 1 and the 0, to represent values. Computers understand only binary numbers; the digits 1 and 0 translate to off and on.

8 Click the **Decimal** option button. Click **View**. Click **Standard**.

9 Click **5**. Click *****. Click **5**. Click **=**. Click **MS**.

You used the memory functions to store and then recall a number. When you close Calculator, everything in the calculator's memory is cleared.

11 Close **Calculator**.

You have returned to the desktop.

10.3 Notepad

You have previously looked at the Notepad text editor. You used it to multitask and to print a file. You can also create simple text documents with Notepad. Remember, a text document is one that has no embedded computer codes. This means that many formatting options are unavailable to you in the Notepad text editor, such as selecting fonts. All word processing programs have embedded codes; all text editors lack embedded codes. As you will later see, at times you need to give direct instructions to Windows 95 itself, but Windows 95 can only recognize text files—those with no special embedded codes. This is why you have Notepad.

Notepad has some minimal editing features such as word wrap, which you can turn on or off. *Word wrap* prevents text from running over into the margins and will automatically move text to the next line, so that you never need to press **Enter**. You can create a file, save it, then reopen it to edit it. You can also create a time log file to track your activities. You can cut, copy, and paste text within Notepad. You can also transfer Notepad text to other word processing, text, or database documents.

10.4 Activity—Using Notepad

1 Place your Data disk in Drive A.

2 Click **Start**. Point at **Programs**. Point at **Accessories**. Click **Notepad**.

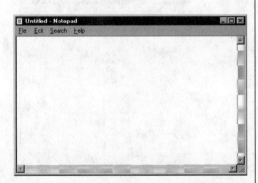

What's happening? You have opened Notepad. If you choose, you can adjust the size of the Notepad window by using the techniques you learned earlier. You are going to keep a log of your work. A log will stamp the current date and time in your document every time you open it.

3 At the insertion point, key in *exactly* the following, making sure you use all upper-case letters:
.LOG

What's happening? You have opened your log file. It is a log file because .LOG is the first line in the file. You now want to save this file to disk.

4   Click **File**.

 You have two choices, Save and Save As. When you choose Save, your file is saved to disk, overwriting the previous file. If you choose Save As, you preserve your original document by creating a new document.

5   Click **Save**.

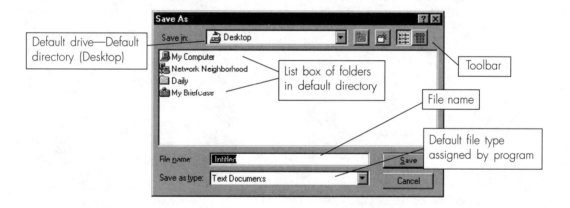

 Although you chose Save, you were presented with the Save As dialog box. A file must first have a name before it can be saved. Every time you save a new file, you see the Save As dialog box. Every time you save a named file, no dialog box appears because the updated file is automatically saved under its original name.

In the Save as type drop-down list box, Text Documents is the default. Text documents use the file extension .txt.

6   Click the down arrow in the **Save in** drop-down list box.

What's happening?   You see the all the drives on your system.

7   Click the **Drive A** icon.

What's happening?   You see all the directories and folders that are available on the Data disk, but only the .txt files are displayed.

8   Click the down arrow in the **Save as type** drop-down list box.

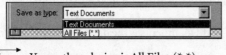

What's happening?   Your other choice is All Files (*.*).

9   Click **All Files (*.*)**.

What's happening?   You see all the folders and files in the root directory of Drive A. In the Save As dialog box, you can also create a new folder.

10   On the toolbar, click the **New Folder** icon which is next to the **Up One Level** icon.

What's happening?   You can now create a new folder.

11   Key in the following: **Chap10** ⌷Enter⌷

What's happening?   You now have a new folder, but you must select it so that you can save your document in it.

12   Double-click **Chap10**.

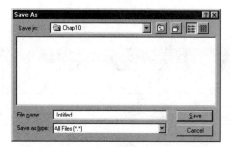

What's happening?   You have an empty folder in which you will save this file.

13   In the **File Name** text box, select **Untitled**, then key in the following: **LOG**

What's happening?   You have named your file. Remember, typing replaces selection. The extension .txt will automatically be added since this file is being created with Notepad.

14   Click **Save**.

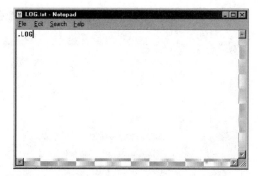

What's happening?   Your file has a name, LOG.txt, which you can see on the Notepad title bar.

15   Close **Notepad**.

16   Open **Notepad**.

17 Click **File**. Click **Open**.

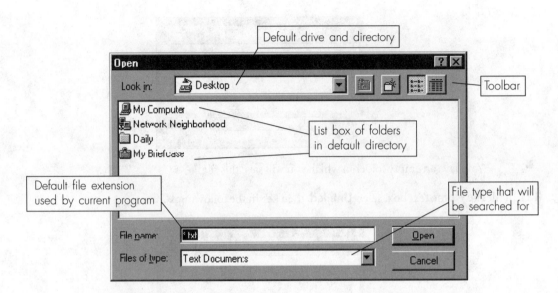

Default drive and directory

Toolbar

List box of folders in default directory

Default file extension used by current program

File type that will be searched for

The Open dialog box looks similar to the Save As dialog box. Once you have learned how to complete a task in one application, you know how to perform this task in all other Windows 95 applications. Because *.txt is shown in the File name text box, only files that have the .txt extension (but have any file name) will be displayed in the dialog box. Notepad only looks for files with its own default extension.

18 Click the down arrow in the **Look in** drop-down list box. Click the **Drive A** icon. Double-click the **Chap10** folder.

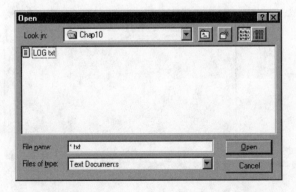

You are searching for all the files with the .txt extension. You see only one displayed in the file list box because it is the only file with a .txt extension in the Chap10 folder. As a matter of fact, it is the only file in that folder altogether.

19   Double-click **LOG.txt**.

 The file opens. You see the current date and time displayed in the file.

20   Key in the following: **I am working with Notepad.** ⏎Enter⏎

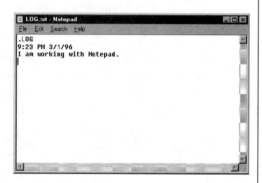

 You have added some text to the file.

21   Click **File**. Click **Save**.

 Since this file has a name, when you clicked File/Save, the updated information was saved to the same file.

22   Click **File**. Click **Open**.

23   Click the **Up One Level** button. Double-click **Stated.txt**. (If the file is not there, copy **Stated.txt** from the **95book** folder from Drive C to the root of the Data disk.)

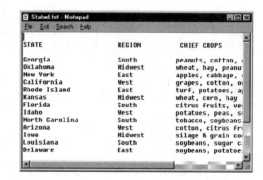

 When you open a file in Notepad, the previous file closes. You can only open one document at a time in Notepad. Depending on the size of your Notepad window, the text of this document may or may not fit in the window.

24   Size the **Notepad** window so it looks as follows:

 You can no longer see all the text.

25   Click **Edit**. Click **Word Wrap**.

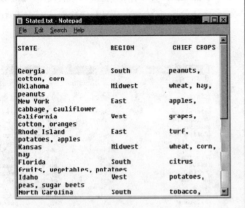

 Word Wrap is set, so the text wraps to fit the window.

26   Click **Search**. Click **Find**.

 The Find dialog box appears. In the Find what text box, you key in what you are looking for. You also have a check box that will, if set, make the search case-sensitive. Using the two option buttons, you may search up or down through your document. Down is the default.

27   In the **Find What** text box, key in the following: **Wheat**

28   Click **Find Next**.

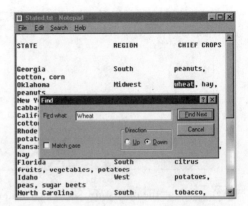

 The Find command located the first occurrence of the word wheat. If you desire, you can continue to search for the next occurrence of your selected text.

29   Click **Cancel**.

30   Click the insertion point in front of **Oklahoma**. Place the cursor after the **s** in **oranges**. Hold the **Shift** key and click.

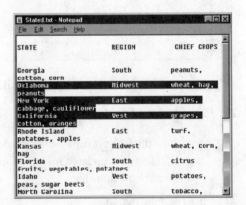

 In order to manipulate text, you must first select it. You know the text is selected because it is highlighted.

31 Click **Edit**. Click **Copy**.

 Windows 95 has a feature called Clipboard that uses an area of memory to store anything copied or cut from a file. Whatever is in Clipboard remains there until you clear the Clipboard, replace it with something else, or turn off the computer.

32 Click **File**. Click **Open**.

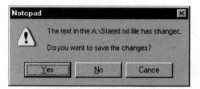

 Notepad is warning you that the Stated.txt file has changed. You do not want to save these changes.

33 Click **No**.

34 Click the down arrow on the **Look in** drop-down list box. Double-click the **Chap10** folder. Double-click **LOG.txt**. Click **Edit**. Click **Paste**.

 Opening your existing LOG.txt file inserted the current date and time. You then selected Edit/Paste, which pasted the information that you copied from Stated.txt to LOG.txt.

35 Click **File**. Click **Save**.

 The new information in the file has been saved.

36 Close **Notepad**.

 You have returned to the desktop.

10.5 Printing and Page Setup in Notepad

To print a Notepad document, you locate it with My Computer or Explorer. Once the file is located and selected, use either the File/Print commands from the menus or the right-click, context-sensitive (shortcut) menus. Either choice will print the document immediately.

You may also open Notepad from the Start/Programs/Accessories menu. From there you can open your document. Once opened, you can print it. The advantage of opening Notepad to print a file is that you can apply page formatting to your document.

You can include a header, a footer, or both on each page. A *header* is text printed on the top of each page, while a *footer* is text printed at the bottom of each page. Typical items in headers and footers are file names, page numbers, and dates. You can also alter the top, bottom, left, and right margins of the document. In order to apply this formatting, you must load Notepad and select File/Page Setup.

10.6 Activity—Page Setup in Notepad

1 Place your Data disk in Drive A.

2 Open **Notepad**.

3 Click **File**. Click **Open**.

4 Click the down arrow in the **Look in** drop-down list box. Click the **Drive A** icon. Double-click the **Chap10** folder.

5 Double-click **LOG.txt**.

6 Click **File**. Click **Page Setup**.

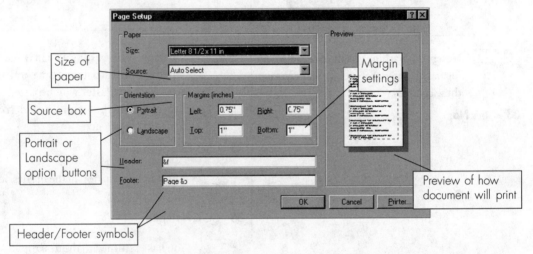

Size of paper

Source box

Portrait or Landscape option buttons

Header/Footer symbols

Margin settings

Preview of how document will print

Your options in the Size and Source drop-down list boxes will depend on which printer you have installed. You also may not have a Portrait or Landscape option. *Portrait* prints in the standard vertical 8½" × 11" format, whereas *landscape* prints "sideways" or in an 11" × 8½" mode. You can change the margin settings. There are default values in the Header and Footer information text boxes. The symbol & indicates that something will be printed. In this case, "&f" means print the file name and "Page &p" means print the word Page and number the pages. To see the available choices, drag the question mark down and click on the Header/Footer text boxes.

7 Click the question mark. Drag it over the header text box and click.

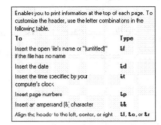

You see the available options.

8 Click outside of the information box to it. Select the text in the **Header** text box, then key in the following: **&cMY LOG FILE**

9 Select the text in the **Footer** text box then key in the following: **&l&f &rPage &p**

10 Change the right and left margins to **1"**.

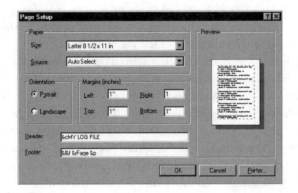

11 Click **OK**. Click **File**. Click **Print**.

```
                         MY LOG FILE
.LOG
9:23 PM 3/1/96
I am working with Notepad.

9:54 PM 3/1/96
Oklahoma          Midwest            wheat, hay, peanuts
New York          East               apples, cabbage, cauliflower
California        West               grapes, cotton, oranges
10:13 PM 3/1/96


LOG.txt                                          Page 1
```

When you changed the margins, the Preview picture in the Page Setup dialog box adjusted to show you the new look of your document. The **&c MY LOG FILE** indicated to center the words at the top of the page (header). The **&l&f** indicated to place the file name at the left side of the bottom of the page (footer). The **&rPage &p** indicated to insert the word Page and the page number at the right side of the bottom of the page.

12 Save the file.

13 Close **Notepad**.

 You have returned to the desktop.

10.7 WordPad

WordPad is a simple word processor that lets the user format a document. You can change the fonts, create special character formatting such as bold or underline, create margins, and insert bullet charts. In addition, you can insert graphics and sound files. WordPad has both a menu bar and a toolbar, but it does not have powerful word processing features, such as the ability to create columns or check spelling.

If you have never used a word processor, there are some things you should know. You must not press **Enter** when a word reaches the right margin. A word processor will word wrap automatically when it encounters a right margin. This action is called a *soft return*. The only time you press **Enter** is to create a new paragraph. This action is called a *hard return*.

A paragraph in word processing is different from the traditional paragraph that you were taught to write in school. The traditional, or English-style, paragraph is typically a group of several sentences. A paragraph begins with a topic sentence, is followed by two or more supporting sentences, and ends with a concluding sentence. The paragraph is usually indented by one tab. In word processing, however, a paragraph is any part of a document that is preceded by one paragraph mark and ends with another. A paragraph can be one character, one page or several pages of text. To WordPad, a paragraph is a unit of information that can be selected as a whole and given individual formatting instructions. The formatting information for the paragraph is contained in the paragraph mark (¶).

For example, if you were keying in an address, you would press **Enter** at the end of each line of the address block. Each line is therefore a separate paragraph. The same is true when you want to indent a paragraph. You do not press the **Space Bar**; you must use the **Tab** key.

When you open WordPad, the WordPad window appears as shown in Figure 10.1. See Table 10.1 for identification of the window's features.

Figure 10.1   WordPad Window

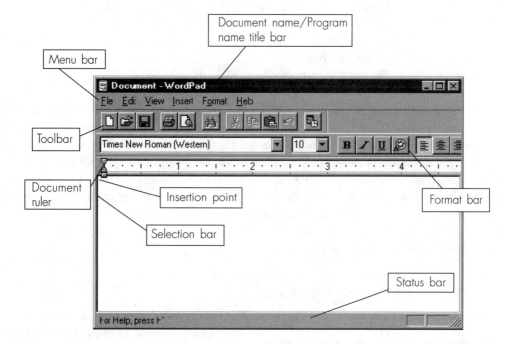

Table 10.1 WordPad Features

Title bar
In applications designed for the Windows 95 docucentric approach, the name of the document appears first, followed by the name of the application. Until this document is named, it is assigned a generic name—Document.

Menu bar
The menu bar provides you choices for the tasks you can accomplish within WordPad.

Toolbar
Each item on the toolbar is a shortcut to one of the menu choices. For instance, if you want to create a new file, you could click File/New or you could click the first toolbar icon, 🗋 , which accomplishes the same task. If you are not sure what an icon represents, hold your pointer over the icon and a ToolTip will appear.

Format toolbar
The Format toolbar, like the standard toolbar, has shortcuts to the Edit and Insert menus. In addition, the Format toolbar provides special character formatting, such as bolding a character.

Document ruler
The *document ruler* displays the margin and tab settings for a document.

Selection bar
The *selection bar* is an imaginary area just outside and to the left of the text in the document. When you are in the selection bar area, your pointer changes shape from an I-beam to an arrow. When you are in the selection bar area, you can take shortcuts with the mouse to select text.

Insertion point   Represented by an I-beam, the insertion point is where you begin keying in text. WordPad works in two modes. The default is *insert mode*. As you key in or edit text, the existing text is pushed to the right. In the other mode, *typeover*, what you key in replaces what is already there. You toggle between these two modes by pressing the **Insert** key.

Status bar   The status bar tells you the status of the document.

WordPad registers the default extension .doc to any document you create in WordPad. As you know, if you are using Explorer or My Computer and double-click a registered file, you will open the application program that created a document as well as the document. Word for Windows has also registered the .doc extension, however. Remember, only one program can "own" a file extension. Thus, although you may have created the document with WordPad, when you double-click any file with the .doc extension, Word will open, not WordPad. This problem can also occur with other registered file extensions to which more than one program claims ownership. Since you want to be able to open the program of your choice, and not necessarily the default program, you need to solve this problem. The following activity will present some alternatives.

10.8 Activity—Choosing Your Program

1   Place the Data disk in Drive A.

2   Click **Start**. Point at **Programs**. Point at **Accessories**. Click **WordPad**.

3   Click **View**.

^{What's happening?}   If each of these items is not set in the View menu, check them now.

4   Click outside the menu to close it.

5   Key in the following: **This is a test.**

6   Click the **File Save** icon on the toolbar.

7   Click the down arrow in the **Save in** drop-down list box. Click the **3½ Floppy (A:)** icon. Double-click the **Chap10** folder.

^{What's happening?}   In the File name text box, Document.doc is listed as the file name. In the Save as type drop-down list box, Word for Windows 6.0 is displayed. This information tells you that the document you just created will be saved as a Word for Windows document.

8   In the **File name** text box, select **Document.doc**, then key in the following: **Test**

9 Click **Save**. Close **WordPad**.

10 Open **Explorer**. On the tree side, double-click the **3½ Floppy (A:)** icon. On the tree side, double-click the **Chap10** folder.

11 On the contents side, right-click **Test.doc**.

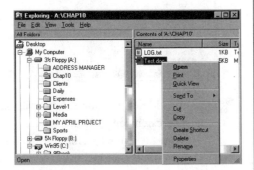

What's happening? The context menu will let you open this file. If you had Word, Word would open, not WordPad. This menu does not give you the option of opening WordPad.

12 Click outside the menu to close it.

13 Click **Test.doc** on the contents side to select it. Hold the [Shift] key and right-click **Test.doc**.

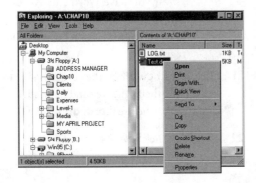

What's happening? A new choice appears, Open With. Open With lets you choose the program you wish to use.

14 Click **Open With**.

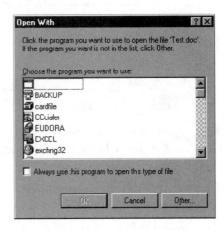

What's happening? Now you can choose your program.

15 Be sure that the check box, **Always use this program to open this type of file** is empty. Locate **WordPad**. Click **WordPad**. Click **OK**.

What's happening? Your Test.doc file opened in WordPad.

16 Click **File**. Click **Save As**.

 What's happening? WordPad remembered your last location, A:\Chap10. In the File name text box is your file name, Test.doc.

17 Select **Test.doc** and key in the following: **Test2.new**

18 Click the down arrow in the **Save as type** drop-down list box.

 What's happening? You have other file types to choose from. You are going to choose the *Rich Text Format (RTF)*. RTF is a text formatting standard that enables a word processing program to create a file encoded with the document's formatting instructions without using any special codes. An RTF file type can be read by another word processing program without losing the formatting.

19 Click **Rich Text Format (RTF)**.

 What's happening? You have made your selection.

20 Click **Save**. Close **WordPad**.

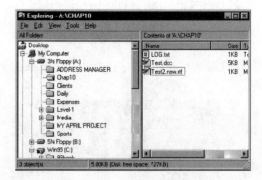

 What's happening? In addition to your assigned file name, the extension .RTF was added so that your file name became Test2.new.rtf. If you double-clicked this file (and if you had Word), Word would open. You will find that file extensions are not the only clue Windows 95 has for knowing what program to open. When you create a data file with any program, in addition to the registered file extension, there is often hidden computer information in the data file that tells Windows 95 what program to open.

If you have Word and WordPad, a simple solution to opening WordPad is to create a file extension for WordPad and register it.

21 Click **Test2.new.rtf** on the contents side to select it. Hold the ⟨**Shift**⟩ key and right-click. Click **Open With**. Choose **WordPad**. Click **OK**.

22 Click **File**. Click **Save As**.

23 In the **File name** text box, select **Test2.new.rtf** and key in the following: **"Test3.pad"**

What's happening? Again, WordPad remembered the last location and the last file type. By using quotation marks, you are telling WordPad to use *only* what you key in and to add no extension.

24 Click **Save**. Close **WordPad**.

What's happening? Because you used quotation marks, your file name is exactly as you named it, test3.pad. Now you want to register .pad as your extension for WordPad.

25 In the **Explorer** window, double-click **Test3.pad**.

What's happening? The extension .pad is unknown to Windows 95, so you are presented with the Open With dialog box. This time the Always use this program to open this file check box is set. Since you want to register this file, you will leave this box checked.

26 Locate **WordPad**. Click it. Click **OK**. Close **WordPad**.

27 Click **View**. Click **Large Icons**.

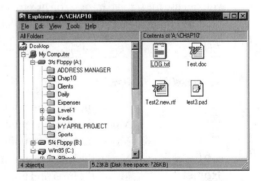

What's happening? The large icons view lets you see the icons clearly. The test3.pad file is no longer an unknown file type.

28 Double-click **test3.pad**.

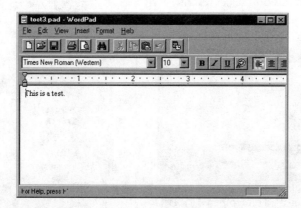

 WordPad opened, as you planned.

29 Click **View**. Click **List**. Close **Explorer**.

 You have returned to the desktop.

10.9 Editing a Document in WordPad

One of the many advantages to using a word processor is the ease of editing a document. You can edit a document using a combination of keyboard and mouse techniques. To edit text, you need to move the insertion point to the proper location in your document. You can move the insertion point using either the keyboard or the mouse. It is usually more convenient to use the keyboard when keying in data and to use the mouse when editing existing text. Taking your hands off the keyboard while you are typing can slow you down. When you use the mouse, you click at the desired location. If you cannot see the location, you can use the scroll bars or scroll box to move about your document. Using the keyboard sometimes requires you to press two keys. Table 10.2 lists ways to move the insertion point using the keyboard.

Table 10.2 Using the Keyboard To Move the Insertion Point

Keystroke(s)	Function
←	Moves the insertion point one character to the left.
→	Moves the insertion point one character to the right.
Ctrl + ←	Moves the insertion point one word to the left.
Ctrl + →	Moves the insertion point one word to the right.
Home	Moves the insertion point to the start of the line.
End	Moves the insertion point to the end of the line.
↑	Moves the insertion point up one line.
↓	Moves the insertion point down one line.
Ctrl + Home	Moves the insertion point to the beginning of the document.
Ctrl + End	Moves the insertion point to the end of the document.

Selecting text is fundamental when you work with WordPad. You must select text to modify it. You know that text is being selected because, as you select it, it becomes highlighted. For instance, if you wanted a word to be in italics, you would first have to select it before you could italicize it. Selecting also allows you to manipulate text. Instead of pressing the **Backspace** key repeatedly to delete a paragraph, you can select the paragraph and press the **Delete** key.

There are many ways to select text. Using the mouse is an easy method. You drag the mouse over the text you wish to select. You can also click the insertion point at the beginning of what you wish to select, move the mouse to the end of the text you wish to select, and hold the **Shift** key while you click the mouse. When working with the mouse, remember that there is an important area on the screen called the selection bar. It is an unmarked column along the left edge of the document window. When you are in the selection bar area, the pointer becomes an arrow. This technique is most useful when you are selecting large amounts of text. Table 10.3 lists techniques for selecting text with the mouse.

Table 10.3 Using the Mouse To Select Text

Text To Be Selected	Mouse Techniques
One or more characters	Click at the first character. Move the mouse to the last character and hold the **Shift** key while you click.
Word	Double-click the word.
Line of text	Move to the selection bar and click at the desired line. To select multiple lines, drag the mouse in the selection bar area.
Paragraph	Move to the selection bar and double-click at the desired paragraph. To select multiple paragraphs, drag the mouse in the selection bar area.
Entire document	Move to the selection bar and hold the **Ctrl** key and click. You may also move to the selection bar and triple-click.

There are also many ways to select text using the keyboard. Essentially, you use the same keyboard selection skills you have learned, but you hold down the **Shift** key. For instance, to move to the end of a line, you press the **End** key. To select to the end of a line, you press both the **Shift** + **End** keys. To select the entire document from the keyboard, hold down the **Ctrl** key and press a.

In addition, the mouse allows you to use the toolbar and format bar, which are shown in Figure 10.2.

Figure 10.2   Format Toolbar

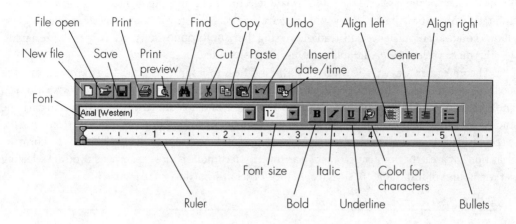

10.10 Activity—Editing a Document in WordPad

1 Place the Data disk in Drive A.

2 Click **Start**. Point at **Programs**. Point at **Accessories**. Click **WordPad**.

3 Click the **File Open** icon.

4 Click the down arrow in the **Look in** drop-down list box. Double-click the **Drive C** icon. Double-click the **95book** folder. Double-click the **Classes** folder.

What's happening?   It appears that there are no files in the C:\95book\Classes folder. However, in the Files of type drop-down list box, you see that it is only looking for .doc files.

5 Click the down arrow in the **Files of type** drop-down list box. Click **All Documents (*.*)**.

What's happening?   You see all the available files.

6 Double-click the **rawgoal.wri** document.

7 Click **File**. Click **Save As**.

8   Click the down arrow in the **Save in** drop-down list box. Click the **3½ Floppy (A)** icon. Double-click the **Chap10** folder.

   You are ready to save the document called rawgoal.wri to A:\Chap10. You will keep the same file name. The .wri file extension, which was originally used for the Write program in Windows 3.1, will always open WordPad.

9   Click the **Save** command button.

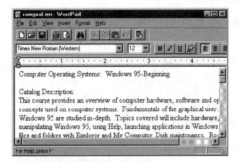

   You are looking at the document on the disk in Drive A.

10   Maximize the window. Click **Edit**. Click **Find**.

11   In the **Find what** text box, key in the following: **COURSE CONTENT**

12   Click **Find Next**. Click **Cancel**.

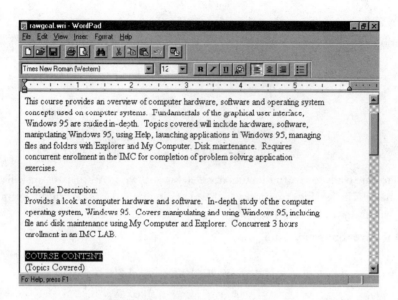

  You located the first occurrence of COURSE CONTENT. As you remember, the techniques you learned in Notepad also work in WordPad.

13   If you cannot see the words, (Topics Covered), scroll until you can. Place the insertion point on the T in Topics and drag until Topics Covered is highlighted.

  You have selected text.

14   Press the **Delete** key.

  You have deleted the words between the two parentheses.

15   Click **Edit**. Click **Undo**.

 You can undo this deletion.

16   Click outside the **(Topics Covered)** area to deselect it.

17   Move the insertion point into the selection bar area. It will assume an arrow shape. Point and click at the **(Topics Covered)** line.

 When your pointer entered the selection bar area, it became an arrow. Since you used the selection bar area, when you pointed and clicked, you selected the entire line including the invisible paragraph marker that contains the formatting instructions.

18   Click **Edit**. Click **Cut**.

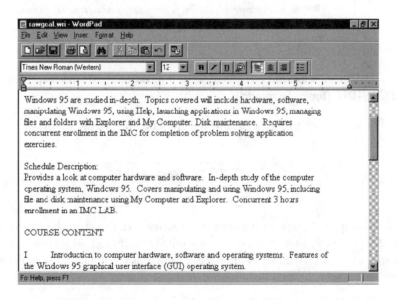

 You have copied the text to the Clipboard.

19 Move the insertion point to the end of **Course Content**. Click **Edit**. Click **Paste**.

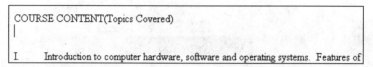

> COURSE CONTENT(Topics Covered)
>
> I. Introduction to computer hardware, software and operating systems. Features of

What's happening? Whatever was on the Clipboard was pasted in the location you specified. You did not insert a space between the letter T in CONTENT and the parenthesis preceding Topics, and when you selected the line, you also selected the "hard return," the invisible paragraph mark. A hard return is just a character that can be deleted like any other character.

20 Press the **Delete** key once.

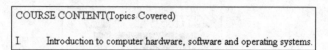

> COURSE CONTENT(Topics Covered)
>
> I. Introduction to computer hardware, software and operating systems.

What's happening? When you pressed the **Delete** key, you deleted one character to the right of the insertion point. The character you deleted was a paragraph marker.

21 Place the insertion point between **T** and **(**. Press the **Space Bar** twice.

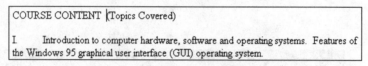

> COURSE CONTENT (Topics Covered)
>
> I. Introduction to computer hardware, software and operating systems. Features of the Windows 95 graphical user interface (GUI) operating system.

What's happening? You inserted two spaces.

22 Move the insertion point into the selection bar area. It will assume an arrow shape. Point and click at the **COURSE CONTENT (Topics Covered)** line.

23 Click the **B**, **I**, and **U** buttons on the **Format** toolbar. Click outside the selected area so it is no longer selected.

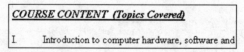

> ***<u>COURSE CONTENT (Topics Covered)</u>***
>
> I. Introduction to computer hardware, software and

What's happening? You have applied character formatting to selected text. You made the text bold, italicized, and underlined. Place your cursor in the underlined text. If you look at the buttons on the Format toolbar, you can see that they are highlighted (appear indented), which means that they are selected.

24 Move the insertion point into the selection bar area. It will assume an arrow shape. Point and click at the **COURSE CONTENT (Topics Covered)** line.

25 Click the **B** and **I** buttons on the **Format** toolbar. Click outside the selected area so it is no longer selected.

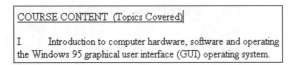

> What's happening? You removed the bold and italic character formatting, but left the underlined character formatting. You can also change the font for a portion of the document or the entire document.

26 Place the insertion point in the selection bar area. Hold the **Ctrl** key and click.

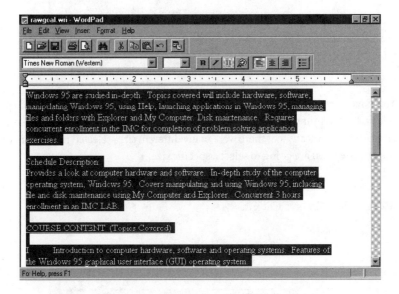

> What's happening? You have selected the entire document.

27 Right-click the mouse.

> What's happening? You have opened the pop-up menu. You can see the Cut, Copy, and Paste commands, which can also be found on the menu bar and the toolbar. Here, you are interested in changing the font.

28 Click **Font**.

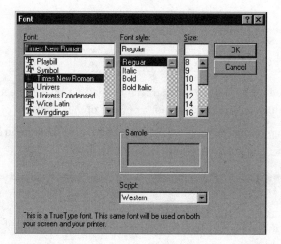

 You have opened the Font dialog box. Times New Roman (note the TrueType font symbol) is selected. It has four styles: regular, italic, bold, and bold italic. The Size text box is empty. Here, the empty text box means that there were many different sizes selected rather than one specific size. In the next step you are going to select a specific size.

29 Scroll to the top of the **Font** list box. Locate **Arial**. Click it.

30 Locate **12** in the **Size** list box. Click it.

 You have selected Arial in the regular font style. You changed the font size to make all the text one size. You have selected your font, its style, and its size. The sample box shows you what this font will look like.

31   Click **OK**.

32   Click in the document window to deselect the text.

33   Scroll until you locate the underlined text, **COURSE OUTLINE (Topics Covered)**.

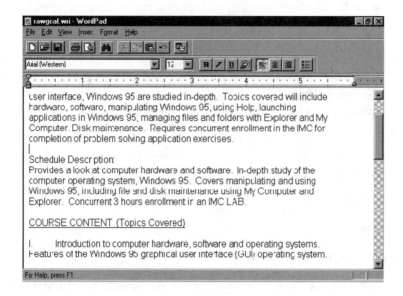

 You have changed the type style of this document. The text that you underlined remains underlined, but now it is in Arial.

34   Click the **Save** icon.

35   Close **WordPad**.

 You have returned to the desktop.

10.11 Formatting Paragraphs and Using Tabs

You have edited and saved a document, Rawgoal.wri. In editing the document, you cut and pasted
portions of the text, changed the character formatting of selected words, and altered the type style of the
entire document. You can also apply formatting styles to specific paragraphs, aligning and indenting
where you wish.

You can change paragraph alignment so that it is left-justified, right-justified, or centered. *Left-justified*,
means that the selected paragraphs will line up on the left margin. *Right-aligned*, or *right-justified*
means that the paragraphs will line up on the right margin. *Centered* means that each line in the
paragraph will be centered between the left and right margins of the document.

Normally, text in a paragraph fills from the left to the right margin. The first line of a paragraph can
be indented by pressing the t key, which moves the first line a preset number of spaces from the left

margin. If your margin is 1 inch and you set a ½ inch tab, the ½ inch tab is set from the left margin. The absolute position of the tab, as measured from the left edge of the paper, is 1.5 inches: 1 inch of margin and ½ inch of tab.

With a *hanging indent*, the first line of the paragraph extends further to the left than the rest of the paragraph. Hanging indents are used for lists, especially for numbered lists. Notice in Figure 10.3 that the text wraps not to the left margin, but to the hanging indent Working. WordPad has an easy way to set hanging indents: the bullet style choice on either the Format menu or the Format toolbar.

Figure 10.3 Hanging Indent

A. Working with the Windows 95 desktop, taskbar, menus, dialog and message boxes, property sheets, icons, toolbars, and buttons.
B. Introduction to the organizational skills necessary for managing information with a computer system.

10.12 Activity—Formatting the Document

1 Place the Data disk in Drive A.

2 Open **WordPad**.

3 Click the **Open** icon on the toolbar.

4 In the **File name** text box, key in the following: **A:\Chap10\rawgoal.wri** Enter

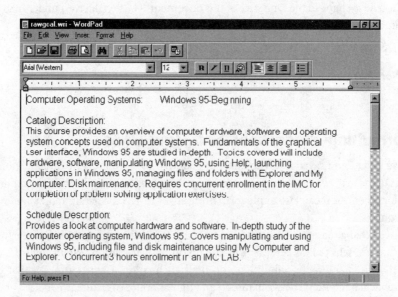

 You have opened your document by keying in the file location and name.

5   If necessary, maximize the **WordPad** window.

6   Select the first line. Click the **Center** icon on the toolbar.

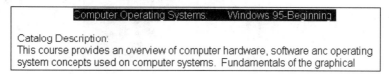

You selected and centered the first paragraph. You are now going to format this title in a larger font.

7   Click the down arrow in the **Size** spin box. Click **14**.

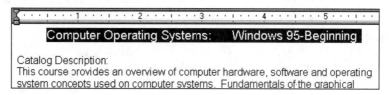

You have increased the size of the font.

8   Click the insertion point in front of the **T** in **This** in the first line. Press the Tab key.

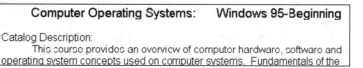

You have indented the first line of the paragraph that begins with the text, This course. The default tabs are at every ½ inch. You observe that this indent is too large and would like to change it to ¼ inch.

9   Click the **.25** dot, which is the second dot on the ruler.

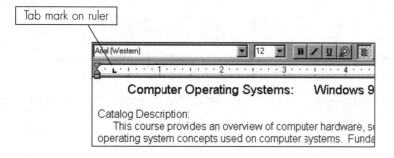

The indent line moved back ¼ inch to the new tab. The tab symbol on the ruler tells you where the tab is set.

10 Click **Format**. Click **Tabs**.

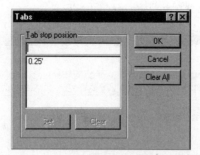

 If your clicking was incorrect, you can set the tab precisely in this dialog box. It is presently set at .25 inches from the left margin of the document.

11 Click **Cancel**.

12 Drag the tab marker down until it disappears from the ruler.

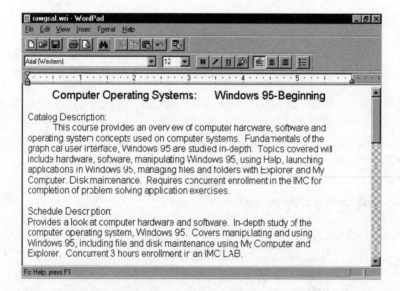

 Dragging the tab marker off the ruler removes it. Your tab for the paragraph is moved back to its ½-inch default setting.

13 Scroll until the words **Schedule Description** are at the top of the window.

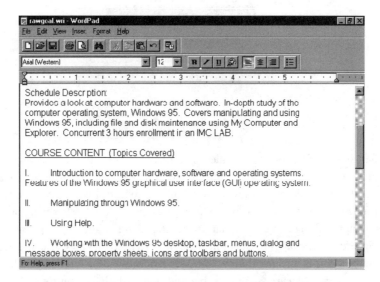

 You would like the paragraph that begins with Provides a look... in a hanging indent form. An easy way to accomplish this is to use the bullet button on the toolbar.

14 Select the entire paragraph that begins with **Provides....** *Hint:* A shortcut to selecting an entire paragraph is to triple-click it. Click the **bullet** button on the toolbar.

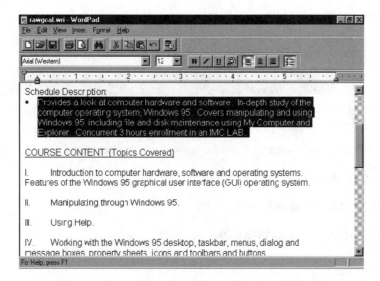

 Instead wrapping to the left margin, the text beginning with computer... wraps to the first indent.

15 Click **Format**. Click **Paragraph**.

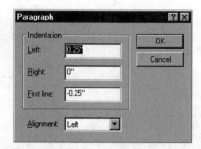

 A hanging indent is sometimes called an outdent. The first line of the paragraph begins at the left margin with a bullet. The remaining lines of the paragraph begin at the .25 tab position. If you wanted the remaining lines to wrap to this temporary margin, you would place a negative number in the First Line text box. The negative number tells WordPad that the first line of the paragraph will align on the left margin, but that all other lines in the paragraph will wrap to the set indent. All lines after the first line wrap negatively, so that they seek the first line set tab rather than the left margin. Since the first line is set at negative .25, as each line of the paragraph reaches the right margin, it will go to the next line and wrap to the left margin less .25 inch. Using the bullet button seemed a lot easier than setting left and first line margins. However, the bullet button does not always work as expected.

In the paragraph that begins with Roman numeral I, you would like the word Features to align with the word Introduction, not with the left margin, as it currently does.

16 Click the **Cancel** command button in the **Paragraph** dialog box.

17 Select the paragraph that begins with Roman numeral **I**. Click the **bullet** button on the toolbar.

 This is not what you wanted. You did not want the bullet symbol, just a hanging indent.

18 Click **Edit**. Click **Undo**. Be sure the paragraph is still selected.

19 Click **Format**. Click **Paragraph**.

20 In the **Left** (margin) text box, key in the following: **.5**

21   In the **First line** text box, key in the following: **-.5**

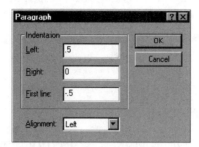

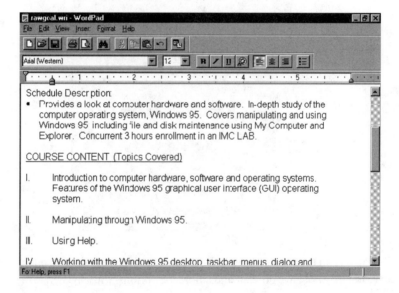

You have set up your hanging indent.

22   Click **OK**. Click outside the paragraph to deselect it.

You now have the hanging indent in your numbered list.

23   Click the **Save** button on the toolbar.

24   Close **WordPad**.

10.13 Printing and Page Setup in WordPad

You can print a document from WordPad in the same manner that you used in Notepad. You can use My Computer or Explorer to locate the file. Once the file is located and selected, you can use either the File/Print commands from the menus or the right-click context-sensitive menus.

In WordPad, the only formatting you can apply to your document is to alter the top, bottom, left, and right margins of the document. You cannot have headers or footers. In order to apply this margin formatting, you must load WordPad and select File/Page Setup.

10.14 Activity—Printing in WordPad

1 Place the Data disk in Drive A.

2 Open **Wordpad**. Click the **File Open** icon.

3 In the **File name** text box, key in the following: **A:\chap10\rawgoal.wri** Enter

4 Click **File**. Click **Page Setup**.

 What's happening?   Your options in the Size and Source drop-down list boxes will depend on the type of printer you have. You may not have portrait and landscape options. You can change the margin settings.

5 Change the right and left margins to **1"**.

6   Click **OK**. Click **File**. Click **Print Preview**.

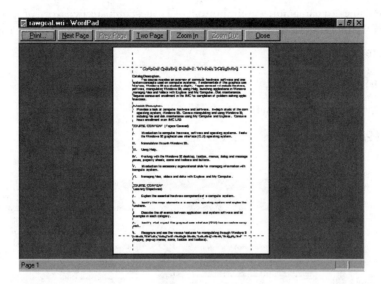

 Your display may or may not appear as above, depending on your installed printer and the screen fonts available to your system. Do not be concerned if your print preview is considerably different from the illustrated example here. Print Preview shows you what text will print on the page. The dotted lines represent the margins. As you can see, the text at the bottom of the page is out of the margin.

7   Click the **Two Page** command button.

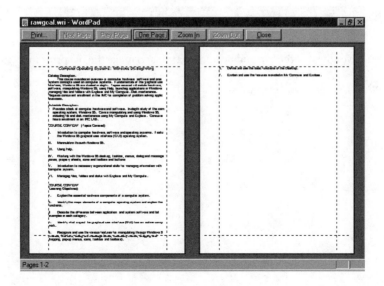

You can see both pages of this document. The top of the second page has a widow. A *widow* occurs when the last line of a paragraph is at the top of the next page; an *orphan* occurs when the first line of a paragraph is at the bottom of a page. Sophisticated word processors automatically fix the unattractive windows and orphans for you, but WordPad has no such feature.

8   Click **Close**.

9   Click **File**. Click **Page Setup**.

10   Change the top and bottom margins to **1.75"**. Click **OK**.

11   Click the **Print Preview** button on the toolbar.

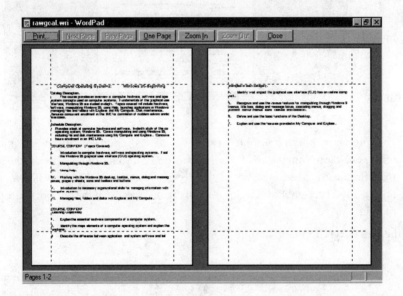

 You have adjusted the top and bottom margins to make the file print more attractively.

12   Click **Print**.

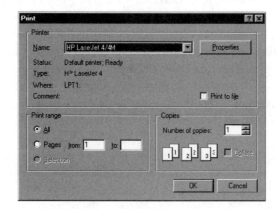

 The Print dialog box has several choices. You can choose how many copies you want to print. You can print all the pages, selected pages, or a selected passage. Currently, All is selected. If you wanted to print only the first page, you would click the Pages option button. In the from box, you would key in 1, and in the to box, you would key in 1. You intend to print the entire document.

13 Click **OK**.

 Your document should print.

14 Click the **Save** button on the toolbar.

15 Close **WordPad**.

 You have returned to the desktop.

10.15 Using Special Symbols—Character Map

Character Map is the accessory that gives you access to special symbols and characters used in application programs. Character Map shows you the character set of each font installed on your system. It displays the assigned keystroke required to create each character from the keyboard. You can easily copy the character from Character Map into an application.

Most keyboards have 101 keys, but every key serves double duty, such as the lowercase a and the uppercase A, or the ' and the ". You get the alternate character by holding down the **Shift** key.

In reality, there are 256 characters available for each font. A coding scheme was developed to assign numeric values to letters, numbers, and other characters. This coding scheme is called ASCII (American Standard Code for Information Interchange). ASCII divides the 256 characters into two sets—standard and extended—of 128 characters each. The standard set is universal. It uses the first thirty-two values for communication and printer control codes. The remaining ninety-six codes are assigned to common punctuation marks, the digits 0 through 9, and the uppercase and lowercase letters of the Roman alphabet. The extended character set, the remaining 128, are assigned to variable sets of characters provided by computer manufacturers and software developers.

Each character in the ASCII character set is assigned a unique number. Thus, both a and A have unique numbers. However, there are more numbers available then keys on the keyboard. For instance, if you wanted to use ½ instead of 1/2, it is not available on your keyboard, but it is typically available in the font set. So how do you access this character? The trick is to know the assigned number. Then be sure the **NumLock** is turned on, hold down the **Alt** key, and press the correct number on the numeric keypad (not the numbers across the top of the keyboard). For instance, you need to know that in a specific font such as Century Schoolbook, ½ has been assigned the number 0189. To access this symbol, you would hold down the **Alt** key, press 0, then 1, then 8, then 9 on the numeric keypad, and then release the **Alt** key.

There are many special symbols available such as a copyright symbol, ©, a registered symbol, ®, foreign characters, and pictures. As you can imagine, it would be very difficult to remember all these numbers. Here is where Character Map can assist you.

10.16 Activity—Using Character Map with WorPad

1   Place the Data disk in Drive A.

2   Open **WordPad**.

3   Click **Start**. Point at **Programs**. Point at **Accessories**. Click **Character Map**.

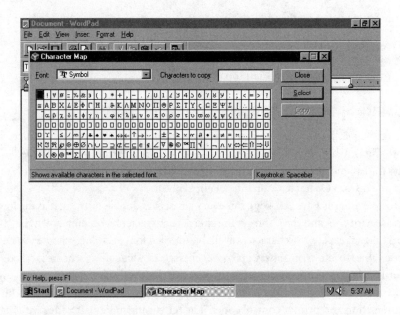

 You have opened both WordPad and Character Map.

4   In the **Font** drop-down list box in **Character Map**, locate **Times New Roman**. Click it.

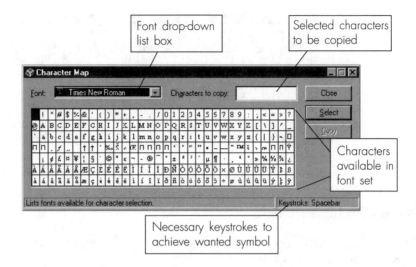

 All the characters available in this set are in the grid. Each one is tiny. You can view a character in a larger format by placing the mouse pointer over it and clicking the mouse button.

5   Click the lowercase **a** (third row, second column).

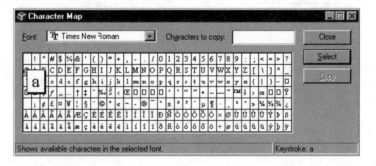

 You see the lowercase a. The keystroke necessary to display the letter a is, of course, the a key. What if you wanted the ¾ symbol?

6 Click the fifth row, second column from the right.

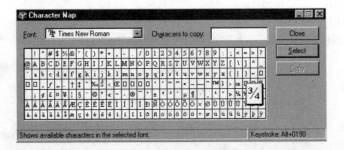

 You have selected the ¾ symbol. The keystroke to insert this into your document is **Alt** + 0190. The bottom right of the dialog box tells you this.

7 Click **WordPad** to make it active.

8 Be sure the **NumLock** key is on. old the **Alt** key. Press **0**, then **1**, then **9**, then **0** on the numeric keypad. Then release the **Alt** key.

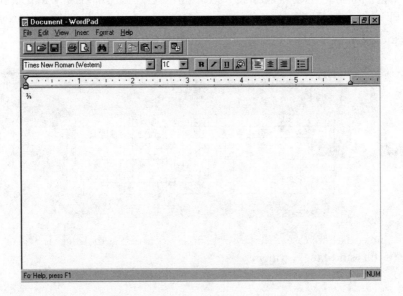

 You inserted the ¾ by using the **Alt** key and the correct number. Notice that the font size is 10 points, which is the WordPad default. Using Character Map can be even easier.

9 Make the **Character Map** window active. Click the **¾**. Click the **Select** command button. Click the **Copy** command button.

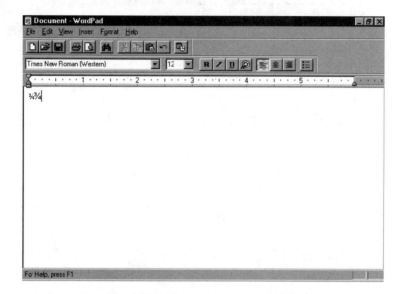

> **What's happening?** You have selected the character you want to copy.

10 Click **WordPad**. Click the **Paste** icon on the toolbar.

> **What's happening?** You pasted ¾ into the document. Notice the font size has changed to 12 points. Characters in the Character Map grid are sized at 12 points. Windows 95 also supplies a font called Wingdings, which provides pictures instead of characters.

11 Click **Character Map**. In the **Font** drop-down list box, locate and click **Wingdings**.

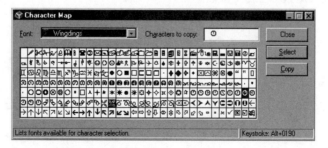

> **What's happening?** In this case, pressing **Alt** + 0190 will generate a picture of a clock ☺.

12 Clear the **Characters to Copy** text box by dragging the mouse over the character in the box and pressing the ⟦**Delete**⟧ key.

13 Locate the floppy disk picture (top row, fourth from right). Click **Select**. Click **Copy**. Click **WordPad**. Press ⟦**Enter**⟧.

14 Click the **Paste** icon on the toolbar.

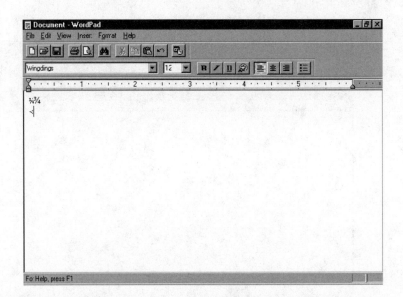

 Instead of the picture of the floppy disk, you see the < symbol because Wingdings font was not selected. The font listed is Times New Roman.

15 Select the entire document.

16 Click the **Font** drop-down list box. Locate and click **Wingdings**.

17 Click the **Size** box. Locate **20**. Click it.

18 Click outside the highlighted area to deselect it.

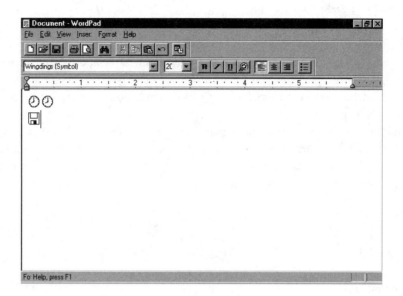

 Now that the correct font is selected, you can see your symbols. The ¾ symbol in Times New Roman is a clock ☺ in the Wingdings font. The < symbol in Times New Roman is the ⊟ in Wingdings.

19 Close **WordPad**. Do not save the document.

20 Close **Character Map**.

 You have returned to the desktop.

Chapter Summary

In this chapter, you learned about some of the accessories provided with Windows 95. These include Calculator, Notepad, WordPad, and Character Map.

Calculator acts like any small, hand-held calculator. It has a standard mode that does simple mathematical calculations. It also has a scientific mode that can perform higher-level functions.

Notepad is a simple ASCII editor used for writing short text documents. It has no embedded codes, and therefore can be used to communicate with the computer system. Placing the word .LOG at the beginning of a file stamps the current date and time on your file. You can also have headers and footers in a Notepad document. The default file extension for Notepad is .txt.

WordPad is a small word processor. The default file extension used with WordPad is .doc. You hold down the **Shift** key while right-clicking to access the Open With option on the shortcut menu. Using quotation marks, you can give your file an exact name; for instance, you can cumstomize a file extension or use none at all. You can register your own file extension for WordPad. WordPad has more editing capabilities than Notepad. WordPad has a toolbar as well as a menu bar. Toolbar buttons are shortcuts to menu commands. In WordPad, you can format characters and paragraphs in styles such as bold or italic. You can set tabs, indents, and hanging indents as well as format paragraphs in a bullet style. In order to manipulate text, you must first select it. WordPad does not allow you to use headers and footers.

Character Map is a tool that provides you access to special symbols and characters, which you can use in application programs such as WordPad. Character Map shows you the character set of each font you have installed on your system. It displays the assigned number of each character's keystroke and allows you to copy the character from Character Map into another application. However, when you paste it into your document, you must be sure the correct font is selected. A character set is not limited to the keys on the keyboard. If you know the ASCII code, you can use the **Alt** key and the numeric code keyed in on the numeric keypad to achieve special symbols. Wingdings is a font comprised of small pictures that can also be pasted into a document.

Key Terms

Centered	Landscape	Selection bar
Document ruler	Left-justified	Soft return
Footer	Orphan	Typeover
Hanging indent	Portrait	Widow
Hard return	Rich Text Format (RTF)	Word wrap
Header	Right-aligned	
Insert mode	Right-justified	

Discussion Questions

1. List and explain two ways that the Calculator can be used.
2. What is the difference between the scientific mode and the standard mode of the Calculator?
3. Explain the purpose and function of Notepad.
4. Define word wrap.
5. What is a time log file? What would be the purpose of creating a time log file?
6. What causes the information in Clipboard to be replaced?
7. What is a header? A footer?
8. What types of information would be found in headers/footers?
9. Explain the purpose and function of WordPad.
10. Why is WordPad considered a simple word processor?
11. How can you make a shortcut menu include both Open and Open With?
12. What technique can you use to ensure that WordPad does not add a file extension to your named file?
13. What type of formatting can be done with WordPad?
14. You have Word for Windows. What would happen if you double-clicked on a file with a .doc extension?
15. When using WordPad, why must you not press **Enter** when a word reaches the right margin?
16. Compare and contrast a soft return versus a hard return.

17. How is a paragraph defined in word processing terms?
18. In computer terms, what is a widow? An orphan?
19. Explain the purpose and function of the selection bar area.
20. Compare and contrast the insert and typeover modes.
21. List and explain three ways that you can align a paragraph.
22. Explain the purpose and function of the Character Map.
23. A character set is not limited to the keys displayed on the keyboard. Explain.
24. What is the Wingdings font? How might you use it?
25. Compare and contrast printing a document using WordPad versus Notepad.

True/False Questions

For each question, circle the letter T if the statement is true or the letter F if the statement is false.

T F 1. A text document has no special embedded codes.

T F 2. In WordPad, each icon on the toolbar is a shortcut to one of the menu choices.

T F 3. In WordPad, the selection bar area is an unmarked column along the left edge of the document window.

T F 4. The only two choices for paragraph alignment are left-justified or right-justified.

T F 5. Each character in the ASCII character set is assigned an unique number.

Completion Questions

Write the correct answer in each blank space provided.

6. Calculator can operate in either _____ or _____ mode.

7. When a page is printed normally with the page taller than it is wide, the page is set to _____ orientation. If the page is printed "sideways," the orientation is _____.

8. If you have keyed in _____ at the beginning of your file, Notepad will stamp the current date and time when the file is opened.

9. If you are in Explorer and hold the **Shift** key when you right-click a file, you will see both Open and _____ on the context menu.

10. In WordPad, bold, italic, and underline are examples of _____ formatting.

Multiple Choice Questions

Circle the letter of the correct answer for each question.

11. In word processing terms, a paragraph is
    a. any text beginning and ending with a paragraph marker.
    b. any text between indents.
    c. any text that begins with an indent.
    d. the text on a single line.

12. Without using Character Map, what key sequence would you use to insert the ® character in a document? (number 0174)

   a. hold the **Ctrl** key, then press 0, 1, 7, 4 on the numeric keypad.

   b. hold the **Alt** key, then press 0, 1, 7, 4 on the numeric keypad.

   c. hold the **Shift** key, then press 0, 1, 7, 4 on the numeric keypad.

   d. none of the above

13. The last line of a paragraph printed at the top of a page is called a(n)

   a. child.

   b. orphan.

   c. parent.

   d. widow.

14. A header is

   a. text printed on the top of each page.

   b. text printed at the bottom of each page.

   c. always a page number.

   d. not available as an option in Notepad.

15. In WordPad, it is possible to set the spacing of the tabs by

   a. clicking on the ruler.

   b. pressing the **Tab** key.

   c. clicking Format, then clicking Tabs, and keying in a tab value.

   d. both a and c

Application Assignments

Problem Set I—At the Computer

Problem A

Open **Calculator**. Be sure you are in standard mode. Multiply 19 × 37. With the results still visible, choose the **scientific** view. Click the **Hex** option button.

1. The hexadecimal (Hex) equivalent of 19 × 37 is

   a. 703

   b. 11

   c. 1010111111

   d. 2BF

Click the **Binary** option button.

2. The binary equivalent of 19×37 is
   a. 703
   b. 11
   c. 1010111111
   d. 2BF

Return **Calculator** to the **standard** mode. Close **Calculator**.

Problem B

Open **Notepad**. Open the **Page Setup** dialog box.

3. The symbol to provide the insertion of the current system date is
   a. &d
   b. %d
   c. @d

Open **Help** for **Notepad**. Click **Help Topics**. Click the **Contents** tab. Double-click **Adding the Time and Date to Documents**.

4. Is there an entry for keeping a log file?
   a. Yes
   b. No

Close **Notepad Help**. Close **Notepad**.

Problem C

Open **WordPad**. Open the document called **Personal.fil** in the **95book** directory.

5. What street does Tai Chan Tran live on?
   a. Lemon.
   b. Lakeview.
   c. Miller.

6. What font is the document presented in?
   a. Times New Roman.
   b. Arial.
   c. Courier.

Close **WordPad**. Do not save the document to disk.

Problem D

Open **Character Map**. Locate and choose the **Wingdings** font.

7. What is the picture in the last column, second row from the bottom?
    a. computer.
    b. disk.
    c. arrow.

Close **Character Map**.

Problem E

For the following assignment:
1. Open Notepad. Open the State1.txt file in the 95book directory.
2. Copy the first three states and their capitals to the Clipboard.
3. Open the LOG.txt document on the Data disk in the Chap10 folder.
4. Save it under a new name, Logging.txt to the Data disk under the Chap10 folder.
5. Include the following changes:
    a. Paste the states from the Clipboard into this document.
    b. Add your name to the document.
    c. Save the document.
    d. Print the document.

Problem F

For the following assignment:
1. Open WordPad. Open the rawgoal.wri file on the Data disk in the Chap10 folder.
2. Save it with the exact name of Final.wri to the Data disk in the Chap10 folder.
3. Include the following changes in Final.wri:
    a. Place your name at the top of the document and right-justify it.
    b. On the line Computer Operating Systems: Windows 95
        1. Change the font size to 16.
        2. Bold the entire line.
    c. Make the text COURSE CONTENT (Topics Covered) 14 points.
    d. Make all the Roman-numbered sections hanging indents. (*Hint:* Do not click at the left margin, but in the body of the text.)
    e. Change COURSE CONTENT (Learning Objectives) to one line.

   f. Make the text COURSE CONTENT (Learning Objectives) 14 points. Underline it.

   g. Make all the numbered paragraphs hanging indents. (*Hint:* You can select more than one paragraph at a time.)

   h. Adjust the printing margins to eliminate all widows and orphans.

   i. Use Character Map to locate the number for the ® symbol. Except for the title, change all occurrences of Windows 95 to Windows 95®. (*Hint:* Use Edit/Replace.)

   j. Save the document with the changes.

   k. Print the document.

Problem Set II—Brief Essay

For all essay questions, you may use Notepad or WordPad for your answer. Print your answer.

1. Compare and contrast WordPad and Notepad. Describe what features you prefer in each. When would you want to use Notepad? WordPad? Justify your decision.

2. What file type is assigned to WordPad documents? What ways can you alter a file's name? Describe the steps you would take to do so. Why would you want to alter file types? Justify your answer.

Problem Set III—Scenario

You are in a study group for your Windows 95 class. Each member of your group has the assignment of outlining a section of this chapter. Select and outline one section for your group. Include keywords and their definitions. Make the document as attractive as possible by using different fonts and font sizes, hanging indents, and bulleted lists. Use bold, italic, or underling for emphasis.

Chapter 11

Windows 95
Accessories—Paint

Chapter Overview

Paint is a graphics application program that allows you to create simple or complex drawings or images. You can import, scan, or alter a picture or drawing in Paint. The images you create can stand alone, or you can copy them into other documents. You could purchase a sophisticated drawing program like Corel Draw, but if your drawing needs are minimal, Paint will meet most of your needs.

Drawing programs, like all programs, store the data you create in files. These files, generically called graphics files, come in a variety of formats which are identified by a file extension. Popular graphics file formats use the extensions .tif, .gif, .pcx, .jpg, and .bmp. Paint creates bitmapped graphics (.bmp) by default. A bitmapped graphic is formed by a pattern of pixels and is limited in resolution by the type of video adapter card and the capability of your monitor. In general, graphics consume a larger amount of memory and disk space than other forms of data. Even minimal graphic files are large.

If you have a color monitor and a color printer, your drawings will appear and print in the colors that your computer system and printer support. If you have a monochrome monitor or a noncolor printer, your drawings will appear in varying shades of gray.

Learning Objectives

1. Explain the purpose and function of Paint.
2. Name and explain the functions of each item found on the Paint screen.
3. List and explain the purpose and functions of the tools that are used in Paint.
4. Explain the purpose and process of importing and exporting graphics.
5. Explain how to create a picture in Paint.
6. Explain how to combine text and pictures in Paint.
7. Explain how to open, save, print, and close files in Paint.
8. Explain how a drawing created with Paint can be used as wallpaper on the Windows 95 desktop.

Student Outcomes

1. Load and exit Paint.
2. Use Paint tools to draw and edit lines, curves, and geometric figures.
3. Import, export, and manipulate graphics.
4. Use Paint to create, edit, save, and print a drawing.
5. Add text and pictures a drawing.
6. Use a drawing created in Paint as a wallpaper.

11.1 Looking at Paint

When you first load Paint, your screen will look as follows:

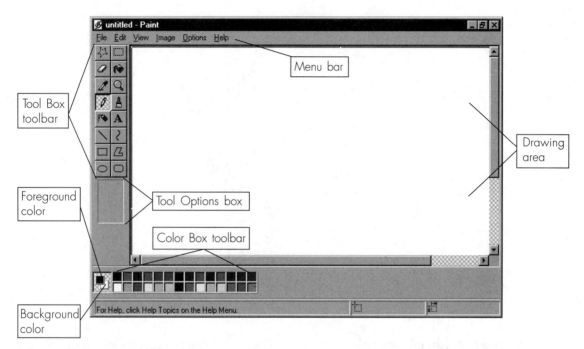

The Paint menu bar has choices that you have seen in other Windows 95 applications, but it also has a new choice called Image. Throughout Windows 95 applications, the location of menu bar choices remains consistent, so File always appears on the left and Help on the right. All the other menu choices are found between File and Help. What they are depends on the application program's purpose. Tasks in a drawing program differ greatly from those in a word processing program, and the menu choices will reflect that.

The next area of importance in Paint is the *Tool Box*. The Tool Box is actually a toolbar from which you select your drawing tool. Below the Tool Box is an area called the *Tool Options box*. When a certain tool is selected, this box provides options for that tool. For instance, if you select the line tool, your line thickness choices will be shown in this area.

The *Color Box* contains the colors you use in Paint. It is also a toolbar. In Paint you must distinguish between background and foreground colors. The *background color* is the color of your drawing area. The *foreground color* is the one with which you draw. The default color choices for Paint are a white background with a black foreground.

The *drawing area* is the canvas on which you create. There is a relationship between the mouse pointer (cursor) and the drawing area. When you open Paint, a default drawing tool is selected, the pencil cursor. When you click in the drawing area, you may begin to draw with that tool. In the Tool Box, you see the pencil icon button indented, indicating that it is the current drawing tool. When you click another tool icon in the Tool Box, your cursor will change to the shape of the selected drawing tool. The Tool Box icons and their names are listed in Figure 11.1.

Figure 11.1   The Tools

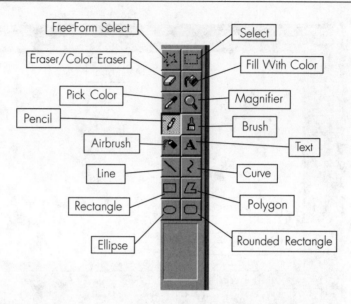

Each tool in the Tool Box has a specific name and purpose. In the activities, the tools will be referred to by their names. If you want to know a tool's function, refer to this table. If you want to know a tool's name, place the pointer over the tool until its ToolTip appears. See Table 11.1.

Table 11.1   Tools

Icon	Tool Name	Purpose
	Free-Form Select	Defines or selects a free-form cutout in a drawing.
	Select	Defines or selects a rectangular cutout in a drawing.
	Eraser/Color Eraser	Changes the foreground color to the background color.

	Fill With Color	Fills a bordered area that with the selected foreground color.
	Pick Color	Picks a color in your drawing and uses it as a foreground color. If you click a color in your drawing with the right mouse button, it will become the background color.
	Magnifier	Magnifies a selected area.
	Pencil	Creates a free-form line in the foreground color. Clicking the right-mouse button creates a free form-line in the background color.
	Brush	Selects a brush shape and draws a free-form brush stroke in the foreground color. Clicking the right-mouse button creates a brush stroke in the background color.
	Airbrush	Creates a spray can effect. The left mouse button sprays the foreground color, and the right mouse button sprays the background color.
	Text	Places text in the drawing for captions and titles.
	Line	Draws a line. You may select the width of the line in the Tool Options box. The left mouse button draws with the foreground color, and the right mouse button draws with the background color.
	Curve	Draws a straight line, then curves it. Each curve has a minimum of one arc and a maximum of two. The left mouse button draws with the foreground color, and the right mouse button draws with the background color.
	Rectangle	Creates a rectangle or square.

Polygon

Draws a shape with an unlimited number of sides. You add sides to a configuration until you return to your starting point. You are essentially connecting straight lines in the selected foreground color.

 Ellipse

Creates a circle or an ellipse.

 Rounded Rectangle

Creates a round-cornered rectangle or square.

The rectangle, polygon, ellipse, and rounded rectangle are considered shape tools. When you select a shape tool, three choices appear in the Tool Options area. Since a shape encloses an area, each choice is considered a *fill style* because the color inside the shape is called the *fill*. Table 11.2 enumerates the choices available for shapes in the Tool Options box.

Table 11.2   Fill Style

Left mouse

❑ Outline in foreground color. No fill color. This option is highlighted, indicating that it is the default.

❑ Outline in foreground color. Fill in background color.

❑ Solid shape in background color. Has no outline.

Right mouse

❑ Outline in background color. No fill color.

❑ Outline in background color. Fill in foreground color.

❑ Solid shape in foreground color. Has no outline.

11.2 About Paint

Paint can edit and create only bitmapped graphics. Your computer screen is divided into small dots called pixels, also called *pels* (picture elements). A bitmap is collected bits of information that create an image when assigned (mapped) to dots on the screen. It is much like a theater marquee where the name of a movie, a message, or a picture is displayed by turning light bulbs on or off in a grid. Paint displays images in a similar way.

When you draw, you are turning the pixels on or off in different colors. There are so many dots that they blend into a picture much like a connect-the-dots image you remember from childhood. Bitmapped graphics are detailed (and take a lot of storage space) because you control the placement and color of each dot. Because a bitmapped graphic has a fixed number of dots, its resolution is fixed. You cannot make it look better by printing it on a high-resolution printer. The resolution is limited by your monitor and video card as well.

11.3 Activity—Opening Paint

1   Click **Start**. Point at **Programs**. Point at **Accessories**. Click **Paint**.

2   Size the window so that it its appearance is similar to the shape below:

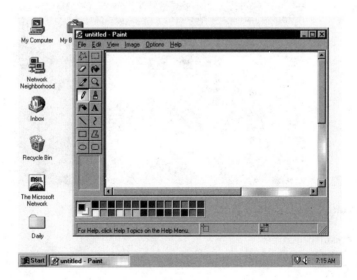

3   Click **File**. Click **Open**. In the **File name** text box, key in the following: **C:\95book\Games\Taipei.bmp** [Enter]

 You opened an existing picture. It is larger than the drawing area. You can use the scroll bars to move up and down within the picture, or you can have the entire picture fill the screen.

4   Click **View**. Click **View Bitmap**.

 Now you can see the entire picture.

5   Click anywhere on the screen.

 You are returned to the previous window. Paint has floating toolbars that you would like to move.

6   In the margin of the **Tool Box** toolbar, click and drag to the left.

7   In the margin of the **Color Box** toolbar, click and drag down.

 You can see more of the picture, and now each toolbar has a title bar. The Tool Box is called Tools, and the Color Box is called Colors. Each toolbar may be closed.

8 Maximize the **Paint** window.

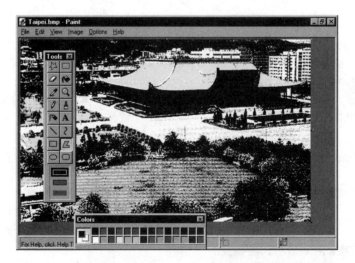

 You have maximized the Paint window and can see all of the picture. The Color Box and Tool Box toolbars are obscuring the picture but can be moved. To "anchor" the toolbars, drag them to the edge of the window.

9   In the margin of the **Tool Box** toolbar, click and drag to the left until the title bar disappears.

10   In the margin of the **Color Box** toolbar, click and drag down until the title bar disappears.

 You have reanchored your toolbars, and the title bars are no longer visible.

11   Close **Paint**. Do not save the picture.

11.4   Picture Characteristics

You just looked at an existing picture. To create a new picture, you need to open Paint. When you open Paint, it has standard settings for the characteristics of the picture you are about to create, like its size and whether it is in color. The default picture is in color, and the default size is the size of your screen (not the size of the window, but of the resolution dimensions of your screen). In the next activity, you will look at your attributes and begin using tools.

11.5   Activity—Creating a New Picture

1   Open the **Paint** program.

2   Click **View**. Click **View Attributes**.

What's happening? Your default settings can be changed. In the example above, the image is in color and the screen resolution is 640 × 480 (pixels).

3   Click **Cancel**.

4   The Pencil should be your selected tool. Drag the mouse across the screen about an inch while holding down the left mouse button.

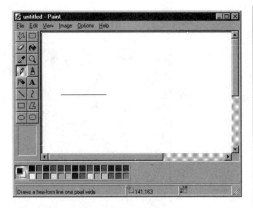

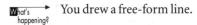

What's happening? You drew a free-form line.

5 Drag the mouse to create a second one-inch line, but do not release the left mouse button. Click the right mouse button once.

What's happening? Whenever you click the right mouse button without releasing the left mouse button, you remove from the screen what you just created.

6 Click the **Brush** tool.

What's happening? In the Tool Options box, you see the choices for shapes and widths of your Brush tool. The selected shape is highlighted.

7 Click the largest square in the **Tool Options** box. Position the in the drawing area near your last line. Hold down the left mouse button and drag the mouse across the drawing area about an inch.

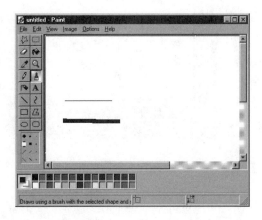

What's happening? You chose a wide brush to draw a wide line.

8   Click **Edit**.

What's happening? ➤ The drop-down Edit menu appears. Undo is not dimmed and is therefore available. You have three levels of Undo, which means you can reverse your last three changes.

9   Click **Undo**.

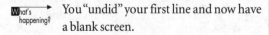

What's happening? ➤ The line you just drew disappeared.

10   Click **Edit**. Click **Undo**.

What's happening? ➤ You "undid" your first line and now have a blank screen.

11   Click **Edit**.

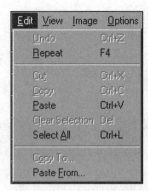

What's happening? ➤ You cannot choose Undo, but Repeat is now available.

12   Click **Repeat**. Click **Edit**. Click **Repeat**.

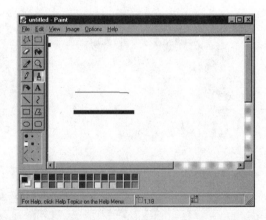

What's happening? ➤ The lines you erased returned to your canvas.

13   Click the **Free-Form Select** tool. Hold down the left mouse button and drag the cursor around the two lines in the canvas. Do not release the left mouse button.

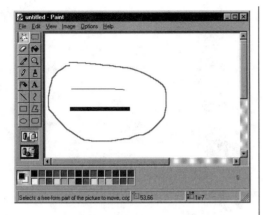

 The shape you created to encircle the two lines is irregular. Even though there are two items enclosed, when you work with them, they are considered one object.

14 Release the left mouse button.

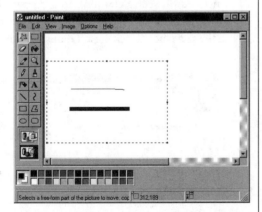

 A dotted line replaced your free-form line. Anything surrounded by a dotted line is selected. Since a dotted line is around your object, you have selected it. Once an object is selected, you can drag it around the screen or cut and paste it to a different location or even to a different document.

15 Place the cursor, now a four-headed arrow, inside the dotted rectangle. Drag the box to the right and down about an inch.

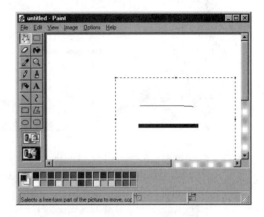

 While you were dragging your selection, the dotted line disappeared. When you reached your new location and released the left mouse button, the dotted line reappeared, indicating that your object (the two lines) is still selected. As long as an object is selected, it can be manipulated.

You have two Select tools, the one you just used and the Select tool located next to it. Instead of a free-form shape, the Select tool uses a rectangular shape.

16 Click the **Select** tool.

17 Holding down the left mouse button, drag the cursor around the two lines on the canvas. When you have selected them, release the left mouse button.

 Your selection is now enclosed by a rectangular dotted line, indicating that you have selected it.

18 Click **Edit**. Click **Copy**.

19 Click **Edit**. Click **Paste**.

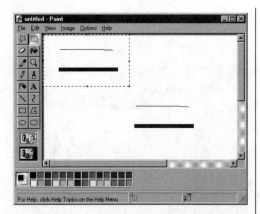

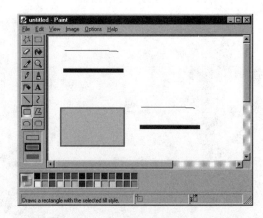

 You saved your object to the Clipboard. Then you pasted it. You now have two copies of your sketch. In the Paint program, Paste will always place whatever is on the Clipboard in the upper-left corner of the drawing area.

20 Place the pointer on the color red, and click the left mouse button.

21 Place the pointer on the color green, and click the right mouse button.

 The left mouse click chose the foreground color, and the right-click chose the background color.

22 Click the **Line** tool. In the **Tool Options** box, pick the middle line for width.

23 Click the **Rectangle** tool. Click the middle fill style in the **Tool Options** box. In an empty area on the screen, hold the left mouse button and drag it down and to the right. As you drag it, you will see the outline of a green box bordered in red. When the box is about one and a half inches by one and a half inches, release the left mouse button.

 You should have a box filled with green (the background color) and outlined in red (the foreground color).

24 Place the pointer on the color blue, and click the left mouse button.

25 Click the **Fill With Color** tool. Your cursor becomes a paint can. Place the tip of the paint can in the green box. Click the left mouse button.

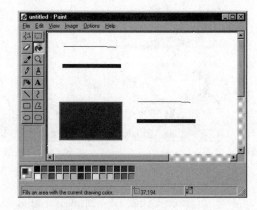

 The color inside the box changed from green to blue.

26 Click the **Eraser/Color Eraser** tool.

27 Hold the left mouse button down and drag across the box.

28 Hold the right mouse button down and drag across the box.

 The cursor changed shape. You could pick a large or small eraser in the Tool Options box. The eraser was filled with green, the background color. The selected background color shows what color the eraser will leave behind. When you dragged the right mouse button, you changed only the foreground color to the background color. Since the fill was the single object in the foreground color (blue), this is the only area that the eraser changed to the background color (green). To limit your changes to a specific color (and nothing else), you change the foreground color to the color you want to erase and the background color to the color you want to replace it with. Click the eraser, and then right-drag the mouse across your selection.

29 Left-click **green**. Right-click **yellow**. Click the **Eraser/Color Eraser** tool. Right-drag it vertically over the box, being sure to drag it over part of the green line.

 Your cursor changed anything green that it touched to yellow, but all other colors remained the same.

30 Click the **Pick Color** tool. Click the red border of the box.

31 Click the **Fill With Color** tool.

32 Move to the bottom black line. Position the tip of the paint can on the line and click.

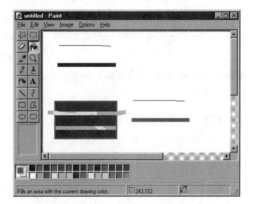

 The Pick Color tool let you select a foreground color from your drawing. If you look at the foreground color in the Color Box, you see your foreground is now red. You then clicked the next tool you wanted to use (the Fill With Color tool) and clicked on an object. The object, a black line, was changed to the foreground color (red).

33 Click on the color **pink** with the left mouse button.

34 Click the **Spray Can** tool.

35 Hold the left mouse button and drag the **Spray Can** cursor across the box. Then hold the right mouse button and drag the **Spray Can** cursor across the box.

 When you dragged the left button a pink (foreground) color effect was produced, and when you used the right mouse button a yellow (background) color effect was produced.

36 Left-click the color **black**. Right-click the color **white**.

37 Click the **Eraser/Color Eraser** tool. Drag it across the box.

 You are "erasing" your box. Actually, you are covering everything with the white background color.

38 Click the **Pencil** tool.

39 Click the **File**. Click **Exit**.

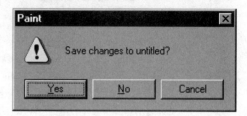

 Paint knows that you have not saved this drawing and, it is giving you an opportunity to do so. You do not want to save this drawing.

40 Click **No**.

 You closed Paint and returned to the desktop.

11.6 The Shape Tools

So far, you have been working with the Pencil, Brush, and Rectangle drawing tools. Pencil and Brush performed much like a pencil and brush you hold in your hand. The Rectangle tool let you work with a predefined shape. In using all these tools, you have also worked with color. You have seen how the cursor changes to the shape of the selected tool. In addition, you worked with the Free-Form Select and Select tools to select, copy, and move an object. The other shape tools work just as easily.

11.7 Activity—Using the Shape Tools

1 Open the **Paint** program.

2 Click the **Ellipse** tool. Click the top fill shape in the **Tool Options** area.

3 Anywhere in the drawing area, hold the left mouse button and drag. When you have an ellipse about one inch high and two inches wide, release the left mouse button.

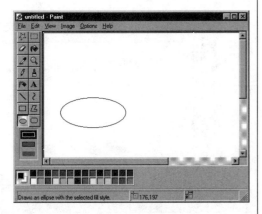

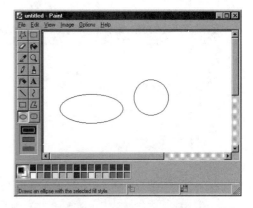

What's happening?→ You have a perfectly round circle instead of an ellipse.

5 Left-click the color **blue**. Right-click the color **pink**.

6 Left-drag to create a half-inch ellipse.

7 Right-drag to create a half-inch ellipse.

What's happening?→ You have an oval-shaped ellipse. If you want to use a shape tool to create an equidistant (of equal sides) circle or a square, hold down the **Shift** key while dragging the mouse.

4 Next to your ellipse, hold down the **Shift** key and the left mouse button, and drag until you have a circle approximately one inch in diameter.

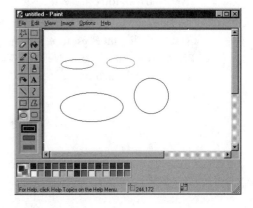

The left-drag gave you a hollow ellipse with a blue (foreground) border. The right-drag gave you a hollow ellipse with a pink (background) border. In both incidences, the first fill style (border with no fill) was selected.

8 Click the middle fill style. Left-drag to create a half-inch ellipse. Right-drag to create a half-inch ellipse.

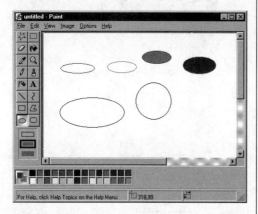

 The left-drag gave you a pink (background color) ellipse with a blue border, whereas the right-drag gave you a blue (foreground color) ellipse with a pink border. In this case, you chose the middle fill style (border and fill in two different colors) for both shapes. The border is very narrow. You can create a wider one.

9 Click the **Line** tool. In the **Tool Options** box, click the largest line. Click the **Ellipse** tool. In an empty area, left-drag to create a half-inch ellipse. Right-drag to create a half-inch ellipse.

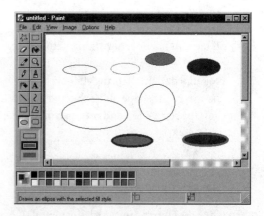

 You have the same shape and fill style, but the borders are larger.

10 Click the bottom fill style in the **Tool Options** box. In an empty spot, left-drag to create a half-inch ellipse. Right-drag to create a half-inch ellipse.

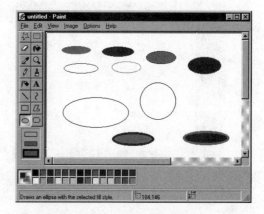

 Left-dragging created an ellipse in the background color (pink) with no border. Right-dragging created an ellipse in the foreground color (blue) with no border. Because you selected the bottom fill style for both (border and fill in the same color), this choice is reflected in the two new ellipses. The Rectangle and Rounded Rectangle work in the same fashion. Holding down the **Shift** key to "square" or "round" your shape also works with all the shape tools.

11   Left-click the color **red**. Right-click the color **green**. Click the **Curve** tool.

12   In an open area, left-drag until you have about a two-inch vertical line. Release the left mouse button.

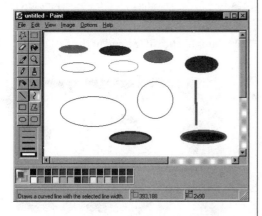

What's happening?   So far, you have a red vertical line. If you wanted it straight, you would have held down the **Shift** key. If you had wanted a green line, you would have right-dragged.

13   The cursor changes to a cross-hair. Place the cross-hair cursor in the middle of the line. Left-drag to the left about an inch. Click the left mouse button.

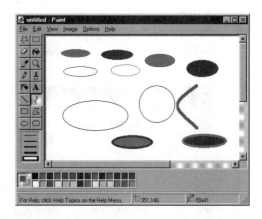

What's happening?   You see your vertical line curving. When you clicked the mouse, you set the line in the curve. If you do not click the mouse, you can make one more curve.

14   In an open area, right-drag the mouse until you have a two-inch horizontal line. Release the mouse button. Place the cross-hair cursor in the middle of the line you just drew. Right-drag down about an inch.

15   Place the cross-hair cursor on the left end of the line. Right-drag up about an inch. Release the mouse button.

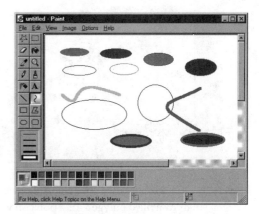

What's happening?   You have made the line curve in two directions. You are limited to two curves and cannot curve it again.

16 Left-click the color **brown**. Right-click the color **yellow**. Click the **Polygon** tool. In the drawing area, left-drag to create a vertical one-inch line.

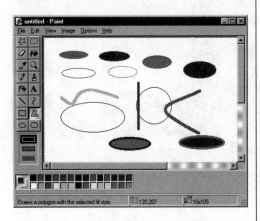

What's happening? → You seem to have drawn a straight line.

17 Place the cross-hair cursor at the bottom of the brown line. Left-drag one inch to the right.

18 Click on top of the first brown line you drew.

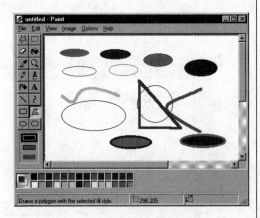

What's happening? → You have drawn a triangle. You can also draw a filled polygon, or a polygon with more than three sides.

19 In the **Tool Options** box, click the middle fill style. You are going to draw a "W." Draw a line. Once

you have drawn your first line, click each point where you want the angles for the "W" to be.

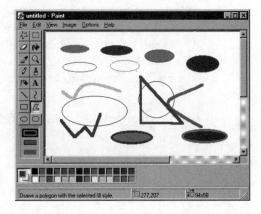

What's happening? → To connect all the lines, double-click at the end of the last line you drew.

20 Double-click at the end of the first line of "W."

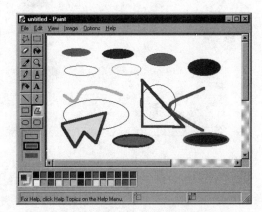

What's happening? → You drew a yellow-filled shape with a brown border. The Polygon tool lets you connect lines to create random shapes.

21 Left-click **black**. Right-click **white**. Click the **Pencil** tool.

22 Close **Paint**. Do not save the drawing.

What's happening? → You have closed Paint and returned to the desktop.

11.8 Importing and Exporting Graphics

So far, you have been using different tools, but none of the drawings has been a work of art. Most of us do not have a lot of artistic talent. You need not be frustrated because there Paint offers a solution. You can *import* (bring in a drawing) or *export* (save to a file on a disk) graphic files. Once you import a graphic, you may alter it. You may also purchase what is called *clip art*. Clip art provides many, typically small, images from which you can choose. You can alter the clip art and then save it as a new drawing.

Graphics files come in many different file formats. You may have heard of some of these formats, such as TIFF (Tagged Image File Format), JPEG (Joint Photographic Experts Group), GIF (Graphic Image File), PCX, or BMP (bitmap) Paint supports the bitmap file format and uses the extension .bmp by default. Paint will open other bitmapped files, such as .pcx, .tif, and .gif. A bitmapped graphic is formed by a pattern of pixels. Its resolution is limited to the type of video adapter card and the capability of your monitor.

11.9 Activity—Using a Graphic

1 Open the **Paint** program.

2 Click **File**. Click **Open**.

3 Click the arrow in the **Look in** drop-down list box.

4 Click the **Drive C** icon. Double-click the **95book** folder.

What's happening? → You have accessed the Open dialog box. The window displays all the folders in the 95book folder, including three bitmap files (.bmp).

5 Double-click **Dancer.bmp**.

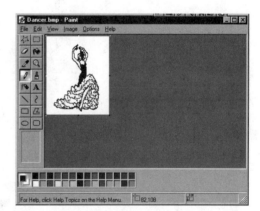

What's happening? → This image appears in the size in which it was saved, and it is extremely small. You can expand the size of the image either by dragging the handles on the edge of the drawing or using the menu.

6 Click **Image**. Click **Attributes**.

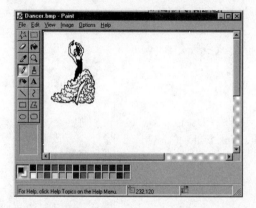

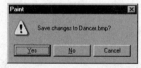

What's happening? You can always alter the size of the drawing canvas by changing its attributes. The attributes are measured in pels (pixels), inches, or centimeters. In this menu, you can also choose a black-and-white image, which is useful if you plan to print the document on a black-and-white printer.

7 Click **Default**. Click **OK**.

What's happening? You have a larger canvas. When you change the attributes, you change the file.

8 Click **File**. Click **New**.

What's happening? You changed the image, but you do not want to save it. You want to create a new drawing and import the graphic into it.

9 Click **No**. Maximize your **Paint** window.

10 Click the **Line** tool. In the **Tool Options** box, select the widest line.

11 Click the **Rectangle** tool. In the middle of the drawing area, create a square with sides measuring approximately three inches.

12 Left-click **green**. Click the **Fill With Color** tool and click in the square.

13 Left-click **black**. Click the **Pencil** tool.

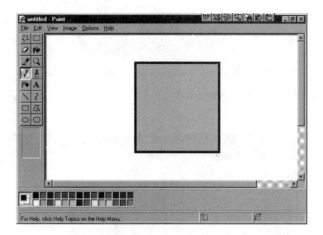

 You have a green square outlined in black.

14 Click **Edit**. Click **Paste From**. Double-click **Dancer.bmp**.

What's happening? Paint remembers that you retrieved the last file from the C:\95book folder and returns you to that window. When you Paste From, you are copying an image into an existing drawing. The dancer is outlined by a dotted line, which means you can drag the image to a desired location. In addition, you can copy the art *opaquely* or *transparently*. Copying it transparently means that your drawing will not obscure the drawing in the background and will pick up the colors of that background. Copying the drawing opaquely means that it will retain its original colors and will obscure whatever is behind it. If you look in the Tool Options box, you will see buttons for these two choices. See Figure 11.2.

Figure 11.2   Tool Options Box Choices

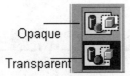

Since the Transparent button is selected, that is how the drawing will be copied.

15   Drag the dancer into the green square.

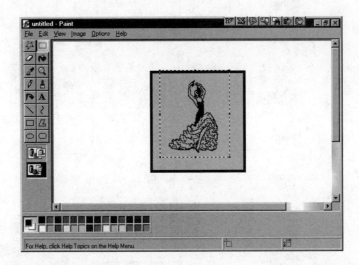

What's
happening?   Because you were in transparent mode, the dancer is completely green. In addition, she fits entirely into your square.

16   Click **Edit**. Click **Undo**.

17   Click **Edit**. Click **Paste From**. Double-click **Dancer.bmp**.

18   Click the **Opaque** button in the **Tool Option** box.

19   Drag the dancer into the box.

What's happening? The dancer and surrounding white area now cover the green area, and both are within the outline of the square.

20 Left-click **green**. Click the **Fill With Color** tool. Click the white background in the box.

21 Left-click **black**. Click the **Pencil** tool.

What's happening? The dancer is now in white and black with a green background. If you select the object, hold the **Ctrl** key, and drag, you will create a copy of the selected object. Although currently set to opaque, you can choose transparent.

22 Click the **Select** tool. Encircle the dancer. Hold the **Ctrl** key and drag her out of the box to the right.

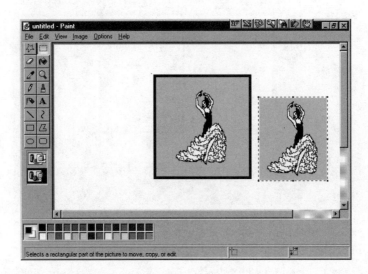

 You copied your image opaquely. You can create a *cutout*, which is the part of a drawing that you cut out. A cutout can be saved to a file and will take less disk space than a full drawing.

23 Encircle the boxed dancer. Include the black border.

24 Click **Edit**. Click **Copy To**.

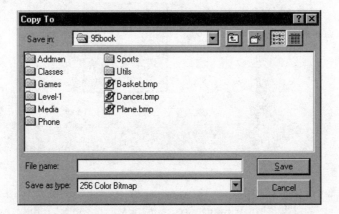

 The Copy To dialog box is asking you where you want to file this cutout.

25 Place the Data disk in Drive A. Click the down arrow in the **Save in** drop-down list box. Double-click the **3½ Floppy (A:)** icon.

26 Click the **Create New Folder** button on the toolbar.

27 Name the folder **Chap11**.

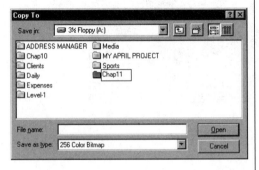

 You created a folder to store your drawings. Chap11 is a short name for Chapter 11, the folder in which you will store Chapter 11 activities and homework.

28 Double-click the **Chap11** folder icon.

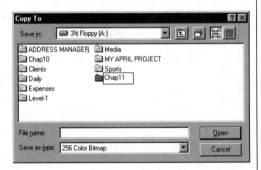

 You are ready to save your file. Graphic files are large, particularly bitmapped files. The size of the file depends on the number of colors chosen when you set up your display properties. The more colors that are in your display, the larger the file will become. One of the ways to reduce the size of a bitmap file is to choose a small number of colors. How your monitor is set up depends on what capabilities your video adapter card and monitor support.

29 Click the down arrow in the **Save as type** drop-down list box.

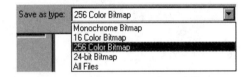

 The 256 Color Bitmap option will create the largest file, whereas Monochrome Bitmap will create the smallest file. A middle ground is the 16 Color Bitmap.

30 Click **16 Color Bitmap**.

31 In the **File name** text box, key in the following: **green.bmp**

32 Click **Save**.

33 Click **File**. Click **New**.

34 Click **No** in the **Save Changes** information box.

35 Open the **green.bmp** file located in the **Chap11** directory of the Data disk.

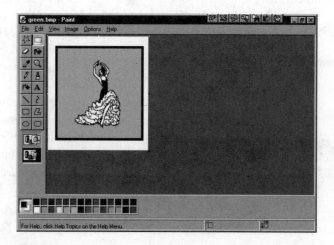

What's
happening? ───▶ You saved your cutout only, not the complete drawing.

36 Close **Paint**.

11.10 Drawing a Picture

In the preceding activities, you experimented with some of the basic drawing and editing tools in Paint. Your next task is to draw a picture that will reinforce your skills and add some techniques to your repertoire. The drawing will be based on simple shapes and techniques. Remember Undo when you get too far afield. This activity should be fun. You can refer to the following finished drawing to get an idea of the way it should look, but your drawing does not have to look *exactly* like this picture.

MY BIRD PICTURE

11.11 Activity—Drawing the Bird

1 Open the **Paint** program.

2 Maximize the **Paint** window.

3 The background color is white and the foreground color is black. Click the **Line** tool. Click the second line from the top in the **Tool Options** box to select the line width.

4 Click the **Ellipse** tool.

5 About two inches from the left and two inches from the bottom of the dragging area, left-drag to the right to create a two and a half-inch oval.

6 About a half inch above and to the right of the oval you just created, left-drag to the right to create an oval about one inch for the head.

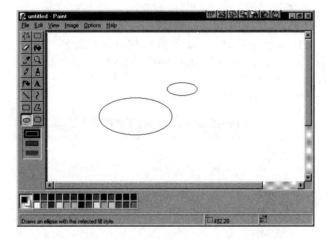

 You have drawn the bird's head and body. If you do not like your ovals, you can click Edit and then click Undo. Now, you are going to draw its neck and legs. Remember, when you have drawn your shape, release the mouse button.

7 Click the **Line** tool. About three-fourths of an inch from the right side of the body, hold down the left mouse button and drag it about two inches down and to the right to form the beginning of the leg.

8 About a half inch from the left side of the body, hold the left mouse button and drag it about one and three-fourths inches down and to the left for the other leg.

 You have drawn the legs. Now you are going to draw the neck.
What's
happening?

9 Place the cross-hair cursor at the bottom of the head oval. Hold the **Shift** key and drag until the line meets the body. Using the same techniques, create another parallel line, making the two lines about one-fourth of an inch apart.

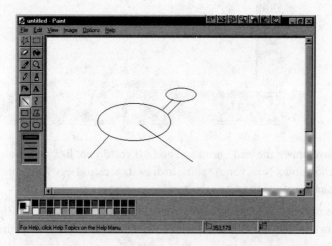

What's
happening?
You have a "straight" neck because you held down the **Shift** key when you dragged the mouse. You do not want to have a line between the neck and body. Although you could use the eraser, Paint allows you to edit a drawing very precisely, one pixel at a time. You must first select and then zoom to the desired location.

10 Click the **Magnifier** and place it over the neck.

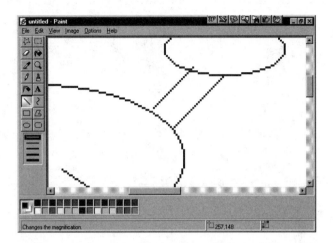

  You have a close-up view of the neck. You can see that one of your neck lines does not completely meet the body. The same line is protruding into the bird's head. You would want to fix this line because, when you color something in Paint and the border is incomplete, your colors will "bleed" to the unbounded area. Your drawing may be different.

11 Click **View**. Point at **Zoom**.

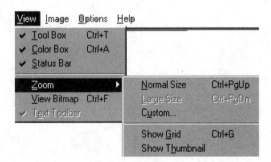

  The cascading menu for Zoom has some choices that make working at the pixel level easier. One is Show Grid and the other is Show Thumbnail.

12 Click **Show Grid**.

13 Click **View**. Point at **Zoom**. Click **Show Thumbnail**.

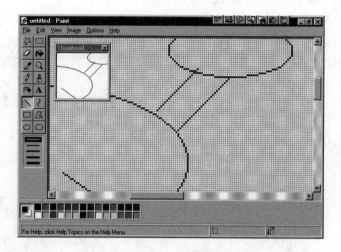

 You have a grid where you can clearly see each pixel in the area you are editing. A left-click places the foreground color in a pixel, and a right-click places the background color in a pixel.

14 Click the **Eraser/Color Eraser** tool. Drag the eraser over the line separating the neck from the body.

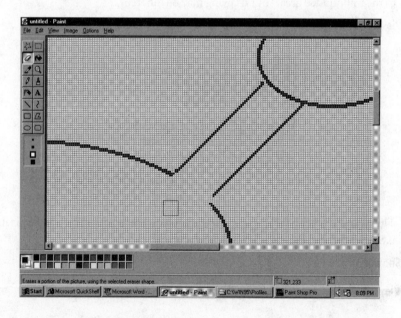

 It is easier to use the eraser than to click each pixel. However, there are still gaps. You want to left-click until there is a complete border.

15 Click the **Pencil** tool. In each place that you see a gap, left-click to place a black pixel in the open area.

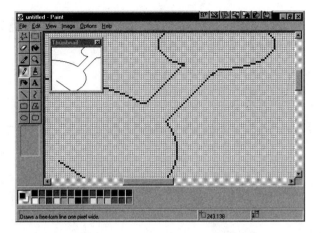

 You have solidly filled in the line.

16 Click **View**. Point at **Zoom**. Click **Normal Size**.

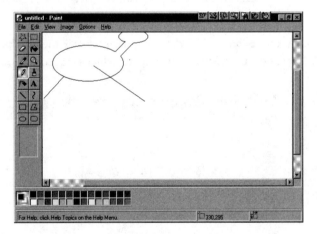

 Your drawing is not quite where it was.

17 Drag the vertical scroll bar up and the horizontal scroll bar to the left.

18 Left-click **black**. Right-click **yellow**. Click the **Polygon** tool. Click the middle fill style in the **Tool Options** box.

19 Move the cursor to the right side of the head to begin drawing the beak. Drag a line out and slightly down about one inch. Release the left mouse button.

20 Place the cross-hair cursor on the head below the first line. Double-click.

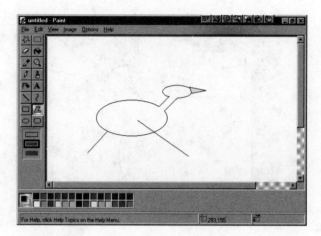

 You should have a yellow beak outlined in black and shaped like a triangle.

21 Click the **Rounded Rectangle** tool. Click the middle fill style in the **Tool Options** box. Place the cross-hair at the bottom of the front leg. Left-drag to the right and down to create a foot. Do the same to the other leg.

22 Right-click **blue**. Click the **Ellipse** tool. Click the middle fill style in the **Tool Options** box. Move the cross-hair to the head. Hold down the **Shift** key to create a small circle for an eye.

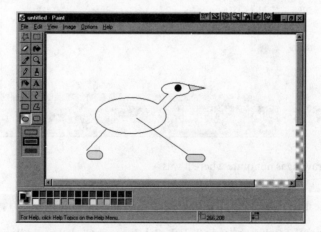

 You have two yellow feet outlined in black and a blue eye outlined in black. You are going to create tail feathers with the Polygon tool. Remember, the easiest way to create a triangle is to draw one line, then double-click at the point where you want a triangle.

23 Left-click the color **black**. Right-click the color **white**. Click the **Polygon** tool. Click the top fill style in the **Tool Options** box. Move the cross-hair to the back end of the large oval, about three-fourths of an inch up and away from the body. Drag about a half-inch line up and to the right.

24 Move the cross-hair to the oval body. Double-click.

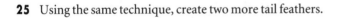 You have quickly created a triangle for the tail feather.

25 Using the same technique, create two more tail feathers.

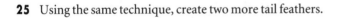 You have a complete set of tail feathers. You can create a wing with the Line and Curve tools.

26   Click the **Curve** tool. In the body of the bird, left-drag a line from front to back. Release the left mouse button. Place the cross-hair in the middle of the new line. Hold the left mouse button and drag up. Release the left mouse button.

27   Click the **Line** tool. Position the cross-hair under the curved line. Left-drag to create a horizontal line below the curve. Release the left mouse button.

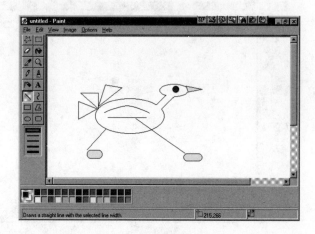

 You have created a wing. This is a good time to save your drawing

28   Click **File**. Click **Save**.

29   Click the down arrow in the **Save in** drop-down list box. Double-click the **3½ Floppy (A:)** icon. Double-click the **Chap11** folder icon.

30   Click the down arrow in the **Save as type** drop-down list box and click **16 Color Bitmap**.

31   In the **File name** text box, key in the following: **Bird.bmp**

32   Click **Save**. Close **Paint**.

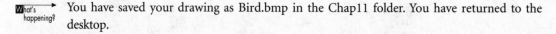 You have saved your drawing as Bird.bmp in the Chap11 folder. You have returned to the desktop.

11.12 Using Text and Other Pictures in a Drawing

Not only can you create, import, and alter drawings, but you can also add text to them. You can choose different fonts and styles for your text. The text itself can be manipulated. You can also import a character from the Wingdings font, manipulate it, and then add it to add to your drawing.

11.13 Activity—Adding Text and Pictures to Your Drawing

1 Open **Paint**. Click **File**.

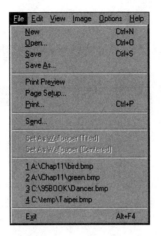

  Paint, like many Windows 95 applications, keeps a list of files that you most recently opened. You may choose from this list. If your lab environment prevents the listing of files, you must open your file by using File/Open and selecting A:\Chap11\Bird.bmp.

2 Click the **A:\Chap11\Bird.bmp** on the file list.

3 Click the **Text** tool. Click above the bird.

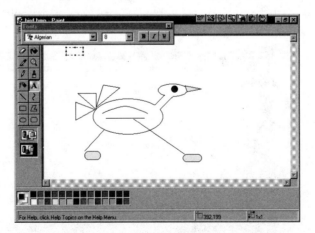

  You retrieved your drawing easily. Then you selected the Text tool. When you clicked in the drawing, you got a small box with a blinking I-beam. Here is where you key in text. The size of the box shows how much room you have to enter text. In addition, the Fonts dialog box has appeared, telling you the font you are using. If you do not see the Fonts dialog box, click View. Then click the Text toolbar. In this case, the font is 8 point Algerian. In the Tool Options box, transparent is the selected option.

4   Choose the **Arial** font. Change its font size to **12**.

5   Using the handles, stretch the box about two inches.

6   Click inside the text box. Key in the following: **MY BIRD PICTURE**

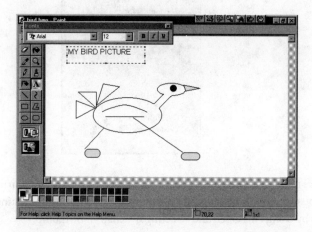

What's happening?   You have aYou keyed text into the text box.

7   Click the **Select** tool. If necessary, move the Fonts dialog box. Encircle the words you just keyed in. Left-drag the selected text to the middle of the picture. When it is in position, click outside the selection.

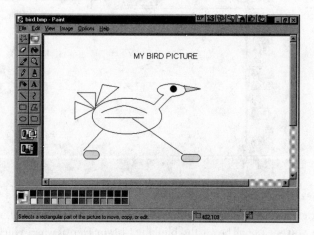

What's happening?   Now that you have centered your text, you want to make it larger.

8   Click the **Select** tool. Encircle the phrase. Click **Image**.

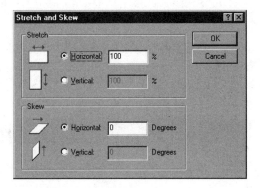 Once you select an object, you can do many things to it. You can flip or rotate it. You can stretch or skew it. You can also reverse its colors.

9   Click **Stretch/Skew**.

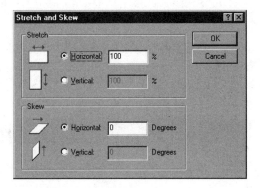

 You want to stretch the letters.

10   In the Stretch **Horizontal** text box, key in **150**.

11   Click the Stretch **Vertical** option button. Key in **150**. Click **OK**. Click outside the selection to deselect it.

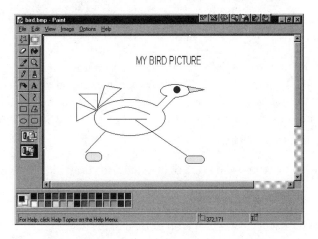

Your letters are larger. You are going to create a flower basket and then use a Wingdings drawing for the flowers.

12 Left-click the color **black**. Right-click the color **red**. Click the **Rectangle** tool. Click the middle fill style in the **Tool Options** box.

13 In the lower-right corner of the drawing area, left-drag up and to the right so that you have about a one-inch square. Release the left mouse button.

14 Left-click **green**. Right-click **green**.

15 Click the **Line** tool. Select the third line from the top as your fill style in the **Tool Options** box. At the top border of the basket, hold the **Shift** key and left-drag up about a half inch to create a stem. Create three of them.

16 Click the **Curve** tool. At the top left of the basket, left-drag the line down and to the left. Release the left mouse button. In the middle of the line, hold down the left mouse button and pull up. Release the left mouse button and click to set the curve.

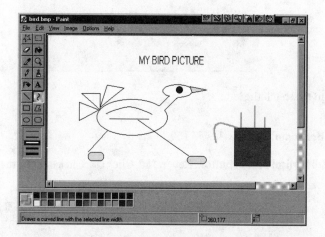

 You created a red rectangle with a black border. When you select the same foreground and background color, as you did for the stems, the object you draw will have no outline or border. You used the Curve tool to draw a droopy stem. Now, you want to add flowers to your stems. Flowers are difficult to draw. You are going to borrow a drawing from Wingdings.

17 Left-click **black**. Right-click **white**.

18 Click the **Text** tool. Click above and to the right of the bird's beak and draw a one-inch square for text.

19 In the **Fonts** box, locate and select **Wingdings**. Change the font size to **36**. Click in the text box.

20 Press the **P**. Press the left bracket, which is to the right of the P.

What's happening? When you clicked in the text box, you saw a large blinking cursor. Each letter you pressed gave you a picture from the Wingdings font. You are going to use the curly brace to get a picture of a flower.

21 Press the **Backspace** key twice to remove the two symbols you just keyed in.

22 Hold the **Shift** key and press the left bracket key. Click outside the text box.

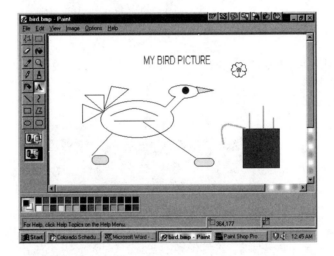

What's happening? You have a flower.

23 Click the **Select** tool. Encircle the flower. Right-click.

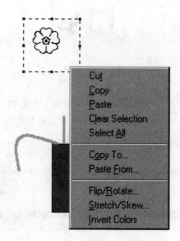

 Right-clicking brings up the shortcut menu.

24   Click **Stretch/Skew**.

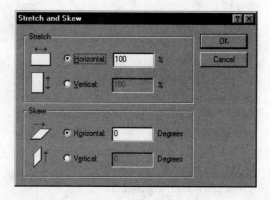

 You have the Stretch and Skew dialog box. You want to stretch the flower.

25   Change the Stretch **Horizontal** number to **125**.

26   Click the Stretch **Vertical** option button and change that number to **125**. Click **OK**.

27   Right-click. Click **Copy**.

28   Right-click. Click **Paste**.

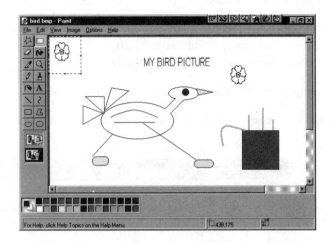

What's
happening? You enlarged the flower and made a copy of it. When you selected Paste, you pasted a flower to the left corner.

29 Drag either flower to a stem.

30 Encircle the other flower and drag it to a stem.

31 Right-click. Click **Paste**. Drag the copy of the flower to another stem.

32 Right-click. Click **Paste**. Drag the copy of the flower to the remaining stem.

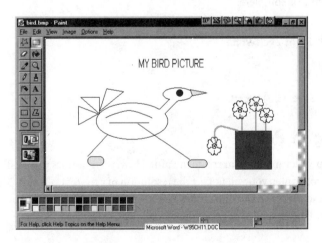

What's
happening? Your flowers are in position. You are now going to color them. Remember to keep the tip of the Fill With Color tool inside the borders of the flowers.

33 Left-click **pink**. Click the **Fill With Color** tool. Place the tip inside a flower. Click the left mouse button.

Hint: If lines in your flowers intersect, you may have to place the tip of the Fill With Color tool in each outlined section in order to color the entire flower. If you have breaks in your lines, you could accidentally color the entire picture. Undo is helpful here.)

34 Color the remaining flowers in colors of your choice, using the above techniques.

35 Left-click **gray**. Click in the bird and color its body, tail feathers, and head. Leave its beak and feet yellow.

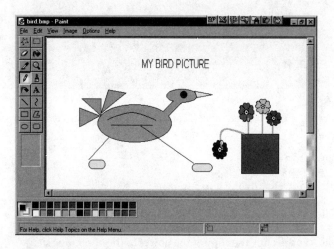

 Your picture is complete.

36 Left-click **black**. Right-click **white**.

37 Click the **Pencil** tool.

38 Click **File**. Click **Save**. Close **Paint**.

11.14 Printing in Paint

You can print any picture that you create in Paint. However, graphics print differently from text. If you have a dot-matrix printer, you will not get the resolution of a more sophisticated printer. Graphic images also take longer to print and use more toner and ink than text images. If you do not have a color printer, your drawing will be in shades of gray.

11.15 Activity—Printing the Bird Picture

Note: You should be in Paint with your bird drawing displayed.

1   Click **File.** Click **Print Preview.**

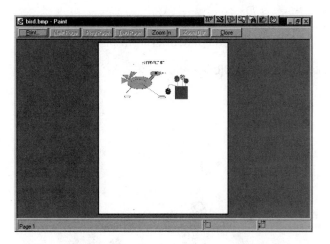

What's
happening?   Print Preview lets you see what your drawing will look like before you print it. If you have your resolution set to 800 × 600, the picture will take two pages to print, even though the second page is blank. If you have your resolution set to 480 × 600, only one page will print. If part of your picture is on the second page, return to the picture and move the flower basket so you can print on one page. In this example, you would like the bird a little further down in the picture.

2   Click **Close.**

3   Click **File.** Click **Page Setup.**

4   Change the top margin to two inches. Click **OK.**

5   Click **File.** Click **Print.**

6   Click **OK.**

7   Click **Save.**

What's
happening?   You printed your drawing. Now you are going to use your drawing as wallpaper for your desktop.

11.16 Using Drawings as Wallpaper

When you selected different wallpapers, your choices were limited to those offered in the Display Properties Background tab. At that time, you learned that wallpapers were bitmapped files (.bmp). In Paint, you created a bitmapped file called Bird.bmp. You can use it as wallpaper.

11.17 Activity—Using a Drawing as Wallpaper

Note: You should be in Paint with your bird drawing displayed.

1   Click **File**. Click **Set as Wallpaper (Centered)**.

2   Minimize **Paint**.

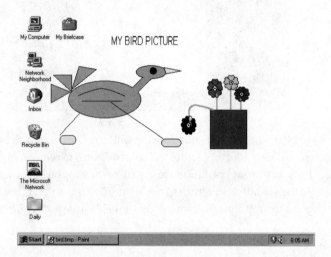

 Since the bird picture occupies the entire screen, you would not have been able to tile it. To create tiled wallpaper, the image should be much smaller.

3   Right-click **Paint** on the taskbar. Click **Close**.

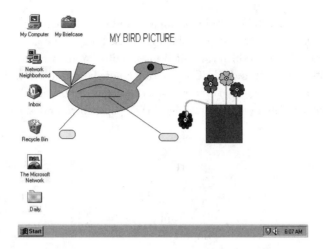

MY BIRD PICTURE

What's
happening? → The bird is still your wallpaper.

4 Right-click the desktop. Click **Properties**.

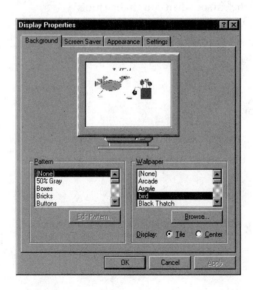

What's
happening? → Bird is now the selected choice.

5 Click **(None)** in the **Wallpaper** list box. Click **OK**.

What's
happening? → The bird is no longer being used as your wallpaper. You can create a wallpaper at any time as long
as you save it to a file. You returned to your desktop without wallpaper.

Chapter Summary

In this chapter, you learned about Paint. You were introduced to different tools and used them to create and edit drawings. You created different shapes and used the color palette to change colors. You imported and exported clip art which you edited and modified. You learned the difference between using File/Open, Edit/Paste From, and Edit/Copy To. You entered text into a drawing and manipulated that text. Using the Wingdings font, you captured a picture and manipulated it. You learned how to save and print your drawings. You used your drawing as a wallpaper for your desktop.

Key Terms

Background color
Clip art
Color Box
Cutout
Drawing area

Export
Fill
Fill style
Foreground color
Import

Opaquely
Pels
Tool Box
Tool Options box
Transparently

Discussion Questions

1. What is Paint?
2. What is a bitmapped file?
3. What is the drawing area?
4. What happens to the cursor when you change tools?
5. Compare and contrast background color with foreground color.
6. What is the purpose of each of the following tools?
   a. Free-Form Select
   b. Select
   c. Eraser/Color Eraser
   d. Fill With Color
   e. Pick Color
   f. Magnifier
   g. Pencil
   h. Brush
   i. Airbrush
   j. Text
   k. Line
   l. Curve
   m. Rectangle
   n. Polygon
   o. Ellipse
   p. Rounded Rectangle

7. What is a fill style? How is it used?
8. What is the function of the Undo command? Why is it important to have this command?
9. Explain two ways to cut out part of your drawing and drag it to a new location.
10. Explain how the Ellipse tool can be used to form a circle.
11. What does it mean to import a graphic? Export a graphic?
12. Compare and contrast opaque and transparent copies.
13. What is the purpose of the Zoom In command when you are drawing a picture?
14. What is the easiest way to draw a triangle?
15. Once a drawing has been created, how do you save it?
16. Identify two characteristics that can be manipulated when incorporating text into your drawing.
17. How can you make a portion of your drawing larger?
18. Explain the purpose and function of the Stretch and Skew dialog box.
19. How could you use a drawing to create a wallpaper?
20. How could you place your wallpaper on the desktop?

True/False Questions

For each question, circle the letter T if the statement is true or the letter F if the statement is false.

T F 1. A disadvantage of importing graphics is that they cannot be altered.

T F 2. Paint can combine text and pictures and save them in a single file.

T F 3. When you paste a selection in Paint, what you pasted will always appear in the upper-left corner of the drawing area.

T F 4. The Eraser/Color Eraser tool can be used to change the foreground color to the background color.

T F 5. Text images take longer to print than graphic images.

Completion Questions

Write the correct answer in each blank space provided.

6. If you don't have the time or talent to create drawings in Paint, _____ provides many small images from which you can choose.

7. When you choose Copy To, you have _____ a graphic. When you choose Paste From, you have _____ a graphic.

8. When you are using the Curve tool, it may be curved a maximum of _____ times.

9. You control the number of sides the _____ tool adds to a configuration.

10. The _____ tool will let you select a color in your drawing and use it as a foreground color.

Multiple Choice Questions

Circle the letter of the correct answer for each question.

11. If you wish your drawing to fill the entire screen, with no tool bars, you may click
  a. View.
  b. View Bitmap.
  c. View. Then click View Bitmap.
  d. View. Then click Full Screen.

12. The following are all shape tools except
  a. Select.
  b. Rectangle.
  c. Rounded Rectangle.
  d. Polygon.

13. To change the foreground color, click a color and then
  a. press the left mouse button.
  b. press the right mouse button.
  c. double-click the left mouse button.
  d. double-click the right mouse button.

14. When you are including text with a drawing, it is possible to alter the text's
  a. font.
  b. size.
  c. style.
  d. all of the above

15. The tool used to make a rectangular selection is the _____ tool.
  a. Free-Form Select
  b. Select
  c. Scissors
  d. Fill

Application Assignments

Problem Set I—At the Computer

Note: Graphic files are very large. You are not required to save the files to disk for Problems B or D. If you want to save the files, it is recommended that you reduce the resolution to 16 Color Bitmap and that you use a new disk.

Problem A

Open **Paint**. Click the **Line** tool. Choose the middle line as your line width in the **Tool Options** box. Left-click **blue**. Right-click **red**. Click the **Ellipse** tool. Choose the top fill style in the **Tool Options** box. Draw an ellipse.

1. The ellipse is
   a. a blue outline with a white interior.
   b. a red outline with a white interior.
   c. a solid blue ellipse.
   d. a solid red ellipse.

Click the **Ellipse** tool. Choose the bottom fill style in the **Tool Options** box. Draw another ellipse.

2. The newly drawn ellipse is
   a. a blue outline with a white interior.
   b. a red outline with a white interior.
   c. a solid blue ellipse.
   d. a solid red ellipse.

Left-click **black**. Right-click **white**. Click **Edit**. Click **Paste From**. In the **File name** text box, key in **C:\95book\Basket.bmp**. Click **Open**.

3. What color is the basket?
   a. Red.
   b. Yellow.
   c. White.
   d. Black.

In the **Tool Options** box, choose the bottom style. Drag the basket over an ellipse.

4. You are dragging the basket
   a. opaquely.
   b. transparently.

Left-click **yellow**. Right-click **pink**. Click the **Eraser/Color Eraser** tool. Right-drag the tool across the entire basket, including the eggs.

5. What happened?
   a. Only the yellow basket became pink.
   b. The yellow basket and all the eggs became pink.
   c. The basket remained yellow, but the eggs became pink.
   d. The basket and eggs became white.

Left-click **black**. Right-click **white**. Close **Paint**. Do not save the picture.

Problem B

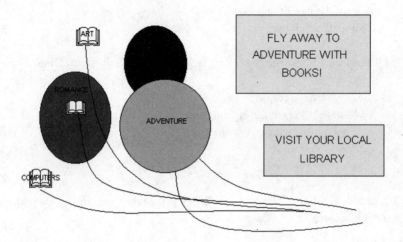

1. Open **Paint** and create a new approximation of the above drawing.
    Some hints on drawing the picture:
    a. The book picture is from Wingdings. You can access it by pressing the **Shift** key and the &
        sign number 7 on the top of the keyboard, not the numeric keypad). The font size is 20 for
        the small book and 26 for the large book.
    b. Use any typeface and size you want for your letters. Remember to make the text box big
        enough so the letters fit. To move text, it is best to key in the words first and use the **Select**
        tool to encircle the words. You can then drag them to the desired location.
    c. Use any colors or gray tones you wish. If you color in the rectangle after you put the words in
        it, use the **Magnifier** to fill in the white spots.
2. Place your name and class section in the upper-right corner.
3. Print the drawing.
4. Close **Paint**.

Problem C

1. Open **Paint**.
2. Click **Edit**. Click **Paste From**. Locate **Plane.bmp** in the **95book** folder. Double-click it.
3. Drag it to the middle of the drawing area.
4. Click the **Text** tool. Change the font to **10**. Key in your name. Click the **Select** tool, encircle your name, and drag it to the banner.
5. Left-click **white**. Use the **Fill With Color** tool to change the plane's body to white.
6. Left-click **black**.
7. Click the **Select** tool and encircle the picture.
8. Right-click. Click **Copy To**.
9. In the **Save as type** drop-down list box, choose **16 Color Bitmap**.
10. In the **File name** text box, key in the following: **A:\Chap11\Mylogo.bmp** [Enter]
11. Close **Paint**. Click **No**. You do not want to save the image.
12. Open **Paint**. Click **File**. Click **Open**.
13. In the **File name** text box, key in the following: **A:\Chap11\Mylogo** [Enter]
14. Click **OK**.
15. Print **Mylogo.bmp**.
16. Close **Paint**.

Problem D

1. Open **Paint**.
2. Create a drawing of your choice.
3. Use as many tools as you can. Import a graphic.
4. If you choose to save the drawing, save it as **Fun.bmp** on a new disk. Do not save it to the Data disk, since you want to conserve space on this disk.
5. Place your name and class section in the upper-right corner using the **Text** tool.
6. Print the picture.
7. Close **Paint**.

Problem Set II—Brief Essay

For all essay questions, you may use Notepad or WordPad for your answer. Print your answer.

1. What purpose does Paint serve? Do you think it was important for Windows 95 to include it as an accessory? Why or why not?

2. What is clip art? Why and how would you use clip art in Paint? What steps would you have to take to use clip art in a drawing that you created?

Problem Set III—Scenario

You want to create a simple map to your house. How could you do this with Paint? You want to include some landmarks, such as stop signs or a gas station. How could you do so? There are arrows in the Wingdings font. The arrow looks like this è, and is achieved by holding the **Alt** key and pressing 0232 on the numeric keypad. How could you find the numbers for arrows pointing in different directions? Answer the above questions, then describe the steps you would take to create a map, including landmarks and directional arrows. Create and print the map.

Chapter 12

Sharing and Exchanging Data between Programs

Chapter Overview

A powerful feature of Windows 95 is the ability to share data, not just *within* a program, but also *between* programs. Sharing data is part of the docucentric approach that Windows 95 takes. You should be concerned with your data, not the program that generates that data. Sharing data between programs lets you focus on what you want to say, not the technology needed to get the data into a document. You can even choose how you want to present your document, including sound or video. All these things are possible in Windows 95. Programs written for Windows 95 provide easy ways to accomplish these goals. Windows 95 enables you to read and convert to other file formats, use the Clipboard for cutting and pasting (static moves and copies of data), and use object linking and embedding (OLE) for dynamic moves and copies of data. Each of these techniques is progressively more sophisticated and reflects the technological improvements of Windows 95.

Learning Objectives

1. Explain the purpose and function of file formats.
2. Define "compound document."
3. Explain the purpose and function of Dynamic Data Exchange.
4. List and explain the three kinds of data exchange.
5. Compare and contrast static and dynamic data exchange.
6. Explain the purpose and function of the Clipboard Viewer.
7. List the steps necessary to print a screen.
8. List ways a screen capture can be altered.
9. When using data exchange, compare and contrast server and client.
10. Describe the purpose of OLE.
11. Explain the purpose and function of embedding objects.
12. Explain the purpose and function of linking objects.
13. Compare and contrast linking and embedding objects.
14. Explain how an embedded object can be edited.
15. Explain the purpose and function of scrap files.

Student Outcomes

1. Use the Clipboard to transfer data between applications.
2. Print a screen.

3. Use Paint to alter a screen capture.
4. Embed an object.
5. If you have a sound card, embed a sound object.
6. Link an object to multiple documents.
7. Create a scrap.
8. Drag and drop a scrap into a document.

12.1   An Introduction to Data Exchange

You use application programs to generate documents (data files). The data must be in a specific format, however, in order for an application program to read, write, display, and print data files. The *file format* (not to be confused with formatting a disk) tells the application program not only what the data is, but also what the data's specific arrangement is within the document. If the application program is a word processor, the file format could include the line and paragraph arrangements, the fonts, the margins, the headers, and the footers. If the application program is a drawing package, the format could include where the drawing is located, the colors, the lines of the drawing, and any text arrangement.

Most application programs have proprietary file formats. Because of these special formats, one application program cannot read a data file created by another application program. For instance, a graphics program such as Paint cannot read data created with a spreadsheet program such as Lotus.

As you become a more sophisticated user, you will want to use several application programs to create compound documents. A *compound document* might be a word processing document with elements from other programs, such as a picture, a video clip, a sound clip, or a table from a spreadsheet. All these elements exist so that you can communicate your ideas effectively. Since each of these elements is created in a different application program, it is extremely complicated to have all these elements appear in one document.

Rather than trying to manipulate the data to create compound documents, there is a better approach—let the software do it. With the improvement of software technology, the technical aspects of data transfer are managed by the software. The principle behind data exchange is objects. An *object* is an entity that you can identify because of its properties, operations, and relationships. In data exchange, the object is data. Essentially, there are three kinds of data exchange: static exchanges, embedding, and linking.

In a *static exchange*, you may move or copy data created with one application program into a document created with a different application program. There are some inconveniences in this kind of data exchange, however. The data, when placed in the new document, cannot be edited. Furthermore, there is no way to return to the original application program to edit the data. To alter the data (object), you would have to recreate the data in the original application program, make your changes, and then copy the data into your document a second time. Thus, if you create a picture in Paint and cut and paste the picture into a WordPad document, you can no longer edit the picture. The picture is no longer connected to Paint, the program that created it.

When you *embed* an object in another document, the object remembers where it came from. When an object is embedded in another document, it can still be edited. For instance, when you double-click a drawing in WordPad, the Paint program appears so that you can edit the drawing (object) in Paint while you are still in WordPad. Embedding breaks down the barriers between the object (data) and the program which created it.

When you *link* an object, the object is not actually in the new document. Instead, the receiving document, called the *container*, keeps the information about where the object came from. Actually, the object is saved as a separate file. Many application programs can access that linked file. Whenever the *linked object* is updated, any document that has a link to that object is also automatically updated. Since the data in the file has the potential of being changed, it is considered dynamic, not static. Thus, if you create a picture in Paint and link it to a WordPad document and a PowerPoint document, when you update the picture in Paint, both the WordPad document and the PowerPoint document will have the updated picture.

12.2   Working with Clipboard

Because file formats are different, one program generally cannot read another program's data. To exchange data among application programs, some standard file formats were developed. When a program can read from and write to a standard file format, the program is described as *supporting* a specific file format. For instance, you created a .bmp file in Paint. The .bmp file extension is a known, standard graphic file format. If you purchase a program that supports the .bmp file format, you know that the new program can read a file created in Paint. Although it would seem that a program can read and write a "foreign" format, it is actually converting the foreign format into its own native format.

Rather than relying on standard file formats to exchange data, Windows provides a feature called the Clipboard. The Clipboard, an area in memory, allows data exchange. There is no icon for Clipboard. When you copy or cut text, a drawing, or any other object, it is automatically placed on the Clipboard. You can copy data created in one application and paste it into another application, using the Clipboard as an intermediary. The Clipboard is more than just a holding area for data; it permits static data exchange by converting the data into a standard format so that another program can read it.

12.3   Activity—Using Clipboard with Wordpad and Paint

1   Open **Paint**. Click **File**. Click **Open**.

2   In the **File name** text box, key in the following:
C:\95book\Personal.fil **Enter**

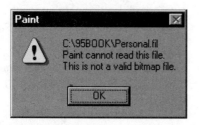

 You cannot open this file in Paint because Paint does not recognize the file format.

3   Click **OK**. Paint should not be maximized.

4   Open **WordPad**. Click **File**. Click **Open**.

5 In the **File name** text box, key in the following: **C:\95book\Dancer.bmp** [Enter]

 WordPad allowed you to open this file because WordPad will let you open any file. However, opening a file is not enough. This file is in the .bmp file format, one that WordPad cannot interpretcorrectly. The data is not displayed as a picture, as it would be in Paint, but in meaningless characters.

6 Click **File**. Click **Open**.

7 In the **File name** text box, key in the following: **C:\95book\Personal.fil** [Enter]

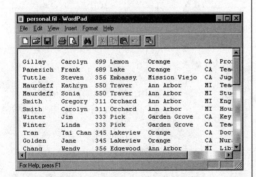

What's happening? WordPad also opened this file. Since this is a text file, WordPad can interpret the format correctly, and the data is displayed in a readable and meaningful

form. A text file, also called an ASCII file, is a standard file format that most programs can read and display properly.

8 Select the last name, **Gillay**.

9 Right-click. Click **Copy**.

10 Click the **Paint** window to make it active.

11 Click **Edit**. Click **Paste**.

What's happening? You see a message box that states the image on the clipboard is larger than the bitmap. Would you like the bitmap enlarged? This dialog box is telling you that your text is being copied as a bitmap, the file format that Paint can recognize.

12 Click **No**.

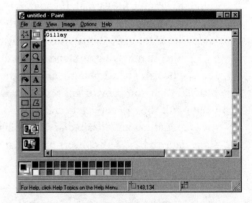

What's happening? The Clipboard has transferred your data from WordPad to Paint. This was done automatically. When you clicked Copy in WordPad, the data was sent to the Clipboard. It was translated into a standard data format that Paint could read. When you clicked Paste in Paint, Paint received the data.

13 Click **File**. Click **Open**. In the **File name** text box, key in the following: **C:\95book\Dancer.bmp** [Enter]

14   Click **No** in the Save File dialog box.

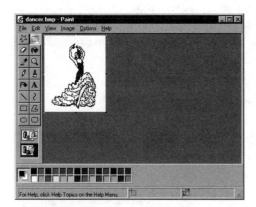

 Since Dance.bmp is a bitmap file, Paint can recognize it.

15   Select the dancer. Click **Edit**. Click **Copy**.

16   Click in **WordPad** to make it active.

17   Click **File**. Click **New**.

 WordPad recognizes three file formats, the ones listed in the dialog box. Text (ASCII) is the most basic of file formats with no special formatting. Rich Text Document (RTF) format has formatting codes that are recognized by many word processors. The Word 6.0 format is one that Microsoft Word specifically recognizes.

18   Click **Rich Text Document**. Click **OK**.

19   Click **No** in the **Save Changes** dialog box.

20   Click **Edit**. Click **Paste**.

 Again, the Clipboard acted as the intermediary and transferred data for you. In each case, the Clipboard took the data and then presented it in a format that the receiving program could accept. You have shared data between programs. By using the Clipboard, Paint could use text generated in WordPad, and WordPad could display a drawing created in Paint.

21   Close all open programs. Do not save any files.

 You have returned to the desktop.

12.4   Clipboard Viewer

What happens in memory is beyond the knowledge of most users. You cannot see what is in memory and, thus, cannot see what is on the Clipboard. You simply use the Clipboard for data exchange. Windows 95 provides a tool called the Clipboard Viewer so that you can look in the Clipboard and see what it has in memory. You can save the contents of the Clipboard to a file as well.

12.5   Activity—Using the Clipboard Viewer

1 Place the Data disk in Drive A.

2 Open **WordPad**. Click **File**. Click **Open**.

3 In the **File name** text box, key in the following: **C:\95book\Personal.fil** `Enter`

4 Select the first three lines of the file. Right-click. Click **Copy**.

5 Click **File**. Click **New**. Click **Rich Text Document**. Click **OK**.

6 Click **File**. Click **Save**. In the **Save in** drop-down list box, click the **3½ Floppy (A:)** icon.

7 Click **Create New Folder**. In the **New Folder** text box, key in the following: **Chap12** `Enter`

8 Double-click the new folder to open it. In the **File name** text box, key in the following: **Person.rtf** `Enter`

9 Size the **WordPad** window so it looks similar to the one shown below.

10 Click **Edit**. Click **Paste**.

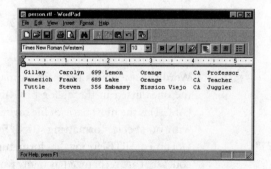

> What's happening?

You have used the Clipboard to copy the information to memory This information is now available.

11 Right-click. Click **Paste**.

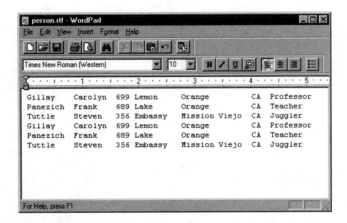

> **What's happening?** Since you did not replace or delete the information in the Clipboard, it is still there for you to use. What is on the Clipboard remains there until you replace it with something else, delete it, or turn off the computer.

12 Select the entire document. Change the font to **Times New Roman**, **14** points.

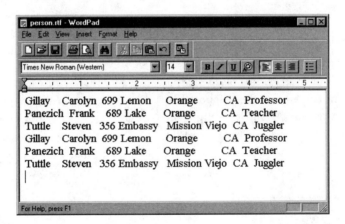

> **What's happening?** You altered the font style and size.

13 Select the first line. Right-click. Click **Copy**.

14 Click **Start**. Point at **Programs**. Point at **Accessories**. Click **Clipboard Viewer**.

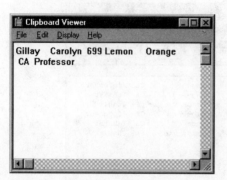

 The text you copied to the Clipboard replaced whatever was there.

15 Click **File** on the **Clipboard Viewer** menu bar.

 You can open an existing file or save the current contents of the Clipboard by choosing Save As and creating a file name. All Clipboard files will have the assigned extension .clp.

16 Click **Edit**.

 The only editing you can do in Clipboard Viewer is to delete the contents of the Clipboard.

17 Click **Display**.

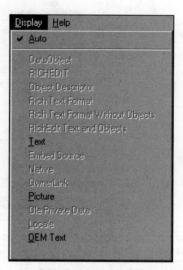

 The Display menu indicates the current data format. It lets you select other formats for viewing your Clipboard data. What choices are available on the menu depends on the application program from which the data was copied. Here, Auto is set, but it is not a file format. Auto means that the Clipboard Viewer will select the format it thinks is the best choice for displaying this data. The format is text since you copied text created in WordPad.

18   Click **Picture**.

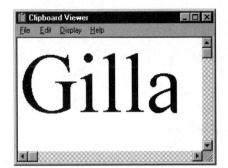

 The Picture format displays the data as a graphic image of the font. The letters are now art.

19   Click **Display**. Click **OEM Text**.

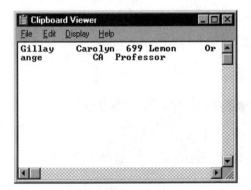

 You have chosen OEM Text. OEM (Other Equipment Manufacturer) displays the data in a character set created by the OEM. You use the OEM Text format when you are copying text from the Clipboard to a DOS application.

20   Click **Display**. Click **Auto**.

21   Open **Paint**. Right-click. Click **Paste**. Click outside the selection to deselect it.

22   Click the **Select** tool. Encircle the words, **Gillay Carolyn**. Drag the object to the middle of the screen.

23   Right-click. Click **Stretch/Skew**.

24   Click the **Horizontal** option button in **Skew**. Key in **20**.

25   Click the **Vertical** option button in **Skew**. Key in **20**.

26   Click **OK**.

 You have skewed the name, which should still be selected.

27   Right-click. Click **Copy**.

28   Click **Clipboard Viewer**.

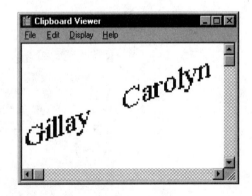

 Your new copy replaced what was there and is now displayed as a picture.

29   Click **Display**.

 Since this display is now a graphic and no longer text, your choices on the menu are different. The Picture format is a graphic image of a text font. A *DIB Bitmap (Device Independent Bitmap)* format is designed to ensure that a bitmapped graphic created in one application can be loaded and displayed in another application exactly the way it appeared in the original application.

30 Click **WordPad**. Move to the bottom of the document.

31 Click **Edit**. Click **Paste Special**.

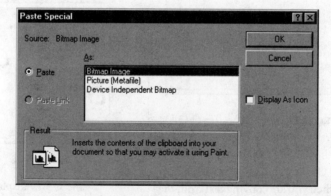

 Since Paint is a Windows 95 application, you would have embedded the picture if you had clicked Paste. In most Windows 95 applications, Paste, by default, is embedding. By choosing Paste Special you have provided yourself with other choices. The default choice is a Bitmap Image. If you look at the Result box at the bottom of the dialog box, you can learn about the result of your action.

32   Click **Picture (Metafile)**. Click **OK**.

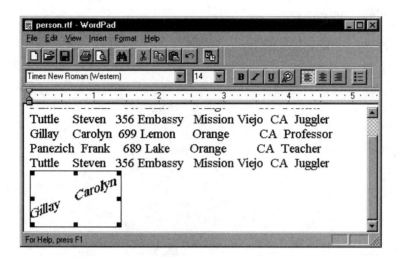

 This choice pasted the information from the Clipboard into your document as a picture. The black squares are sizing handles. You cannot edit the information inside the box, but you can adjust the size by dragging the handles.

33   Click outside the box to deselect it. Click **File**. Click **Save**.

34   Close **WordPad** and the **Clipboard Viewer**.

35   Close **Paint**. Do not save the document.

 You have returned to the desktop. You have used the Clipboard to transfer data between applications.

12.6   Printing the Screen

You sometimes need to print a screen. If you were creating documentation (instructions on how to accomplish a task on a computer), you might like to include a picture of the screen in your text. This process is called a *screen capture*, or a *screen dump*. You might also want to print the screen so that you would have a hard copy to use. For example, if you had a computer problem and wanted to show an expert what happened on your screen when the problem occurred, you would do a screen capture.

To capture a screen, you press the S key. To capture the active window, press **Alt** and the letter s. When you do either of these, the picture of the screen goes to the Clipboard. In order to print the screen, you have to paste it into a document created in an application program. It is essential that the application program be able to accept graphics (pictures).

12.7   Activity—Creating a Screen Capture

1   Press the **Print Screen** key.

2   Open **Notepad**.

3   Click **Edit**.

Paste is not available. Notepad cannot accept graphic images.

4   Click outside the menu to deselect it. Close **Notepad**.

5   Open **WordPad**.

6   Click **Edit**. Click **Paste**.

7   Touch **Ctrl** + **Home** to move to the top of the document.

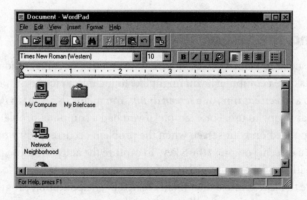

By pressing the **Print Screen** key, you copied the entire screen to the Clipboard. You opened WordPad, which can handle graphics. You then pasted the screen capture into WordPad. Now, you can create a hard copy of this document. *Note:* If you are using a dot-matrix printer, you may want to skip this next step because it will take a long time to print the graphic.

8   Click the **Print** icon on the toolbar.

What's
happening?   You should have a hard copy of the screen.

9   Minimize **WordPad**.

10   Double-click **My Computer**.

11   Press [**Alt**] + [**Print Screen**]. Close **My Computer**.

12   Restore **WordPad**. Maximize it.

13   Click the **New** icon on the toolbar. Click **Rich Text Document**. Click **OK**.

14   In the dialog box that appears, click **No**.

15   Click the **Paste** icon on the toolbar. Scroll until you can see the top of the document.

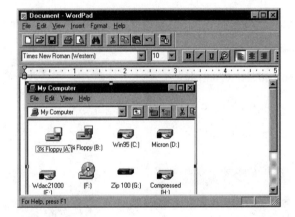

What's
happening?   By pressing the [**Alt**] + [**Print Screen**] keys, you captured only the active window, which was the My Computer window in this example.

16   Close **WordPad**. Do not save the file.

17 Close **My Computer**.

What's
happening? → You have returned to the desktop.

12.8   Altering a Screen Capture

When you capture a screen, you can paste it into a graphic package such as Paint and edit it like any other drawing. You can alter the graphic, change its colors, or skew it. You can cut and paste it to another document or save it as a file.

12.9   Activity—Altering a Screen Capture with Paint

1 Double-click **My Computer**. Double-click the **Control Panel** folder.

2 Scroll until you can see the icon labeled System.

3 Press **Alt** + **Print Screen**.

4 Close **Control Panel**.

5 Open **Paint**. Maximize it. Click **Edit**. Click **Paste**.

6 Scroll until you can see the System icon.

7 Click outside the picture to deselect it.

What's
happening? → You pasted the entire window into Paint.

8 Click the **Select** tool. Cut out only the System icon and its label.

9 Click **Edit**. Click **Cut**.

10 Click **File**. Click **New**. In the dialog box that appears, click **No**.

11 Click **Edit**. Click **Paste**.

What's
happening? → You have a picture of just the System icon. Now that it is selected, you can alter it.

12 Drag the icon to the middle of the screen.

13 Click the **Select** tool. Encircle the letters. Drag them above the picture of the computer.

14 Click the **Rectangle** tool and draw a frame around the letters.

15 Click the **Rectangle** tool again. Box in the entire picture.

 You have moved and boxed in the letters and the picture.

16 Left-click red. Click the **Fill With Color** tool. Click inside the large box, but not the one with the letters.

17 Click the point of the **Fill With Color** tool inside the blue computer screen.

 You have a red background with a red computer screen. You have altered a screen dump. If you wished, you could save this or cut it out and paste it into another document.

18 Left-click black. Click the **Pencil** tool.

19 Close **Paint**. Do not save the picture.

12.10 An Introduction to OLE Technology

The Clipboard allows for only the simplest type of data exchange. More sophisticated technologies exist. In any kind of data exchange, there are two parts to the transaction: the program that supplies the data, and the other program that receives the data. The *server application* is the program that creates the data, and the *client application* is the program that receives the data. If you create a drawing in Paint and embed (paste) that drawing in a WordPad document, you have a supplying document, or *source document*, (the Paint picture) and a receiving document, or *destination document* (the WordPad document). The destination document is also known as the client or the container.

Remember, you are copying an object. In our example, the picture in Paint is the object. Paint is the server application. As you will see, object is the key concept in data exchange.

Data exchange technology was introduced in Windows in the form of *DDE* (*Dynamic Data Exchange*). Microsoft, along with other software and hardware manufacturers, developed a set of standards that was used in Windows to support data exchange. A *standard* is a set of detailed technical guidelines used to establish conformity in software or hardware development. Microsoft then shared the standards so that other software developers could use them when writing their programs designed for Windows.

Because of this collaboration, DDE made it easier to create a compound document. A compound document, as stated earlier, is a document with different elements from different programs. Although each element is created in a different application program, DDE allowed the user to put all these elements into one document. However, DDE was just an early form of this technology.

DDE was supplanted by object linking and embedding (OLE, pronounced Oh-lay). OLE was introduced to improve data exchange. In fact, sometimes OLE is called DDE that works. The principle behind OLE is objects. Remember, an object is an entity that a user can identify because of its properties, operations, and relationships. In object linking and embedding, the object is data. Data can have characteristics (such as animation) and behavior (such as moving on the screen when you click it), but from a software point of view, data is an object.

OLE allows documents created in applications to embed or to link data (objects). When you embed an object in another document, the object remembers what program created it. Thus, you may edit the embedded object in the destination document. For our example, when you select and double-click the drawing in WordPad, the Paint program appears. You can make changes to the drawing (object) in Paint while you are in WordPad. This process is called in-place editing, which is defined later.

When you link an object, the object is not actually in the new document. Instead, the receiving document or container keeps the information about where the object came from. Remember, the object must then be saved in a separate file first. If you link that object to many documents, each one accesses the object, which is actually a file. Whenever the linked object is updated, any document that has a link to that object is automatically updated.

With the release of OLE 2, the latest standard, OLE is no longer an acronym for object linking and embedding. Now the standard includes the following:

In-place editing: When you edit embedded objects, you never leave the client application. The containing program's menus and toolbars are temporarily replaced by those of the object's source program.

Cross-application dragging and dropping: When you select an object, you can drag it out of the server application and drop it into a client document.

Container objects: Objects can contain other objects. Thus, the WordPad document could contain not only the Paint object, but also a sound object and a video object. The WordPad document is then considered a compound document.

OLE automation: You can create scripts or macros that move data between two or more applications by using a programming language such as Visual Basic or Visual Basic for Applications.

OLE technology is a big part of Windows 95. Application software that incorporates and uses Object Linking and Embedding is called *OLE-aware*, or *OLE-compliant*. Some application programs are only servers, others only clients. Some high-end applications, such as the Microsoft Office Professional suite that includes Word, Excel, PowerPoint, and Access can function as both client and server applications. In Windows 95, Paint is a server application and WordPad is a client application.

12.11 Linking and Embedding

When you embed an object, the object is part of the client document. You no longer have any connection to the source document. Whatever changes you make to the object in WordPad are not reflected in the source document in Paint. There does not even have to be a source document. The connection is only to the server application.

For example, imagine that you create a drawing in Paint. You select it and copy it to the Clipboard. You open WordPad and click Edit/Paste. You have two copies of the object (drawing), one in Paint and one in WordPad. You close Paint. You return to WordPad. You add text to the document. Now, you want to change the drawing. You select the object (the drawing) and double-click it. The Paint menu and toolbars appear in place of the WordPad menus and toolbars, even though you are still in WordPad. You edit your drawing. When you are finished, you return to WordPad.

On the other hand, linking an object does not create another copy of the object. Instead, you create a reference or a "link" to the document that contains the data. Thus, when you edit a linked object, you are altering the original information in the original source document with the original source application. The updating can be instantaneous (*automatic links* or *hot links*) or only when you request the update (*manual links* or *cold links*).

Say, for example, that you open Paint, create a drawing, and save it. In linking, you must save the drawing to disk as a file. You then click Edit/Copy. You close Paint. You open WordPad, select Paste Special, and choose Paste Link. You have only *one* copy of the object (drawing)—the data file you saved to disk. You add text to the document. Now, you want to change your drawing. You select the object (the picture) and double-click it. The server application Paint opens, and you edit your original saved file. When you are finished, you return to WordPad.

When you link an object, the object is not part of the client document. There is only a reference, or a pointer, to the original source document. You work with the source document only. Whatever changes you make to the object are reflected in the source document. There must be a source document on the disk.

Linking an object has another advantage. Many programs can use the same link. For example, your object is a logo for your company and is linked to many documents, such as a word processing document and a graphic presentation document. Whenever you update the logo, all documents that are linked to the object immediately have the updated version. Only one copy of the logo exists as a file.

Figure 12.1   *Embedding Objects*

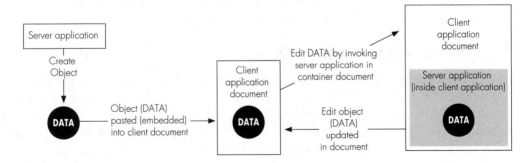

Figure 12.2   Linking Objects

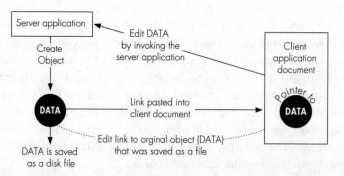

The decision between linking or embedding an object depends on your end purpose. If you want only one copy of an object that belongs to the client document, you would choose to embed the object. Embedding an object is permanent and portable. Because the embedded object resides in the client container, you do not have to worry about the source document. Furthermore, any changes you make to the object will occur only in the current document. Usually when you click Paste, the default is to embed, if the document and the object are OLE-aware. However, this is not always true. Sometimes, the default is to link. If you want to ensure that you are embedding an object, select Paste Special. Usually, the choice on the Paste Special menu will have the word object somewhere in its name.

If, on the other hand, several destination documents are going to use the object and you want each destination document to reflect any changes, you would choose to link the object. Object linking allows you to have only one correct copy of an object. All editing changes are incorporated into whatever destination documents are linked to the object. Documents that use a linked object take up less disk space. Only the pointers to objects are stored in the container document, not the objects themselves. Furthermore, if you are on a network, a linked object can be available to everyone, whereas an embedded object cannot. A disadvantage to linking is that if something happens to the object file, your link is worthless. If all of your documents are linked to a file (the object) and you delete that file, then the documents will only have a pointer, but no object.

12.12 Embedding an Existing Object

An embedded object is data that has been created with a server application program. It may or may not be saved as a file. The object may be part of a document, such as selected rows and columns generated in a spreadsheet program like Excel, or it can be the entire document, such as a drawing created in Paint. You embed an object when you wish to customize it in a specific client application. If you save your original object to a file, you will not affect it. You are only altering what is in your current document.

12.13 Activity—How to Embed an Existing Object

1 Place the Data disk in Drive A.

2 Open **My Computer**. Double-click the **3½ Floppy (A:)** icon.

3 Delete the **ADDRESS MANAGER** and **Clients** folders on your Data disk.

4 In the dialog boxes that appear, click **Yes**.

5 When the folders and files have been deleted, arrange your icons by name and close **My Computer**.

 You made room on your Data disk for new files.

6 Open **WordPad**. Click the **Open** icon on the toolbar.

7 In the **File name** box, key in the following: **A:\Chap12\Person.rtf** Enter

8 Locate the text that is skewed. Double-click it.

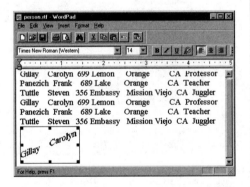

 Nothing happens. You pasted this graphic from Paint into WordPad as a static picture. Thus, you cannot edit it.

9 Click the **New** icon on the toolbar. Click **Rich Text Document**. Click **OK**.

10 Change the point size of the font to **12**.

11 Key in the following text:

Enter
Enter
Enter

Frank and Carolyn Panezich invite you to a dinner dance to celebrate their 10th wedding anniversary. The festivities will be held on November 23rd beginning at 6:00 P.M. at Claes Seafood, Etc., located at 1234 Pacific Coast Highway, Laguna Beach, CA 93669. Enter
Enter
Black Tie Enter
RSVP Enter

 You have created a party invitation. The WordPad screen should look as follows:

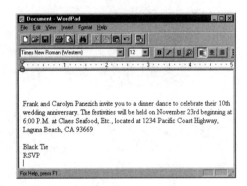

12 Press Ctrl + Home to move to the top of the document.

13 Click **Insert**. Click **Object**.

 Windows 95 maintains a registry of all the programs capable of providing an embedded object. Your list may be different, depending on what programs you have installed on your system. You have the choice of creating a new object (Create New) or using one that already exists (Create from File).

14 Click **Create from File**.

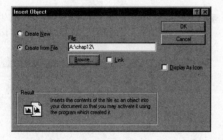

 WordPad remembers that the last place you were was in A:\Chap12. You want to use the drawing Green.bmp, which you created in the last chapter.

15 Key in the following: **A:\Chap11\Green.bmp** **Enter**

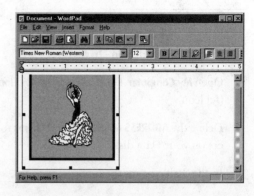

 You inserted your object from a file created earlier. You want to save this file.

16 Click the **Save** icon.

17 In the **File name** text box, key in the following: **A:\Chap12\invite** **Enter**

18 Click once on the picture of the dancer, if it is not selected.

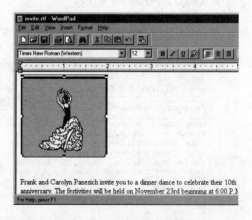

 You can tell that the drawing is selected because it is highlighted and has sizing handles.

19 Click the **Center** icon on the toolbar.

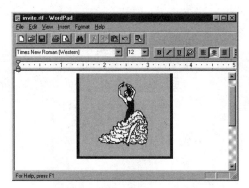

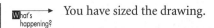 You have a centered picture in your in-vitation. You decide that you are going to change the background color. In addition, you want to add some text to the drawing and make the drawing bigger.

20 Drag the center-left sizing handle and make the drawing reach the one inch mark on the ruler.

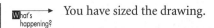 You have sized the drawing.

21 Double-click the drawing.

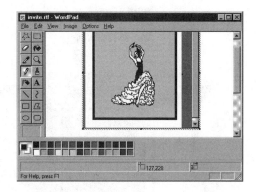

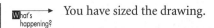 If you look at the title bar, you are still in WordPad, but the menus and toolbars are for Paint, the server application. You are doing in-place editing. You did not have to leave WordPad and load Paint to edit this drawing.

22 Left-click gray. Click the **Fill With Color** tool. Place the tip of the tool in the background and click.

23 Left-click **red**.

24 Click the **Text** tool. Create a text box large enough for the following text:

> **Happy**
>
> **Tenth**
>
> **Anniversary**

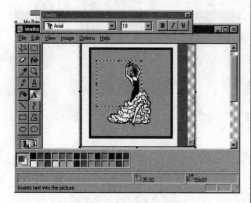

 Now you are ready to key in text.

25 Click **B** for bold on the **Font** toolbar.

26 Press **Enter** once.

27 Key in the following: **Happy** **Enter** **Tenth** **Enter** **Anniversary** **Enter**

28 Click outside the text box.

 You have altered your drawing.

29 Left-click black. Click the **Pencil** tool.

30 Click outside the picture.

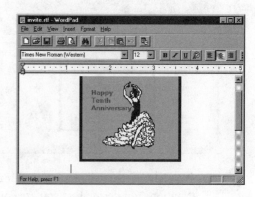

 Your invitation now has an edited drawing.

31 Click the **Save** icon. Close **WordPad**.

32 Open **Paint**. Click File. Click Open.

33 In the **File name** text box, key in the following: **A:\Chap11\Green.bmp** **Enter**

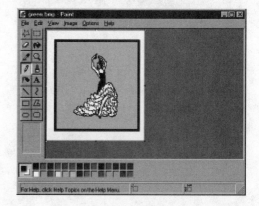

 Your original object stored as Green.bmp has not changed. You edited only the embedded copy of the object in the document called Invite.rtf.

34 Close **Paint**.

 You have returned to the desktop.

12.14 Embedding a New Object

In the last activity, you retrieved an object you had previously created and embedded. When you are working with a document, you often realize that you would like to accomplish a task that your current application does not allow. For instance, you are in WordPad and want to create a drawing. You do not need to exit WordPad and open Paint. You can create and embed an object directly from WordPad.

12.15   Activity—How to Insert a New Embedded Object

1 Open **WordPad**.

2 Click the **Open** icon. In the **File name** text box, key in the following: **A:\Chap12\Invite.rtf** **Enter**

3 Press **Ctrl** + **End** to move to the bottom of the document.

4 Click at the end of **Black Tie**. Press the **Space Bar** twice.

5 Click **Insert**. Click **Object**.

 This time, the Create New button was set. You do not have a file. You simply want to create a drawing that will be embedded in this document. The default choice, Bitmap Image, will open Paint.

6 Click **Bitmap Image**. Click **OK**.

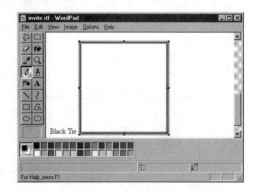

 Again, you are doing in-place editing. You are in WordPad, but have Paint's menus and toolbars.

7 Click **Image**. Click **Attributes**.

8 Be sure **Pels** is selected. Place **60** in both the **Width** and **Height** boxes.

9 Click **OK**.

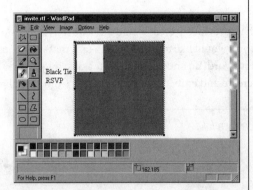

What's
happening? → You want the drawing to be small, so that it will fit next to the words Black Tie.

10 Click the **Polygon** tool. Click the last fill style in the **Tool Options** box. Right-click black. Create two triangles shaped like a tie.

What's
happening? → You have a small drawing of a tie.

11 Right-click **white**. Click the **Pencil** tool.

12 Click outside the picture to return to **WordPad**.

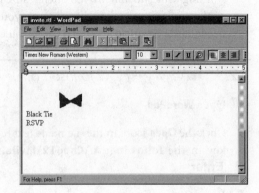

What's
happening? → You now have a drawing of a black tie. You embedded a drawing you just created. This drawing does not exist anywhere as a file, but since you embedding, it does not have to exist as a file.

13 Save the document. Close **WordPad**.

12.16 Editing Objects

Once you embed an object, you can not only edit the object's data, but also its characteristics. You can have the object appear as an icon. The advantage to this is that it not only takes up less room on the screen, but it also takes less space on the disk. If an object is represented by an icon, Windows 95 compresses the image data and then decompresses it when you return it to its real size, which you can do by double-clicking it. Anyone who uses the document can choose whether or not to open the icon to see the information. For instance, you might create a report in Word containing financial calculation objects created in Excel. If you changed the objects to icons in the Word document, only those interested in the numbers would open the icon to see the data. You can also change an object's icon or label.

12.17 Activity—Editing Objects

1 Open **Paint**.

2 Click **Image**. Click **Attributes**. Click **Default**. Click **OK**.

3 Click the **Rectangle** tool. Create a hollow square of about two inches by two inches.

4 Left-click pink. Click the **Fill With Color** tool. Click inside the rectangle you just created.

5 Left-click black. Click the **Text** tool. Create a text box outside the colored rectangle. Click the **B** for bold and set the point size **12**. In the text box, key in the following: **THIS IS A TEST.**

6 Click the **Pencil** tool. Click the **Select** tool. Encircle the letters and drag them to the middle of the rectangle. Click outside the rectangle to deselect it.

What's happening? → You have created a small sample drawing.

7 Click the **Select** tool. Encircle the rectangle. Right-click. Click **Copy**.

8 Close **Paint**. Do not save the image.

9 Open **WordPad**.

10 Click **Edit**. Click **Paste Special**.

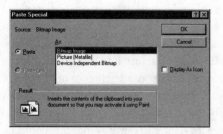

The default is a bitmap image.

11 Click the **Display As Icon** check box to set it. Click **OK**.

Instead of having a drawing, you have an icon representing your drawing.

12 Click outside the sizing box. Double-click the icon.

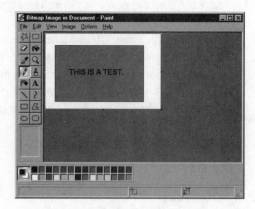

By double-clicking the icon, you caused the image to appear.

13 Click the **Text** tool. In the pink rectangle, draw a text box. Key in the following: **TEST**

14 Click outside the text box.

15 Click **File**.

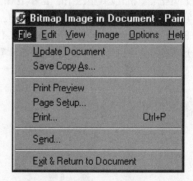

You have changed the drawing. You want to update your document with the change and then return to WordPad.

16 Click **Update Document**.

17 Click **File**. Click **Exit & Return to Document**.

18 Right-click the icon.

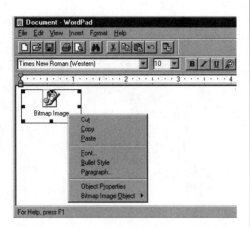

What's happening? You returned to your WordPad document. You then opened the shortcut menu by right-clicking the icon. Since the icon is an object, it has properties. In addition, it is a Bitmap Image Object that can be altered.

19 Click **Object Properties**. Click the **View** tab.

What's happening? Here is where you can change the display back to the actual picture instead of an icon. You can also change the icon or its label. You are going to do both.

20 Click **Change Icon**.

What's happening? You have your choice of icons. You can use the current icon, choose the default for a bitmap image, or choose from a file. Icons are stored in files. You can see the path name to the current icon file in the text box above the icon choices.

21 Click a different icon. In the Label text box, key in the following: **MY SAMPLE DRAWING**

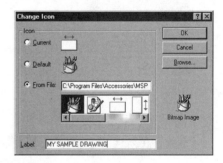

What's happening? You have made your changes.

22 Click **OK**.

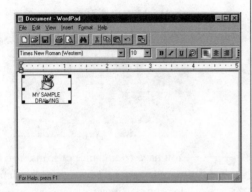

> **What's happening?** You have changed both your icon and your label.

23 Right-click the object. Click **Bitmap Image Object**.

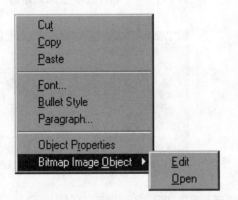

> **What's happening?** You can edit or open your object. If you choose Open, you will open Paint and your drawing will appear.

24 Click **Edit**.

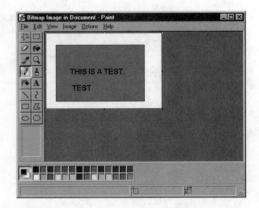

> **What's happening?** You can now do in-place editing.

25 Click the **Ellipse** tool. Draw a circle around the text, **THIS IS A TEST**. Click the **Pencil** tool.

> **What's happening?** You have altered your drawing.

26 Click **File**. Click **Exit & Return to Document**.

27 Right-click the object. Click **Object Properties**. Click the **View** tab. Click the **Display as editable information** command button. Click **OK**. Click outside the drawing to deselect it.

What's happening? → Your object is an icon. You want it to be your drawing.

What's happening? → Your drawing is no longer an icon, but a picture.

28 Close **WordPad**. Do not save the document.

12.18 Sound Objects

Although you have been embedding a drawing, you are not limited to this type of object. You may also embed a sound clip, a video clip, or other types of multimedia objects. The multimedia objects are most useful when embedded in documents created with presentation software packages such as PowerPoint. These packages are designed for public speaking, sales reports, and other types of public presentations. Adding video and sound can greatly increase the impact of presentations. Because these objects "play," there are some hardware requirements. You must have a sound card and video display capable of using these objects.

12.19 Activity—Embedding a Sound Object

Note: If you do not have a sound card, you will not be able to do this activity.

1 Open **WordPad**.

2 Key in the following: **This is a test of embedding a sound file.** Enter Enter

3 Click **Insert**. Click **Object**. Click **Create from File**. Click **Browse**.

4 Locate the **Windows** folder. Double-click it.

> *What's happening?* When you installed Windows 95, you also installed sound files. They are usually kept in the Media folder, under the Windows folder.

5 Double-click **Media**.

> *What's happening?* Again, the files in this folder are dependent on what choices you made when you installed Windows 95. In this example, files that begin with Jungle are additional sound files. Sound files have the extension of .wav. Some basic sounds come with Windows 95, such as the Chimes.wav or the Ding.wav files. These are the sound files that make your computer chime when you exit Windows.

6 Click **Chord.wav**. Click **Insert**.

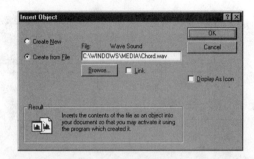

> *What's happening?* You are ready to embed your sound object.

7 Click the check box for **Display As Icon** to set it. Click **OK**. Click outside the icon to deselect it.

> *What's happening?* You have a sound object. A sound file is displayed only as an icon.

8 Double-click the **Wave Sound** icon.

> *What's happening?* You should have heard the sound of a chord.

9 Right-click the **Wave Sound** icon. Click **Object Properties**. Click the **View** tab.

10 Click the **Change Icon** button. Choose the second icon. In the **Label** text box, key in the following: **Double-click to hear a chord.**

> **What's happening?** You have selected a different icon and changed the text for the label.

11 Click **OK**. Click **OK**. Click outside the icon to deselect it.

> **What's happening?** Your icon looks different, but works the same way.

12 Double-click the icon.

> **What's happening?** You hear the chord.

13 Right-click the icon. Point to the **Wave Sound** object. Click **Edit**.

> **What's happening?** You can also edit sound. You are now editing in-place.

14 Click **Effects** on the menu bar of the **Sound Object in Document** window.

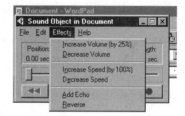

> **What's happening?** Sound editing or any kind of media editing can be, and usually is, complex. You need the proper hardware and software installed. Furthermore, sound and media files are very large. In this case, you are going to do a simple edit on the chord sound. You are going to increase the speed of the sound.

15 Click **Increase Speed (by 100%)**. Close the **Sound Object in Document** window.

16 Double-click the **Sound** icon.

> **What's happening?** The sound should be different because you speeded up its playback.

17 Click **File**. Click **Print**.

> **What's happening?** Your image printed exactly as it appeared on the screen. When you have an object displayed as an icon on the screen, a picture of the icon is printed, not the object itself.

18   Close **WordPad**. Do not save the document.

   You have returned to the desktop.

12.20   Linking an Object

When you choose to link an object, you are working with a single object that must be saved to disk as a file. When you modify the object, you are modifying the original file and any changes you make to it will occur in documents that are linked to that object. You will be affecting the source document and will use the original server application.

12.21   Activity—Linking the Basket Picture

1   Place the Data disk in Drive A. Open **Paint**.

2   Click **File**. Click **Open**. In the **File name** text box, key in the following: **C:\95book\Basket.bmp** Enter

3   Click the **Select** tool. Encircle the basket. Click **Edit**. Click **Copy To**.

4   In the **File name** text box, key in the following: **A:\Chap12\Basket**

5   Click the down arrow in the **Save as type** box. Click **16 Color Bitmap**. Click **Save**.

   You have selected data—an object. You saved it as a file to the Data disk because you are going to link this object. Remember, the first requirement in linking an object is to create a file for that object.

6   Close **Paint**. Open **WordPad**.

7   Click **Insert**. Click **Object**. Click **Create from File**. Click **Browse**.

8   In the **File name** text box, key in the following: **A:\Chap12\Basket.bmp**

9   Click **Insert**.

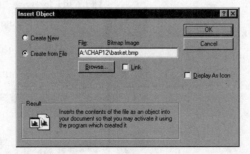

   You want to link the basket file.

10 Click the **Link** check box to set it. Click **OK**. Double-click the basket picture in **WordPad**. (*Note:* arrange the two open widows so you can see both of them. You may have to adjust borders.)

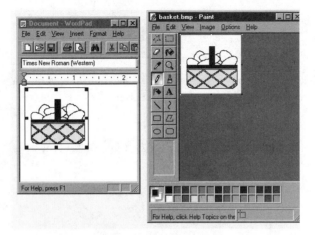

  You opened WordPad and inserted a Paint object. Remember, Paint is the server application, and WordPad is the client application. You then linked your object. When you double-clicked the object in WordPad, the Paint program opened and became the active window. You are not doing in-place editing; you are editing the actual file called A:\Chap12\Basket.bmp.

11 Left-click **yellow**. Right-click **white**. Click the **Eraser/Color Eraser** tool. Right-drag the eraser over the basket. When the yellow basket is white, release the right mouse button.

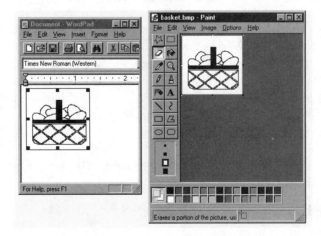

  Your linked object in WordPad changed to reflect the changes made to the object in Paint.

12   Close **Paint**.

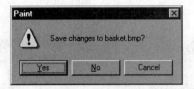

 Note that the dialog box is asking you if you want to save your changes in Paint, not WordPad. The object you are changing is the Basket.bmp file.

13   Click **Yes**.

14   Click the basket object in **WordPad**. Right-click. Click **Object Properties**. Click the **Link** tab.

 Because this is a linked object, you have a new tab, Link. Although the Automatically option button is selected in the Update section, sometimes this does not happen. As of yet, this feature does not always work as advertised. When selected, the Manually option button updates only when you click on the Update Now button. The Open Source button would open Paint and the Break Link button would break the connection between the document and the object file. You would be embedding the object if you chose Break Link.

15   Click **Cancel**.

16   Click **Save As**. Change the file type to **Rich Text Format (RTF)**. In the **File name** text box, key in the following: **A:\Chap12\First.rtf** Enter

17   Close **WordPad**.

 You have returned to the desktop.

12.22 Linking to Many Documents

In the last activity, you created an object, the Basket.bmp file. When you inserted the object in WordPad, you linked it, you did not embed it. The only noticeable difference between linking and embedding was that when you edited the object, you opened Paint itself instead of editing in-place. At this point, however, you have not seen the power of linking. You can see the advantages of linking over embedding when your object is linked to several documents.

12.23 Activity—A Linked Object in Two Documents

1 Open **WordPad**. Click **File**. Click **New**. Click **Rich Text Document**.

2 Click **Insert**. Click **Object**. Click **Create from File**. Click **Browse**.

3 In the **File name** text box, key in the following: **A:\Chap12\Basket.bmp** Enter

4 Click the **Link** check box to set it. Click **OK**.

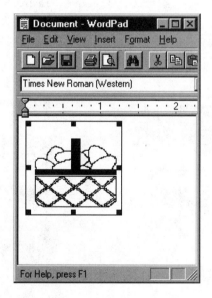

 You have linked your object in your new document.

5 Double-click the basket picture in **WordPad**.

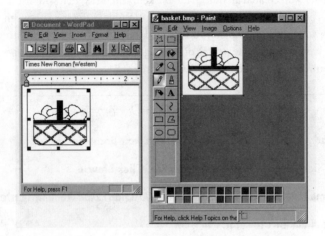

What's
happening?   →   The Paint program again opened and became the active window.

6 Left-click **pink**. Click the **Fill With Color** tool. Color two eggs pink. Left-click **blue**. Color two different eggs blue.

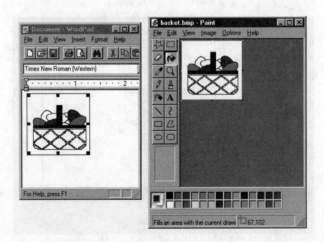

What's
happening?   →   As you changed your egg colors, the object in WordPad also changed colors.

7 Left-click black. Close **Paint**. Click **Yes** to save the changes.

8 Click to deselect the picture in **WordPad**. Press [Enter].

9 Key in the following under the basket: **This is my second basket picture.**

  You have a new document with your linked object in it.

10 Click **Save**. In the **File name** text box, key in the following: **A:\Chap12\Second.rtf** [Enter]

11 Click **File**. Click **Open**. In the **File name** text box, key in the following: **A:\Chap12\First.rtf** [Enter]

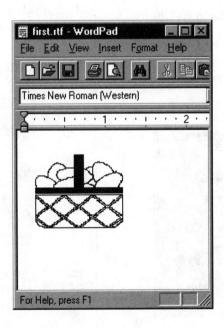

  You closed your second document, the one with the colored eggs. You then opened your first document with no colored eggs. Although you updated the Basket.bmp file, this document's object is not updated with the colored eggs.

12   Double-click the picture.

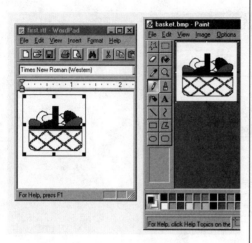

  By double-clicking the picture, you updated the object in your original WordPad file.

13   Close **WordPad**. Click **Yes** to save the file.

14   In Paint, left-click **green**. Click the **Fill With Color** tool. Change some of the diamond-shaped areas on the side of the basket to green. Left-click **black**.

  You closed the WordPad document, but Paint remained opened. You made changes to your object, the Basket.bmp file.

15   Close **Paint** and save the changes to the disk.

16   Open **WordPad**. Open the file called **A:\Chap12\Second.rtf**.

  Although you altered your object, in this document, your linked object was not updated.

17   Right-click the object. Click **Object Properties**. Click the **Link** tab.

  You can update from the property sheet as well.

18 Click **Update Now**. Click **Close**.

 Your document is updated. Any document that uses the object will only be using the contents of the one file, Basket.bmp. You can alter the object within a document or by going directly to the server document to edit the file.

19 Click **Save**.

20 Close **WordPad**.

 You have returned to the desktop.

12.24 Scraps

In many OLE applications, you can select some text, a picture, or any object and drag it onto the desktop or into a folder. When you perform this action, you have created a scrap. A *scrap* is a file that is created when you drag part of a document to the desktop or to a folder on the desktop. When you drag a scrap onto the desktop, Windows 95 gives it a name based on its contents or source. You can rename the scrap the same way you rename any file. A scrap file must originate in a program that supports OLE. There are two methods for creating scrap files: the copy and paste method or the drag-and-drop method. The easiest way to create a scrap is by dragging and dropping, but the source program must be able to support this technique. If this technique is not supported by the source program, you can still create a scrap by selecting the object and clicking Copy. You may then right-click on the desktop and choose Paste.

12.25   Activity—Creating and Using Scraps

1   Open **Paint**.

2   Create a stop sign in **Paint** that looks approximately like the drawing below:

 You have a small drawing, and you are going to turn it into a scrap. Paint does not support drag-and-drop scraps.

3   Click the **Select** tool. Encircle the stop sign. Right-click. Click **Copy**.

4   Close **Paint**. Do not save the document.

5   In an open area on the desktop, right-click. Click **Paste**.

 You have created a scrap.

6   Open **WordPad**. Click **New**. Click **Rich Text Document**. Click **OK**. Size the **WordPad** window so you can see the scrap on the desktop.

7   Left-drag the scrap into the WordPad document. When you are in the document, release the left mouse button.

 You have dragged and dropped the scrap into your document. WordPad supports the dragging and dropping of scraps to and from the desktop.

8   Click outside the picture to deselect it. Press **Enter**.

9   Key in the following: **Now is the time for all good men to come to the aid of their party.**

10   Select this line. Left-drag out of **WordPad** and onto the desktop. When you are on the desktop, release the left mouse button.

 You have created a new scrap with WordPad. Its name contains the first few words of the sentence.

11   In **WordPad**, click the new button on the toolbar. Do not save the current document.

12   Choose **Rich Text Document**. Click **OK**.

13   Left-drag the **WordPad** scrap into the **WordPad** document. When you are in the **WordPad** document, release the left mouse button.

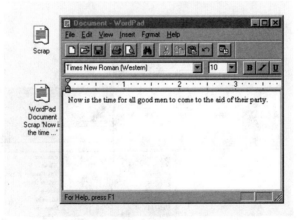

 You have dragged and dropped the scrap back into WordPad.

14 Press **Enter** to move to the next line in **WordPad**.

15 Open **My Computer**. Open the **95book** folder.

16 Arrange the **WordPad** window and the **My Computer** window so that you can see both. You may have to adjust borders.

17 In the **95book** folder, locate the file called **Document Scrap 'STATE CAPITALS...'**

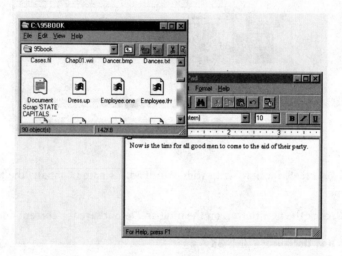

What's happening? → A scrap can be located in a folder.

18 Left-drag the **WordPad Document Scrap** into **WordPad**.

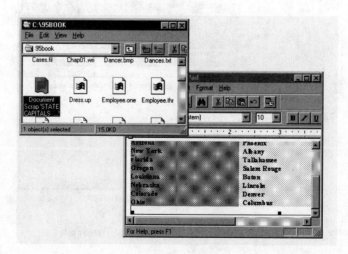

When you left-drag a scrap into a document, the scrap remains located where it was. You are not moving the scrap from one folder to another, but are copying it into a document.

19 Maximize **WordPad**.

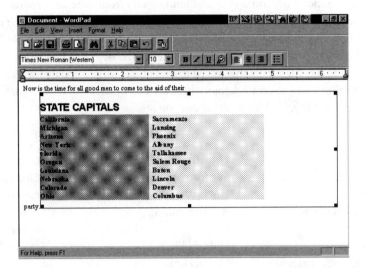

 This file has errors in it. The capital of Oregon is Salem, not Salem Rouge. The capital of Louisiana is Baton Rouge, not Baton. This file is a Microsoft Word object. If you do not have Word for Windows, you cannot edit the text in this object.

20 Click outside the selection to deselect it. Press **Enter** to move to the next line.

21 Restore **WordPad**. Close **WordPad**. Do not save the document.

22 Close the **My Computer** window.

23 Drag the scraps on the desktop to the **Recycle Bin**. Empty the **Recycle Bin**.

 You have returned the desktop to its previous state.

Chapter Summary

In this chapter you learned about sharing data between programs. You were introduced to the different file formats programs use for their data files. You learned more about the Clipboard, a place in temporary memory that allows you to copy and paste information to and from Windows 95 programs. You were introduced to Clipboard Viewer, the tool which allows you to see what is currently on the Clipboard. You learned to print both the screen and an active window, and to alter screen captures with Paint.

You were introduced to object linking and embedding. OLE focuses on data (the object). You learned the basics of linking and embedding objects so that you could link or embed an object created in one program and place it in another document created with another program. The source application is the program that creates the data, and the client application is the one that receives the data. Compound documents are containers that hold objects from different programs. When you embed an object, any OLE-compliant program allows in-place editing of a copy of the object. The object is changed in that document only. To link an object, you must first save it as a file. The object does not appear in the client document; it is only a pointer to the object. When you edit the object, you are editing the saved file. All documents linked to that object will be updated with the new information. Windows 95 allows you to create scraps which are bits of data (an object) that can be dragged and dropped to the desktop, a folder, or other documents.

Key Terms

Automatic links	Embed	Scrap
Client application	File format	Screen capture
Cold links	Hot links	Screen dump
Compound document	In-place editing	Server application
Container	Link	Source document
Container objects	Linked object	Standard
Cross-application dragging and dropping	Manual links	Static exchange
	Object	Supporting
Destination document	Object linking and embedding (OLE)	
DIB Bitmap (Device Independent Bitmap)	OLE-aware	
Dynamic Data Exchange (DDE)	OLE automation	
	OLE-compliant	

Discussion Questions

1. What is a file format?
2. Why are application programs unable to read data files created by a different application programs?
3. A program can be described as supporting a specific file format. Explain.
4. What is a compound document?
5. What is an object?
6. List and explain the three kinds of data exchange.
7. What is a static exchange?
8. Explain the purpose and function of embedding an object.
9. Explain the purpose and function of linking an object.
10. Compare and contrast linking and embedding.
11. When would you use linking?
12. When would you use embedding?
13. Compare and contrast static exchange with dynamic data exchange.

14. What is the purpose of Clipboard?
15. Compare and contrast the Clipboard and the Clipboard Viewer.
16. What is a screen dump?
17. How can you print a screen in Windows?
18. In what ways can you alter a screen capture?
19. In data exchange, there are two parts to the transaction. Name the parts and explain their functions.
20. What is the difference between the source document and the destination document?
21. What is a standard?
22. Explain the purpose and function of OLE.
23. Explain the following terms: in-place editing, cross-application drag and drop, container object, and OLE automation.
24. Explain how to embed an object.
25. If an object is embedded, what will happen to the source document when changes are made to the embedded object?
26. Linking an object does not create another copy of the object. Explain.
27. Compare and contrast linking and embedding an object.
28. Why would you want to have an object appear as an icon?
29. What is a scrap?
30. Explain the purpose and function of scraps.
31. Name two ways you can create a scrap.

True/False Questions

For each question, circle the letter T if the statement is true or the letter F if the statement is false.

T   F   1. All application programs use the same type of file format for their data files.
T   F   2. OLE is an acronym for Object Linking and Executing.
T   F   3. You must open the Clipboard before you can copy data to it.
T   F   4. When you embed an object and edit it, you are editing only the object in the destination document.
T   F   5. If you link an object, you create a reference to the object file.

Completion Questions

Write the correct answer in each blank space provided.

6. The program supplying the linked or edited data is called the _____ .
7. If you wish to save the contents of the Clipboard Viewer, the default file extension assigned is _____ .
8. You _____ an object when you place the actual data in the client document.
9. You _____ an object when you place a reference to the data in the client document.
10. In order to link an object, it must be first _____ as a file.

Multiple Choice Questions

Circle the letter of the correct answer for each question.

11. An example of a compound document is a
    a. Notepad file.
    b. WordPad document with many different fonts.
    c. WordPad document with a Paint picture in it.
    d. none of the above

12. The Clipboard can contain how many objects at one time?
    a. one.
    b. two.
    c. eight.
    d. It depends on how much memory you have.

13. You double-click an object and the program's toolbars change to those found in the source program so that you can edit the object. This process is called
    a. a static exchange.
    b. embedding.
    c. linking.
    d. in-place editing.

14. How do pressing **Alt** + **Print Screen** differ from pressing **Print Screen** only?
    a. Pressing **Alt** + **Print Screen** changes the screen capture into a screen dump.
    b. Pressing **Alt** + **Print Screen** automatically sends the screen capture to a file.
    c. Pressing **Alt** + **Print Screen** captures the active window, whereas pressing **Print Screen** captures the entire screen.
    d. Pressing **Alt** + **Print Screen** captures the entire screen, whereas pressing captures the active window.

15. Which statement is true about a linked object?
    a. The object can be edited in the client document without affecting the original object.
    b. There are two copies of the object, one saved as a file and the other placed in the client document.
    c. The object must be first be saved to disk as a file before it can be linked.
    d. both a and c

Application Assignments

Problem Set I—At the Computer

Problem A

Open **WordPad**. Open the following document: **C:\95book\Media\Books\Mystery.bks**. Select all the text in the file. Copy the text. Open a new file in **WordPad**. Paste the text into the new document.

1. You cut and pasted text from one document to another. To accomplish this task, you used the
   a. embedding technique.
   b. OLE technique.
   c. Clipboard.
   d. Clipboard Viewer.

2. In this task, the data exchange was an example of a _____ exchange.
   a. static
   b. dynamic

Close **WordPad**. Do not save the changes in the original file. Do not save the data to disk.

Problem B

Open **WordPad**. Open the following file: **C:\95Book\Media\Books\Pulitzer.bks**.

3. The winner of the 1991 Pulitzer prize was
   a. Peter Taylor.
   b. Anne Tyler.
   c. John Updike.

Press **Alt** + **Print Screen**. Close **WordPad**. Open **Paint**. Click **Edit**. Click **Paste**.

4. Paint now has a copy (screen capture) of the
   a. WordPad window.
   b. entire desktop.
   c. text only in the WordPad document.

Close **Paint**. Do not save the file to disk.

Problem C

Place the Data disk in Drive A. Open **WordPad**. Change the point size to **14**. Key in the following line of text: **You are cordially invited to the grand opening of a new hobby store, Planes and Stuff.** Press **Enter** two times. Save the file as a **Rich Text Document**. Name it **A:\chap12\plane.rtf**. Insert an object created from the file **C:\95book\plane.bmp**. Select the object in your document and click the **Center** icon on the toolbar.

5. The following has occurred:
   a. Only the drawing became centered.
   b. The text and the drawing became centered.

Double-click the drawing.

6. You have
   a. closed WordPad and opened Paint.
   b. displayed the menus and toolbars for WordPad.
   c. displayed the menus and toolbars for Paint.
   d. kept WordPad open but also opened Paint.

Click the **Text** tool. Click in the banner. Change the point size to **12** and click **Bold** and **Italic**. In the banner, key in the following words: **Planes and Stuff**. Click outside the text box. Return to **WordPad**.

7. You have
   a. embedded the plane object in Plane.rtf.
   b. linked the plane object in Plane.rtf.

8. The following statement is true:
   a. The words Planes and Stuff appear on the banner in both the C:\95book\Plane.bmp and A:\Chap12\Plane.rtf files.
   b. The words Planes and Stuff appear on the banner in C:\95book\Plane.bmp only.
   c. The words Planes and Stuff appear on the banner in A:\Chap12\Plane.rtf only.

Save the file. Close **WordPad**.

Problem D

Open **Paint**. Open the following file: **C:\95book\Plane.bmp**. Save the file as a **16 Color Bitmap** to the Data disk as **A:\Chap12\Logo.bmp**. Close **Paint**. Open **WordPad**. Save the new **WordPad** file as a **Rich Text Document** to the Data disk as **A:\Chap12\Logo.rtf**. Change the point size to **16**. Key in your name and your class section on two separate lines. Center both lines. Press **Enter** twice. Insert and link the object created from the file **A:\Chap12\Logo.bmp**. Double-click the picture.

9. You have
   a. closed WordPad and opened Paint.
   b. closed Paint and opened WordPad.
   c. kept WordPad open and also opened Paint.

In the banner, add the text: **Windows 95**. Center the object. Close **Paint**. Save all changes.

10. You have
    a. embedded the plane object in Logo.rtf.
    b. linked the plane object in Logo.rtf.

11. The following statement is true:
    a. The A:\Chap12\Logo.bmp file was updated to include the words Windows 95 on the banner.
    b. The A:\Chap12\Logo.bmp file was not updated to include the words Windows 95 on the banner.

Save the file. Close **WordPad**.

Problem E

For the following assignment:
1. Open **WordPad**.
2. Open the document **A:\Chap12\Plane.rtf**.
3. Place your name and class section at the top of the document.
4. Save the document.
5. Print it.

Problem F

For the following assignment:
1. Open **WordPad**.
2. Open the document **A:\Chap12\Logo.rtf**.
3. Left-justify your name and class section.
4. Save the document.
5. Print it.

Problem G

For the following assignment:
1. Open **Paint**.
2. Open the document **A:\Chap12\Logo.bmp**.
3. Change the color of the plane to grey.
4. Left-click **black**. Right-click **white**.
5. Close the document. Save the changes.
6. Close **Paint**.
7. Open **WordPad**. Open the document **A:\Chap12\Logo.rtf**.
8. Right-justify your name and class section.
9. Open the **plane** object. Add the word **Plane** in the banner. (If it does not fit in the banner, place the word **Plane** somewhere in the plane object.)
10. Close **Paint**, saving all changes.
11. Save the **WordPad** document.
12. Print it.
13. Close **WordPad**.

Problem H

For the following assignment:

1. Open **Explorer**.
2. In **C:\95book**, locate the scrap labeled **Worksheet Scrap**.
3. Open a new **WordPad** document in the **Rich Text Format**.
4. Key in your name and class section.
5. Drag and drop the scrap into the new document under your name and class section.
6. Save the document as **A:\Chap12\Exp.rtf**.
7. Print the document.
8. Close **WordPad**. Close **Explorer**.

Problem Set II—Brief Essay

For all essay questions, use Notepad or WordPad for your answer. Print your answer.

1. Compare and contrast embedding and linking objects. What are the advantages of embedding an object? Linking an object? When and why would you use each method?
2. What is the purpose of the Clipboard? How can you see its contents? How is it used in sharing data among applications? Consider the following statement: Including the Clipboard and Clipboard Viewer was an asset to Windows 95. Agree or disagree, and provide your reasons for your position.

Problem Set III—Scenario

You work for a company called Balloons and Baskets. The company creates gift baskets and gift balloons for special occasions. You have just been assigned to create a logo for the company's letterhead. A logo is a design that incorporates text and graphics and indicates the purpose of the company. Create a sample letterhead, linking the Basket.bmp object in the Chap12 folder on the Data disk. Alter the Basket.bmp object in the most attractive way you can. The company's name, address, and phone number are: Balloons and Baskets, 1223 Chapman Avenue, Orange, CA 92869, (714) 555-8999. In addition, write a memo to your employer, Ms. Bette Peat, describing the steps you took to create the letterhead. In the memo, include a link to the Basket.bmp file. Save both documents to the Chap12 folder. Print both documents.

Chapter 13

File and System Maintenance

Chapter Overview

By running certain programs designed to keep your disk in good working order, you can learn much about your system and optimize the performance of your hard disk. You can synchronize your files, repair disk errors, store files more efficiently, see what resources your computer is using, back up and restore files, and gain more space on your disks.

In this chapter, you will learn to use different file and system programs. Briefcase will let you synchronize files between computers. You will learn how to use ScanDisk to obtain statistical information about a disk and to repair disk errors. You will use the Disk Defragmenter to optimize the storage of files on a disk. The Resource Meter and System Monitor will let you view the use of your computer resources. The Backup program will allow you to back up and restore files for data protection. You will use DriveSpace to compress your disks to gain additional space. You will also learn about Plug-and-Play.

Learning Objectives

1. Explain the purpose and function of Briefcase.
2. Explain what lost clusters and cross-linked files are, how they occur, and how to correct these problems.
3. Explain the purpose and function of ScanDisk.
4. Compare and contrast contiguous and noncontiguous files.
5. Explain how the Disk Defragmenter can help optimize disk performance.
6. List and explain the two functions of disk caching programs.
7. Explain the purposes and functions of virtual memory and swap files.
9. Explain the purposes and functions of the System Monitor and the Resource Meter.
8. Compare and contrast full and incremental backups.
9. Explain the importance of and procedures for backing up, restoring, and comparing files.
10. List and explain the purposes and functions of the two types of disk compression programs.
11. Explain the purpose and function of DriveSpace.
12. Explain the purpose and function of Plug and Play.

Student Outcomes

1. Create and use a briefcase.
2. Use ScanDisk to repair disk problems.
3. Use the Disk Defragmenter to optimize disk performance.
4. Obtain information about virtual memory.

5. Use the Resource Meter and System Monitor to display how your system is being used.
6. Back up files.
7. Restore and compare files.

13.1   Synchronizing Files

Today, mobile computing is becoming more and more prevalent. You might have a desktop computer both at home and at the office and a notebook computer as well. You are working on a project at the office and may want to transfer those files to your home computer. If you are going out of town, you may want to transfer those files to your notebook. You will have created multiple copies of the same files. With all of this transferring, it becomes difficult to know which set of files is the most current.

Windows 95 provides a utility program called Briefcase that assists you in *synchronizing files*. When you synchronize files, you want to compare the dates and times of the various copies of these files to identify the most current copy. Instead of your having to determine which file is most current, Briefcase will automatically update your files so that they are all identical. It can tell you which files have changed so that you can select which version you wish to keep. You can create more than one briefcase.

Essentially, Briefcase allows you to move your files to a floppy disk, modify those files when you are away from your original machine, and then update the original files when you return to your computer. One major drawback to using Briefcase occurs when you have a large file or files that will not fit onto a floppy disk. In that case, Briefcase cannot help you out.

If you chose a typical installation when you installed Windows 95, you did not install Briefcase. To install it, use Add/Remove Programs in the Control Panel. Once you have installed Briefcase from the Add/Remove Programs, you will no longer find it listed in Accessories. Instead, Briefcase is added to all your Send To shortcut menus, as well as to the right-click shortcut menu of the desktop as a New option. You create new briefcases from the right-click menu.

When working with your computer in a professional environment, you will primarily be working on the hard disk. But since you are in a learning environment, you are going to learn to use Briefcase in an artificial environment so that you do not harm files or folders on the hard disk. Thus, you will create a temporary folder on the desktop, copy files to it, and then copy those files to the Briefcase. If you were working on the hard disk, you would not need to create a temporary folder to store the copied files. You would drag and drop the files you wished to synchronize directly from their folder on the hard drive into the Briefcase.

13.2   Activity—Using Briefcase

Note: Check with your lab instructor to see if you can do this activity.

1   Right-click the desktop. Point to **New**. Click **Folder**. Name the folder **Temp**.

2   Open **Explorer**. In the **95book** directory, select **April.txt** and **Bye.txt**.

3   Click **Edit**. Click **Copy**. Close **Explorer**.

4   Double-click **Temp**. Click **Edit**. Click **Paste**.

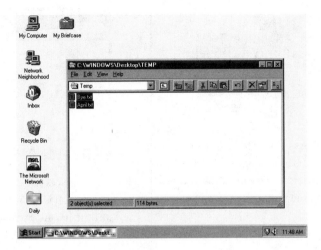

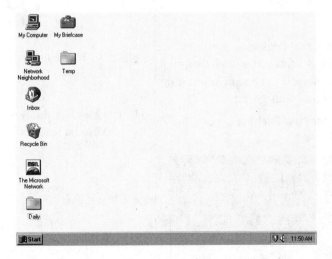 You have created a folder and placed two files in it.

5   Close the **Temp** window. Arrange the icons by name on the desktop.

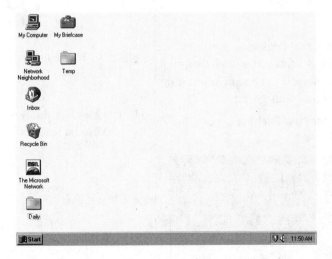

 You see your new folder on the desktop. You may also see the My Briefcase icon. Rather than using My Briefcase, you are going to create a new briefcase. You can have more than one briefcase, and you can create a new briefcase at any time.

6   Right-click on the desktop. Point to **New**.

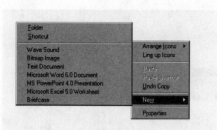

> **What's happening?** If Briefcase is not listed on the menu, then Briefcase was not installed. On this system, Briefcase was installed and is a choice on the menu.

7   Click **Briefcase**.

> **What's happening?** You have two briefcases, My Briefcase and New Briefcase. This is how you create a briefcase if you do not have one or if you want another.

8   Double-click the **New Briefcase** icon.

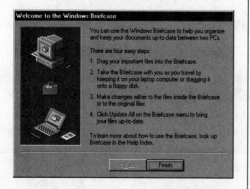

> **What's happening?** A screen appears telling you about Briefcase and how to use it.

9   Click **Finish**.

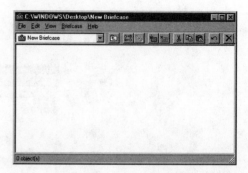

> **What's happening?** Briefcase is a directory created on the desktop. It is not just a regular folder, because it has its own command on the menu bar.

10   Close **New Briefcase**. Right-click **New Briefcase**. Click **Rename**. Key in the following in the **Rename** text box: **Testing** [Enter]

> **What's happening?** You changed the name from New Briefcase to Testing.

11   Double-click the **Temp** folder. Click **April.txt** and **Bye.txt** to select them.

12 Drag them to the **Testing briefcase** icon. Double-click the **Testing briefcase**.

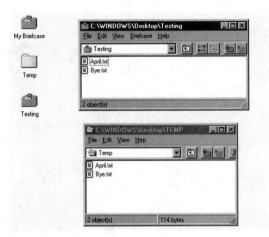

What's happening? Although you left-dragged the files, you did not move them, but copied them to the Testing briefcase.

13 Close the **Testing briefcase** window. Close the **Temp** window. Place the Data disk in Drive A.

14 Right-click the **Testing briefcase**. Point to **Send To**. Click the **3½ Floppy (A:)** icon.

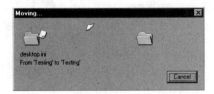

What's happening? Because this is a Briefcase operation, the Testing briefcase was moved to the disk in Drive A, not copied. If you look on your desktop, you will no longer see the Testing briefcase icon.

15 Double-click My Computer. Double-click Drive A.

 → The Testing briefcase is now on Drive A.

16 Double-click the **Testing** briefcase. Double-click **April.txt**.

17 At the bottom of the file, add the following line: **I AM USING BRIEFCASE**.

What's happening? → In the Testing briefcase, you opened the file April.txt and added text to it.

18 Click **File**. Click **Save**. Close **NotePad**. Click the **Up One Level** button to move to the top of the Drive A structure.

What's happening? → You have updated a file on the floppy disk drive. Now, you want to update your original file.

19 Drag the **Testing** briefcase to the desktop.

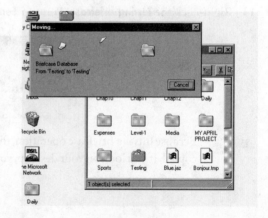

What's happening? → You are moving the Testing briefcase back to the desktop.

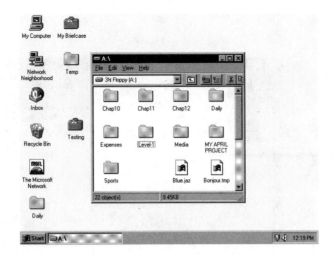

What's happening? The Testing briefcase is no longer on Drive A but on the desktop.

20 Close the **Drive A** window.

21 Double-click the **Testing** briefcase icon. Click **Briefcase** on the menu bar.

What's happening? You are going to update your files.

22 Click **Update All**.

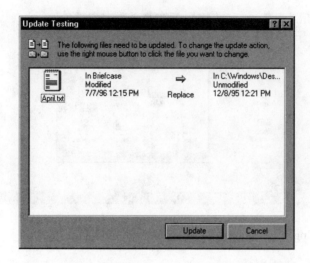

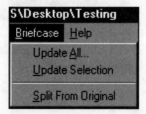

You are informed of the file that changed. You are asked if you want to update the file in the C:\Windows\Desktop\Temp folder with the file from the floppy disk.

23 Click **Update**.

24 Click **April.txt** to select it. Click **Briefcase** on the menu bar.

You have some additional choices. You may choose to update only a specific file. You also have a Split From Original choice. If you choose this option, you will have two separate files that are no longer related.

25 Click outside the menu to close it. Close the **Testing briefcase** window.

26 Double-click the **Temp** folder. Double-click **April.txt**.

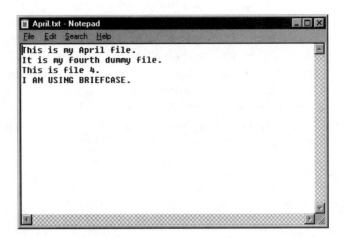

The file April.txt was updated. Your files are now synchronized.

27 Close **Notepad**. Close the **Temp** folder window.

28 Drag the **Testing** briefcase and **Temp** folder into the **Recycle Bin**. Empty the **Recycle Bin**.

You have removed this briefcase, but you can create a new one at any time.

13.3   Protecting Your Data

It is probably no surprise to you that errors can happen on a computer. Errors that you have no control over can cause havoc to your data. Remember, the FAT is the map to all the data on your disk. If the FAT is damaged, you lose access to your data. The FAT can be damaged for a variety of reasons, including a bad spot on a disk or a power surge. A FAT can become corrupted and can report bogus errors such as an incorrect file size, lost clusters, or a cross-linked file. To solve this problem, you are provided with the ScanDisk program, which can correct a host of errors.

It is recommended that ScanDisk be run on a regular basis to prevent errors. Before you run ScanDisk, it is important to close any programs that are open, including screen savers, Microsoft Office, and virus-checking programs. Since ScanDisk is dealing with the FAT and the root directory table, open programs can cause a loss of data, corrupt files, and produce a host of other catastrophic errors.

13.4   Lost Clusters

The file allocation table (FAT) and directory work in conjunction. Every file has an entry in the directory table. The file entry in the directory table points to the first starting cluster in the FAT. If the file is longer than one cluster, which it usually is, the FAT has a pointer that leads it to the next cluster and the next cluster and so on. These pointers *chain* all the data together in a file. If the chain is broken (a lost pointer), the disk ends up with *lost clusters*, which means that these clusters are incorrectly marked as used in the FAT and unavailable for new data. In other words, the FAT knows that the clusters are occupied by data, but does not know to which file the clusters belong. Look at Figure 13.1. The FAT looks normal. Clusters 3, 4, and 6 are a chain. But the FAT does not know to which file this chain belongs. There is no entry in the directory. Hence, these are lost clusters.

Figure 13.1   Lost Clusters

Root Directory Table

File Name	File Extension	Date	Time	Other Info	Starting Cluster Number

File Allocation Table

Cluster Number	Status
1	in use
2	in use
3	4
4	6
5	in use
6	end

Clusters 3, 4, and 6 have data, are linked together,
but have no file entry in the directory table.

Since these lost clusters belong to no file, they cannot be retrieved. The data becomes useless. Windows 95 cannot write other data to these lost clusters, so you lose space on the disk. This phenomenon occurs for a variety of reasons. The most common explanation is that a user did not exit a program properly. Often, when you interrupt this process, the data will not be properly written to the disk. Other times, power failures or power surges cause clusters to be lost.

ScanDisk offers two options to repairing lost clusters: Convert to files or Free. The first option will convert lost file fragments into files so that you may view the contents to determine whether there is any data in them that you want. The files are stored in the root directory and have names such as File0000.chk, File0001.chk, and so on. ScanDisk increments the numbers to make each converted file unique. If you choose this option, once the process is complete, you will have recovered your data. The data in these files is often useless. You typically delete these files to free up disk space. See Figure 13.2.

Figure 13.2   Repairing Lost Clusters and Converting Them to Files

Root Directory Table

File Name	File Extension	Date	Time	Other Info	Starting Cluster Number
FILE0000	CHK	4-15-94	11:23		3

File Allocation Table

Cluster Number	Status
1	in use
2	in use
3	4
4	6
5	in use
6	end

Clusters 3, 4, and 6 now belong to FILE0000.CHK after you choose Y.

The second option is to choose Free. The process is the same, but this alternative causes ScanDisk to automatically delete these files for you. ScanDisk places 0s in the lost clusters, making them empty and available once again. The lost fragments are gone. Figure 13.3 demonstrates this.

Figure 13.3 Repairing Lost Clusters by Choosing the Free Option

Root Directory Table

File Name	File Extension	Date	Time	Other Info	Starting Cluster Number

File Allocation Table

Cluster Number	Status
1	in use
2	in use
3	0
4	0
5	in use
6	0

Choosing N frees up clusters 3, 4, and 6 for data but does not assign a file entry for them in the root directory table.

13.5   Cross-Linked Files

A cross-link occurs when two or more files claim the same cluster simultaneously. The files that are affected are called *cross-linked files*. The data in a crossed-linked cluster is usually correct for only one of the cross-linked files, but it may not be correct for any of them. Figure 13.4 gives an example of what happens when files are cross-linked.

Figure 13.4   Cross-Linked Files

Root Directory Table

File Name	File Extension	Date	Time	Other Info	Starting Cluster Number
MY	FIL	4-15-94	11:23		1
HIS	FIL	4-15-94	11:23		3

File Allocation Table

Cluster Number	Status
1	MY.FIL
2	MY.FIL
3	HIS.FIL
4	**MY.FIL HIS.FIL**
5	HIS FIL
6	MY.FIL

In the example above, My.fil thinks it owns clusters 1, 2, 4, and 6. His.fil thinks it owns clusters 3, 4, and 5. Thus, both My.fil and His.fil think that cluster 4 is part of their chain. If you try to use or delete a cross-linked file, you may further damage the data in them, or your program may fail. ScanDisk offers three options to correct cross-linked files: Delete, Make Copies, or Ignore. Delete and Ignore are self-explanatory. Make Copies is an attempt to save the data. ScanDisk will make a separate copy of each cross-linked cluster for each affected file.

ScanDisk will also repair problems with DriveSpace drives. DriveSpace is a software solution provided by Windows 95 that increases your existing disk space by compressing a disk. A disk compression program does not actually make your hard disk larger; instead, it pulls some software tricks to make it seem as if your disk is larger.

13.6 Activity—Using Scandisk

Note: The Data disk should be in Drive A.

1 Double-click **My Computer**. Right-click the **Drive A** icon. Click **Properties**. Click **Tools**.

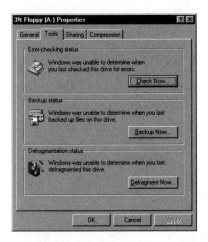

 You are interested in the Error-checking status. Windows 95 does not know the last time you checked this disk. When you choose Error-checking status, you are invoking the ScanDisk program.

2 Click **Check Now** in the **Error-checking** status box.

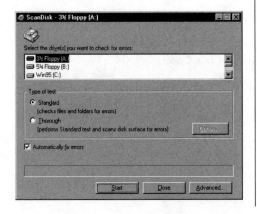

 Since Drive A was already selected from My Computer, it is highlighted in the Select the drive(s) list box. You have two options under Type of test: Standard or Thorough. You can choose between speed and completeness. The Standard test is acceptable for the usual testing of a disk. You use Thorough occasionally or when you think you might have a disk problem. Thorough takes a much longer time to run because it individually tests each sector of your disk to see if it is reliable enough to hold data. If ScanDisk has any trouble reading or writing to a sector during this test, it will try to move the data to a known good sector. In addition, the Automatically fix errors check box may be set to insure that errors are fixed automatically.

3 Click **Thorough** to set it. Click the **Options** command button.

 If you choose Thorough, you can make other choices. You can speed up the time that Thorough takes by selecting System area only (it checks the FAT and directory tracks) or Data area only (it checks the part of the disk that actually contains data). For the most reliable test, you would check System and data areas. If you choose Do not perform write-testing, your disk will only be checked for readability, not writablity. You probably will not use the last choice, because if you have errors, you should have them corrected.

4 Click **Cancel**. Click **Standard** to set it. Click **Automatically fix errors** to unset it.

5 Click **Advanced**.

 Each area has option buttons. If you wish to know what each option does, click and drag the question mark to the option you want to know about and click again. The default settings are acceptable.

6 Set the options to match those shown in the screen capture following Step 5.

7 Click **OK**.

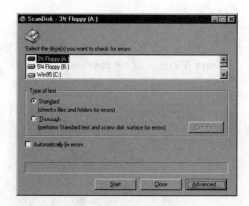

 You have selected your options. Be sure Drive A is selected.

8 Click **Start**.

 ScanDisk has completed its test and has found no problems with the disk in Drive A.

9 Click **Close**. Click **OK**.

10 Close the **My Computer** window.

11 Click **Start**. Point at **Programs**. Point at **Accessories**. Point at **System Tools**.

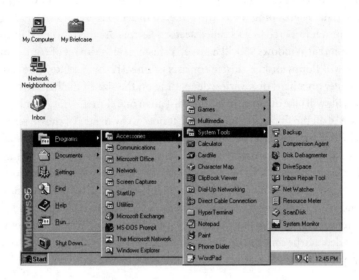

What's happening? → You may also use menus to use ScanDisk.

12 Click **ScanDisk**.

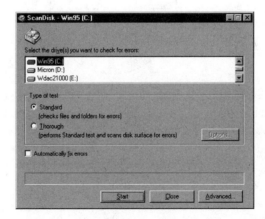

What's happening? → As you see, you are back at the same dialog box. The only difference is that Drive C is the default drive to be checked.

13 Click **Close**.

13.7   Contiguous and Noncontiguous Files

Contiguous means being in contact or touching. What does this have to do with files? Windows 95 keeps track of data by grouping them into a file. In order to store and retrieve the files, Windows 95 divides a disk into numbered blocks called sectors. Sectors are then grouped into clusters. A cluster is the smallest unit that Windows 95 will handle. A cluster is always a set of contiguous sectors. On a 1.2-MB or a 1.44-MB floppy disk, a cluster consists of one 512-byte sector. The number of sectors that make up a cluster on a hard disk varies, depending on the size of the hard drive.

Usually, a file will take up more space on a disk than one cluster. Thus, Windows 95 has to keep track of the location of all the file's parts on the disk. It does so by means of the directory and the FAT.

The FAT (file allocation table) keeps a record of the cluster numbers each file occupies. As Windows 95 begins to write files on a new disk, it makes an entry in the disk's directory for that file and updates the FAT with the cluster numbers used to store that file. Windows 95 writes the data to disk based on the next empty cluster. As Windows 95 begins to write the file to a disk, it writes the information in adjacent clusters. Windows 95 wants all the file information to be next to each other and, thus, tries to write to adjacent clusters because it is easier to retrieve or store information when it is together. When this occurs, the file is considered to be **contiguous**. For example, if you began writing a letter to your senator, it would be stored on your disk in the manner shown in Figure 13.5.

Figure 13.5   One File in Clusters

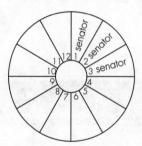

The clusters with nothing in them are simply empty spaces on the disk. Now, you decide to write a letter to your mother. Windows 95 writes this new file to the next adjacent cluster, which would begin with cluster 4, as shown in Figure 13.6.

Figure 13.6   Contiguous Files in Clusters

These two files, Senator and Mom are contiguous. Each part of each file follows on the disk. Now, you decide to add a comment to your senator letter, making the Senator file bigger. When Windows 95 tries to write the letter to the disk, it looks for the next empty cluster, which is cluster 7. It would appear as shown in Figure 13.7.

Figure 13.7   Noncontiguous Files in Clusters

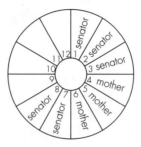

The parts of the file named Senator are separated. The process becomes more complicated as you add and delete files. For example, if you delete the file Senator, the FAT marks clusters 1, 2, 3, 7, and 8 as available, even though the data actually remain on the disk. When you delete files, only the entries in the directory table and FAT are altered, to save time in the deletion process. You then decide to develop a Phone file, as shown in Figure 13.8.

Figure 13.8   Adding a File

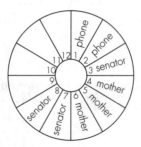

Next, you decide to write a letter to your friends Joe and Mary, add to the Phone file, and add to the letter to your mother. The disk would look like the one in Figure 13.9.

Figure 13.9   Adding More Files

The parts of these files are broken up and are no longer stored in adjacent clusters. They are now known as *noncontiguous* or *fragmented files*. If the disk is comprised of noncontiguous files, it can be called a *fragmented disk*. Windows 95 will take longer to read noncontiguous files because the read/write heads must move around the disk to find all the parts of a file.

13.8   Optimizing Performance on Disks

To fix a fragmented disk, you need a defragmenting utility program, sometimes called a defragger or a disk optimization program. Sometimes these programs are called disk compression programs, but that is a misnomer. These programs do not compress data. Defragging programs literally move data around on the disk to make files contiguous. These programs that must rewrite the directory table and the FAT so that the new locations of the files are available. In its System Tools menu, Windows 95 provides a utility called Disk Defragmenter. Figure 13.10, Defragging a Disk, shows what a disk looks like before and after you run the utility. EOF stands for the special end of file marker.

Figure 13.10   Defragging a Disk

Before Defragmentation			After Defragmentation		
FAT Clusters	Pointers	Data	FAT Clusters	Pointers	Data
1	2	MYFILE.TXT	1	2	MYFILE.TXT
2	4	MYFILE.TXT	2	3	MYFILE.TXT
3	5	YOUR.FIL	3	4	MYFILE.TXT
4	9	MYFILE.TXT	4	EOF	MYFILE.TXT
5	7	YOUR.FIL	5	6	YOUR.FIL
6	8	THIS.ONE	6	7	YOUR.FIL
7	EOF	YOUR.FIL	7	EOF	YOUR.FIL
8	10	THIS.ONE	8	9	THIS.ONE
9	EOF	MYFILE.TXT	9	10	THIS.ONE
10	EOF	THIS.ONE	10	EOF	THIS.ONE

The Disk Defragmenter program gives the user you several choices. You can pick full defragmentation, which takes the longest. It moves files around until they are stored contiguously on the disk. All files with data in them are moved to the front of the disk for fastest access time, freeing up a large amount of space. There are no spaces between the files. If you simply defragment the files, it will also make the files contiguous. However, it will not move the files to the front of the disk and it will leave spaces between the files, if necessary. This is much faster to run than the full optimization. You may also choose to consolidate free space only for maximum efficiency in the storage of new files. The Disk Defragmenter will make a recommendation as to which method it prefers, but you can always override it.

You should run ScanDisk prior to running the Disk Defragmenter. Like ScanDisk, you should also close any open programs such as screen savers or virus checking programs prior to running Disk Defragmenter. In addition, you should be sure to have plenty of time to run the Disk Defragmenter. A good time to run the program is overnight when you are away from the computer. If you run it every couple of weeks, depending on your computer use, the program will not take as long to run, because it has less to do.

You *must* use the Disk Defragmenter program that comes with Windows 95. Although Disk Defragmenter is safe, it is directly manipulating your disk. Therefore, you should back your disk up before beginning the Disk Defragmenter. You can use the program on compressed disks, but not on a network drive.

13.9   Activity—Using the Disk Defragmenter

1   Place the Data disk in Drive A.

2   Double-click **My Computer**. Right-click the **Drive A** icon. Click **Properties**. Click the **Tools** tab.

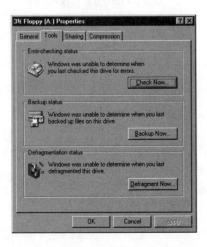

 When you look at the Tools tab, you are informed of when the disk in question was last checked for errors, backed up, or defragged. You can start any of these operations from this property sheet, or you can choose to use the menus.

3   Close the property sheet. Close the **My Computer** window.

4 Click **Start**. Point at **Programs**. Point at **Accessories**. Point at **System Tools**. Click **Disk Defragmenter**.

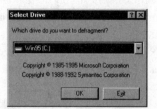

What's happening? → You are asked which drive you want to defragment.

5 Click the down arrow in the drop-down list box. Click **Drive A**. Click **OK**.

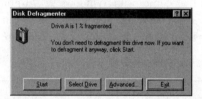

What's happening? → In this example, the Disk Defragmenter program is telling you that you do not need to defragment this disk. However, you may do so if you want.

6 Click **Advanced**.

What's happening? → Here is the place to make choices. In addition to choosing a defragmentation method, you may also choose to check for disk errors and to save your settings.

7 Unset **Check drive for errors**. Set **This time only. Next time use the defaults again.**

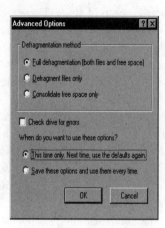

What's happening? → You have made your selection.

8 Click **OK**. Click **Start**.

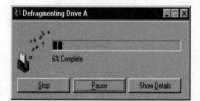

What's happening? → A progress box tells you how close to completion the process is.

9 Click **Show Details**.

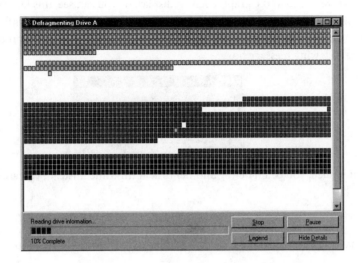

 You see a graphic of what is happening on the disk in Drive A. Different colored squares are being moved around. Files are being read and then written to a new area. You can find out what each color means.

10 Click **Legend**.

 The colors change as different operations occur. The color chart tells you what each color means.

11   Click **Close**.

 You have returned to the graphic screen display. As you can see, this takes some time. You can imagine how long it could take for a gigabyte hard drive. This is why users like to defrag the hard disk when they do not intend to use the computer for a while. When the process is complete, you see the following message box:

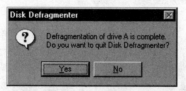

 If you wished, you could defrag another disk at this time. Instead, you are going to stop.

12   Click **Yes**.

 You have defragmented the Data disk and have returned to the desktop.

13.10 Disk Caching

Disk caches occupy an area in memory that Windows 95 looks to for necessary information before going to disk. Disk caches are used because it is faster to go to memory than to go to disk. When you use *disk caching*, your system has to access the hard disk less frequently. Disk caching programs have two functions, read caches and write caches. A *read cache* intercepts, makes a copy, and places into memory whatever file you have read. When a program makes a request to Windows 95 for data, the caching program intercepts the request and checks to see if it already has the requested information in memory. If it does, it passes the data to the program. If the cache does not have the required information, it reads the disk, keeps a copy of the requested information in the cache, and passes the data to the program. See Figure 13.11.

Tom: Figure 15.1 DOS pwp, page 717

Caching programs are smart. They assume that if you read a sector of the disk, you will probably want to read the same sector again soon. They also assume that you will probably want the next sector of data, even if you have not yet asked for it, so they will also load that sector. They try to set priorities by anticipating what you might need. As the cache gets filled, the caching program will discard the oldest or least used data. If you have not previously asked for the data, the disk will have to be read.

When the caching program finds what it needs in memory, it is considered a "hit." You can think of a hit as an incident when the caching program has the data in memory and a disk read is avoided, therefore saving processing time. A "miss" would be the opposite—the data was not in memory and a disk read was mandatory, taking processing time. Read caching is very safe. Since the data is also on disk, even if you have a power failure while using a cache program, your data is safe.

Write caching is the opposite of read caching. When a program wants to write data to disk, the cache makes a copy of it and holds the data in the memory cache until a specified time period has elapsed or the system is less busy, at which time the data is written to disk with a minimum impact on performance. Thus, when you save a file to disk, instead of replacing the file on the hard drive, Windows 95 simply writes back to the saved file in cache memory, and the file in the cache is marked as *dirty data*. Write caching can be more dangerous than read caching, since you may think that the data was saved when in fact it was not. However, anything that reduces the number of times a disk has to be accessed and that improves performance is a benefit.

Caching is a very important element in the multitasking Windows 95 environment. When you are running many programs at the same time, Windows 95 has a big job to do. It must keep each program happy and supply it with the data it needs (disk reads) or take the data from the program to save to disk (disk writes). The Windows 95 file system must keep track of all these program requests so that the user thinks things are happening simultaneously.

Windows 95 has a new disk caching system called VCACHE (virtual cache), which decides how to handle caching according to the demands of the system. The caching program does not use a fixed size in memory for the cache. Windows 95 takes whatever free memory you have for disk caching. As memory fills up with programs, Windows 95 allocates less memory to disk caching. Windows 95 uses read caching with data from all sources—floppy drives, hard drives, CD-ROM drives, and network drives. However, it cannot write cache CD-ROMS or network drives.

13.11 Virtual Memory and the Swap File

In order to boost performance, Windows 95 uses what is called *virtual memory*. Where disk buffering uses memory to improve performance, virtual memory uses the hard disk as "scratch space" when it runs out of memory. When you are running several programs and begin to run out of memory, Windows 95 moves programs from memory to a special *swap file* on the hard disk. When memory is freed up, Windows 95 restores those programs in the swap file back to memory. Windows 95 uses your hard disk as an extension of computer memory. This "memory" on the hard drive is called virtual memory.

Programs today are so large that when they are loaded into memory, not all parts of them are used. For instance, if you are using a word processor and a drawing package such as Paint, both programs are in memory. If the word processor has a spell-checking feature that you are not currently using, Windows 95 will place that unused portion of the program in the swap file. Later, when you wish to spell-check your document, Windows 95 might place the unused Stretch/Skew portion of the Paint program in the swap file so that it can reload the spelling checker. Usually, the only portions of a program that need to be in memory are those that are actively being used.

To handle this exchange, Windows 95 creates a temporary swap file. The swap file begins small, but increases in size as necessary. Windows 95 increases and decreases the swap file as needed. By default, Windows 95 places the swap file on the same disk on which Windows 95 is installed.

Windows 95 automatically handles settings for disk caching and virtual memory. There is seldom a reason to change the settings. If you are curious about the settings, you can look at them in the System Properties dialog box. The best solution to memory and disk resources is to have as much memory and as large a hard drive as you can.

13.12 Activity—Looking at Virtual Memory and Disk Caching

1 Double-click **My Computer**. Double-click **Control Panel**. Double-click the **System** icon.

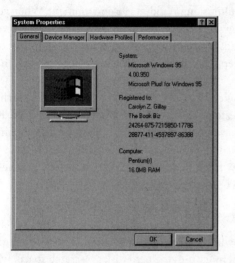

 This tabbed dialog box gives you information about your system. Your report will vary, depending on your system. On this computer system, Windows 95 and Microsoft Plus! are installed. It is a Pentium computer with 16 MB of memory.

2 Click the **Performance** tab.

 The Performance property sheet gives information about how much memory is installed on this computer and other details about the 32-bit access file system that is installed. As far as Windows 95 is concerned, this computer is configured for the best performance.

3 Click **File System**.

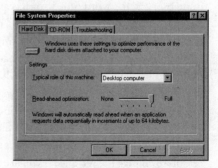

 The only settings you have to make for disk caching are the type of computer you are using and the optimization, which can range from none to full.

4 Click the down arrow in the **Typical role of this machine** drop-down list box.

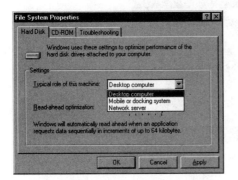

 Your choices are a desktop computer, a laptop, or a network computer.

5 If you have a **CD-ROM** tab, click it; otherwise look at the example.

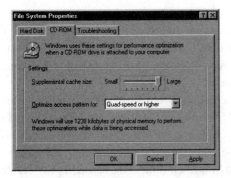

 On this system, the Supplemental cache size is set to Large, although the range can be set from Small to Large.

6 Click the down arrow in the **Optimize access pattern for** drop-down list box.

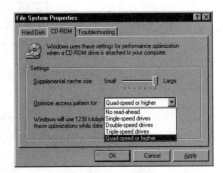

 Your choices for CD-ROM disk caching are No read-ahead, which is no caching, and ranges for the type of CD-ROM drive you have.

7 Click outside the drop-down list box to close it. Click the **Troubleshooting** tab.

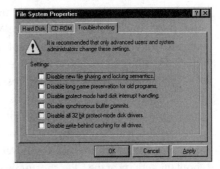

 There is a warning icon and a warning message informing you that unless you know what you are doing, you should not change these settings. This statement is absolutely true. The only setting you might change is to set Disable write-behind caching for all drives. You would only do this if you had an unstable power supply and were worried about having cached data written to the hard disk. Remember, write caching is more dangerous than read caching.

8 Click **Cancel**. Click the **Virtual Memory** tab.

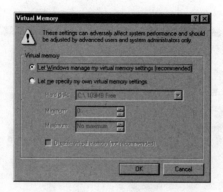

 Let Windows manage my virtual memory settings is set. This is as it should be. Again, unless you have a very specific set of circumstances, Windows 95 knows best how to manage virtual memory.

9 Click **Cancel**. Close **System Properties**. Close the **Control Panel** window.

13.13 Monitoring Your System

Windows 95 provides two programs, the Resource Meter and System Monitor, to monitor the resources of your system. The Resource Meter provides a graphical display of the use of system resources and your resource use percentage. It also reports on the GDI (Graphical Device Interface), which describes the graphical resource use percentage.

The System Monitor tracks the file system, the kernel, and the memory manager. By monitoring the file system, this program provides statistics about different speeds of disk access, both reads and writes. It also can track dirty data, the data written back to cache and not yet written to disk. The *kernel* is the core of the operating system. It is the portion of the system that manages files and memory, launches applications, and allocates resources. When System Monitor monitors the kernel, it provides statistics about the activity of the CPU, the number of virtual machines, and the number of threads. By monitoring the memory manager, it provides statistical data on such topics as the disk cache size and available memory. System Monitor provides these displays in a variety of chart formats to show how your system is being used.

13.14 Activity—Using the Resource Meter and System Monitor

1 Click **Start**. Point at **Programs**. Point at **Accessories**. Point at **System Tools**. Click **Resource Meter**.

> **What's happening?** If you have never used this program before, you may get this information box. You are informed that by running this program, you are increasing your use of system resources.

2 Click **OK**.

> **What's happening?** Nothing seems to be happening. Look at the taskbar.

> **What's happening?** The green icon is the resource meter.

3 Place the pointer over the icon until a **ToolTip** appears.

> **What's happening?** By placing the mouse pointer over the icon, you see that the System has 82% free resources, you have 88% free, and the GDI (Graphic Device Interface) has 82% free. Your numbers will vary. The system resources are what Windows 95 requires to run, the user is what you have for free memory, and the GDI is the necessary resource for drawing windows and so forth.

4 Right-click the **Resource Meter** icon.

> **What's happening?** You opened the menu. Your choices are Details or Exit the Resource Meter program.

5 Click **Details**.

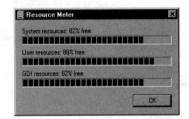

> **What's happening?** You see a graphical chart reflecting the same information you saw when you held the mouse pointer over the icon.

6 Click **OK**.

7 Right-click the **Resource Meter** icon on the taskbar. Click **Exit**.

> **What's happening?** You have closed the Resource Meter program.

8 Click **Start**. Point at **Programs**. Point at **Accessories**. Point at **System Tools**. Click **System Monitor**.

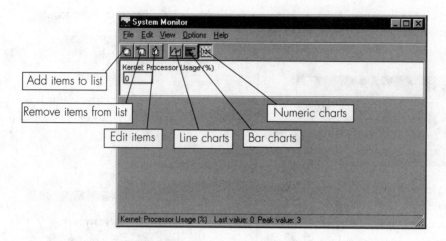

> **What's happening?** You have opened the System Monitor. You can use the menus or the buttons on the toolbar.

9 Click **View**.

> **What's happening?** In this example, Toolbar, Status Bar, and Numeric Charts are set.

10 If they are not set on your menu, set **Toolbar**, **Status Bar**, and **Numeric Chart**.

11 Click the **Add** button on the toolbar.

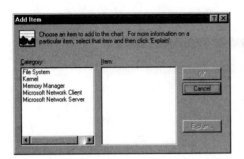

What's happening?

You see a list of the items you can view. If you are not on a Microsoft network, you will not see the two network entries.

12 In the **Category** list box, click **File System**.

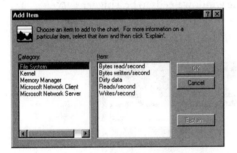

What's happening?

You can track data about each item in the list to the right. To select an item, you must click it. You can hold down the c key to select more than one item.

13 Click **Bytes read/second**. Click the **Explain** command button.

What's happening?

When you select an item and click Explain, you get a brief description of what you are monitoring.

14 Click **OK**.

15 Click **Bytes/written second**. Hold the [Ctrl] key down and click **Dirty data**. Click **OK**.

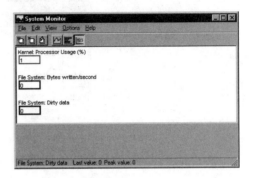

What's happening?

You have selected two items to track.

16 Click the **Remove Item** button.

What's happening?

To remove items, select them and click OK.

17 Click **Cancel**. Click **Add**. Click **Kernel**. Click **Processor Usage**. Click **OK**.

18 Click **Add**. Click **Memory Manager**. Click **Disk cache size**. Hold the Ctrl key and click **Free Memory**. Click **OK**.

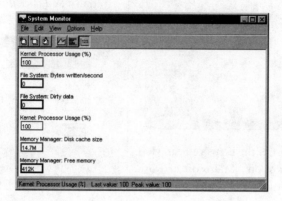

 You are tracking some of your computer resources. You will see the numbers change as activity occurs. *Note:* If you do not see the labels, the window needs to be a bigger size.

19 Click the **Line Charts** button on the toolbar.

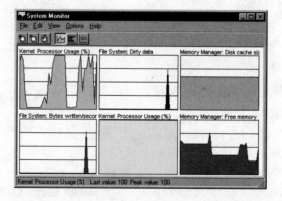

 You have a graphical image of what is happening on your system. Again, by using this tool, you can see which programs and operations place a heavy load on your system.

20 Click the **Bar Chart** button on the toolbar.

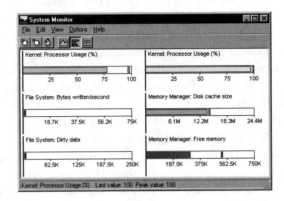

What's
happening? You are looking at the same data in a different graphical view.

21 Close **System Monitor**.

What's
happening? You have returned to the desktop.

13.15 Backing Up Data

Backing up data is a critical task that users all too often neglect. When things go wrong, either through your error or the computer's, rather than having to try and recreate data, you can turn to your backups, but only if you have created them. A *backup* is nothing more than a duplicate of the file or files that are on a disk copied to a medium such as floppy disks or a tape. You retrieve the files by restoring them, which again, simply means copying them back to the original media. When you copy a file to a floppy disk, you are in effect backing it up. But you usually want to back up your entire hard disk or all your folders. Although you can back up your entire hard disk to floppy disks, it is a very laborious and time-consuming process in this era of 1-GB hard drives. Thus, most users opt to have a tape backup unit. Special tapes must be purchased for use in the tape hardware.

As you use your computer and programs, you create data. For instance, you are writing a book and you create your first chapter, saving it as a file to the hard disk. You back up in January. It is now April, and you have completed ten chapters. You accidentally delete the folder that contains your chapters. You do not want to rewrite those chapters and, furthermore, you cannot. You turn to your backup. But you have a major problem. The only file you can restore is that first chapter you created in January. The rest of your work is gone. This is why backing up your data files regularly is so critical. The reason for backing up your entire hard drive may not be as obvious, but it is equally important.

As you work with Windows 95, you create settings, install new programs, and delete old programs. You are also adding and making changes to the system Registry that controls the Windows 95 environment. If the Registry becomes corrupt, you will not be able to boot into Windows 95. The system itself is ever changing. But things happen. If, for instance, you install a new program and it does something to your hard drive, such as causing another program not to work (or worse), you would like to return to the working system you had prior to your installation. If the problem is serious, you might have to reformat your hard drive. It can literally take hours, if not days, to reinstall all of your software. If you have backed up your system, you can simply restore what you had before, and a major catastrophe becomes a minor inconvenience.

There are two major backup types, full and incremental, and there are two types of full backups. A *full backup* copies all the selected files from the hard drive to the backup media, regardless of when or whether anything has changed. A *full system backup* copies everything from the hard drive to the backup media, regardless of when or whether anything has changed and, most importantly, copies the system files, including the Registry. An *incremental backup* only copies the files that have changed since the last full backup. If you do a second incremental backup, it would only copy the files that have changed since the last incremental backup. You should have a regular backup schedule. The timing of your backups depends on how much you use your computer and how often you change things. A typical backup schedule might be that once a week you perform a full backup and that every day you perform an incremental backup. If you need to restore your data, you need all of the backups, both the full and the incremental. If you are on a network, the network administrator will take care of the full backup; you need only be concerned about your data files.

When you do backups, it is a good idea to have more than one copy of your backup media. For instance, if you do a full system backup once a week and incremental backups daily, you would want at least two sets of tapes. One week, you would back up on one set of tapes, the following week you would use the other set of tapes. Thus, if Murphy's law is in effect for you—your hard disk and your tape backup tape are both corrupted—you will be able to restore files from the other week's tapes. The files may not be the most current, but at least you will not have to recreate everything from scratch. Another word of warning: Store at least one copy of your backup media away from your computer. If you have your backup tapes at the office and you have a fire or theft, you will lose everything. If you have another set at home, you can recover what was lost at work.

Windows 95 provides a backup program called Backup in the System Tools. It is licensed from Colorado Memory Systems, the manufacturer of many tape backup units. Using Backup, you can back up your files to QIC (quarter-inch cartridge) tape drives or the new larger tape sizes, to local or remote hard drives, or even to floppy disks. You can create a file set (list of files) that describes the files you want to back up. Once you have created a file set, you can drag and drop it onto the Backup icon. With Backup, you can do full backups or incremental backups, or you can back up only those files that have changed since a certain date, regardless of whether they have changed since your last backup.

Backup also has other uses. You can use Backup to archive data. If your hard disk starts filling up and you want to make more room on it, you can use Backup to copy seldom-used files to a backup media and then delete them from the hard drive. If you need these files at a later date, you can simply restore them. You can also use Backup to transfer programs and files to other computers. If you purchase a new computer, you can back up your old computer and restore to your new computer. This way, your new system will look the same as your old system, including the arrangement of your desktop.

The first time you use Backup, it automatically creates a file set to be backed up that includes your entire hard drive and the Registry. All file sets are saved to the hard disk.

13.16 Activity—Using Backup

Since using Backup requires writing information to the hard disk, and since each system is unique, these steps are only one example of how to use Backup. Should you choose to complete this activity on your own computer, be aware that you are only going to do an incremental backup of some files. *Under no circumstances should you do this activity if you are on a network.*

Note: You should have a newly formatted floppy disk. Do not use your Data or Activities disks for this activity.

1 Click **Start**. Point at **Programs**. Point at **Accessories**. Point at **System Tools**. Click **Backup**.

What's happening? The introduction screen tells you what Backup does. If you set the check box, you will not see this screen again.

2 Click **OK**.

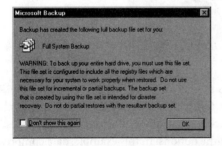

What's happening? Your full backup file set has been created. Again, you have the choice of not seeing this window again. Note: You may next see a dialog box informing you that Microsoft Backup did not detect a tape

drive. If you do not have a tape drive, click OK. Otherwise, follow the instructions on the screen.

3 Click **OK**.

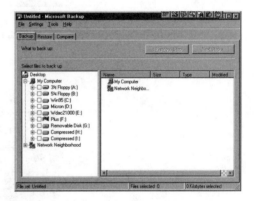

What's happening? You have opened the Backup program. It has three tabs, Backup, Restore, and Compare. The Backup window looks somewhat like the Explorer window. The left pane is the structure of your disk and the right pane shows the files in the folders. In front of each item is an empty check box. To select an item, click in the check box. To expand an entry, double-click the item of interest.

4   Click **Settings**. Click **Options**.

What's
happening? → You have two options to customize how you back up, restore, and compare your files.

5   Click the **Backup** tab.

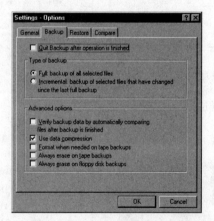

What's
happening? → Many options are now available to you. Your first choice is whether you want the Backup program to quit automatically when it has finished backing up files. The second choice is whether you want a full or incremental backup. The other choices are check boxes, which means you may choose some, all, or none of the options. In this example, data compression is set. This setting will pack as much data as possible onto a disk or a tape. You can use the question mark on the title bar to explain any choices you do not understand. There is no choice for formatting floppy disks, so your blank disks should always be formatted.

6   Set **Always erase on floppy disk backups**. Click **OK**.

7 Double-click the **Drive C** icon. Double-click the **95book** folder.

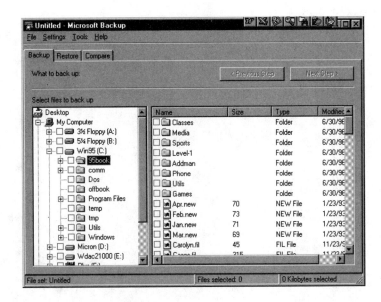

You have opened the 95book folder and can select individual files to back up or an entire folder. The message at the top of the tab states What to back up.

8 Click in the check box for **Apr.new**, **Feb.new**, **Jan.new**, and **Mar.new**.

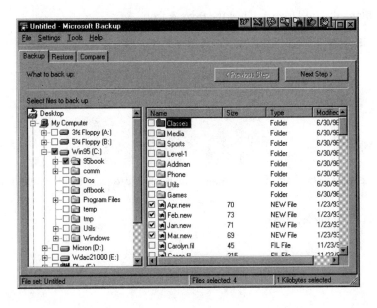

You have selected the files you wish to back up by placing a check in each box preceding the file.

9   Click **Next Step**.

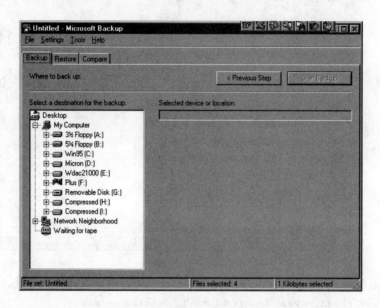

 Backup wants to know where you are going to back up your selected files.

10   Place the blank disk in Drive A. Click the **Drive A** icon.

11   Click **Start Backup**.

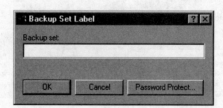

 Since this is a backup of selected files, the Backup program needs a label for the file set.

12   Key in the following: **MONTHS**

13 Click **OK**.

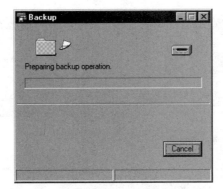

A window tells you that Backup is getting ready to do its job. Another window shows the progress of the backup. When it is complete, you see the following information box.

14 Click **OK**.

What's
happening? You see the progress bar as well as the device to which the files were copied.

15   Click **OK**.

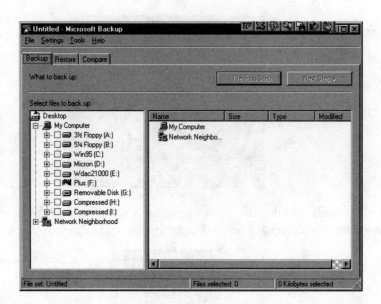

   Your backup is complete.

16   Close **Backup**.

   You have returned to the desktop.

13.17 Restoring Files

Backup has an option called Restore so that you can copy some or all of your files to your original disk, another disk, or another directory. Restore lets you choose whether want to copy from the backup tape or disks. Backup also includes a Compare utility, which ensures that the files on the backup media are indeed identical to the source files.

Restoring files is as easy as backing them up with the Backup program. You merely choose Restore and choose the kind of restoring you want.

13.18 Activity—Comparing and Restoring Files

Since using Restore requires writing information to the hard disk, and since each system is unique, these steps are one example of how to use Restore and Compare. Should you choose to complete this activity on your own computer, be aware that you are only going to do an incremental restore of some files. *Under no circumstances should you do this activity if you are on a network.*

Note: You should have the backup disk to which you just backed files in Drive A. Do not use your Data or Activities disks for this activity.

1 Click **Start**. Point at **Programs**. Point at **Accessories**. Point at **System Tools**. Click **Backup**.

2 Click **OK**. Click **OK** to any dialog boxes that appear. These appear if you have not turned them off.

3 Click the **Compare** tab.

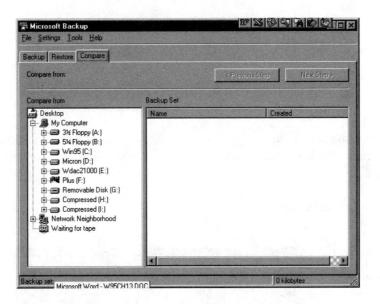

 This screen looks similar to the Backup screen. In this case, you are going to compare the files on the floppy disk to the files on the hard disk.

4   Click **Settings**. Click **Options**. Click the **Compare** tab.

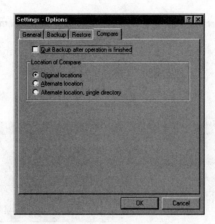

  Again, you have the option of quitting when you have finished your comparison. You can also compare files in different locations. In this case, you are going to accept the defaults.

5   Click **OK**.

6   Double-click the **Drive A** icon.

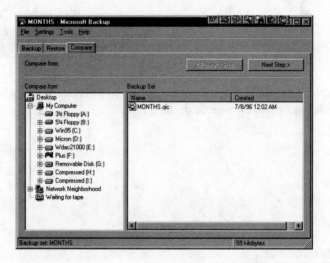

  You can see the file set you created, MONTHS.qic, in the right pane.

7 Double-click **MONTHS.qic**.

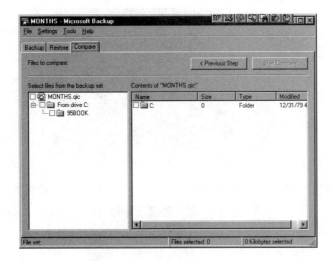

What's happening? In the left pane is the file set you wish to compare and the drive and directory from which the files came. The right pane also shows the drive from which the files came.

8 Click the check box in front of **95BOOK**.

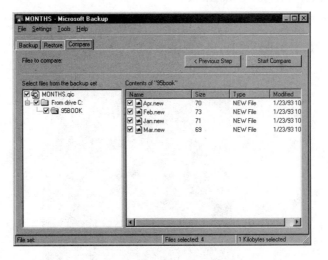

What's happening? The files you wish to compare are selected. You are comparing the files on the disk in Drive A in the backup set called MONTHS.qic to the files located in the 95BOOK directory on Drive C.

9   Click **Start Compare**.

 The operation begins. When it is complete, you see the following message box.

10   Click **OK**. Click **OK**.

 You have returned to the Backup program. Since you received no error messages, you know that the files are indeed identical.

11   Click the **Restore** tab.

12   Click **Settings**. Click **Options**. Click the **Restore** tab.

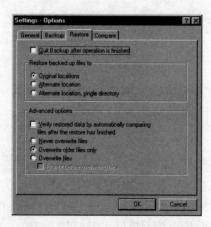

 Again, you have a choice as to how you want to restore your files. The default is to overwrite older files.

13 Click **Overwrite files**. Click **Prompt before overwriting files**. Click **OK**.

14 Double-click the **Drive A** icon.

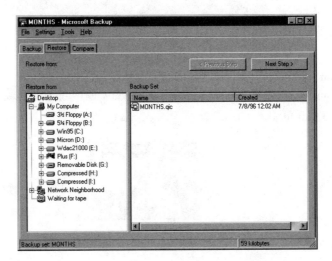

Since you have only one backup set on Drive A, that is all that is displayed.

15 Double-click **MONTHS.qic**.

16 Click the **95BOOK** checkbox.

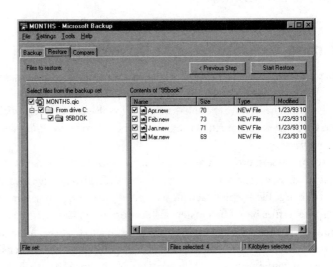

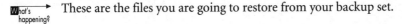
These are the files you are going to restore from your backup set.

17 Click **Start Restore**.

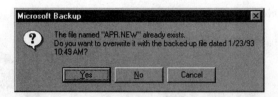

Since one of the options you selected in Restore was to be prompted before any file was over-written, you now are presented with a message box allowing you to make this choice.

18 Click **Yes** to all four files.

The operation is complete. Your files have been restored.

19 Click **OK**.

You have returned to the Backup program.

20 Close **Backup**.

You have returned to the desktop.

13.19 Optimizing Disk Space with DriveSpace

As program files and data files get larger, lack of disk space increasingly becomes a problem. Once, a 100-MB hard drive was considered enormous. Today, most new computers come with at least a 500-MB hard drive. Still, you can never have enough disk space. To solve this problem, *disk compression programs* have come into vogue. Disk compression programs come in two types: *offline compression* and *real-time* or *on-the-fly compression*.

An offline compression program reads in data from an uncompressed file and outputs it to a new compressed file. Usually, offline compression programs can also archive files. Archiving can combine several files into one large file, keeping each file separate within the combination. Remember, Windows 95 allocates disk space to files based on clusters (allocation units) and that the cluster (512 bytes) is the smallest amount of space that Windows 95 can read from and write to. A file that is one byte long will actually occupy a different amount of space on a disk, depending on the cluster size assigned to that disk type. Thus, a file that contains only one byte of data will occupy 512 bytes on a high-density disk (one sector equals a cluster); 8192 bytes (sixteen sectors make up a cluster) or even 32,678 bytes (sixty-four sectors make up a cluster) on a hard disk. *Cluster overhang* occurs when a file occupies more space on the disk than the data requires. Since offline compression programs place many files in one file, it minimizes cluster overhang.

Offline disk compression programs can also save space within a file. Disk compression utility programs store repeated data in less space. For instance, in this paragraph, the word *the* appears many times. A disk compression program can analyze the data in a file, develop a binary shorthand for every occurrence of *the*, and create a **token** to represent it. When a file is compressed, the tokens represent repeated characters, and the file occupies less space on the disk. When you uncompress the file, the tokens are read and the original characters are restored.

On-the-fly compression works in the background. As you use files, you are unaware of the compression and uncompression of data. Such a process is considered *transparent to the user*. On-the-fly compression works for a variety of reasons. Normally, to access a file, you must access a disk drive. Disk drives are mechanical devices and are slower than electronic memory. Although it may seem fast to you as Windows 95 loads files from disk to memory or from memory to disk, there is plenty of time to compress and uncompress files on-the-fly because compressed files are smaller and take less time to read or write. The compressing or uncompressing takes place in memory, which is fast. In fact, on-the-fly compression can actually improve disk performance and be faster because it can take longer to read and write a file to disk than it does to compress and uncompress it.

The most popular offline compression program is a shareware program called PKZIP, which has a corresponding program called PKUNZIP. These two programs are extremely useful because they help you control which files are compressed or uncompressed. You can manipulate compressed files the same way you manage all files; you can copy them or send them over a modem to another user. The disadvantage to PKZIP is that, before you can use the files, you must manually uncompress each with PKUNZIP. As you can imagine, this is time-consuming and unwieldy unless you are backing up files on a floppy disk or compressing a file to send over a modem.

There are many other popular on-the-fly compression programs including Stacker and SuperStor. DOS 6.0 introduced DoubleSpace, which was replaced by DriveSpace. Windows 95 also includes an improved version of DriveSpace. Once installed, DriveSpace uses a file called Drvspace.bin to provide access to the compressed disk. If you delete this file, you lose access to your compressed drive.

DriveSpace creates a compressed drive called a *compressed volume file* (*CVF*). When you install DriveSpace, it creates a new disk drive and assigns a drive letter to it. For instance, if you have a hard Drive C and floppy Drives A and B, DriveSpace skips the next four letters and assigns Drive H to the new drive. The new Drive H is a logical, not a physical, drive. DriveSpace "jumps" drive letters to avoid conflict with other drives you may have. If you want to have more than one compressed drive, a CVF is created for each new drive. Each CVF is located on an uncompressed drive, which is referred to as the host drive. A CVF is stored in the root directory of the host drive and has the file name Drvspace.001. Thus, if you install DriveSpace on the above system, Drive C is the compressed drive and Drive H is the host drive with Drvspace.001 as the compressed Drive C. If you delete the file Drvspace.001, you are deleting the file that holds all your data. If you have more than one DriveSpace drive, the next file name would be Drvspace.002, and so forth.

DriveSpace can compress data because it does not allocate whole clusters to a file. DriveSpace allocates sectors to a file one at a time. Although a DriveSpace drive emulates a "real" disk drive with a FAT and a directory table, it does not require that every cluster have the same number of sectors, unlike physical drives. You only need enough sectors to store your data. Thus, if you had a file that required only five sectors, DriveSpace would allocate exactly five sectors, not the sixty-four sectors that are required on a hard disk. This, in itself, saves enormous amounts of space.

In addition, as with offline compression programs, DriveSpace compresses data by using tokens to represent repeated data. The key to DriveSpace's data compression is its ability to search quickly for a string of bytes, identify them as repetitive, and replace the bytes with tokens. A lot of duplication of data is required before data compression is worthwhile. Most data files gain about a 2:1 ratio. In other words, you gain twice as much disk space by using disk compression. However, not all files compress at this rate. Sound files or executable programs do not benefit as much by compression, and you will seldom see any improvement in the space saved. The version of DriveSpace that comes with Windows 95 only allows the maximum compressed drive size to be 512 MB or less. If you have a 1-GB drive, you will have to divide it into smaller portions. However, if you purchase Microsoft Plus!, it improves DriveSpace and allows you to compress drives of up to 2 GB. Furthermore, the compression ratio runs about 4:1, even further increasing your drive space.

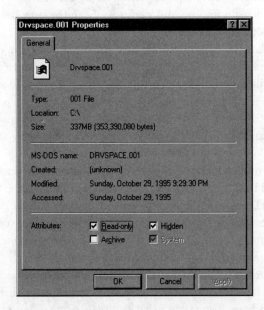

The above example shows the DriveSpace file called Drvspace.001. It occupies about 337 MB of the actual hard drive. This is the CVF file. If you deleted this file, you would delete all your data. This CVF file translates as logical Drive H on this system.

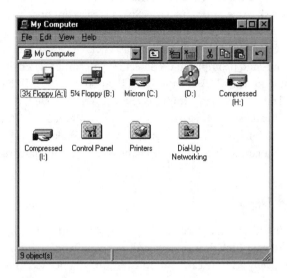

When you open My Computer, any drive that is compressed is so labeled. If you look at the properties of the drive, you see the gains made by using DriveSpace.

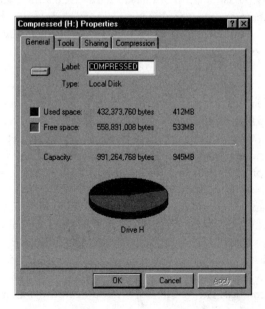

The 337 MB that the CVF file physically occupies translates into a drive with about 945 MB of space you can use for files, almost triple the space had you not compressed the drive.

Although you can uncompress a compressed drive, it is a difficult process, particularly if you have used up your disk space. Installing DriveSpace is easy, but once you install it, it is not so easy to uninstall. Remember, if you ever deleted the CVF file, you would have deleted everything on it.

To install DriveSpace, you go to System Tools, click DriveSpace, and click Drive/Compress. You then follow the menus and prompts on the screen. If you compress a drive with data on it, it typically takes about a minute for each MB of data. Thus, if you had an 80-MB hard drive that you wished to compress, it would take about eighty minutes. Once it is compressed, you will have a new drive that is about 160 MB, or if you use the Microsoft Plus! version, about 320 MB. Before you compress a hard drive, you should do a full system backup. Once you have installed DriveSpace, you can use DriveSpace to perform other changes, such as compressing floppy drives or changing the size of the compressed drive.

13.20 Plug and Play

Prior to Windows 95, adding new hardware to your system could be a nightmare. If you wanted to add a new piece of hardware such as a sound card, not only would you have to take the cover off the computer and physically add the card, but in addition, you needed to make software changes. Each hardware component needs access to system resources such as IRQ and DMA channels. An IRQ (Interrupt Request Line) signals the CPU to get its attention. DMA (Direct Memory Access) devices use DMA channels to access memory directly, rather than going through the CPU. If different devices contend for the same IRQ or DMA channel, you can have a hardware conflict, which means that the hardware does not work. Furthermore, most hardware devices often need software support contained in driver files that must also be installed. They are called drivers because they "drive" the hardware. A user needs a fair amount of technical expertise to adjust these settings so that the hardware devices would work.

Plug and Play is an industry standard developed by Intel and Microsoft, with help from other computer industry leaders, that automates adding new hardware to your computer. Because Windows 95 supports Plug and Play, adding new hardware to your system requires almost no thought. You install the hardware. Then, when you boot the system, Windows 95 can detect that you have added a new hardware device. Windows 95 will make the appropriate adjustments to your system. Hence, the name—you plug it in and it plays. But, like any new standard, Plug and Play does not always work. Sometimes it is called Plug and Pray.

In order for Plug and Play to work, you must have a computer that has a Plug and Play-compatible BIOS (Basic Input Output System). The device you are going to install also needs to be Plug and Play-compatible. Windows 95 is Plug and Play-compatible. Most computers manufactured after 1994 have a Plug and Play-compatible BIOS. Hardware that is not Plug and Play-compatible is called *legacy hardware*. If you have an older computer or an older device, you still can get help from Window 95 in resolving hardware conflicts. The Add/Remove Hardware wizard in Control Panel will attempt to assist you in solving hardware conflicts.

13.21 Activity—Looking at Plug and Play

1 Open **Control Panel**. Double-click the **System** icon.

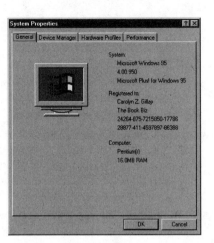

 You are looking at the System Properties.

2 Click the **Device Manager** tab. Scroll to the bottom until you see **System Devices**.

 These are the various devices attached to your computer system.

3 Double-click **System Devices**.

 You will see that on this system, one of the entries is Plug and Play BIOS. This computer is compatible with Plug and Play. You may see an ISA Plug and Play BIOS or ISA Plug and Play bus on older systems. You can look at the properties of this device, refresh the connections, remove it, or print the details about it.

4 Click **Plug and Play BIOS**. Click **Properties**.

5 Click the **Driver** tab, if available.

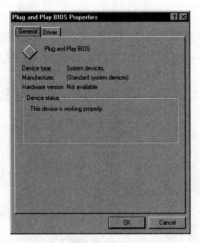

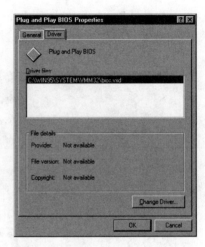

 This device is working properly. Not all devices will have a Driver tab as the device may or may not have a driver.

 This is the piece of software that drives this device. You can look at each device on your system and review its properties and other attributes.

6 Click **Cancel**. Click **Cancel**. Close **Control Panel**.

 You have returned to the desktop.

Chapter Summary

In this chapter, you learned that in today's world of multiple computers, keeping files in sync can be difficult. Windows 95 provides a tool called Briefcase. Briefcase can be dragged to a disk or transported to another computer. When you return to your original computer, you drag the Briefcase back to the desktop and choose Update. Your files are automatically updated.

You also learned that errors can happen to files. These errors include cross-linked files, when two files claim the same cluster, and lost clusters, which belong to no file. ScanDisk can repair these errors, as well as check a disk for bad spots or other errors.

You leaned that contiguous files are those that have been written to the disk in adjacent clusters. Noncontiguous files have been written in nonadjacent sectors and thereby create a fragmented disk. Fragmented disks slow your access to the disk. The Disk Defragmenter will repair fragmented files.

Another tool that helps disk performance is disk caching. Windows 95 has a new disk caching system called VCACHE (virtual cache). In addition, when Windows 95 runs out of memory, it uses a swap file on the hard disk as virtual memory. You can review disk caching and swap file specifications by using the System icon in Control Panel and looking at the Performance tab. Windows 95 also provides some tools that allow you to monitor the use of resources on your system constantly. These include the Resource Meter and the System Monitor.

Another important aspect of any computer user's routine should be the regular backing up of data. You can easily accomplish this in Windows 95 with the Backup program. This program allows you to complete either full or incremental backups. You can back up the whole system or just selected files. You can also compare the backed-up files to the originals and restore the files.

To gain more disk space, you can use the DriveSpace program that comes with Windows 95. DriveSpace is an on-the-fly compression program that compresses and uncompresses data as you use it. The version of DriveSpace that comes with Windows 95 can double the available space on your hard drive.

Windows 95 supports Plug and Play. Plug and Play means that when you install new hardware, Windows 95 automatically detects it so you do not have to make any hardware or software decisions. Your computer must have a Plug and Play BIOS and the device you install must be Plug and Play-compatible. If you have legacy hardware, you can use the Add/Remove Hardware wizard to assist you in installing devices.

Key Terms

Backup	Full backup	On-the-fly compression
Chain	Full system backup	Plug and Play
Cluster overhang	Fragmented disks	Read cache
Compressed volume file	Fragmented files	Real time compression
(CVF)	Incremental backup	Swap file
Contiguous	Kernel	Synchronizing files
Cross-linked files	Legacy hardware	Token
Dirty data	Lost clusters	Transparent to the user
Disk caching	Noncontiguous	Virtual memory
Disk compression	Offline compression	Write cache

Discussion Questions

1. The Briefcase allows you to synchronize your files. Explain.
2. What is a lost cluster? How does it occur? How can you correct the problem?
3. List and explain two problems that lost clusters create on your disk.
4. What is a cross-linked file? How does it occur? How can you correct the problem of cross-linked files?
5. Explain the purpose and function of ScanDisk.
6. Compare and contrast contiguous and noncontiguous files.
7. List and explain at least one disadvantage of having a fragmented disk.
8. How does Disk Defragmenter help optimize disk performance?
9. List and explain the two factors that should be considered before defragging your disk.
10. Explain the purpose and function of disk caches.

11. Compare and contrast a read cache and a write cache.
12. What happens when a cache reaches its capacity?
13. When using cache programs, what is a "hit?" a "miss?"
14. Why is write caching more dangerous than read caching?
15. Explain the purpose and function of virtual memory.
16. How do swap files work? What is their function?
17. Explain the purpose and function of the System Monitor.
18. Explain the purpose and function of the Resource Meter.
19. Why is it important to back up data? programs?
20. Compare and contrast full and incremental backups.
21. Why is it wise to have more than one copy of your backup media?
22. Explain the purpose and function of the Backup program.
23. The two purposes of backing up files are to recover files from disaster and to archive files. Explain.
24. Explain how you can restore files.
25. What can you do to create more disk space short of buying a new hard drive?
26. What is a disk compression program?
27. List and explain the two types of disk compression methods.
28. Why and how does DriveSpace compress data?
29. Explain the purpose and function of Plug and Play.
30. What are the requirements needed in order for Plug and Play to work?

True/False Questions

For each question, circle the letter T if the statement is true or the letter F if the statement is false.

T   F   1. You may updates files using Briefcase so they are all identical.
T   F   2. Data that is in lost clusters typically has no value, and wastes valuable disk space.
T   F   3. ScanDisk can be used to optimize the storage of files on a disk.
T   F   4. A defragging program such as Disk Defragmenter compresses data.
T   F   5. The disk caching program discards the oldest or least-used data as the cache gets filled.

Completion Questions

Write the correct answer in each blank space provided.

6. Two or more files that share the same cluster are said to be _____ files.
7. When all information for a file is in adjacent clusters, that file is considered a(n) _____ file.
8. It is possible to turn lost clusters into files by using the _____ program.
9. The program included with Windows 95 that provides graphic representation of resource usage is the _____.
10. A backup that only backs up files that have changed since the last full backup is called a(n) _____ backup.

Multiple Choice Questions

Circle the letter of the correct answer for each question.

11. A file named File0002.chk is most likely to be
    a. the FAT.
    b. lost clusters converted into a file.
    c. a file without a name in the FAT.
    d. none of the above

12. Before running the Disk Defragmenter program, be sure you have
    a. plenty of time.
    b. a backup of important files.
    c. a floppy in the drive.
    d. both a and b

13. A read cache stores data in memory
    a. so that the disk does not have to be read every time data is needed.
    b. until the system is rebooted.
    c. both and b
    d. neither a nor b

14. DriveSpace
    a. optimizes and increases disk space.
    b. optimizes memory usage.
    c. allows disk space to act like memory.
    d. allows memory to act like a disk cache.

15. Which of the following statements is true?
    a. In order to install new hardware, you must open the Plug and Play program.
    b. Plug and Play makes it easy to install new hardware.
    c. If you have legacy hardware, you cannot use Plug and Play.
    d. When using Plug and Play, you must manually install any needed device drivers.

Application Assignments

For all essay questions, use Notepad or WordPad for your answer. Print your answer.

Problem A

Compare and contrast Briefcase and the Backup program. Which would you use in what circumstances? Why? Describe the advantages and disadvantages to each.

Problem B

The following options are chosen in ScanDisk. Briefly describe the purpose of each chosen option. Determine and explain which options you think are the best to use when using ScanDisk.

Problem C

The following options are chosen in Disk Defragmenter. Briefly describe the purpose of each chosen option. Determine and explain which options you think are best when using Disk Defragmenter.

Problem D

You are the owner of a small business. Your keep your business records on a computer. Develop a plan to schedule ScanDisk and Disk Defragmenter on your computer. Defend the reasons for your choices.

Problem E

You are the owner of a small business. You have an accounting program installed on the computer. The accounting program is kept in a directory called Quicken. You keep your accounting data files in a directory called Accounting. You are using a word processing program called Word for Windows. The program files are kept in a folder called Winword. You also have business letters created in Word that are kept in a folder called Letters. You also use Word to create invoices and you keep those data files in a directory called Invoices.

Develop a backup plan for your computer system. Include which files and directories you would back up and how often.

Problem Set I—At the Computer

Open the **Resource Meter**. Open the **System Monitor**. Look at the results of each screen. Open **WordPad**. Open **Paint**. Open **Calculator**.Open **Solitaire**.

Look again at the results of the Resource Meter and System Monitor. Do you see any changes? Describe any differences between the results of the Resource Meter and the System Monitor before and after you opened the programs. Describe what advantages and disadvantages there are to using the Resource Meter and System Monitor. Print the document you just created. Close all open programs.

Chapter 14

Command Syntax and Running MS-DOS

Chapter Overview

Although the Windows 95 environment has improved users' communications with their computer systems, there are still many MS-DOS application programs. Users continue to want to run these programs and they still can. Windows 95 allows the user to run DOS-based programs in the same ways as they run Windows 95 programs. The DOS programs can even run in a window.

Windows 95 comes with MS-DOS 7.0. There is a command choice on the Start/Programs menu so the user can access the DOS prompt. DOS is a command line interface that uses syntax and parameters. Many Windows 95 commands can also be run from the command line, using syntax and parameters. There are still some functions that are easier to perform in DOS. Windows 95 does not have certain capabilities that DOS does.

You can control the boot process. You can either boot in the normal way by beginning with Windows 95, or you can choose to change these options and boot into your old operating system or to MS-DOS 7.0.

Learning Objectives

1. Explain the purpose and function of DOS and why it is used in Windows 95.
2. Define command syntax.
3. Explain what parameters are and how they are used.
4. Explain the purpose and use of the DIR command.
5. Define global specifications and identify their symbols.
6. Explain how parameters are used with Explorer.
7. Explain the purpose and function of redirection.
8. Explain the purposes and functions of the COPY, REN, and DEL commands.
9. Compare and contrast using DOS commands and Explorer to manipulate files.
10. Explain the purpose and function of Autoexec.bat and Config.sys.
11. Explain the purpose and function of the boot process.
12. Explain how to control the boot process by altering the MSDOS.SYS file.

Student Outcomes

1. Start, use, and exit MS-DOS in Windows 95.
2. Read a syntax diagram and be able to name and explain what each part signifies.
3. Use the DIR command.
4. Use global specifications with the DIR command.
5. Create a desktop shortcut using Explorer.
6. Use redirection to create a file and print a list of files in a directory.
7. Use the COPY, REN, and DEL commands to copy, rename, and delete files.

14.1 DOS Lives

Introduced in 1981, DOS (PC-DOS or MS-DOS) was the first major operating system used on IBM and IBM-compatible microcomputers. MS-DOS was developed by Microsoft and licensed to IBM, who called it IBM PC-DOS. Other computer manufacturers licensed MS-DOS from Microsoft without changing the name. PC-DOS and MS-DOS are virtually identical, and all versions are generically referred to as DOS. Updated versions of DOS were periodically introduced. DOS 1.0 was the first version, with DOS 7.0 being the most recent.

DOS is a character-based operating system. With DOS, you work at what is known as the command line. You must know the exact command you want and how to use it. DOS was considered user-unfriendly. In order to make computers easier to use, Windows 3.0, 3.1, and 3.11 were introduced. Windows 3.0 through 3.11 are graphical user interfaces, the predecessors to Windows 95. When the first versions of Windows were released, they provided an operating environment that was a shell around DOS. You still had to load DOS and then load Windows. Thus, you had to have a copy of DOS to run Windows. In one sense, Windows 95 replaces DOS; you do not need a copy of DOS to run Windows 95. But, in fact, Windows 95 ships with an upgraded version of DOS and does install DOS.

Essentially, installing Windows 95 also means installing MS-DOS 7.0. What happens to all your old DOS system files depends on how you install Windows 95. If you upgrade to Windows 95 and overwrite your existing Windows directory, Windows 95 will rename the old DOS system and configuration files. In addition, a large number of DOS utility programs will either be removed or upgraded with new Windows 95 versions. Windows 95 also replaces your hard disk's boot sector. If you install Windows 95 to a new directory, you can return to the version of DOS that was on your system prior to installing Windows 95.

Although Windows 95 is designed to shield the user from the world of arcane DOS commands, configuration files, and the old necessary memory management techniques, you may still have programs that need to run under DOS. Many games in particular need to run under DOS. Another reason for running DOS is that although many tasks are easier to accomplish in Windows 95, some are easier to accomplish while in DOS. Three immediate examples come to mind. First, there is no way to copy a file in Windows 95 and give it a new name in one step. You have to copy the file and then rename the copy. Second, there is no easy way to copy a group of files and give them new names in one step. Third, there is no simple way to rename a group of files in Windows 95. In Explorer, you can rename only one file at a time. At times like this, you will find it much easier to drop into or shell out to DOS and accomplish your tasks there.

Unlike Windows 95, DOS was never designed as a multitasking environment. Thus, applications written for DOS want to take control of the entire computer. Windows 95 lets you launch and run DOS applications inside virtual machines where each DOS application thinks it has a machine of its own. Since the virtual machines are separate from one another, you can run several DOS applications at once. Windows 95 settles any conflict between the applications over which one can write to the screen or read from the disk. Thus, your DOS applications behave as if they are the only programs running on the computer. On the whole, you should run DOS applications from within Windows 95 unless they do not work.

MS-DOS 7.0 supports long file names. It will let you access network resources. You can run Windows programs from the command line. The following is a list of programs you should not run in Windows 95: FDISK, CHKDSK, CHKDSK /F, the DOS version of ScanDisk, the DOS version of Backup, or any third-party disk optimization programs unless they were written specifically for Windows 95. A *third-party program* is one written by a company other than Microsoft.

The two most important things to know about working with a DOS-based program in Windows 95 are how to start the program and how to exit the program.

14.2   Activity—Running MS-DOS Programs in Windows 95

1   Open **Windows Explorer**.

2   Double-click **95book**. Double-click **Phone**.

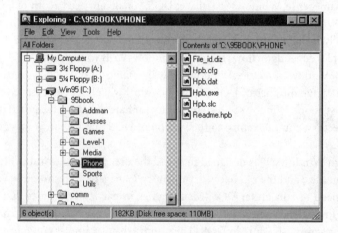

 You have opened the Phone folder. In it is a DOS-based program. You know which is the program because it has the file extension .exe. Its file name is Hpb, which is a shareware program that lets you keep track of names and addresses. Since this program was not designed for Windows, it has a DOS icon.

3   Double-click the **Hpb.exe** icon.

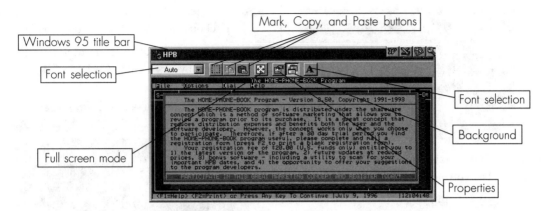

A DOS box opened. Even though this is not a Windows 95 program, it opened in a window. You can choose your font size and the type of font. You can mark, copy, and paste information to and from the Clipboard. You are currently in background mode. But you can switch to full screen mode. Full screen mode means the application will take up the entire screen and will not appear in a window. You are looking at registration information for this program.

4   Press **Enter**.

This program can only work with one data file. Hpb.exe loaded HPB.DAT, its data file. The information on the screen, such as Acme-Fly-By-Night, Inc. with the phone numbers, is the data. If you wanted to add data to the file, you would have to learn how to use this program.

5   Click the **Full Screen** button.

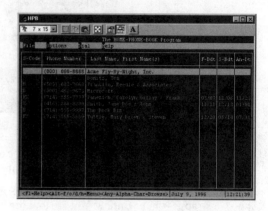

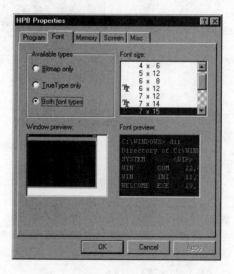

 You can change the size of the grid by choosing one of the available choices.

8   Scroll until you locate **7 × 15**, or the nearest size available for your monitor. Click it.

 The program is no longer in a window. It takes up the entire screen.

6   Press **Alt** + **Enter**.

 By pressing **Alt** + **Enter**, you returned the program to a window. It does not matter if you use the program in full screen mode or in a window. However, if you want to use any of the Windows 95 features, you must be in a DOS window. For instance, if you are in a window and the font is small and difficult to read, you can change the size of the font with the control of Windows 95.

7   Click the down arrow in the **Font** drop-down list box.

 As you can see, the font size changed. In order to accommodate the new font size, the window size increased.

9   Click the **Font** button on the toolbar.

 You are looking at the Font property sheet. Currently, both TrueType and Bitmap fonts are selected.

10   Click **Bitmap only**.

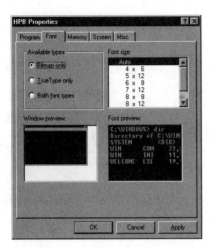

> *What's happening?* → Your choices are more limited when you choose Bitmap only.

11   Locate **8 × 12**. Click it to select it. Click **Apply**. Click **OK**.

> *What's happening?* → Your font and window are much larger. You can also select text and copy it to another application. However, in a DOS box, you must first mark it before you can copy it.

12   Click the **Mark** button on the toolbar.

> *What's happening?* → You see a blinking white box at the top left of the black area of the screen. That is your marker.

13   Click the mouse on the last line of the text (**Tuttle, Mary Brown & Steven**) and drag it to the end of the line.

> *What's happening?* → You have selected the text.

14   Click the **Copy** button on the toolbar.

15   Open **Notepad**. Click **Edit**. Click **Paste**.

> *What's happening?* → You copied the data from the HPB program to Notepad.

16   Close **Notepad**. Do not save the data.

> *What's happening?* → You have returned to the HPB window.

17   Click the **Close** button on the Windows **95** title bar.

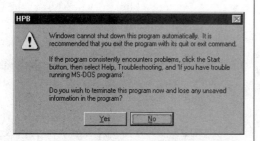

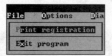 Unlike programs designed for Windows 95, you do not close a DOS-based program using the Close button. You only use this button if the DOS-based program misbehaves and you cannot get out of it any other way. You need to use the DOS program's commands to exit it.

18 Click **No**.

19 Press **Alt** + **F**.

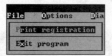

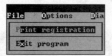 You dropped down the File menu for this program. You are in DOS mode. You need to exit a DOS program through the program itself, not through Windows 95.

20 Press **X**.

21 Close the **Explorer** window.

 You have closed HPB and Explorer and returned to the desktop. You may also start a program from the Start menu.

22 Click **Start**. Click **Run**.

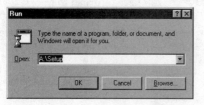

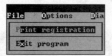 The Run command on the Start menu is asking you what program you want to run. This is considered a command line. You must key in the command that you wish to execute.

23 Key in the following: **C:\95book\phone\hpb.exe**

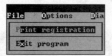 You are going to Run the program. You are telling the Run command line where the program is located.

24 Click **OK**.

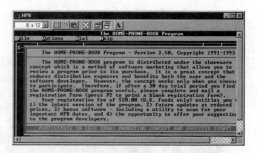

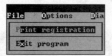 You specified what program you wanted to run.

25 Press **Enter**. Press **Alt** + **F**. Press **X**.

26 Open **Explorer**. Double-click **95book**. Double-click **Phone**. Right-click **Hpb.exe**. Click **Properties**. Click the **Program** tab.

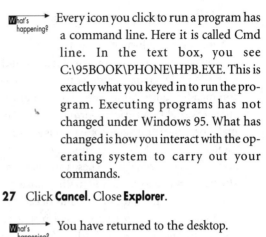 Every icon you click to run a program has a command line. Here it is called Cmd line. In the text box, you see C:\95BOOK\PHONE\HPB.EXE. This is exactly what you keyed in to run the program. Executing programs has not changed under Windows 95. What has changed is how you interact with the operating system to carry out your commands.

27 Click **Cancel**. Close **Explorer**.

You have returned to the desktop.

14.3 Command Syntax

Using DOS commands is very different from using Windows 95. Where Windows 95 is a graphical user interface, DOS is a character-based operating system. Because of this, you must know the command syntax of DOS in order to be able to use it. All languages have rules or conventions for speaking or writing. The *syntax*, or order of a language, is important. For example, in English, the noun (person, place, or thing) is followed by the verb (the action). In another language, however, the syntax or order might be different; first comes the verb, then the noun.

Computers also communicate with language, but you must speak the computer's language and follow its *command syntax* exactly because the computer has a very limited understanding of language. You cannot key in any word and expect the computer to understand. You can only key in a word or words that the computer recognizes. Window 95 hides the details of the commands and instead presents you with icons and menus. But when you are using DOS or the Run command on the Start menu, you are not protected in this way. You must use the computer's vocabulary with the proper syntax. The computer cannot guess what you mean. For example, if I said, "Going I store," people would probably understand. But if I keyed in an incorrect word or put correct words in the wrong order, the computer would respond with the message, Bad command or file name. This statement is the computer equivalent of "I do not understand."

In computer language, the command can be compared with a verb, the action you wish to take. In Windows 95, you use the Explorer or My Computer to list or view your files on your disk. When you use DOS, you use the command DIR to list your files. You must key in DIR at the command prompt. In doing so, you are asking DOS to run the program called DIR that lets you see the table of contents or the directory of a disk.

14.4 What are Parameters?

A *parameter* is information that you want a command to have. In Windows 95, to list your files alphabetically by name, you use Explorer and then choose View/Arrange Icons/by Name from the menu. With DOS commands, you can do the same thing, but you need to know the parameters. Some commands require parameters, while other commands let you add them when needed. Some parameters are variable. A *variable parameter* is one to which you supply the value. This process is similar to a math formula. For instance, x + y = z is a simple formula. You can plug in whatever values you wish for x and y. If x = 1 and y = 2, you know the value of z. These values are variable; x can equal 5 and y can equal 3, which makes z equal to 8. These variables can have any other numerical value you wish to use. You can also have z = 10 and x = 5, and mathematically establish the value of y. No matter what x, y, and z equal, you will be able to establish the value of each.

Other parameters are fixed. For instance, if the formula reads x + 5 = z, then x is the variable parameter, and 5 is the fixed value. You can change the value of x but not the value of 5.

When you are working with some DOS commands, you can add one or more qualifiers or modifiers to the command to make it more specific. These qualifiers are the parameters. This process is the same in English. If I give my son my credit card and tell him, "Go buy," I have given him an open-ended statement—he can buy anything (making him one happy guy). However, if I add a qualifier, "Go buy shoes," I have limited what he can do. This is precisely what parameters do to a command.

14.5 Reading a Syntax Diagram

DOS is like a foreign language. How do you know what the commands are, what the syntax is, and what the parameters are? The syntax information is provided through online Help. You issue the name of the command followed by a /?. If you do not know the name of the command, you can key in FASTHELP at the command prompt. However, FASTHELP may not be available to you, depending on how you installed Windows 95.

The command *syntax diagrams* tell you how to enter the command with its optional or mandatory parameters. However, you need to be able to interpret these syntax diagrams. They can also be found in other software applications. As a matter of fact, if you get into the nuts and bolts of Windows 95, you will find that it, too, has commands with syntax diagrams that can be run from the Start/Run menu.

An example of a DOS command is DIR. When you key in DIR, you get a list of files. If you key in DIR /?, you will see a syntax diagram. Here is a brief example of the formal command syntax diagram:

DIR [DRIVE:][PATH][FILENAME] [/P] [/W]

The first entry is the command name. You may only use DIR. You cannot substitute another word, such as DIRECTORY or INDEX. Then, you have items that follow the command. In this case, everything is in brackets except DIR, indicating that these parameters (the items in brackets) are optional. Whenever you see brackets, you know you can choose whether or not to include parameters.

14.6 Using Fixed Parameters with the DIR Command

DIR is one of the commands with *optional parameters*. Two *fixed parameters* allow you to control the way the operating system displays the table of contents on the disk: /W for "wide display" and /P for "pause display." In the DIR command syntax diagram, the /W and the /P are in brackets. You never key in the brackets, only the / (forward slash or slash), also known as a *switch*, and the W or P. You must be careful to use the forward slash (/). The \ is a backslash and is always referred to as such. The word slash by itself always refers to the forward slash.

When you key in DIR, the files scroll by so quickly that you cannot read them. There is an efficient way to solve this problem by using the /P parameter. The /P parameter will display one screen of information at a time. It will also give you a prompt to which you must respond before it will display another screenful of information.

14.7 Activity—Using DIR in the DOS Box

1 Click **Start**. Point at **Programs**. Click **MS-DOS Prompt**.	**2** Key in the following: **C:\WINDOWS>DIR** Enter

 You have dropped into DOS. If you look at the screen, you will see the C:\WINDOWS> with a blinking cursor following it. This is known as the prompt, because it is "prompting" you to do something. (On your screen, the prompt may look like C:\WIN95> or [H:\WINDOWS].) Being in a character-based operating system does not mean that the rules of an operating system have changed. You are on a default drive (C) in a default directory (Windows). If you want to see the files in this directory, you need to issue a command. You must key in information and press Enter. There is nothing to click.

 You are looking at the files and folders (directories) in the default directory. As you remember, in Windows 95, all files receive a DOS file name that follows rigid rules—there should be a file name of no more than eight characters, followed by a period, followed by a file extension (file type) with no more than a three characters. There must be no spaces in the file name. If you have a file with a long file name, the DOS name is in a column on the left with the long file name to the far right. Remember, to create a DOS file name, the long file name is truncated. The long file name For Your Information.cpe will become FORYOU~1.CPE in DOS. Essentially, Windows 95 takes the first six characters and truncates the rest of the file name. It uses the ~1 to designate similar files. The numbers increase so each file has a unique name. Thus, if you had a file called For Your Pleasure.cpe and For Your Wonder.cpe, the DOS file names would become FORYOU~2.CPE and FORYOU~3.CPE. As you can see, DOS file names are exceedingly cryptic. See Figure 14.1 for a description of the parts of the screen.

Figure 14.1 Parts of the DOS Screen

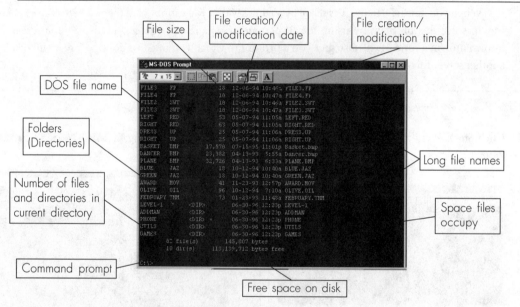

3 Key in the following: **C:\WINDOWS>DIR /P** **Enter**

What's happening? → By using the /P parameter, you have stopped the screen display from scrolling.

4 Press **Enter** until you have returned to the command prompt.

5 Place the Data disk in Drive A. Key in the following: **C:\WINDOWS>DIR A:** **Enter**

 The default drive and directory are still C:\WINDOWS, but you are looking at the files and folders on Drive A. Your directory list may differ slightly from the one shown above, depending on the work you completed in previous chapters. If you want to look inside a folder, you must key in the path name.

6 Key in the following: **C:\WINDOWS>DIR A:\CHAP11** **Enter**

 You substituted A:\CHAP11 for [DRIVE:][PATH] in the syntax diagram. If you want to change default drives, you key in the drive letter followed by a colon.

7 Key in the following: **C:\WINDOWS>A:** **Enter**

 Now Drive A is the default drive and the root directory is the default directory. You can tell this by looking at the system prompt (A:\>). If you wanted to look in the directory CHAP11, you would not have to include the drive letter since you are already in Drive A. DOS will always assume the default drive and directory unless you specify otherwise.

8 Key in the following: **A:\>C:** **Enter**

What's happening? ➜ DOS remembers the last directory you were in before you changed drives. You can also change directories. The command is CD [PATH].

9 Key in the following: **C:\WINDOWS>CD ** Enter

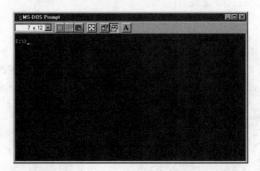

What's happening? ➜ You have changed the default directory to the root of C (C:\).

10 Key in the following: **C:\>CD 95BOOK\LEVEL-1\LEVEL-2\LEVEL-3** Enter

What's happening? ➜ You changed the default directory to LEVEL-3, which is under LEVEL-2, which is under LEVEL-1, which is under 95BOOK, which is under the root of C. To move down the directory tree, you must key in the entire path name. However, if you want to move up the tree, you may take a shortcut. If you key in CD .. you will move up one level. If you key in CD ... you will move up two levels, if you key CD .... you will move up three levels, and so on. Thus, in this example, if you wanted to move up to the 95BOOK directory, you would key in CD .... in order to reach that level.

11 Key in the following: **C:\95BOOK\LEVEL-1\LEVEL-2\LEVEL-3>CD ....** Enter

You have moved up three levels and the default directory is now 95BOOK.

12 Key in the following: **C:\95BOOK>EXIT** Enter

DOS is a program. You must exit it to return to Windows 95.

14.8 Global File Specifications—Wildcards, the ?, and the *

Using the DIR command and a file specification, you can find one specific file that matches what you key in. Every time you wish to locate a file, you can key in the entire file specification. Often, however, you wish to work with a group of files that have similar names or a group of files whose names you do not know. DOS has a "shorthand" system that allows you to operate on a group of files rather than a single file. This system is formally called *global file specifications*; informally, it is called using *wildcards*. These are the same wildcards that can be used in Windows 95 when using Find. Conceptually, wildcards are similar to playing cards, where the joker can stand for any card of your choice. In DOS, the question mark (?) and the asterisk (*) are the wildcards. These symbols stand for unknowns. The * represents or substitutes for a group of characters; the ? represents or substitutes for a single character. Many commands allow you to use global file specifications. You will use the DIR command to explore the use of wildcards.

14.9 Activity—DIR and Wildcards

1 Click **Start**. Point at **Programs**. Point at **MS-DOS Prompt**.

2 Key in the following: **C:\WINDOWS> Cd \95BOOK** Enter

You are in DOS. You made the default directory C:\95BOOK.

3   Key in the following: **C:\95BOOK>DIR *.txt** [Enter]

 You asked DOS what files have an extension of .txt and are located in the 95BOOK directory. You did not know anything about the file names, only the file extension. DOS searched the table of contents of C:\95BOOK. Since you did not include a drive or a path, DOS assumed the default drive and directory. The command found eleven files that matched *.txt. Now, how does the question mark differ from the asterisk?

4   Key in the following: **C:\95BOOK>DIR ?????.txt** [Enter]

 This time, you asked your question differently. You still asked for any file that had the file extension of .txt in the 95BOOK directory. However, you used the ? five times. DOS responds to this by looking for any file name that starts with any letter and has a file name no longer than five characters. It can be less than five characters but no more than five. Thus, the ????? represented five characters. You then separated the file name from the file extension with a period, which tells DOS that any file with the extension .txt is fine. This time, only three files matched your request. Note how the above screen display differs from the screen display in Step 3. This time, you do not see any file name longer than five characters. Although the ? is helpful in specific cases, the * is generally used more often. In fact, ????????.??? is the same as *.*.

5   Key in the following: **C:\95BOOK>DIR Exp*.*** [Enter]

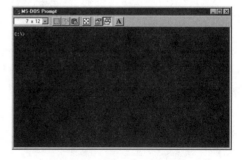

You asked DOS to show you all the files (DIR) located in the 95BOOK directory that start with the letters Exp. The *.* following the Exp represents the rest of the file name and the file extension. Some budget files appear. The letters EXP mean expenses, followed by the year (93, 94, or 95) and the month (JANuary, FEBruary, or MARch). The file extension is .DAT, meaning data is in these files; they are not programs. You may not be interested in all the files. In this case, you want to know what expense files you have in your directory for 1993.

6 Key in the following: **C:\95BOOK>DIR EXP93*.*** **Enter**

You asked for all the files (DIR) in the 95BOOK folder that were expense files for 1993. The rest of the information in the file names was represented by *.*. On your screen, you got the 1993 files. Suppose you are interested in all the files

with data about January. You included JAN in the file names to indicate the kind of data in the files. You no longer care about the year, only the month.

7 Key in the following: **C:\95BOOK>DIR EXP*JAN.*** **Enter**

You asked for a file name that specifically starts with EXP and ends with JAN. The middle two characters, represented by the first *, could be a number of characters between EXP and JAN. The second * acts as a place holder. You could use the question mark and key in the command as DIR EXP??JAN.*. That request would be asking for files with only two characters between EXP and JAN.

8 Key in the following: **C:\95BOOK>CD ** **Enter**

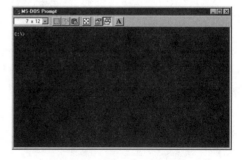

You returned to the root directory of C.

9 Key in the following: **C:\>EXIT** **Enter**

You are back at the Windows 95 desktop.

14.10 Explorer Parameters

Explorer is also a command that can be executed using Run. Its syntax is:

Explorer.exe [/n],[/e],[options],[folder]

The parameters have the following meanings:

/n   will open a new Explorer window.

/e   will expand a folder to display its contents.

When you use [options], you may use either of the following:

/root selects a folder as the root of a folder tree; or

/select highlights a folder and displays the folder's parent.

The [folder] can be any folder name or path, such as C:\95book or C:\Windows. The commas are required between the switches. These parameters allow you to customize where and how Explorer will display a window. You can also create shortcuts that will reflect an often used Explorer view.

14.11 Activity—Using Explorer Parameters

1   Click **Start**. Click **Run**. In the command line box, key in the following: **Explorer /n,/e,/root,C:\95book**

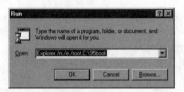

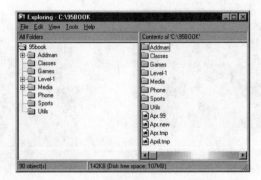

What's happening? → You are asking to open Explorer with C:\95book as the open Explorer window. The commas are required. To ensure the correct path, you could also key in C:\Windows\Explorer.exe /n,/e,/root,C:\95book.

2   Click **OK**.

What's happening? → As you can see, your Explorer window opened and expanded the 95book directory.

3 Close the **Explorer** window.

4 Click **Start**. Click **Run**. In the command line box, key in the following: **Explorer /n,/e,/select, C:\95book** **Enter**

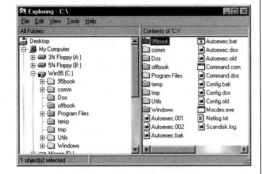

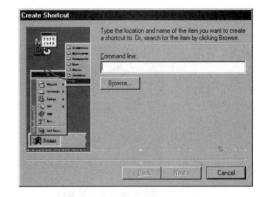

What's happening? Now the Explorer window opened with 95book highlighted in the Contents pane. You can use this feature to your advantage. For instance, you would like to access the desktop, but you have opened and maximized several windows and cannot see the desktop. To do this, you would have to minimize your open windows. There is an alternative, however. You can create a shortcut to the desktop and place it on the Start menu.

5 Close the open Explorer window.

6 Right-click the desktop. Point to **New**. Click **Shortcut**.

What's happening? You opened the Create Shortcut dialog box.

7 In the **Command line** text box, key in the following: **Explorer /root,**

8 Click **Next**.

9 In the **Select name for shortcut** box, key in the following: **Desktop**

10 Click **Finish**.

Desktop

What's happening? You now have a shortcut to the Desktop on the desktop.

11 Drag the shortcut to the **Desktop** to the **Start** menu and drop it.

12 Click the **Start** menu.

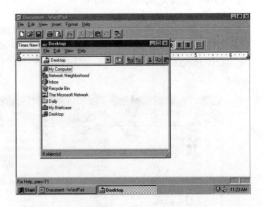

 You have a shortcut to the Desktop on the Start menu.

13   Open **WordPad**. Maximize it.

14   Click the **Start** menu. Click **Desktop**.

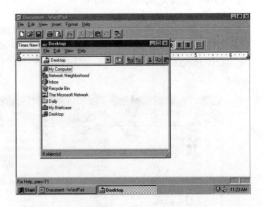 You now can reach the Desktop from wherever you are. You can change the view to large icons if you prefer.

15   Close the **Desktop** window. Close **WordPad**.

16   Remove the **Desktop** shortcut from the desktop and from the **Start** menu. (Right click the **Taskbar**. Click **Properties**. Click **Start Menu** tab. Click **Remove**. Click **Desktop**. Click **Remove**.)

You have returned to the desktop.

14.12 Redirection

DOS knows what you want it to do because you key in commands. DOS always looks to the keyboard for input. The keyboard is considered the standard input device. After DOS executes the command, it writes the output to the screen, which is considered the standard output device. DOS has a feature called *redirection*, which allows you to tell DOS that instead of writing the output to the standard output device, it should write the information to another place that you specify. Typically, this is to a file or to the printer. Redirection does not work with all DOS commands, but it does work with the DIR command, since DIR gets its input from the keyboard and writes to the screen.

To tell DOS to write information somewhere else, the syntax is COMMAND > DESTINATION. The command is what you usually key in, such as DIR *.TXT. Then you use the "greater than" symbol, >, to tell DOS to write to a specific place. If you want the output to be sent to a particular file, you would key in DIR *.TXT > MY.FIL. If you want the output to go to the printer, you tell DOS by using the reserved name for the printer, PRN or LPT1, and keying in DIR *.TXT > LPT1. For instance, you want a hard copy of files in one directory so you can compare it to another directory to see if you have duplicate files. You cannot accomplish this task in Windows 95, but you can use DOS for this purpose.

14.13 Activity—Redirecting Output to a File

Note: You should be in the DOS box. The Data disk is in Drive A. The default directory should be C.

1   Key in the following: **C:\>A:** **Enter**

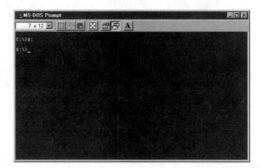

2   Key in the following: **A:\>DIR *.txt** **Enter**

What's
happening?   You asked for all the files on the Data disk with the file extension of .txt. The output is displayed
on the screen. Three files meet your criteria. Keying in the command and seeing the output
displayed on the screen is the usual process. Figure 14.1 illustrates this process.

Figure 14.1   *Standard Input/Output*

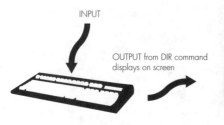

INPUT

OUTPUT from DIR command
displays on screen

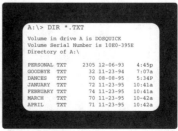

3 Key in the following: **A:\>DIR *.txt > my.hw** [Enter]

This time, you instructed DOS to send the output to a file called my.hw instead of displaying the output on the screen. Notice that redirection is an "instead of" procedure. You either have the results of the DIR command displayed on the screen *or* you send it to a file. Figure 14.2 shows what happens during redirection.

Figure 14.2   Redirection

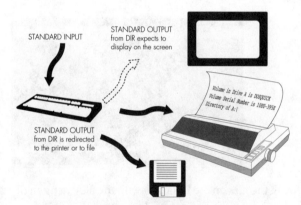

4 Key in the following: **A:\>DIR my.hw** [Enter]

You now have a file with the contents of the DIR command you issued in Step 3.

14.14 Redirecting Output to the Printer

You have seen that you can redirect output to a file. You can also redirect output to the printer. You can redirect the output of the DIR command to the printer to get a printout. However, you cannot use any name as you did when redirecting output to a file. DOS is specific and names its devices. You know that disk drive names are always letters of the alphabet followed by a colon. Printers also have names. The printer device name is PRN, LPT1, or LPT2. Usually, PRN and LPT1 are synonymous.

Prior to completing the next activity, check with your lab instructor to see if there are any special procedures to be used in your lab. Sometimes, for instance, a networked environment will not let you use the device name PRN. Instead, you must use the alternate device name, LPT1. Be sure to use the number 1 and not the lowercase letter l. Furthermore, in a networked environment, there is often a shared network printer and you *cannot* redirect the output to the printer in the manner described below.

14.15 Activity—Redirecting the Output of the DIR Command to the Printer

Note 1: *Do not do* this activity until you have checked with your lab instructor for any special instructions prior to proceeding. You may not be able to do it at all. If you cannot do it, simply read the activity.

Note 2: You should be in the DOS box. The Data disk is in Drive A. The A:\> is displayed as the default drive and the default directory.

Note 3: Be sure the printer is turned on before you begin this activity.

1 Key in the following: **A:\>DIR *.txt** **Enter**

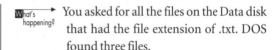 You asked for all the files on the Data disk that had the file extension of .txt. DOS found three files.

2 Key in the following: **A:\>DIR *.txt > PRN** **Enter**

This time, you instructed DOS to send the output to an output device, namely the printer instead of to the screen. The printer should be printing and nothing new should be appearing on the screen. If you have a dot-matrix printer, the lines in the directory printed and then the printer stopped at that point. The printer did not advance to the beginning of a new page. If you wanted this printout or hard copy, you would have to go to the printer and roll the platen until the perforated line appeared and you could tear off the page. If you have an ink jet printer or a laser printer, the situation is even stranger. No paper appeared at all. In order to feed the paper manually, you would have to go to the printer, turn the online button off, press the form-feed button, and then turn the online button back on.

In all these cases, you are finding a hardware solution to a problem; you are manipulating the hardware to get the desired results. With computers, there is always an easier way. What you want is a software solution, or, a way of making the computer do the work. The problem in printing a page is that a computer has no idea what a page is or when it has finished printing. Thus, you want to send a signal to the printer that the page is done and to prepare a new page. This signal is known as a form feed. Most printers universally use **Ctrl** + L as the signal for a form feed. You cannot do this with a shared printer or a networked printer. In these situations, see your lab administrator for instructions on getting your hard copy. You can use the form-feed signal on a stand-alone printer. To send this signal from the computer, you will use redirection and a command called ECHO. ECHO can send a signal to the printer if you so instruct it. Remember, when you see the notation of **Ctrl** + L, it means to hold down the **Ctrl** key and press the letter L.

3   Key in the following: **A:\>ECHO** **Ctrl** **+ L > PRN**

 The paper should eject. Look at the screen. What you keyed in, **Ctrl** + L, appeared on the screen as ^L. Thus, the signal to the printer meant one thing, but the signal to the screen was something else. If this procedure did not work for you, you will need to roll the paper manually on a dot-matrix printer. For a laser printer, take the following steps: turn off the online button, press the form-feed button, and turn on the online button.

14.16 Copying and Renaming Files

In Windows 95, although you can copy and rename files and folders when you open a folder window in Explorer or in My Computer, there are certain limitations. For instance, when you copy a file, you cannot give it a new name. If you are in the same folder, the default file name is a copy of the old file name. You must copy the file and then rename it, which is a two-step process. If you want to copy a group of files and give them a new name, you cannot do it in one step. Although you can easily copy a group of files, the files keep the same names. You must rename each file individually. You also cannot give a whole group of files new names in Windows 95.

For instance, if you were in Windows 95 and wished to copy a group of files with the extension .txt to a floppy disk for archival purposes, but wanted to give them the extension .old, you could select the files, click Send To, and choose Drive A. On the floppy disk, the files would all have the extension .txt. You would have to change each file individually from .txt to .old. When you have tasks like this to perform, it is easier to do them in DOS.

If you do not give a destination name, DOS will assume the default and keep the old file name. With the COPY command, you retain the original file and make a copy. You start with one file and end with two. With the REN command, you start with one file and end up with the same file under a new name.

The rename command, REN, does not let you specify a new drive or path for FILENAME2. Remember, you are not making a copy of a file, but using the same file. The file does not move in the process of renaming. You use the DEL command to delete files.

The COPY syntax in DOS is:

COPY   [DRIVE:][PATH]FILENAME   [DRIVE:][PATH] FILENAME
        or conceptually
COPY   source   destination

The REN command has a similar syntax:

REN   [DRIVE:][PATH] FILENAME1   FILENAME 2

The syntax for the DEL command is:

DEL   [DRIVE:][PATH] FILENAME

14.17 Activity—Using COPY, REN, and DEL

Note: You should be in the DOS box. The Data disk is in Drive A. The A:\> is displayed as the default drive and the default directory.

1   Key in the following: **A:\>COPY my.hw your.txt** **[Enter]**

2   Key in the following: **A:\> COPY my.hw your.hw** **[Enter]**

3   Key in the following: **A:\>DIR your*.*** **[Enter]**

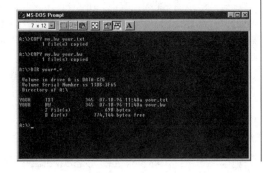

 You issued three commands. In the first instance, you told DOS to copy the file called my.hw to a new file called your.txt. You saw the message "1 file(s) copied" to let you know that your copy was successful. You then told DOS to copy my.hw to a file called your.hw. Again, you saw the message that the file was copied correctly. Last, you asked for all the files that begin with "your". You see the files listed on the screen. You can also copy a group of files and give them new names.

4   Key in the following: **A:\>COPY your*.* hist*.*** **[Enter]**

5   Key in the following: **A:\>DIR hist*.*** **[Enter]**

What's happening? → You copied the two files, your.txt and your.hw, and gave them a new name.

6 Key in the following: **A:\>DIR *.hw** [Enter]

7 Key in the following: **A:\>COPY *.hw *.old** [Enter]

What's happening? → You copied the two files with the .hw extension and kept the same file names, but gave them a new extension of .old. Renaming files is just as easy. If you only need to rename one file, it is just as easy to do it in Windows 95. However, if you want to rename a group of files, there is no way to do this in Windows 95. This is where DOS comes in handy.

8 Key in the following: **A:\>REN *.old *.new** [Enter]

9 Key in the following: **A:\>DIR *.old** [Enter]

10 Key in the following: **A:\>DIR *.new** [Enter]

What's happening? → You renamed all the files with the .old file extension to the same file names, but gave them a new extension of .new. You then used the DIR command to see that there are no more files with the .old file extension, only those with the .new file extension. You can also delete files easily.

11 Key in the following: **A:\>DEL *.new** [Enter]

12 Key in the following: **A:\>DIR *.new** [Enter]

What's happening? → You have deleted any file that had the .new extension. These files were deleted without going to the Recycle Bin. They are are gone and irretrievable. This can be good if you are certain you want to delete the files, but bad if you accidentally deleted the wrong files.

13 Key in the following: **A:\>EXIT** [Enter]

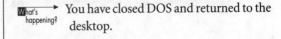

What's happening? → You have closed DOS and returned to the desktop.

14.18 Controlling the Boot Process

In the days of using only MS-DOS, users created batch files. A batch file is a file with a series of commands that execute automatically. Most users had one particular batch file called AUTOEXEC.BAT, which means automatically execute. When the system was booted and the operating system was loaded into memory, one of the last things DOS did was to look for AUTOEXEC.BAT on the booting disk. If DOS found it, this file would take precedence and DOS would automatically run it. What made the AUTOEXEC.BAT file special was that it always ran when you booted the system. Thus, only one AUTOEXEC.BAT file could be on any one booting disk. In order for AUTOEXEC.BAT to be automatic, it had to be on the booting disk, Drive A or Drive C. It also had to be located in the root directory of the booting disk.

This file was typically used for startup routines. An AUTOEXEC.BAT file contained specific commands that a user wanted to execute. In other words, it was a custom program designed by the user. Users typically made their AUTOEXEC.BAT include lines that would change the PROMPT, set the PATH, and execute any program with which they wanted to begin their work session.

Another important file was called CONFIG.SYS. This file configured the system and would set up different hardware and software specific to that computer system. When the user installed new hardware or software, a line often had to be placed in the CONFIG.SYS file so that DOS would know how to handle the device.

Fortunately, with Windows 95, you no longer need AUTOEXEC.BAT or CONFIG.SYS. Windows 95 automatically configures your devices and sets up what you need. If you upgraded from DOS or Windows 3.0 through 3.11, Windows 95 leaves the AUTOEXEC.BAT file and the CONFIG.SYS on the booting disk, but no longer uses them. Still, some things never change.

It is always good to have a bootable floppy system disk so that if something goes wrong, you can always boot with the floppy disk. When you installed Windows 95, it asked you if you wanted to create a Start Up disk and recommended that you do so. If you did not create one when you installed Windows 95, you can go to Control Panel and choose Add/Remove Programs. One of the tabs is called Start Up Disk. You can create a Start Up disk there.

In MS-DOS, there were two hidden system files called IO.SYS and MSDOS.SYS. These files, along with COMMAND.COM, were the operating system files. In Windows 95, the functions of IO.SYS and MSDOS.SYS are handled by the file called Io.sys. MSDOS.SYS still exists, but it is now an ASCII file that can be edited. Under no circumstances should you edit these files in a lab or networked environment. If you change the settings in the MSDOS.SYS file, you can control your booting process. However, before you begin changing anything in this file, you should make a backup copy of it, and you should have a Start Up disk. The file is a hidden, system, read-only file, so you would need to change the attributes. An easy way to do it is to go to the MS-DOS program and key in the following:

    C:\WINDOWS>CD \
    C:\>ATTRIB -r -s -h MSDOS.SYS
    C:\>EDIT MSDOS.SYS

The ATTRIB command line has a "-r" to remove the read-only protection, a "-s" to remove its system status, and a "-h" to unhide the file.

When you open the file, it looks something like this. You do not want to change the first lines. The only lines you want to change, add, or modify are those listed under the section heading [Options]. This file must be 1024 bytes because some programs make assumptions about the original MSDOS.SYS file and expect it to be this size. When you have completed your changes, you press **Alt** + S to save the file and then exit. At that point, you would want to make the file a hidden, read-only file again. You would key in the commands:

C:\>ATTRIB +r +s +h MSDOS.SYS

The ATTRIB command line has a "+r" to add the read-only protection, a "+s" to add its system status, and a "+h" to hide the file. Table 14.1 gives you the option names and explains what the settings mean. The option names must be keyed in exactly as listed. Each is followed by an equal sign and a value so a sample option would look like: BootKeys=0

Table 14.1   Option Names and Settings

Option Name	Setting
BootKeys	=0 Disables the boot keys. =1 Enables the boot keys, **F5**, **F6**, and **F8** when the Starting Windows 95 message appears. Default is 1.
BootDelay	=n Here, n is the number of seconds to wait after displaying the Starting Windows 95 message and before booting the system. Default is two seconds.
BootMulti	=0 Disables the **F4** key. =1 Enables the **F4** key and boots you into your previous version of DOS without going through the Startup menu. If BootKeys is disabled, this will not work. Default is 0.

BootMenu	=0 The boot menu appears only if user presses **F8** when the Starting Windows 95 message appears. =1 Boot menu automatically appears at bootup. You do not begin with Windows 95. Default is 0.
BootMenuDelay	=n Here, n is the number of seconds Windows 95 will wait after displaying the Boot menu and before selecting the default option. =0 Safe-boot option is disabled. =1 CONFIG.SYS and AUTOEXEC.BAT files are not processed. Default is 0.
BootMenuDefault	=n Here, n is the number of menu options you wish to boot by default after the number of selected seconds. Default is one second.
BootWin	=0 Starts previous version of DOS. Windows 95 Msdos.sys file is renamed Msdos.w40 the next time you boot the system. Original DOS system files are restored prior to booting. =1 Starts Windows 95. Default is 1.
Logo	=0 Disables the Windows 95 logo. If you press x during the boot process, you will also disable the logo. =1 Displays the Windows 95 logo. Default is 1.
BootGUI	=0 Boots to MS-DOS 7.0. From this prompt, you can start Windows 95 by keying in WIN. =1 Boots into Windows 95. Default is 1.
BootSafe	=0 Safe-boot option is disabled. =1 The CONFIG.SYS and AUTOEXEC.BAT files are not processed. Default is 1.
DisableLog	=0 Record of all files processed and loaded during boot is written to a file called Bootleg.txt. =1 Bootleg.txt is not written. Default is 0.

After you set the options in Msdos.sys, Windows 95 allows you to press certain function keys to perform different functions in the booting process. When you see the message Starting Windows 95 ..., you can use the function keys. These keys have the following results:

F4	If you press the **F4** key, place Windows 95 in a new directory and do not overwrite the old Windows directory, you will boot back to your last version of MS-DOS. In this case, any lines in the CONFIG.SYS file and the AUTOEXEC.BAT file will be executed.
F5	If you press the **F5** key, Windows 95 bypasses your CONFIG.SYS and AUTOEXEC BAT files and then boots as directed by the options in the Msdos.sys file if the option is set in Msdos.sys. Otherwise, it boots into safe mode.
Shift + **F5**	If you press the **Shift** and the **F5** keys, Windows 95 bypasses your CONFIG.SYS and AUTOEXEC BAT files and then boots to the MS-DOS 7.0 command prompt, regardless of any options in the Msdos.sys file.
F6	If you press the **F6** key, Windows 95 bypasses your CONFIG.SYS and AUTOEXEC.BAT files, then loads Windows 95, regardless of any of the options in the Msdos.sys file.
F8	If you press the **F8** key, you will activate the Windows 95 Boot menu screen.
Shift + **F8**	If you press the **Shift** + **F8** keys, Windows 95 processes your CONFIG.SYS and AUTOEXEC.BAT files one line at a time, asking you for confirmation before executing each line. This is known as interactive booting.

Chapter Summary

You learned that you can run MS-DOS programs in Windows 95. All you need to do is locate the program and double-click it. MS-DOS-based programs run in a window. You can change the window's font and size. You can copy data from a non-Windows program to a Windows 95 program by using the Mark and Copy commands. To switch between a window and full-screen view, press **Alt** + **Enter**. You must exit from the MS-DOS program by keying in EXIT at the command prompt to return to Windows 95.

You can run MS-DOS by choosing the MS-DOS program on the Application menus. You are then running DOS as a virtual machine. You must use the DOS commands and understand the syntax diagram. However, there are some tasks that are easier to accomplish in DOS, such as copying a file and giving it a new name, copying a group of files, and renaming a group of files. You can also print a directory listing of files by redirecting the output to the printer.

It is very important to have a Start Up disk so you can boot your system from a floppy disk. You can create the disk by using the Add/Remove object in Control Panel. You can also control the boot process by altering the Msdos.sys file. You should back this file up before you begin altering it. Once you have altered it, you can press different function keys to return to your old version of DOS, go to the boot menu, or boot to DOS 7.0 instead of Windows 95.

Key Terms

Command syntax
Fixed parameters
Global file specifications
Interactive booting
Optional parameters

Parameter
Redirection
Switch
Syntax
Syntax diagram

Variable parameters
Virtual machines
Wild cards

Discussion Questions

1. Why is it important to understand how DOS functions?
2. Explain the purpose and function of DOS.
3. List and explain two reasons for running DOS.
4. Identify and explain one task that is easier to run in DOS rather than in Windows 95.
5. What is the advantage of running a DOS application in a virtual machine?
6. Identify two ways to run a DOS-based program.
7. How can you change a font in a DOS window?
8. Define command syntax. Why is it important to know the syntax when using a command?
9. Why is it important to know the command syntax of DOS?
10. Why is it important to understand syntax when using Windows 95?
11. Explain the purpose and function of the DIR command in DOS.
12. What are parameters? How are they used?
13. Compare and contrast variable parameters and fixed parameters.
14. When using DOS, how can you get help on a topic?
15. Identify each item in this diagram and explain its purpose.
      DIR [DRIVE:][PATH][FILENAME] [/P] [/W]
16. What do brackets indicate in a syntax diagram?
17. List and explain two optional parameters found in DIR.
18. Define global file specifications. When would you use them?
19. Why and how would you use Explorer parameters in the Run command box?
20. How and why would you want to make a shortcut to the desktop?
21. Explain the purpose and function of redirection.
22. Redirection does not work with all DOS commands, but it does work with DIR. Explain.
23. What happens when you redirect output to the printer?
24. List and explain two limitations in copying and renaming files and folders in Explorer or My Computer.

25. Compare and contrast copying and renaming files in DOS and performing the same tasks in Windows 95.
26. Explain the purpose and function of the AUTOEXEC.BAT and CONFIG.SYS files.
27. Why is it wise to have a bootable floppy system disk?
28. When using Windows 95, how can you control your booting process?
29. Why would you want to control the booting process?
30. List three function keys that can be used when starting Windows 95 and explain what will occur when those function keys are pressed.

True/False Questions

For each question, circle the letter T if the statement is true or the letter F if the statement is false.

T   F   1.   In DOS, the DIR command is used to see the directory of a disk.
T   F   2.   A variable parameter is one in which you supply the value.
T   F   3.   The command syntax diagram tells you how to enter a command.
T   F   4.   Command syntax is only used with DOS commands, never in Windows 95.
T   F   5.   When using wildcards, the question mark symbol represents a group of characters.

Completion Questions

Write the correct answer in each blank space provided.

6. Windows 95 runs DOS in what is called a(n) _____ machine.
7. DOS is a(n) _____ operating system, whereas Windows 95 is a(n) _____ operating system.
8. The order of a command line is considered the command _____.
9. You can tell which parameters are optional because they are enclosed in _____.
10. You may send the output of the DIR command to the printer by using _____.

Multiple Choice Questions

Circle the letter of the correct answer for each question.

11. Before a text can be copied from a DOS application you must
    a. restart the computer in MS-DOS mode.
    b. mark the text.
    c. run the program in a window.
    d. both b and c
12. The DOS command for listing files that is equivalent to Explorer or My Computer is
    a. EXPLORE.
    b. LIST.
    c. DIR.
    d. INDEX.

13. The file that can be edited that determines how Windows 95 boots is
    a. Autoexec.bat
    b. Config.sys
    c. Io.sys
    d. Msdos.sys
14. It would be easier to use DOS than Windows 95 to perform tasks when
    a. you want to use a graphical interface.
    b. the task is more difficult or more time-consuming in Windows 95.
    c. the task involves long file names.
    d. never; all tasks are easier in Windows 95.
15. The / (forward slash) in a DOS command is known as known as
    a. an operator.
    b. an option bar.
    c. a switch.
    d. none of the above

Application Assignments

Problem Set I—At the Computer

Problem A

Open **Explorer**. Open the **95book** folder. Double-click the **Games** folder, then **Mlshut.exe**. Press Enter.

1. What is the name of this game?
   a. Mshut.exe
   b. Msshut.hlp
   c. Shut the Box.
   d. Microsoft Shut the Box.

2. The game is dedicated to
   a. my family.
   b. game lovers.
   c. computer users.

Press Enter. When it asks for a player name, press the Esc key. Press **Y** to exit the game. Press Enter.

    3. A dialog box appears. Its title bar states:
       a. Fatal Error-Mlshut.
       b. Exit-Mlshut.
       c. Finished-Mlshut.

Click **OK**. Click the **Close** button on the **DOS** window.

Problem B

Open the **MS-DOS Prompt**. Key in the following: **CD 95BOOK** [Enter]

    4. Find the file called PERSONAL.FIL. How many bytes does it have?
       a. 3.
       b. 317.
       c. 2307.
       d. 3057.

Find all the files that have the file extension .BMP in the 95BOOK folder.

    5. How many files are there?
       a. One.
       b. Two.
       c. Three.
       d. Four.

Find all the files that begin with the letter E and whose file extension ends in a letter t.

    6. How many files are there?
       a. Three.
       b. Six
       c. Nine.
       d. Twelve.

Locate the file called **BYE.TXT** in the **95BOOK** folder.

    7. What time is displayed?
       a. 10:45
       b. 10:45a
       c. 10:45p
       d. 22.45

Exit the **MS-DOS Prompt** and return to the desktop.

Problem C

Place the Data disk in Drive A. Open the **MS-DOS Prompt**. Key in the following: **CD 95BOOK** [Enter] Copy all the files that begin with the letter b to the root directory of the Data disk. Overwrite any files, if necessary.

8. What command did you use?
   a. COPY B*.* A:\
   b. COPY B*.*
   c. COPY A:B*.* C:\95BOOK

9. How many files were copied?
   a. One.
   b. Two.
   c. Three.
   d. Four.
   e. Five.

Exit the **MS-DOS Prompt** and return to the desktop

Problem D

For the following assignment:
1. Place the Data disk in Drive A.
2. Open the **MS-DOS Prompt**.
3. Key in the following: **A:** [Enter]
4. Key in the following: **CD ** [Enter]
5. Copy all the files that end with the file extension .txt to a new set of files that have the same file name but the extension of .czg.
6. Use the DIR command to locate only the files that have the extension of .czg.
7. Redirect the output of this command to the printer.

Problem E

For the following assignment:
1. Open the **MS-DOS Prompt**.
2. Key in the following: **A:** [Enter] and **CD ** [Enter]
3. Rename all the files that begin with **YOUR** and have any file extension to a new set of files with the new file name **FRANK** but the same file extensions.
4. Use the DIR command to locate only the files with the file name **FRANK** and any extension.
5. Redirect the output of this command to the printer.
6. Delete all the files that have the file name **FRANK**.

Problem Set II—Brief Essay

For all essay questions, use Notepad or WordPad for your answer. Print your answer.

1. Compare and contrast using the DOS and Windows 95 interfaces. Which do you prefer? Why?
2. Agree or disagree with the statement, "Learning command syntax is not important in Windows 95." Explain your reasons for your choice.

Problem Set III—Scenario

You have two DOS-based programs on your system. One is an address program and the other is a game. Describe how you would run these programs in the Windows 95 environment. Explain why you selected the option you did. You now decide that you want a shortcut for these programs. How could you create a shortcut? Describe the steps you would take.

Chapter 15

Multimedia, Microsoft Exchange, MSN, and the Internet

Chapter Overview

Windows 95 provides a lot of support for multimedia. Multimedia can be a combination of video, sound, and recordings. You must have the proper hardware to use multimedia in Windows 95. If you have the correct hardware, you can play audio CDs and customize your recordings to suit your preferences.

In Windows 95, you can play videos by using the Media Player. You can do a small amount of editing of sound and video clips as well. You can embed video and sound clips in documents.

Windows 95 provides Microsoft Exchange, which is a central place to create, send, and receive faxes and electronic mail. When you install Microsoft Exchange, it sets up an Inbox on your desktop in which you can keep mail, send mail, and do other types of electronic communications. Windows 95 also provides a character-based communications package called HyperTerminal, which allows you to communicate with online services and other computers so that you can send and receive files.

Windows 95 provides the Microsoft Network, a commercial service that you can choose to install. MSN allows you access to forums, bulletin boards, electronic mail, and other such resources.

Should you choose to install it, the Internet Explorer allows you to connect to networks and travel the information superhighway. Here, you have access to libraries, commercial vendors, forums, chat groups, and other such amenities.

Learning Objectives

1. Define multimedia, explain the role of the multimedia consortium, and explain Windows 95's role in the support of multimedia services.
2. Explain how the CD Player can be used to play an audio CD.
3. List the devices in the CD Player and explain how they can control the sound levels and balances of a CD.
4. Explain the purpose and function of Video for Windows.
5. Explain the purpose and function of the Media Player.
6. Explain how to edit and embed video and sound objects in a document.
7. Explain the function and advantages of using the Phone Dialer.
8. Explain the purpose and function of Microsoft Exchange and the Personal Address book provided by Microsoft Exchange.
9. Explain how to send and receive a fax in Microsoft Exchange.
10. Explain the purpose of HyperTerminal.
11. Explain the purpose and function of The Microsoft Network (MSN).
12. Explain the purpose and function of the Internet.

Student Outcomes

1. Use the CD Player to play an audio disc, if hardware permits.
2. Use the Media Player application program to play a video clip.
3. Edit and embed a video clip, if hardware permits.
4. Use the Phone Dialer, if hardware permits.
5. Identify and explain the function of each item in the Inbox window.
6. Use Address Book to send a message, if hardware permits.
7. Use Microsoft Exchange to create and prepare a fax for transmission, if hardware permits.
8. Use HyperTerminal to connect to another computer, if hardware permits.
9. Use MSN, if hardware permits.
10. Use the Internet Explorer to log on to the Internet, if hardware permits.

15.1   Multimedia

In order to use multimedia, you need the proper hardware. In general, this includes the capability of running Windows 95 (memory and disk storage availability), a CD-ROM drive, a sound card, and speakers. If you want to record anything, you also need a microphone. Windows 95 makes it easy to install these devices with the Add New Hardware wizard in Control Panel. A multimedia consortium called *MPC* (*Multimedia Personal Computer*) has set standards for multimedia. The latest version is called *MPC-2*. Any hardware device or software that meets this consortium's standards should work correctly. Nearly every computer today that has a CD-ROM drive and a sound card does meet the MPC standards.

Windows 95 allows you to play existing videos, sound, audio CDs, and animation clips. If you want to edit or create multimedia productions, you need additional software and need to learn many new skills.

15.2   AutoPlay

If you have a computer with the proper multimedia hardware, you have the feature called *AutoPlay*. Every time you insert a CD into your CD-ROM drive, Windows 95 is aware of it. Windows 95 inspects the CD to see what it is. Windows 95 makes the assumption that if you insert a CD into the CD-ROM drive, you are planning to use it immediately. One of three things will happen next:

1. If the CD is a program that has not been installed, Windows 95 automatically begins installing the program.
2. If the CD is a program that has been installed, Windows 95 immediately starts that program.
3. If it is an audio CD, Windows 95 immediately begins playing it.

If you do not want Windows 95 to immediately start the disc, hold down the **Shift** key when you insert the disc. This will bypass AutoPlay.

15.3   CD Player

In addition to loading software, the CD Player can also play and program audio CDs. You insert any CD into the CD Player, and it automatically starts playing the CD. Once you have inserted the audio CD, you can store the names of the CD, artists, and musical selection on each one. You can alter the order in which the selections play, remove selections you do not like, and have the selections played randomly. The associations are made for that specific compact disc so the next time you insert the disc, all your settings will be restored.

If you have purchased a compact audiodisc that is labeled "enhanced CD," you do not have to enter the artist and selection titles manually. This is taken care of for you. Furthermore, if the audiodisc is an enhanced CD, you will see all types of advanced features. For instance, you may see spots to click on the album cover. When you click, you may receive facts about the artist, the selection, the lyrics, or other information that the CD manufacturer has placed on the audio CD.

15.4   Activity—Using the CD Player

1 Place an audiodisc in the CD Player.

 Your selection should automatically start playing. In this example, you are looking at a George Strait disc—Greatest Hits, Volume II.

2 Click **Start**. Point at **Programs**. Point at **Multimedia**. Click **Player**.

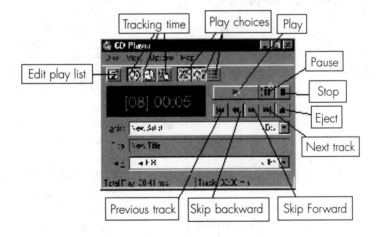

 As you can see, this looks similar to a physical CD player that you operate by pressing the appropriate buttons.

3 Click the **Edit Play List** button.

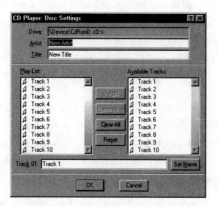

What's happening? Here, you can key in the information for your CD since this is not an enhanced CD. The device drive name is specified. You can key the artist and album names into the text boxes.

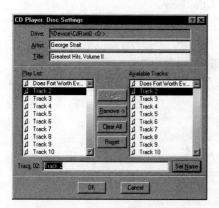

What's happening? You click a track you like in the Play List pane. Then, you key in the selection titles in the Track text box at the bottom of the window. This is how it looks when it is completed:

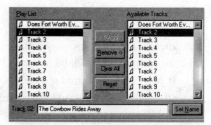

What's happening? Once you have keyed in the title, you click the Set Name command button. The following is a completed CD listing:

What's happening? If you want to change the order in which the selections will be played, you can drag them into the Play List pane. In the example, "All My Ex's Live in Texas" will be dragged upwards. You see the arrow and music staff as you move the selection up. You can drop it anywhere you want. It does not have to be the first selection.

 In this example, "All My Ex's Live in Texas" is now in the second position. If you want a song to play more than once, click the selection in the Available Tracks pane.

 Once you have selected an available track, the Add button becomes available. Click the Add button.

 Now the selection will play twice. You can drag it in the list to where you want

it to play. To remove a selection, click it in the Play List pane.

 Now the Remove button becomes available. When you remove a track, you are only preventing it from playing, not removing it from the CD.

4 Click **OK**.

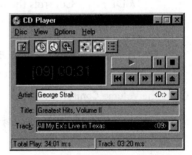

 You have returned to the CD Player window. If you wish to continue listening to your audio CD, minimize it. If you want to play this CD later, close the CD Player without ejecting the disc. To reactivate it, click Start/Programs/Accessories/Multimedia/CD Player and the Play button. You can also control the volume level.

5 Click **View**. Click **Volume Control**.

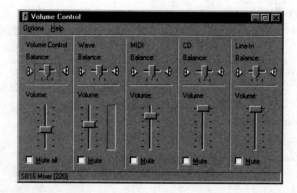

  You can control all levels in the Volume Control window. You may have more or fewer selections. Depending on what device you are using, you may be able to control the sound levels and balance. The following is a list of options you may be able to adjust:

Volume	Controls the entire sound, no matter what device you are using.
Wave	Controls the wave table sound volume. *Wave* sounds are realistic sounds, unlike *FM synthesis* sounds, which less expensive sound cards and/or older computers use.
MIDI	Controls the *MIDI* (*Musical Instrument Digital Interface*) sound, which reproduces musical instruments and other such sounds.
CD	Controls the volume of the audio CD when using CD Player.
Line-in	Controls any device that you connect to your sound card such as a microphone or a stereo's output.

6 Close the **Volume Control** window.

7 Minimize the **CD Player**.

8   Double-click the **My Computer** icon. Double-click **Control Panel**. Double-click the **Multimedia** icon.

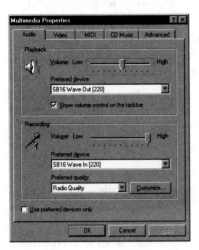

You see the Multimedia property sheet. Audio is selected. In the Playback area, a check box allows you to set the volume control on the taskbar. If you had a microphone, you could adjust the volume and sound level of your recording.

9   Click the **CD Music** tab.

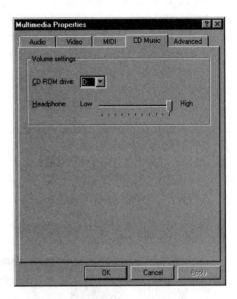

As you can see, your CD-ROM drive letter is listed. If you had more than one CD-ROM drive, you could change it. You could also change the Headphone volume level, if you had headphones.

10   Close the property sheet.

11   Close the **My Computer** window.

You have returned to the desktop.

15.5   Video in Windows 95

Prior to the release of Windows 95, Microsoft allowed users to play videos with a product called Video for Windows. Most multimedia products at that time included a run-time version of Video for Windows. Windows 95 also includes Video for Windows. This means that it supports full-motion video. It can display video in a full-screen resolution or in a smaller window. Video is much smoother in Windows 95 because the way it handles the playback has been improved. Of course, video is hardware dependent. How your video will play back on your system depends on both the speed of your processor and the speed of your CD-ROM drive. The first releases of CD-ROMs were double-speed. Today, they are most commonly quad-speed, and the latest available speed is called 6X. You may also want what is called a video accelerator card, which speeds up the drawing of graphics.

15.6   Using Media Player

Windows 95 includes a Media Player application program. Media Player allows you to play sound files, Microsoft Multimedia Movie Player files, Video for Windows files, and MIDI sequencer files. You will find that most videos fall into one of these categories. Windows 95 recognizes the type of file by its extension and knows what to do with it. The extension .avi means Video for Windows, .wav means sound wave files, and .mid or .mi mean MIDI sequencer files. All of these file types are "playable." Each provides a different kind of audio and video quality. Windows 95 automatically recognizes the sound sources and selects the correct playing software for you.

15.7   Activity—Playing a Video Clip

Note: If you did not purchase the CD-ROM version of Windows 95, you will not be able to locate these files.

1   Insert the Windows 95 installation CD-ROM.

 Because of AutoPlay, the above screen appears.

2   Double-click **Cool Video Clips**.

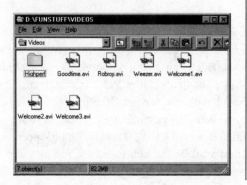

What's happening? You see the available video choices. Each is a file with the .avi file extension. The high-performance folder, Highperf, contains the same .avi files, but their quality may be a little better, depending on your hardware.

3   Double-click **Goodtime.avi**.

What's happening? You see and hear a music video.

4   Close **Goodtime.avi**.

5   Double-click **Welcome1.avi**.

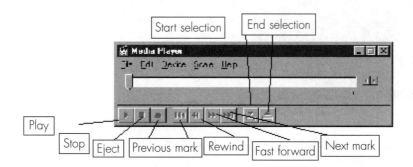   Again, you are playing a video clip with motion, color, and sound.

6   Close **Welcome1.avi**.

7   Close the **D:\FUNSTUFF** window.

8   Minimize **Windows 95 CD-ROM** window.

15.8   Editing and Embedding Video and Sound Objects

Just as you embedded a sound object in Chapter 12, you can also insert a video clip or part of a video clip in any document that supports OLE. You can embed it or link it, depending on your needs. In this case, you will use Media Player, which is located in Multimedia.

15.9   Activity—Embedding Part of a Video Clip in WordPad

Note: The Windows 95 CD-ROM disc should be in your CD-ROM drive.

1   Click **Start**. Point at **Programs**. Point at **Accessories**. Point at **Multimedia**. Click **Media Player**.

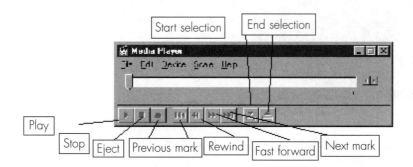

You have opened the Media Player. The Start Selection and End Selection buttons allow you to choose which section of a clip you wish to include in your document. You can include the entire clip or part of it.

2   Click **File**. Click **Open**.

 If you installed Microsoft Plus!, you will see a collection of clips in the Media window. These are all sound clips, which you can determine from the .mi, .mid, and .wav file extensions.

3   In the **File name** text box, key in the following: **D:\Funstuff\Videos\Welcome1.avi** [Enter]

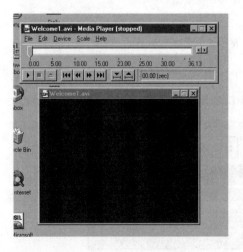

 You have opened the Welcome1.avi window. You cannot maximize it. However, you can make the window larger if you want. If you do, you may lose some picture quality.

4   Click the **Play** button.

 As the video clip plays, the scale in Media Player reflects how many seconds have elapsed. The butterfly appears at approximately five seconds.

5   Click **Scale**. Click **Frames**.

6   Replay the video clip.

 The butterfly appears at about frame 50. The man and butterfly appear in about frame 100. You decide that you want to include a video clip of the butterfly and man from about frame 100 to about frame 150.

7   Drag the slider to **100**. Click the **Start Selection** button.

8 Drag the slider to **150**. Click the **End Selection** button.

What's
happening? → You have selected your clip.

9 Click **Edit**. Click **Copy Object**.

10 Click **Start**. Point at **Programs**. Point at **Accessories**. Click **WordPad**.

11 Key in the following: **This is my video clip.** [Enter]

12 Click **Edit**. Click **Paste**.

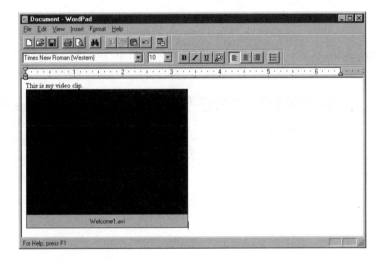

What's
happening? → You have pasted the entire image into WordPad. If you want only an icon, you must change the properties.

13 Right-click the object. Click **Object Properties**. Click the **View** tab.

What's happening? → You want to display the image as an icon in your document.

14 Click **Display as icon**. Click **Apply**. Click **OK**. Click outside the object to deselect it.

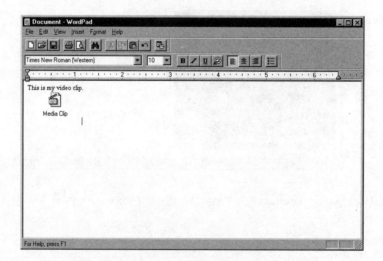

What's happening? → Now it is displayed as an icon. You can also change the object's name or icon.

15 Double-click the icon.

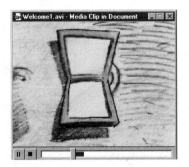

As you can see, only the selected portion of the video clip played in your document, not the entire clip.

16 Close **WordPad**. Do not save the document.

17 Close **Media Player**.

15.10 Phone Dialer

Phone Dialer is a tool located in the Accessories folder. In order to use it, you must have a modem connected to your phone line. Phone Dialer dials a number for the purpose of voice communication. It allows you to pick up your handset to speak once the number is dialed. You can keep often used numbers in Speed Dialer and just click a number. If you need to prefix a phone number with a calling card number or use a long distance access code, you will find Phone Dialer useful. Phone Dialer also keeps a log of the phone calls you have made.

15.11 Activity—Using Phone Dialer

1 Click **Start**. Point at **Programs**. Point at **Accessories**. Click **Phone Dialer**.

What's
happening? → The Phone Dialer window appears. In order to use it, you would click each number, then click Dial.

2 Key in a phone number. Click **Dial**.

What's
happening? → Two message boxes appear. One tells you that Phone Dialer does not have a log entry for the number you are calling. The other initiates the phone call. You can choose either Talk or Hang Up.

3 Click **Hang Up**.

4 Click a speed dial button.

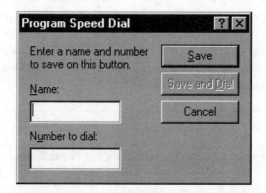

What's
happening? → Here, you fill in a name and number.

5 Key in a name and a number.

What's happening? ➤ You can dial right now or save your number.

6 Click **Save**.

What's happening? ➤ Now you can simply click Steven's button to call him.

7 Click **Tools**. Click **Show Log**.

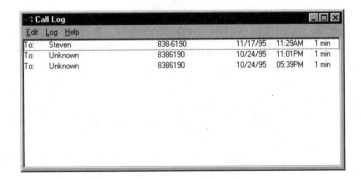

What's happening? → The log lets you can see whom you called and how long you talked.

8 Close the **Call Log** window.

9 Click **Edit**. Click **Speed Dial**.

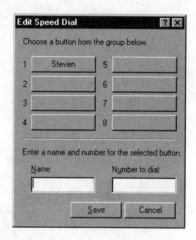

What's happening? → You can alter any speed dialing settings here.

10 Click **Cancel**. Close **Phone Dialer**.

15.12 Microsoft Exchange

Windows 95 comes with some tools, such as Microsoft Exchange, that allow you to exchange electronic mail and to send and receive faxes. Microsoft Exchange must be installed as a component of Windows 95. When you install Microsoft Exchange, it places a universal Inbox on your desktop.

Today, people communicate more and more by electronic mail, or *e-mail*. To receive and generate e-mail, you must belong to a service such as CompuServe, America online, or a provider such as MSN (The Microsoft Network) that provides access to the Internet. These online services provide access to a wealth of information ranging from world events to specific computer hardware questions. You can "chat" online with people all over the world about topics of interest to you, or you can send e-mail.

If you belong to a service or more than one service, you can log on to your provider or providers every day to send and receive your electronic mail. Because you are charged for each moment you are online, it is best to compose your messages offline. *Online* means that you have connected via your modem to your service. *Offline* means you are no longer connected to your service. Once you are online, you simply "mail" your e-mail, which takes a very short period of time.

You also want to be able to receive your mail and read it offline. The universal Inbox provided by Microsoft Exchange is a place to store, receive, and send all electronic mail. When you receive messages in your Inbox, an Inbox icon appears on your taskbar indicating that you have new mail.

Microsoft Exchange also provides a Personal Address Book where you can keep names, addresses, and notes about people or services. The only service that comes with Windows 95 is MSN. If you wish to belong to a different service or an additional one, such as America Online or CompuServe, you need to contact those organizations.

15.13 Activity—Using Microsoft Exchange

1 Double-click the **Inbox** icon on the desktop.

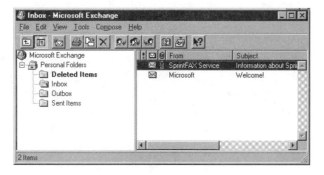

 The Microsoft Exchange window appears, followed immediately by the Inbox - Microsoft Exchange window. If you had any incoming messages, they would appear in the second window.

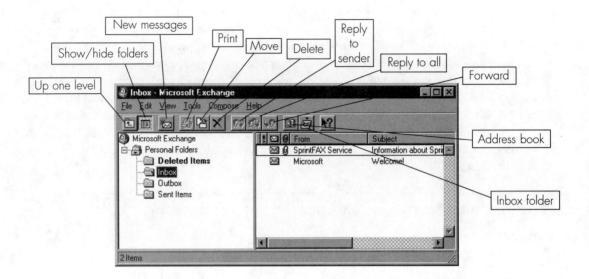

What's happening? The Inbox window is a folder window. The toolbar buttons provide easily accessible choices.

2 Click the **Inbox** folder in the left pane.

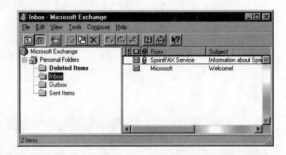

What's happening? The sealed envelope next to an item indicates that you have not yet read that message. A paper clip next to an item indicates that the file contains an embedded object. If you double-clicked the Sprint folder, you would be connected to Sprint automatically, which is trying to sell you their online service. Since this is a folder window, you can manipulate the window size.

3 Right-click the **Microsoft** envelope.

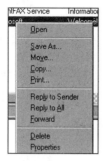

What's happening? → In addition to the usual choices, you also can Forward or Reply to this message.

4 Double-click the **Microsoft** envelope.

What's happening? → Since this is a folder, you can drag it, copy it, or move it to any location you wish. If you wanted to delete it, you could drag it to the Deleted Items folder. The items would remain in the folder until you opened that folder and deleted them.

6 Close **Microsoft Exchange**.

What's happening? → You are welcomed to the Microsoft Exchange and given information about the various services it provides.

15.14 Using Address Book and Sending a Message

In order to use the Address Book, you must have Microsoft Exchange installed. If you are on a network using the Windows workgroup, you can have two Address Books. The Postoffice Address Book serves the users in a workgroup. The Personal Address Book serves any individual user. Most users compile and create a Personal Address Book and use it as the default. The Personal Address Book is used for receiving faxes and e-mail. You can use the Address Book to create and send messages. You can create mail and send it to others using MSN or another online service.

15.15 Activity—Using Address Book and Sending a Message

1   Click **Start**. Point at **Programs**. Click **Microsoft Exchange**.

2   Click **Tools**. Click **Address Book**.

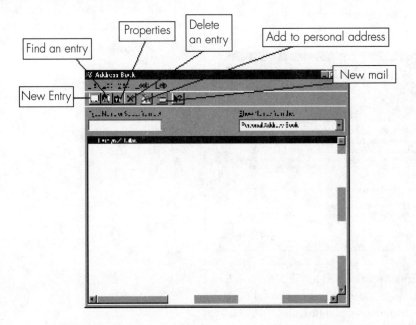

 You have opened the Address Book.

3 Click the **New Entry** icon on the toolbar.

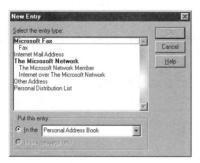

Now, you have to decide what kind of entry this is going to be. To send things by fax/modem, you must have access to an online service. You would choose Fax if you were sending a document as a fax. If you need to send copies of a document to many people, such as a distribution list in an office environment, you could choose Personal Distribution List. This would create one entry to distribute a fax or e-mail to many people. In this case, you are going to use the Internet selection.

4 Double-click **Internet Mail Address**.

5 Key in a name and an Internet address.

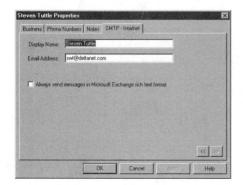

You have keyed in a name with an Internet address. You can input more

information, such as a home or work address and phone or fax numbers.

6 Click the **Business** tab.

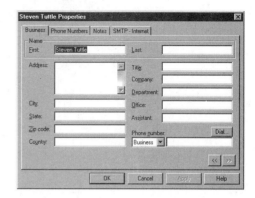

As you can see, you can include address information.

7 Click the **Phone Numbers** tab.

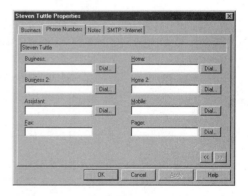

You can enter a multiplicity of numbers for this individual.

8 Click **OK**. Close the **Address Book**.

9   Click the **Outbox** folder in the **Microsoft Exchange** window's left pane. Click **Compose**. Click **New Message**.

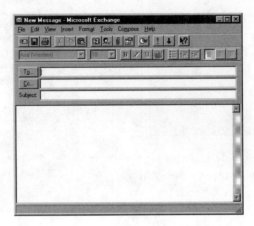

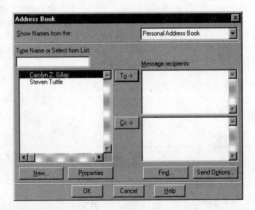   You can create your message here.

10   Double-click the **To** button.

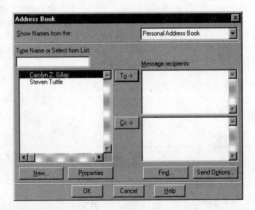

    You may select a person from your address book.

11   Click a person. Click **To**. Click **OK**.

12 In the **Subject** text box, key in the following: **TEST** Tab

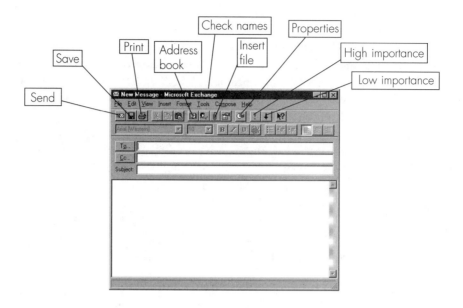

By pressing the Tab key, you move to the area where you can create your message.

13 Key in the following: **THIS IS A TEST.**

14 Click the **Send** button.

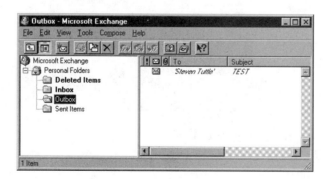

Your message is in the Outbox. To send it, you would need to be connected to an online service

15 Close **Microsoft Exchange**.

15.16 Faxes in Microsoft Exchange

Installing Microsoft Exchange allows you to send and receive faxes. You must have a fax/modem in order to do so. When you install your fax/modem, you will be able to select that fax/modem within a Windows 95 word processor by using WordPad or by running the Fax wizard so that you can send a fax directly from the Microsoft Exchange. If the person receiving the fax also has Windows 95 installed, the document itself is sent so the recipient receives a document file in the Inbox. If the recipient has a standard fax machine, then he or she receives a paper standard fax. The minute you activate Microsoft Exchange, you will see a fax machine icon on your taskbar.

The easiest way to create a fax document is to use a word processor such as WordPad. You then choose File/Print. However, instead of selecting your printer, you select the Microsoft Fax option. If you have already created a document and saved it to disk, you can fax directly from Microsoft Exchange to any recipient in your Personal Address Book.

15.17 Activity—Creating a Fax

1   Click **Start**. Point at **Programs**. Point at **Accessories**. Click **WordPad**.

2   Key in the following: **THIS IS A TEST.**

3   Click **File**. Click **Print**.

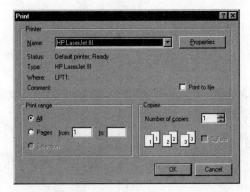

 → Your default printer is selected.

4   Click the arrow in the **Name** drop-down list box.

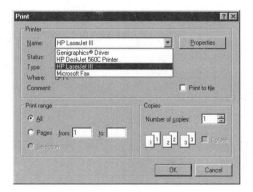

You have several choices.

5   Click **Microsoft Fax**. Click **OK**.

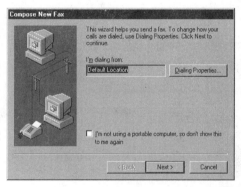

You see a message that the document is printing to the Microsoft Fax. You are then presented with the Compose New Fax dialog box.

6 Click **Next**.

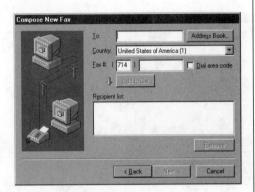

What's happening? If you have the recipient's name and fax number in your Personal Address Book, you can use that. Otherwise, you can just key in a name and fax number.

7 Key in a name and fax number. Click **Next**.

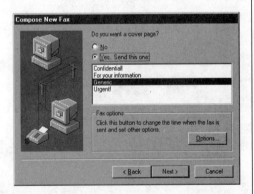

What's happening? You are given the opportunity to include a cover page. By clicking the Options button, you can also establish the time, urgency, and other characteristics of the fax.

8 Click **Next**.

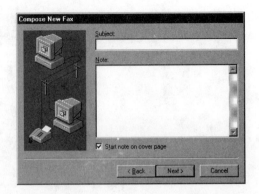

What's happening? You can include information here about the subject and add any notes you wish.

9 Click **Next**.

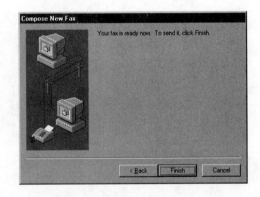

What's happening? Your fax is ready to be sent. If you wanted to send it, you would click Finish.

10 Click **Cancel**.

11 Close **WordPad**. Do not save the document.

15.18 HyperTerminal

In order to communicate with other computers, you need an electronic communications package. If you wish to communicate with an online service such as CompuServe, MSN, or America Online, you need a computer, a modem, and a software communications package. Typically, commercial online services provide free communications software. However, you must pay for the service you choose. If you want to communicate with another computer user to *upload* (send) or *download* (receive) a file or files, you and the person with whom you want to communicate both need computers, modems, and electronic communications software with which to communicate. You may want to communicate with *bulletin board services* (*BBSs*) which are electronic bulletin boards that provide different services. They can contain different kinds of software, such as games that you can download. Some are provided by software manufacturers for users to download the newest drivers and patches (fixes to software bugs). In all cases, you need a computer, a modem, and the communications software.

Windows 95 provides HyperTerminal as its built-in electronic communications software. Connecting online can be a difficult, technical task. HyperTerminal eliminates some of the initial setup requirements for communicating with remote computers. However, HyperTerminal is a character-based communications software package. It does the initial communications, but you still need to know what the other computer needs when you log in. Most people who use online services use the graphics-based software that such services provide. Those who want to simplify their communication with other users purchase other software packages, such as ProComm Plus for Windows, which are graphics-based communications packages and are easier to use.

15.19 Activity—Using HyperTerminal

1 Click **Start**. Point at **Programs**. Point at **Accessories**. Click **HyperTerminal**.

2 Double-click the **CompuServe** icon.

 When you double-click the CompuServe icon, HyperTerminal opens with the 800 number ready and available for you. If you click Dial, you see the following dialog box followed by the CompuServe log on screen. It asks you questions to which you need answers. When you connect to a service with the appropriate graphics software, such as MSN, the questions are in plain English and allow you to connect easily to the services.

As you can see, some commercial providers of electronic mail and online services, such as AT&T Mail or CompuServe, give users icons with which to log on to their services.

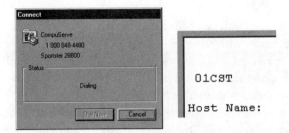

3 Click **Cancel**.

4 Double-click the **Hypertrm** icon.

 If you want to connect with another computer, you can assign a name and an icon to that computer. HyperTerminal saves the connection information in a *connection profile*. Once you have set up a profile, you only need to click its icon to access it.

5 Key in the following: **WORK**

 You have given your connection a name and an icon. Now you need to give this profile a phone number.

6 Click **OK**.

> **What's happening?** The information you key into the Phone Number dialog box provides your default country code, your default area code, and the name of your modem.

7 Key in the following: **555-1111**

8 Click **OK**.

> **What's happening?** Your computer is ready to connect to the mythical number you keyed in.

9 Click **Cancel**. Close the **HyperTerminal** window.

> **What's happening?** HyperTerminal wants to know if you want to save this profile.

10 Click **Yes**.

> **What's happening?** Now, you have a profile for your work number. The next time you need to dial work, you can simply click the WORK profile to be connected.

11 Drag the **WORK** icon to the **Recycle Bin**.

12 Close the **HyperTerminal** window.

> **What's happening?** You have returned to the desktop.

15.20 MSN—The Microsoft Network

When you purchase Windows 95, one of the installation options you have is to install the MSN network (The Microsoft Network). MSN is a commercial online service that competes with CompuServe, America Online, and Genie, among others. MSN gives users access to electronic mail, news, movie reviews, sports information, and games. It provides forums, places for people to communicate by computer. In forums, people might address technical issues, working together to solve computer problems. They might also chat about some subject of interest. People leave messages, receive messages, or chat "live." When you chat live, you key in questions and answers, which are displayed on your monitor along with other people's questions and answers.

Like all commercial services, MSN charges you for your connection time to the service. When you sign up, you must tell Microsoft how you want to pay for the service. Different forums and services will have additional charges. The cost for using MSN depends on what services are currently being offered. These services will expand with time. The cost of basic access to MSN is competitive with other online services. However, be aware that if you choose to visit certain sites, you will incur an additional charge.

When you sign up with MSN, you create a member ID by which people will know you on MSN. In addition, you provide a password. Only you know what the password is so that no one else can access your account. A password should be easy to remember yet covert. For instance, you might use your mother's maiden name or the name of the city you live in spelled backward to fool possible password thieves. When you deal with online services, it is very important that you have a fast modem. A modem comes in a speed called a baud rate, which is the speed of the computerized telephone connection. Today, with graphics becoming a bigger part of communications, a 14.4 modem is a minimum, with a 28.8 modem preferred.

15.21 Activity—Using MSN

Note: The next activity assumes that you have joined MSN.

1   Double-click the **MSN** icon on the desktop.

 You are ready to dial into MSN.

2   Click **Connect.**

3   Right-click the **MSN** icon on the taskbar.

 You can send mail, look for files, or go to your favorite places once you know where they are. MSN Central is the main directory to MSN and gives you overall choices.

4   Click **Go to MSN Central.**

 Each of the choices takes you to other places. MSN Today is current news and events, E-mail allows you to send and receive mail, Member Assistance helps you with membership information, and Categories provides a list of available topics.

5 Click **MSN Today**.

 What's happening?   You see a list of current topics of interest. If you wanted to see more information, you would click on the topic of interest.

6 Close the **MSN Today** window.

7 Click **Categories** in the **MSN Central** window.

 What's happening?   As you can see, there is a wide list of categories from which to choose.

8 Double-click **Arts & Entertainment**.

 What's happening?   You now have many choices about the arts.

9 Double-click **Movies**.

 What's happening?   Now all the topics relate to movies. You can look at reviews, talk to other people about movies, and learn how to write a movie, among other things.

10   Click **File** on the Movies menu bar.

 MSN provides directory windows. It is a hierarchical structure. To back up one screen at a time, you click Up One Level. If this is a site you wish to visit a lot, you can add it to Favorite Places. You can also create a shortcut. If you did this, clicking on the shortcut would take you directly to the Movies window. You can also log off, which is called Sign Out in this menu.

11   Click **Up One Level**.

 You return to the previous screen.

12   Click **File**. Click **Sign Out**.

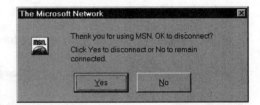

 Before you log off, MSN asks if you want to disconnect.

13   Click **Yes**.

 You have closed MSN and returned to the desktop.

15.22 The Internet

The *Internet* is an enormous, worldwide network of computers—a network of networks. By connecting to this network, you become connected with all the people sitting at their computers. There are more than 20 million people connected to the Internet. You can access the government, colleges, universities, and other educational institutions. You can connect with companies and particular individuals. These sources provide information to anyone who wants it and provide a place for you to purchase items of interest.

The primary areas of interest are e-mail, chat lines, forums, and the World Wide Web (WWW). The Web, as it is known colloquially, is an interconnected collection of more than 50,000 Web sites, called home pages. It is growing at the rate of a 1000 a day. You can even create your own home page. There is a White House home page, a Grateful Dead home page, and a home page for just about any subject that you can imagine. Home pages usually have *hypertext links*. This means it works like a huge encyclopedia; when you click an item, it "leaps" you to the subject of interest. Thus, if you were interested in mystery books, by knowing the address of a mystery home page, such as http://www.clulass.com, you would be taken to a home page. There, you could click on Authors and it would take you immediately to a list of authors. Once on that page, you could click on your favorite author and you would be taken to that home page. You would be "surfing the net."

Commercial sites end in .com, educational sites end in .edu, and government sites end in .gov. You will use an index to these sites called Yahoo. Its address is http://www.yahoo.com.

When you install MSN, you can choose to create an icon to the Internet on the desktop. You will then be able to connect to the net by double-clicking the Internet icon.

15.23 Activity—Using the Internet

Note: It is assumed that you have installed the Internet using MSN.

1   Double-click the **Internet** icon.

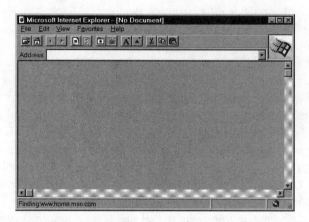

> **What's happening?** → If you look at the bottom of the screen, you see that MSN is looking for www.home.msn.com. Home is the home page for the MSN Internet Explorer.

> **What's happening?** → Once again, you need to connect to MSN, which is the gateway to the Internet. You can use Internet providers other than MSN, but you must sign up with those providers and pay their fees.

2   Click **Connect**.

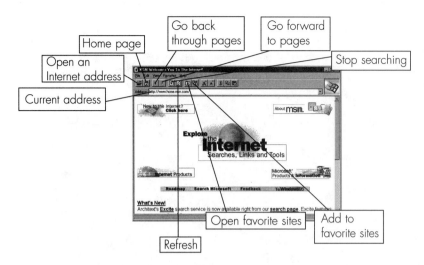

Home page

Go back through pages

Go forward to pages

Open an Internet address

Stop searching

Current address

Open favorite sites

Add to favorite sites

Refresh

What's happening? You have entered the Microsoft Internet Explorer. If you look in the Address text box, you see your "home," which is http://www.home.msn.com. This is the address to which you will come home. You can click on any of the pictures, which will take you to a new site. You can also click any underlined term in the window; each one is a hypertext entry that will take you to another place.

3 Click the **Open** button on the toolbar.

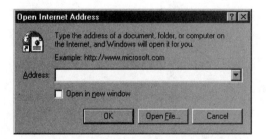

What's happening? If you know where you want to go, you can key in the address here.

4 In the **Address** text box, key in the following: **http://www.yahoo.com**

5 Click **OK**.

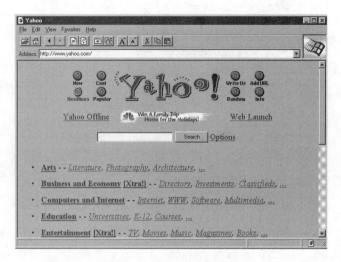

What's
happening?
Yahoo is an index to the different sites on the net. Each time you click an underlined term, you will be taken to an index of those sites.

6 Click **Computers and Internet**.

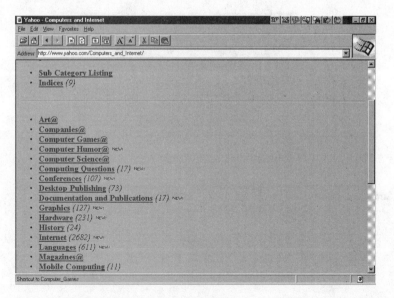

What's
happening?
Each one of these topics will take you to another topic. The number in parentheses after the site name tells you how many entries there are.

7   Click **Computer Humor**.

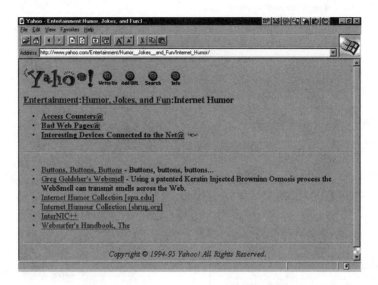

 What's happening? → As you can see, each click takes you to another Web site. You can back up one page at a time.

8   Click the **Back** button on the toolbar.

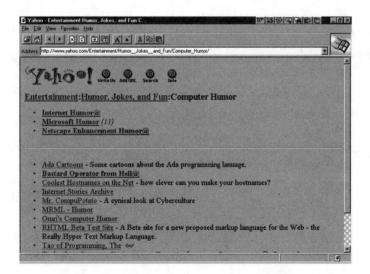

What's happening? → You have returned to the previous page. You can also return to your home page quickly.

9   Click **File**. Click **Open Start Page**.

   You can also change the address in the Address text box to advance to a new site.

10   Select **home.msn.com** in the **Open** text box.

   Typing replaces selection here.

11   Key in the following: **fbeedle.com**

   You have keyed in the home page address of this book's publisher, Franklin, Beedle & Associates.

12   Press [Enter].

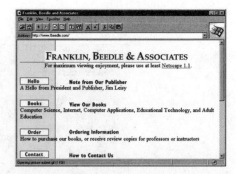

   On the Franklin, Beedle home page, you can write to the publisher, see the available books, and order books, among other things.

13   Click the **Back** button.

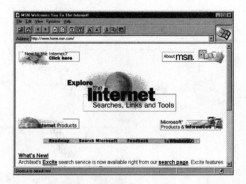

   You have returned to your home page. Remember, you are being charged for your connect time.

14   Close the **Internet Explorer** window.

15   Close your connection.

   You have returned to the desktop.

Chapter Summary

In this chapter, you learned that Windows 95 has a feature called AutoPlay. When you insert a CD into your CD-ROM player, AutoPlay automatically knows whether it has received an audio or a program CD and will take the appropriate action. You can play audio CDs and create a Play List that suits your listening pleasure. You can control the volume of any device in Windows 95.

Media Player allows you to play sound files, video clips, and MIDI sequencer files. By using file extensions, Windows 95 automatically recognizes the sound sources and selects the correct playing device. You can embed a video or sound clip in a document that supports OLE. You can insert a portion of a sound or video clip in a document that will play when the user clicks on it in the document.

Windows 95 provides an accessory called Phone Dialer that dials a number for voice communication. It will keep a log of the calls you make.

Windows 95 provides Microsoft Exchange, which gives you an Inbox. The Inbox allows you to send and receive all your e-mail, regardless of what online services you have. You can also create and keep a Personal Address Book for names, addresses, and phone numbers. You can include e-mail addresses in the Personal Phone Book. Microsoft Exchange also allows you to create, send, and receive faxes. You can use a word processor to create faxes and send them from the word processing package after you install Microsoft Exchange. HyperTerminal is the communications software provided with Windows 95 that allows you to connect with other computers or online services. However, HyperTerminal is character-based, rather than graphics-based, software. Hence, even though you can use HyperTerminal to connect, you still need to know more information to complete your transactions.

MSN, The Microsoft Network, competes with other online services such as CompuServe or America Online. MSN provides access to services such as electronic mail, news, movie and book reviews, chat groups, forums, and bulletin boards. Forums provide information or discussion about topics ranging from current events to computer software questions. To use MSN, you must also join the service and pay a fee for using it.

The Internet is a network of networks. On it, you can access institutions such as governmental agencies, educational agencies, and other types of organizations. The Internet gives you access to e-mail, forums and chat groups, and Web sites (or home pages) that cover a wide variety of topics. Home pages provide hypertext links. By clicking them, you can go to the next subject of interest. You can choose to install and use the Internet Explorer that comes with Microsoft Explorer. You access the Internet through MSN.

Key Terms

AutoPlay	Hypertext links	MPC-2
Bulletin board services (BBS)	Internet	Offline
Connection profile	MIDI (Musical Instrument	Online
Download	Digital Interface)	Upload
E-mail	MPC (Multimedia Personal	Wave
FM Synthesis	Computer)	

Discussion Questions

1. Define multimedia.
2. What hardware is necessary to use multimedia?
3. Explain the purpose and function of the Add New Hardware wizard.
4. Explain the importance of setting standards for multimedia.
5. What is Windows 95's role in multimedia?
6. Explain how AutoPlay functions.
7. If you do not want Windows 95 to start playing an inserted disc immediately, what should you do?
8. Explain the purpose and function of the CD Player.
9. If you have an enhanced CD, you get extra features. Explain.
10. Choose two of the five devices in the CD Player and list and explain how they control the sound levels and balances of your CD function.
11. Video is hardware dependent. Explain.
12. What determines how your video will play back on your system?
13. Explain the purpose and function of the Media Player application program.
14. How does the Media Player application program determine what to do with a file?
15. What type of file will have the extension .avi? .wav? .mid?
16. When you are embedding part of a video clip in WordPad, you cannot maximize the video window. Why?
17. List and explain the two main advantages of using Phone Dialer.
18. Explain the purpose and function of Microsoft Exchange.
19. What is e-mail?
20. How can you send and receive e-mail?
21. What does it mean to be online? Offline?
22. What is the purpose of the universal Inbox?
23. Windows 95 comes with MSN. How can you join another services and cancel MSN?
24. Explain how to send and receive faxes in Microsoft Exchange.
25. When communicating with another computer, what is the difference between uploading and downloading?
26. Explain the purpose and function of HyperTerminal.
27. What is MSN? What types of services does it provide?
28. What is a forum?
29. Why would you want to have a fast modem when using online services?
30. List and describe two uses of the Internet.
31. What is the World Wide Web?
32. What is a home page?
33. What does it mean to "surf the net?"
34. Why is MSN considered to be the gateway to the Internet? What other services provide access to the Internet?
35. Describe the function and purpose of Yahoo.

True/False Questions

For each question, circle the letter T if the statement is true or the letter F if the statement is false.

T   F   1. When Microsoft Exchange is activated, a fax machine icon will be seen on your taskbar.

T   F   2. It is possible to explore the Internet using Microsoft Exchange.

T   F   3. The Phone Dialer will keep a log of the phone calls you make.

T   F   4. If you send a fax to a computer user who does not have Microsoft Exchange installed, the fax will be lost.

T   F   5. HyperTerminal is a character-based communication software package.

Completion Questions

Write the correct answer in the blank space provided.

6. A special type of CD that contains the artist's name, track titles, and other multimedia features is known as a(an) _____ CD.

7. _____ are provided by online services and allow users to communicate via the computer.

8. When you use Video for Windows, you may want to purchase and install a(n) _____ card to speed up the drawing of graphics.

9. When you wish to send files to another user, you need to _____ those files. To receive files, you _____ them.

10. Two of the hardware pieces necessary to use mulitmedia include _____ and _____ .

Multiple Choice

Circle the letter of the correct answer for each question.

11. The feature of Windows 95 that inspects a CD when it is inserted into the CD-ROM drive is
    a. AutoRun.
    b. AutoPlay.
    c. CD Watch.
    d. Plug and Play.

12. Microsoft Exchange can be used to do all of the following, *except*
    a. explore the Internet.
    b. receive e-mail.
    c. send e-mail.
    d. send and receive faxes.

13. To copy information from a Video for Windows (.avi) file, you must
    a. right-click the video window while the clip is running and select Copy.
    b. use the Start and End Selection buttons in Media Player to select the frames, and then select Copy from the Edit menu.
    c. drag the Media Player slider to select the clip, then select Copy from the Edit menu.
    d. do nothing; video cannot be copied.

14. From its name, you know that http://www.ibm.com is
    a. a World Wide Web site.
    b. a public organization.
    c. a commercial organization.
    d. both a and c
15. All faxes that you receive automatically are placed in the
    a. Inbox.
    b. New Mail folder.
    c. Special Fax folder.
    d. none of the above

Application Assignments

Problem Set I—Brief Essay

For all essay questions, use Notepad or WordPad to create your answer. Print your answer.

1. Describe the benefits of AutoPlay. If possible, create a Play List for a compact disc. Describe the steps you took to do so.
2. Discuss the advantages and disadvantages of embedding video and sound clips in a document. Give examples of when this feature could be useful. Give examples of when this feature would not be useful.
3. If possible, create a document and embed a sound or video clip. Edit the video or sound clip to play only a portion of it. Describe the steps you took to accomplish this task.
4. Describe the purpose of Phone Dialer. If possible, create some speed dialing entries. Describe when and how you would use Phone Dialer. Describe when and how you would use the Call Log.
5. Discuss the advantages and disadvantages of using Microsoft Exchange. Describe the steps you would take to send e-mail, receive e-mail, send a fax, receive a fax. Describe the advantages and disadvantages of creating a Personal Address Book. Describe how it can be used with Microsoft Exchange.
6. Describe the purpose of MSN, The Microsoft Network. Discuss why you would or would not want to join MSN. Give examples of how MSN could be of use to you in your home, school, or business. If possible, compare and contrast the advantages of joining MSN, CompuServe, America Online, or another online provider. What would influence your decision?
7. Describe the purpose of the Internet. Discuss why you would or would not want to use the Internet. Give examples of how the Internet could be of use to you in your home, school, or business. Who or what do you think can most benefit from using the Internet? Explain your answer.

Installing the Activities Disk
Files onto Your Hard Drive

If you are doing your work in a lab environment, you do not need to do this, since the 95book directory has already been installed for you. But if you are working on your own computer, you will need to load the 95book directory onto your hard drive to do the activities and exercises beginning with Chapter 4. To install the files, take the following steps:

1 Boot into Windows 95.

2 Place the Activities disk in the correct drive.

3 Click **Start**. Click **Run**.

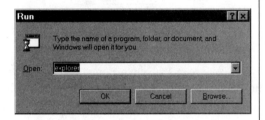

 There may or may not be highlighted text in the Open text box. If there is highlighted text in the box and you key in the following, typing will replace what is selected. If there is text in the box that is not highlighted, drag the mouse over the text to highlight it. Then you can key in the command in Step 4. If you have more than one hard drive and wish to install the files on a drive other than Drive C, you may install the files by substituting your chosen drive letter for C.

4 Key in the following: **A:\PUT C:**

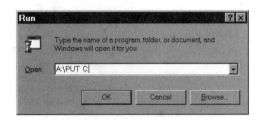

 You have issued the command to copy the files from the Activities disk to Drive C. You must be sure to install the files onto Drive C, rather than just copy them. There are zipped (compressed) files on the Activities disk that will be unzipped (uncompressed) when they are copied to your hard disk. Furthermore, not all the files on the Activities disk will be copied to the hard disk.

5 Click **OK**.

 You will see the above DOS box with PUT on the title bar.

6 Press Enter.

 As the files are being copied, you will see various messages. When the copy is complete, you will see the screen below:

7 Click the **Close** button (the in the upper-right corner of the title bar.)

 You have installed the files to the hard disk. If you are in a lab environment, do not delete the 95book folder. If are working on your own computer, however, you may remove the 95book folder at the end of the course. To remove the 95book directory from the hard drive, you may use Explorer or My Computer. Select the 95book folder and drag it to the Recycle Bin.

Shareware Programs Provided with the Textbook

Several programs on the Activities disk that are installed to the 95book directory are shareware programs. Shareware programs are for trial purposes only. If you find the programs useful and would like to keep them, you must register them and pay the registration fee.

Home Phone Book Shareware Program

Home Phone Book, version 2.5 is provided by:

Thomas E. Bonitz
7903 Kona Circle
Papillion, NE 68128

If you like Home Phone Book, please send $20.00 to Thomas E. Bonitz at the above address.

The Address Manager Program

Address Manager, version 3.0 is provided by:

Wilson WindowWare, Inc.
2701 California Avenue SW, Suite 212
Seattle, WA 98116

If you like Address Manager, please send $39.95 plus shipping and handling to the above address.

Microlink Shareware: Shut the Box

Shut the Box is provided by:

Bob Lancaster
P. O. Box 5612
Hacienda Heights, CA 91745

If you like this game, please send $5.00 to Bob Lancaster at the above address.

Cipher Shareware Program

Cipher, version 2.0 is provided by:

Brad Trupp
75 Nicollet Avenue
Winnipeg, Manitoba
Canada, R2M 4X6

If you like Cipher, please register by sending a picture postcard of your town or city to the above address. Indicate which program you are registering and where you found it.

Taipei Shareware Program

Taipei, version 5.0 is provided by:

David Norris
17911 NE 101st Court
Redmond, WA 98052

If you like Taipei, please send $10.00 to the above address.

Spider Solitaire Shareware Program

Spider Solitaire, version 93.06.20 is provided by:

John A. Junod
267 Hillwood Street
Martinez, GA 30907

If you like Spider Solitaire, please send $5.00 to the above address.

Timekard Shareware Program

Timekard, version 1.x is provided by:

Tarton Software
143 Horstman Drive
Scotia, NY 12302

If you like Timekard, please send $24.95 to the above address.

Index